上海市浦东新区统计局
SHANGHAI PUDONG NEW AREA STATISTICAL BUREAU
国家统计局浦东调查队
PUDONG SURVEY TEAM OF NATIONAL STATISTICS BUREAU

上海浦东新区统计年鉴 2015

SHANGHAI PUDONG NEW AREA STATISTICAL YEARBOOK

(总第22期 No.22)

中国统计出版社
China Statistics Press

智慧浦东 Intelligent Pudong

新区生产总值(亿元)
Gross Output Value of Pudong New Area (100 million yuan)

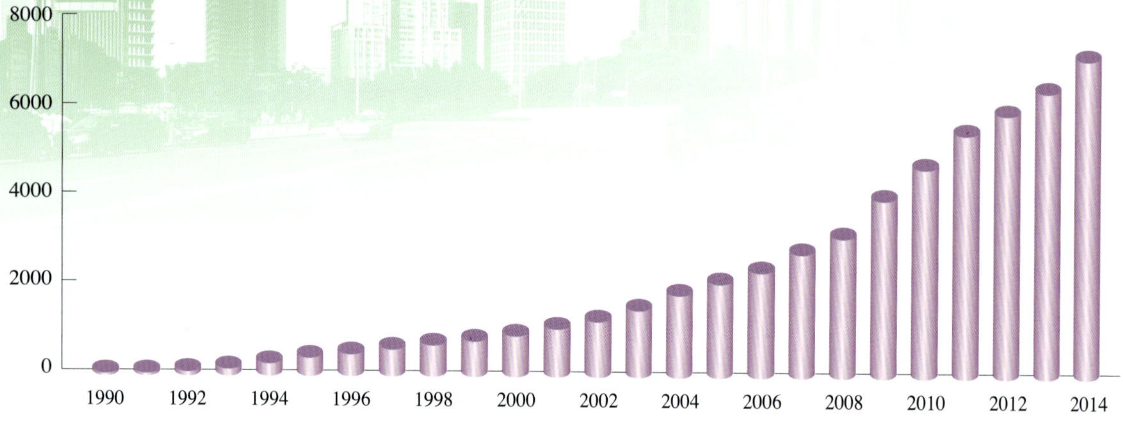

新区生产总值构成(%)
Composition of GDP of PNA (%)

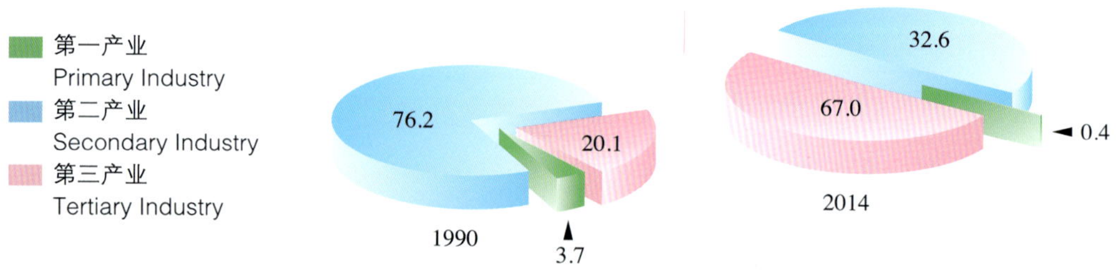

第三产业增加值构成(%)
Composition of Value Added of Tertiary Industry (%)

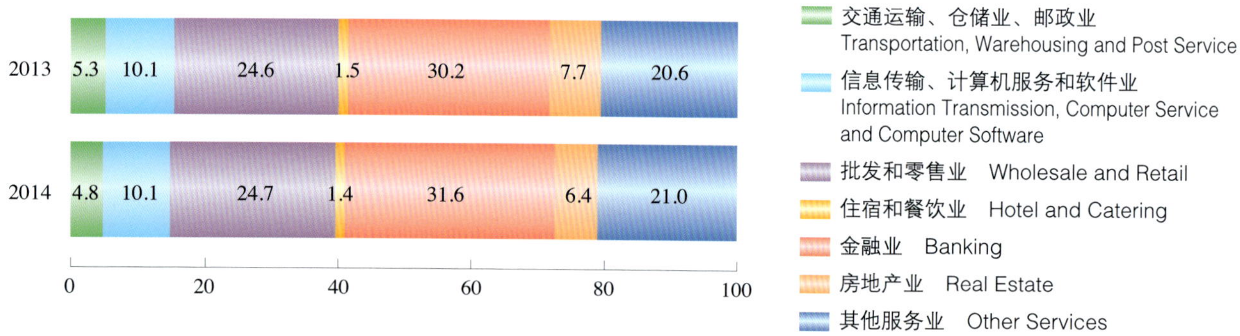

财政收入(亿元)
Fiscal Revenue (100 million yuan)

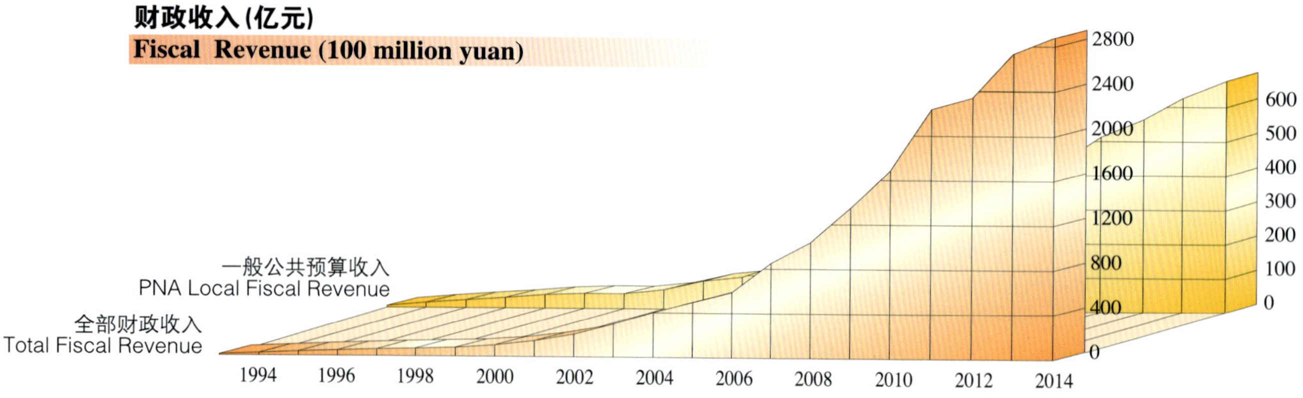

农业总产值(亿元)
Gross Output Value of Agriculture (100 million yuan)

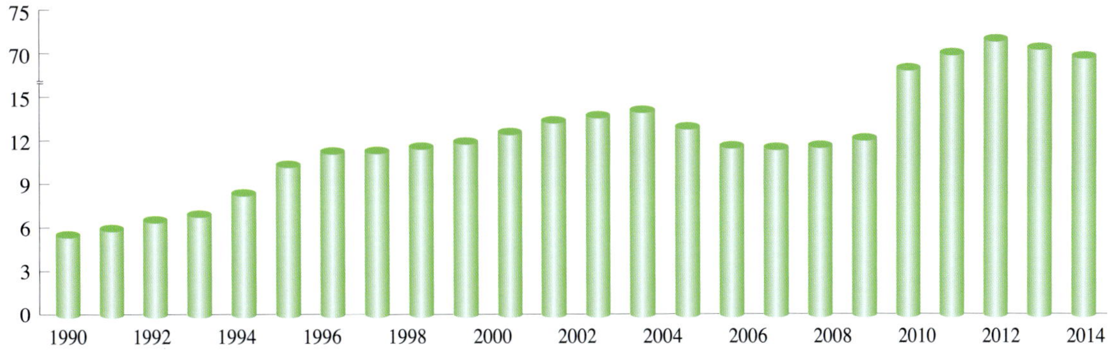

进出口货物总值(亿美元)
Total Value of Imports and Exports (USD 100 million)

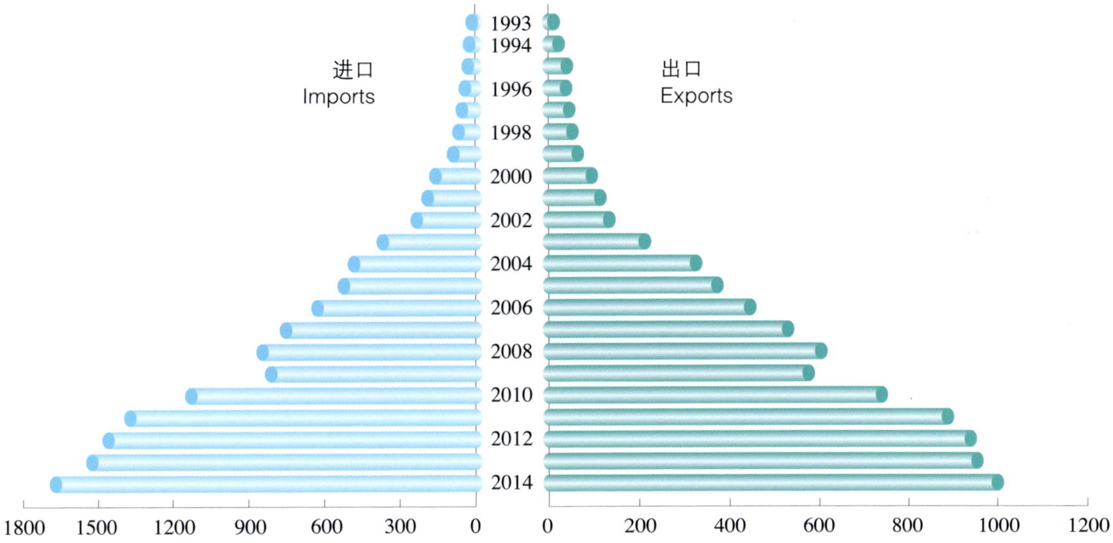

2014年六个工业重点发展行业产值构成(%)
Composition of Gross Output Value of Six Key Industries in 2014 (%)

城市基础设施投资额构成(%)
Composition of Urban Infrastructure Investment (%)

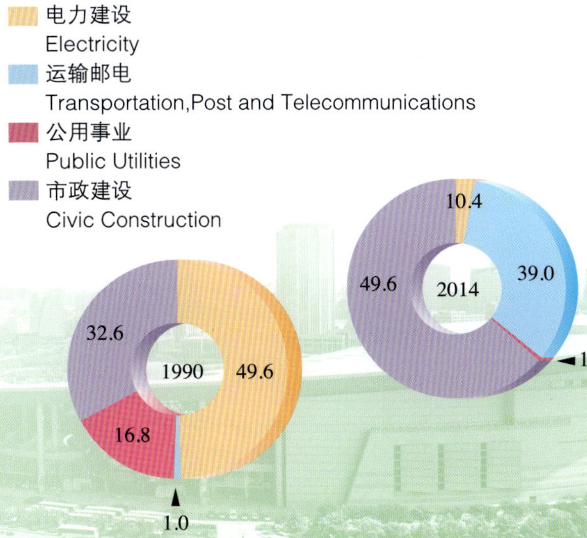

固定资产投资和城市基础设施投资(亿元)
Total Investment in Fixed Assets and Urban Infrastructure (100 million yuan)

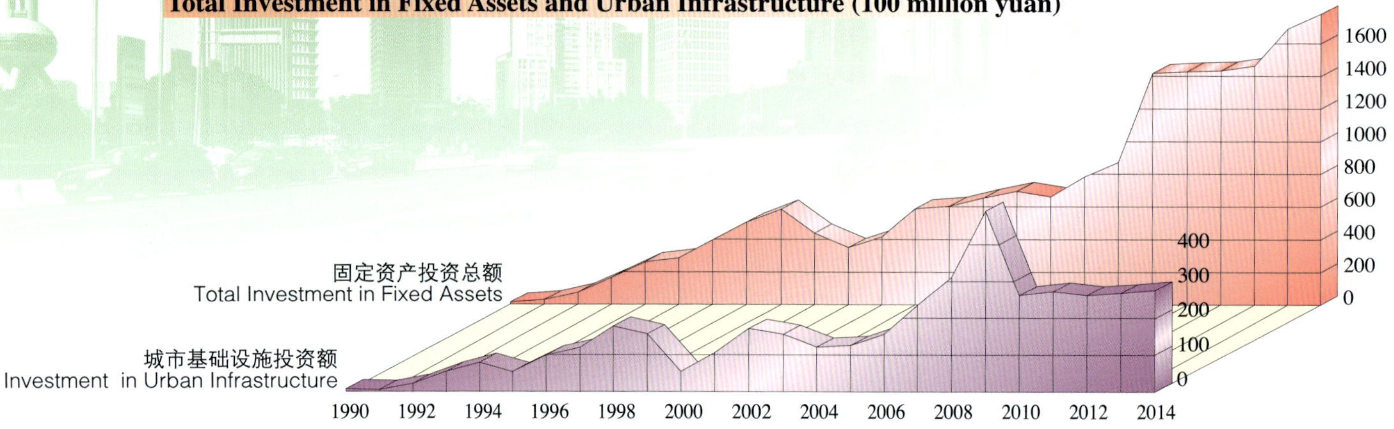

中外资银行本外币存贷款年末余额(亿元)
Balance of RMB and Foreign Currencies Deposits and Loans in Chinese and Foreign Banks (100 million yuan)

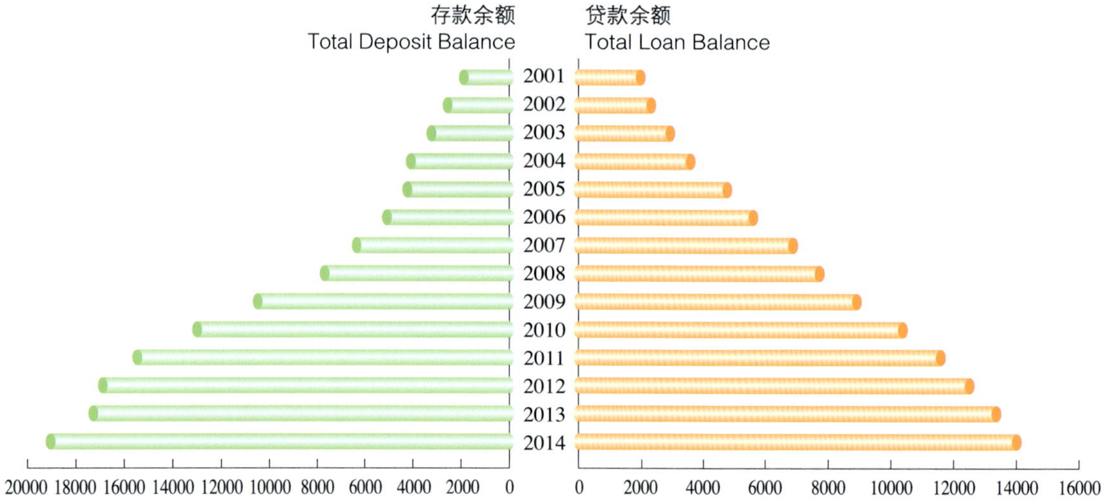

上海证券交易所市价总值(亿元)
Market Value of Shanghai Stock Exchange (100 million yuan)

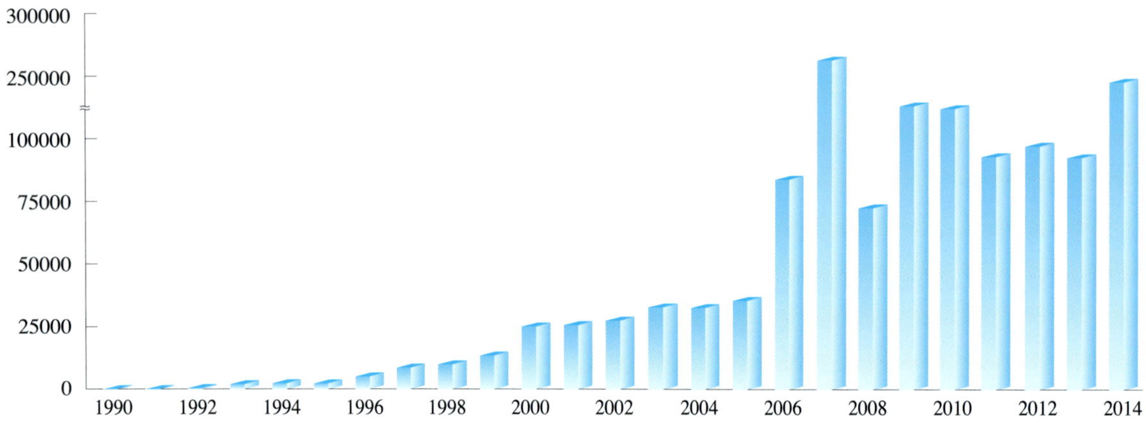

社会消费品零售总额(亿元)
Total Retail Sales of Consumer Goods (100 million yuan)

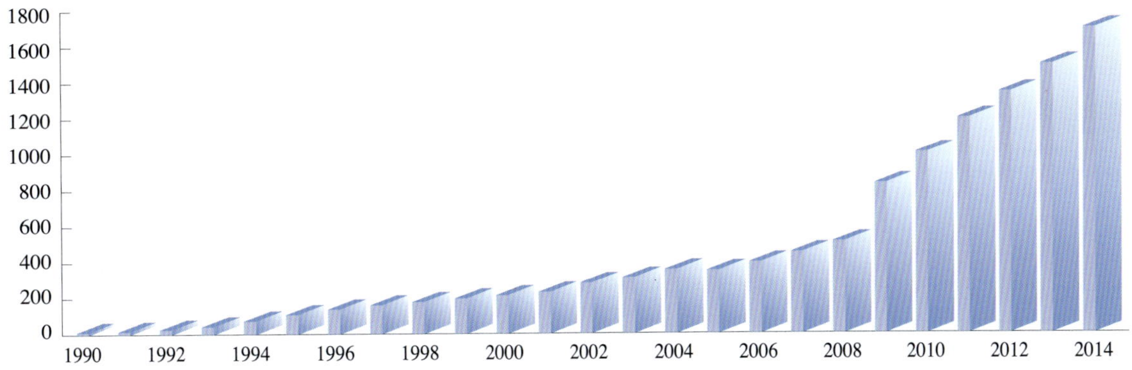

外商合同投资额的投资方式构成(%)
Composition of Contract Value of Foreign Investment by Ways of Investment (%)

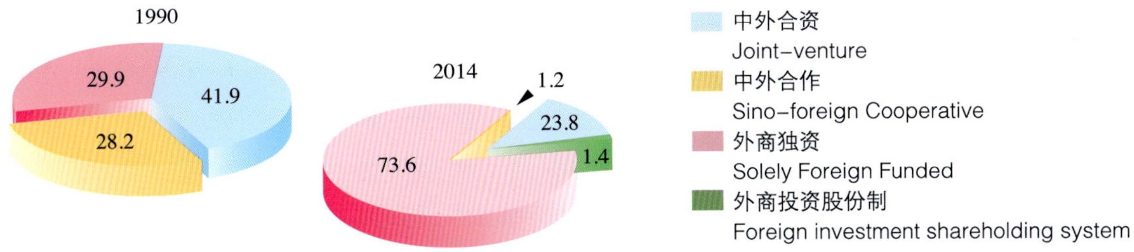

居民储蓄存款年末余额(亿元)
Resident Savings Deposit (100 million yuan)

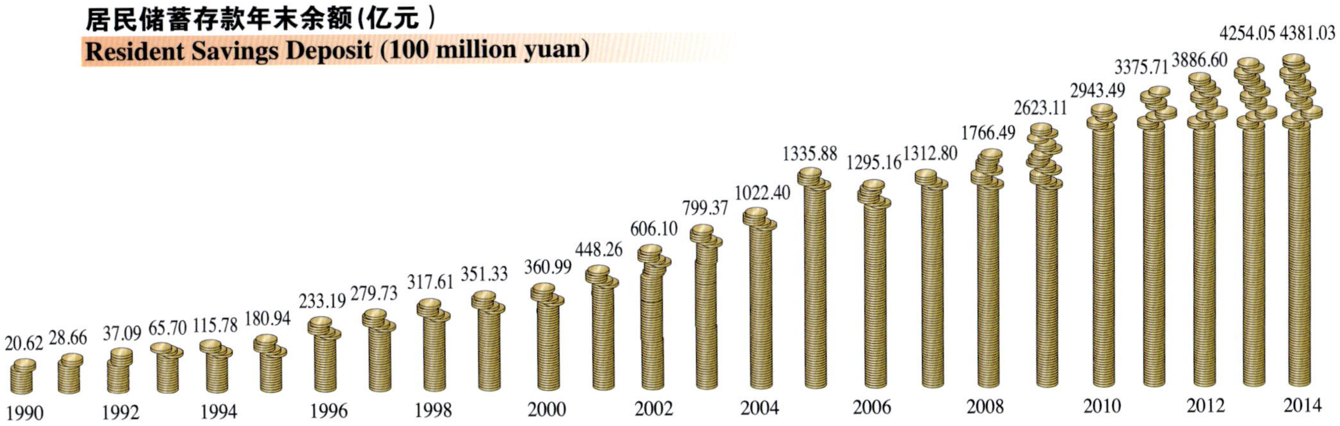

2014年城镇居民家庭消费支出构成(%)
Composition of Consumption Expenditure of Urban Families in 2014 (%)

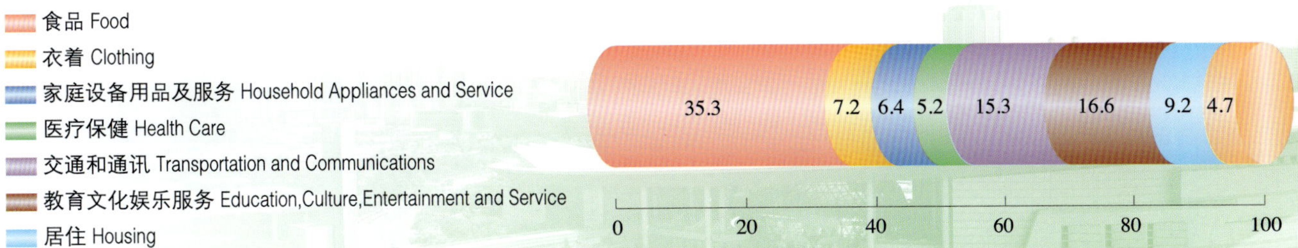

2014年农村居民家庭收入构成(%)
Income Composition of Urban Residents in 2014 (%)

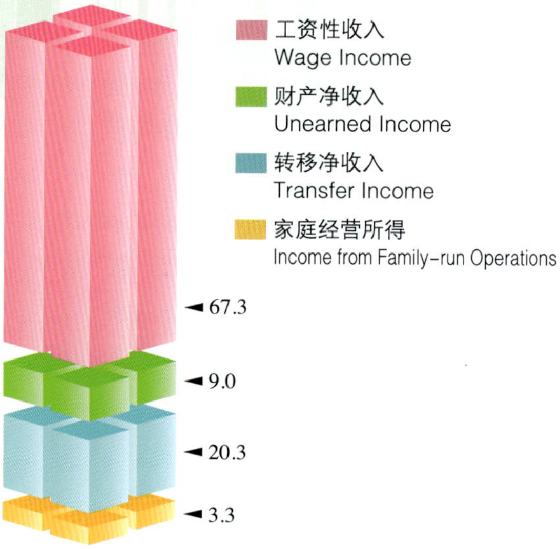

从业人员三次产业构成(%)
Employed Persons by Industry (%)

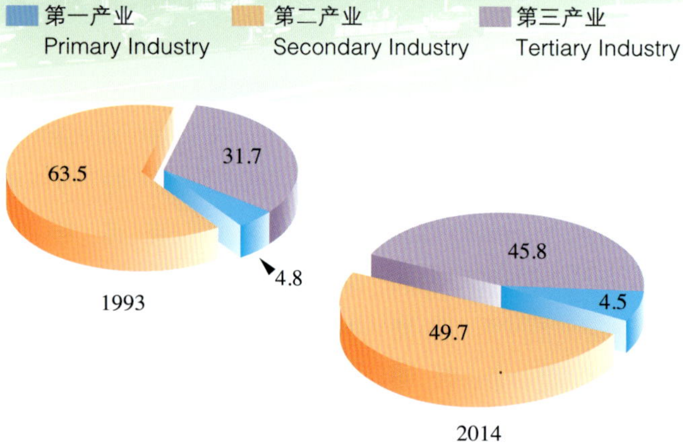

人口自然增长率和净迁移率(‰)
Natural Growth Rate and Net Migration Rate of Population (‰)

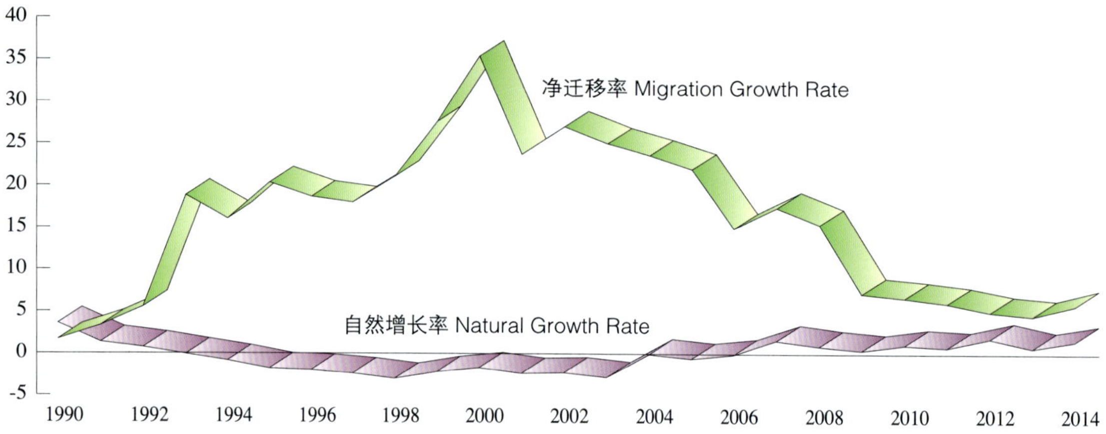

集装箱吞吐量(万标箱)
Container Handling Capacity (10000TEU)

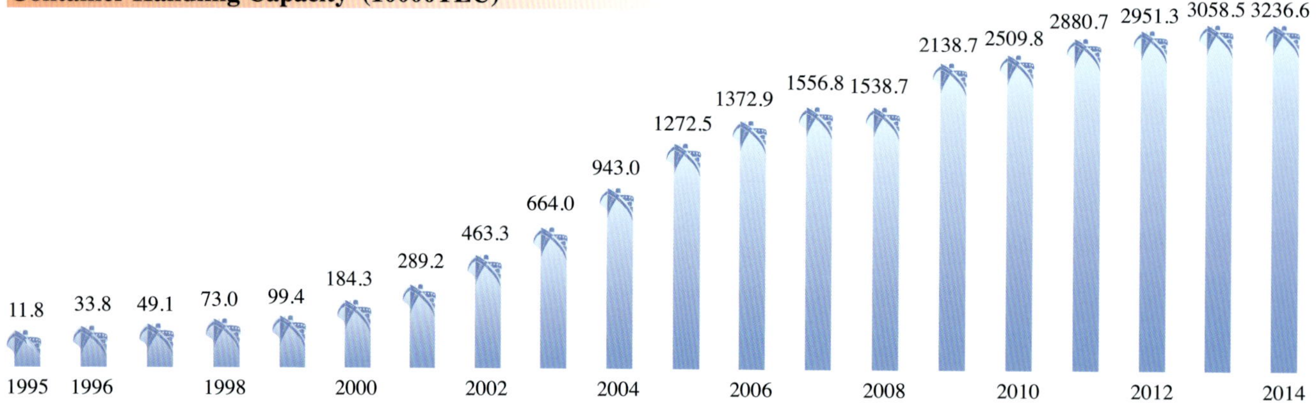

人均公共绿地面积(平方米)
Public Green Space Per Capita (sq.m)

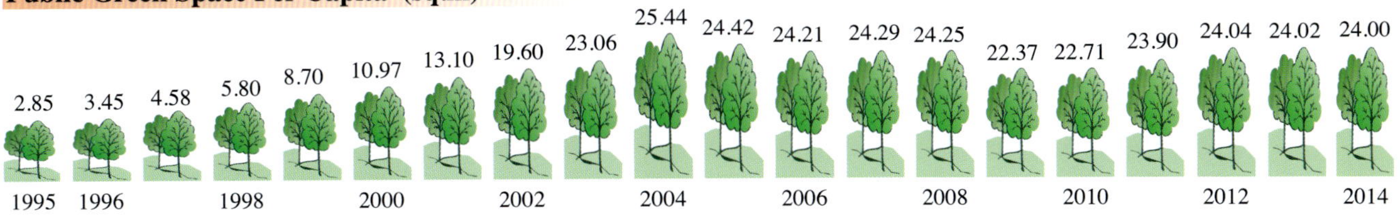

水电消耗情况
Consumption of Tap Water and Electricity

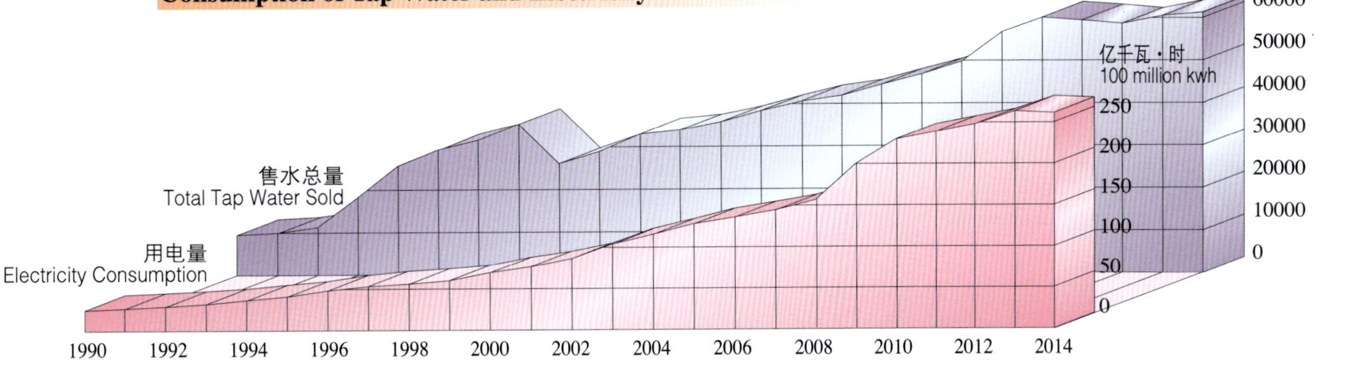

2014年前十位疾病死亡原因构成(%)
Composition of Top 10 Death-Causing Diseases in 2014 (%)

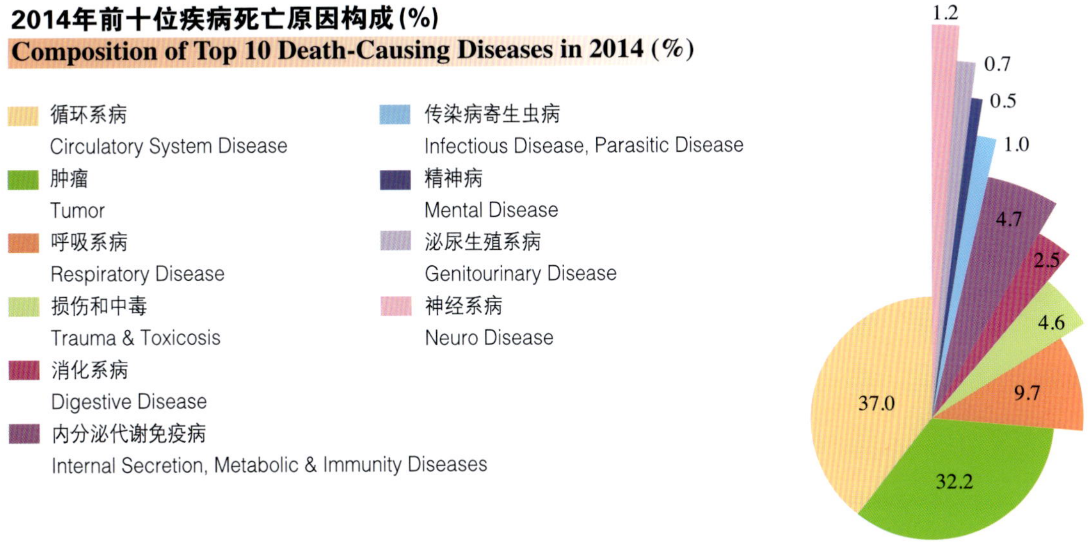

各级学校在校学生数构成(%)
Composition of Students Enrollment by Various Schools (%)

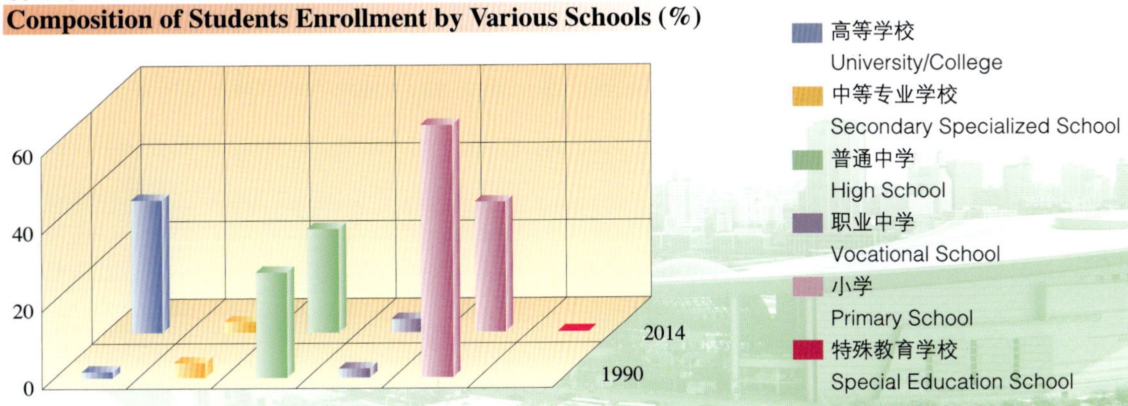

编者说明

一、《上海浦东新区统计年鉴—2015》是一部集浦东新区资料于一体的大型工具书。全书通过大量的统计数据,以中英文对照的形式记录了浦东新区开发开放以来社会经济发展的历程,全面展示了2014年浦东新区在二次创业的新阶段中,经济、社会、科技和重点开发区等各方面的发展变化。年鉴为各级领导、理论研究和实际工作者,以及国内外各界关心浦东开发开放的人士了解浦东、研究浦东、参与浦东开发建设提供了案头工具。

二、2009年,浦东新区行政体制发生重大变化。4月24日,国务院批准南汇区行政区域划入浦东新区。5月6日,上海市人民政府正式宣布两区合并。由于两区以前年度很多数据在统计方法、统计口径、统计范围等方面的不一致,数据无法简单相加,追溯存在一定难度。因此除特别注明外,本年鉴自2009年起,统计数据均为新浦东数据(即含原南汇地区),以前年度仍为原浦东数据。

三、2011年和2012年,浦东新区进行部分街镇行政区划调整。2011年10月28日,上海市人民政府批准撤销川沙新镇、六灶镇建制,设立新的川沙新镇;撤销祝桥镇建制,设立新的祝桥镇,其行政区域范围作相应调整。2012年8月30日,经批准撤销申港街道、芦潮港镇建制,设立南汇新城镇,同时行政区域范围也作相应调整。

四、本年鉴中平均增长速度根据每年的环比增长速度相乘再开方得到。

五、全书内容分为二十一个篇目。内含:1. 综合; 2. 人口; 3. 固定资产投资; 4. 招商引资; 5. 农业; 6. 工业; 7. 建筑业; 8. 金融业及要素市场; 9. 房地产; 10. 国内外贸易; 11. 服务、旅游和住宿业; 12. 科学技术; 13. 人民生活; 14. 就业与社会保障; 15. 教育; 16. 文化和体育; 17. 卫生; 18. 法律、社会治安及其他; 19. 城市建设和环境保护; 20. 重点开发区和街镇; 21. 上海市统计资料。

六、资料中使用的度量衡单位均采用国际统一标准计量单位。

七、本年鉴部分数据总计数或相对数由于单位取舍不同,产生的计算误差均未作机械调整。

八、浦东新区在行政管理体制上于1995年11月撤乡建镇,实行镇管村体制。因此,本年鉴中有关“镇”和“镇及镇以上工业”等指标含义与全国的“乡”和“乡及乡以上工业”等指标的含义相同。

九、本年鉴中的符号使用说明:“#”表示某一指标的其中主要项;“…”表示数据不足本表最小计量单位数;“空格”表示该项统计指标数据不详或无该项数据或数据为零。

十、根据国务院和国家统计局有关我国GDP核算和数据发布制度的规定,浦东新区国内生产总值自2004年起更名为“浦东新区生产总值”,简称“新区生产总值”。

十一、本年鉴中各项增加值和总产值绝对数均按当年价格计算,增长速度按可比价格计算。

十二、在使用统计资料时，凡与本年鉴有出入的，均以本年鉴为准。

十三、《上海浦东新区统计年鉴》公开出版以来，受到国内外广大读者的爱护和支持，对此我们深表谢意，并竭诚欢迎读者继续对本年鉴的不足之处给予批评和指正。

本年鉴的编制得到了上海市统计局、浦东新区各委、办、局及各开发区管委会等有关单位的大力支持，在此一并表示谢意。

EDITOR'S NOTE

Ⅰ. Statistical Yearbook of Shanghai Pudong New Area (PNA) — 2015 is a large, comprehensive reference book. With great amount of data and in both Chinese and English versions, it records recent years' social and economic development in PNA. It describes the changes in economy, society, science and technology, and key development zones in PNA's new stage of "Second Startup for Business" in 2014. It is a desktop tool - book meant for leaders at all levels, theorists, practitioners, and people at home and abroad who are interested in PNA, want to do research work on Pudong and intend to participate in its development and its construction.

Ⅱ. Great changes happened to the administrative system of Pudong New Area in 2009. On April 24, the State Council approved to add the administrative area of Nanhui District into Pudong New Area. On May 6, the Shanghai Municipal government formally announced the combination of these two districts. Because of data of previous years in these two districts can not be added simply while they had been produced with different statistical methods, approached and areas and it is hard to trace them. Unless specified, the statistical data in this Yearbook are those of new PNA (including former Nanhui District) since 2009, and the data of previous years are those of former PNA.

Ⅲ. In 2011 and 2012, administrative divisions of some towns in PNA were readjusted. On October 28, 2011, Shanghai People's Government approved the establishment of the new Chuansha New Town after rescinding the former Chuansha New Town and Liuzao Town, approved the establishment of the new Zhuqiao Town after rescinding the former Zhuqiao Town, and readjusted the administrative divisions of these two new towns. On August 30, 2012, the municipal government approved the establishment of the new Nanhui New Town after rescinding Shengang Sub - district and Luchaogang Town, and readjusted its administrative division.

Ⅳ. The annual average growth rate in this Yearbook is extracted from the multiplication of the annual chain growth rates.

Ⅴ. This book falls into nineteen chapters: 1. General Survey; 2. Population; 3. Investment in Fixed Assets; 4. Business Promotion and Foreign - fund Attraction; 5. Agriculture; 6. Industry; 7. Construction; 8. Finance and Banking, and Factor Markets; 9. Real Estate; 10. Domestic and Foreign Trades; 11. Services, Tourism and Hotels; 12. Science and Technology; 13. People's Livelihood; 14. Employment and Social Security; 15. Education; 16. Culture and Sports; 17. Public Health; 18. Laws, Public Order and Others; 19. Urban Construction and Environmental Protection; 20. Key Development Zones and Sub - districts and Towns; 21. Statistics of Shanghai Municipality.

Ⅵ. The units of measurement in this book are consistent with international standards.

Ⅶ. No adjustment has been made to correct the deviations of some of the figures in the Yearbook caused by different methods used in rounding.

Ⅷ. In November 1995, PNA rescinded township system and adopted town system. Villages are supervised by towns in the town system. Therefore, in this book, the meanings of "town" and "town and town - above industry" are the same as "township" and "township and township - above industry" in other Chinese statistical books.

Ⅸ. Notations used in this Yearbook:

"#" indicates the major item of a certain indicator,

"…" indicates the figure which is too small to be measured by the smallest unit in the table,

"blank" indicates the data unavailable or none in certain statistical indicator.

Ⅹ. According to relevant stipulations by the State Council and National Bureau of Statistics, GDP of Pudong New Area is to be renamed as Gross Output Value of Pudong New Area, shortened as PNA Gross Output Value starting from 2004.

Ⅺ. All added values and gross output vales in the Yearbook are listed in terms of current prices while growth rates listed in terms of comparable prices.

XII. If any statistical data from other sources conflict with the data in the present Yearbook, data in the present Yearbook shall apply.

XIII. The publication of Pudong New Area Statistical Yearbook has received great attention. Our gratitude and appreciation go to all the readers who have offered their comments. We welcome and are open to more comments and suggestions from our readers when presenting this new edition.

We appreciate the great support and efforts of Shanghai Statistics Bureau, all the commissions, offices and bureaus, and administrations of all the development zones in PNA during compilation of the present Yearbook.

目　　录
CONTENTS

综　述
ABSTRACT

第一篇　综　合
CHAPTER 1　GENERAL SURVEY

第二篇　人　口

CHAPTER 2 POPULATION

第三篇　固定资产投资

CHAPTER 3 INVESTMENT IN FIXED ASSETS

第四篇　招商引资

CHAPTER 4　BUSINESS PROMOTION AND FOREIGN-FUND ATTRACTION

第五篇　农　业

CHAPTER 5　AGRICULTURE

第六篇　工　业
CHAPTER 6 INDUSTRY

第七篇　建筑业
CHAPTER　7　CONSTRUCTION

第八篇　金融业及要素市场
CHAPTER　8　FINANCIAL INDUSTRY AND FACTOR MARKETS

第九篇　房地产
CHAPTER　9　REAL ESTATE

第十篇　国内外贸易

CHAPTER 10　DOMESTIC AND FOREIGN TRADES

第十一篇　服务、旅游和住宿业
CHAPTER　11　SERVICES, TOURISM AND HOTELS

第十二篇　科学技术
CHAPTER　12　SCIENCE AND TECHNOLOGY

第十三篇　人民生活
CHAPTER　13　PEOPLE'S LIVELIHOOD

第十四篇　就业与社会保障
CHAPTER　14　EMPLOYMENT AND SOCIAL SECURITY

第十五篇　教　育
CHAPTER 15　EDUCATION

第十六篇　文化和体育
CHAPTER 16　CULTURE AND SPORTS

第十七篇 卫 生
CHAPTER 17 PUBLIC HEALTH

第十八篇 法律、社会治安及其他
CHAPTER 18 LAWS, PUBLIC ORDER AND OTHERS

第十九篇 城市建设和环境保护
CHAPTER 19 URBAN CONSTRUCTIONS AND ENVIRONMENTAL PROTECTION

第二十篇 重点开发区和街镇
CHAPTER 20 KEY DEVELOPMENT ZONES AND SUB－DISTRICTS AND TOWNS

第二十一篇　上海市统计资料
CHAPTER 21 STATISTICS OF SHANGHAI MUNICIPALITY

2014年浦东新区经济和社会发展情况

2014年，面对复杂多变的外部环境，浦东新区积极贯彻党的十八届三中全会精神，根据市委、市政府的总体部署，坚持创新驱动发展、经济转型升级，扎实推进“稳增长、促改革、调结构、惠民生”的各项工作，经济社会发展平稳有序，年度计划执行情况总体良好，约束性指标全面完成，多数预期性指标得以实现。

一、经济转型升级步伐加快

1、经济运行总体平稳。2014年，新区实现地区生产总值7109.74亿元，增长9.3%，增幅比上年小幅下降，但高于全市增幅2.3个百分点。经济运行质量和效益继续提升，全年一般公共预算收入达到684.51亿元，增长12.1%。投资规模再创新高，2014年，全社会固定资产投资完成1765.73亿元，增长5.2%，超额完成全年目标。在自贸试验区资本集聚效应的带动下，招商引资保持良好势头，全年合同外资达到143.07亿美元，增长93.6%；新增内资企业注册资本6062.32亿元，增长2.4倍。

2、产业结构进一步优化。2014年，第三产业实现增加值4760.63亿元，增长12.7%，占GDP比重达到67.0%，比上年提高2.6个百分点，已超过“十二五”规划预期目标。第三产业中，金融、信息服务业等现代服务业增速相对较快，电子商务、互联网服务等新兴业态发展迅速。工业内部结构进一步优化，“三大三新”行业中除整体增加值率相对较低的电子信息产品制造业下降1.3%外，其他重点行业增长速度均快于工业平均水平。战略性新兴产业（制造业）产值增长8.8%，高于全市平均增幅3.3百分点，占全市比重达32%。

3、重点区域建设继续加快。陆家嘴、张江和金桥地区加快集聚高端项目、推进转型升级；临港地区落实“双特机制”、实施“南下战略”，高标准推进区域开发；国际旅游度假区全力推进迪士尼乐园建设；世博园区及前滩地区形态和功能开发全面推进。

二、核心功能进一步拓展提升

1、金融功能进一步提升。2014年底，中外资银行本外币存贷款余额分别增长9.7%和4.7%。在国债、股票和基金的拉动下，证券市场成交额增长48.1%。金融机构加快集聚，金砖国家开发银行总部、中国农业银行上海管理总部落户。全年新增监管类金融机构50家，股权投资及管理企业963家、融资租赁企业267家、财富管理企业73家、金融专业服务机构594家。新兴金融业态蓬勃发展，出台相关政策，推动新纳入监管的第三方支付及移动支付等互联网金融机构进一步集聚。

2、航运功能继续增强。2014年，港口货物吞吐量和集装箱吞吐量分别增长4.3%和5.8%。机场货邮吞吐量由上年的下降逆转为增长8.7%。洋山港水水中转箱量和国际中转箱量分别增长5.7%和5.1%，占比达到49.7%和11%。上海南盛堡船舶管理有限公司等5家外资船舶管理公司、大地航运保险运营中心、中外运长航航运事业部等重点航运服务企业落户。上海亚洲船级社中心、中国贸促会上海海损理算中心、上海海事司法鉴定中心等航运功能性机构入驻。中国海运大厦、洋泾国际航运服务创新试验区等项目建设正式启动。

3、贸易功能稳步发展。2014年，实现商品销售总额27640.16亿元，增长15.0%，增幅高于上年2.2个百分点，高于全市3.6个百分点。社会消费品零售总额1740.23亿元，增长8.9%，增速逐月回升。世博源等新增商业设施和周浦万达等区域型商圈销售良好。全年外贸进出口总额2678.71亿美元，增长7.3%。贸易结构继续优化，电子商务交易额和服务贸易总额均达到两位数增长。积极发展跨境电子商务，东方电子支付、快钱、盛付通、通联支付等4家第三方支付机构参与了自贸区跨境电子商务人民币支付结算试点。

4、总部功能不断升级。实施总部企业外汇集中管理、人民币资金池政策，优化总部运营环境，促进一批企业区域总部的设立。引导和协助已落户浦东的总部企业升级为亚太区总部。2014年底，累计获认定的跨国公司地区总部达229家，占全市的46.7%。

三、区域创新体系不断完善

1、创新创业环境继续优化。探索扩大代持股专项资金的政策受益覆盖面。完善集成电路产业链保税监管模式，推进再制造产业改革试点。积极推进孵化基地建设，加大对孵化器、在孵企业和苗圃项目的扶持力度，在南汇工业园、临港软件园和北蔡、航头、泥城等区域布局新建孵化器。推动科技金融服务平台建设，完善科技企业与金融机构的交流对接机制。全面推进国家知识产权试点城区建设，不断优化知识产权发展环境。科技企业信用体系进一步完善。

2、创新成效进一步显现。全年专利授权数达到10896件，其中发明专利3139件，每百万人发明专利授权数达到576件。罗氏、安进、杜邦等跨国公司创新中心相继落户。新认定高新技术成果转化项目139个，认定技术交易合同2753件，交易金额179.5亿元。获得各类科技奖励160项，其中12个项目获国家科技进步奖。深入推进“千人计划”引才工程，入选“千人计划”专家283人，其中国家级148人、市级135人。

四、以自贸试验区带动综合配套改革取得新进展

1、自贸试验区内外联动进一步加强。主动建立对接联动机制，积极配合全市制定推广自贸试验区改革经验的实施方案。深化跨国公司总部外汇资金集中运营管理试点，总部企业的集中报关试点范围进一步扩大。延伸自贸试验区保税展示交易功能，推动森兰商都进口商品展示平台正式运营，形成“前店后库”的商业模式。促进上海国际黄金交易中心推出国际板业务。完善信托登记制度的地方规范性文件，推动全国性信托登记服务机构落户浦东。推进商业保理业务创新，首创商业保理企业信用评级机制。

2、政府管理体制改革取得突破。成立全国首家实现专利、商标、版权的集中管理和综合执法的知识产权局。进一步推进工商、质监、食药监及价格监督检查组成的市场监管体制改革。借鉴负面清单管理理念，优化外资项目审批流程，实现外资审批、企业登记、组织机构代码证办理、税务登记和食品前置审批“五证联办”，并在全国首创推动海关加入“一口受理”流程，实现外资设立和变更环节审批“六联动”。推进区级机关编制下沉，各区级机关行政编制精简率达到15%，内设机构精简率近16%。完善建设项目审批制度，建立陆家嘴、张江、金桥、世博和自贸试验区（含森兰区域）等“4+1”区域审批平台，建立“建设项目网上联合审批系统”，完善政府投资项目代建制管理制度。国资国企改革有序推进，制订国资国企改革意见，部分企业率先启动分类改革试点。

五、社会民生持续改善

1、居民收入保持较快增长。城乡居民可支配收入分别达49629元和21814元，增长9.8%和11.7%，均超过全市平均水平。农村居民收入增速继续高于城镇居民收入，城乡居民收入差距有所改善。

2、就业和社会保障工作深入推进。实施就业优先战略和更加积极的就业政策，确保就业形势保持基本稳定。社会保障力度不断加大，城乡居民养老保险制度合并实施，全区城乡居保参保人数14.5万人。切实落实重大工程项目被征地人员社会保障政策，近6.3万名征地养老纳入镇保人员参加本市镇保门急诊统筹。加快推进社会养老服务体系建设，新增养老床位1241张，新建6家老年人日间服务中心、10家老年人助餐点，完成266户“适老性”住房改造和79家标准化老年活动室建设，为5.83万名老人开展社区居家养老服务，为2.63万名高龄老人提供家庭互助服务。进一步加快保障性住房建设，245万平方米保障性住房（区级）已全部开工建设，全年竣工174.86万平方米。

3、教育事业取得新发展。新开办中小幼学校19所，36所急需建造的公建配套学校开工15所、竣工1所。积极推进“区级新优质学校创建”和第一批10所区级特色高中创建等工作。与全市多所著名高校开展战略合作，实现全市教育资源与新区发展的深度融合。积极促进教育培训等开放领域项目在自贸区落地，鼓励并支持中外合作经营性培训机构发展。与商飞公司、临港集团、唐镇电子商务港等联合开展校企合作培训。

4、医疗服务水平进一步改善。浦南医院综合楼建成，东方医院改扩建、七院医技综合楼新建项目积极推进，祝桥区域医疗中心、新场综合医疗卫生中心前期工作启动，花木、金桥、高行、泥城等社区卫生服务中心建设项目有序实施。落户在国际医学园区的质子重离子医院和国际医学中心开业试运营，新区医疗服务的能级进一步提升。深化公立医院改革，完善公立医疗机构综合评价体系。以全科医生为核心，形成居民健康管理

团队工作机制,推广慢性病自我管理模式。推进国家中医药综合改革试验区建设。继续实施60岁以上老人接种肺炎疫苗、新生儿疾病筛查等国家及上海市重大公共卫生服务项目。

5、文化软实力逐步提升。公共文化设施建设积极推进,谢稚柳陈佩秋艺术馆、航头大居文化活动中心和广电中心等项目稳步实施。努力打造文化活动品牌,成功举办上海夏季音乐节、"三林塘"上海民俗文化节等重大文化活动。文化创意产业发展平稳,重点园区(基地)建设和功能平台集聚加速,张江国家数字出版基地三期、三林老街文化创意园区等一批文化创意集聚区全面开工。

6、体育事业稳步发展。推进川沙体育场征地改扩建、周浦体育中心新建等重点项目建设。继续推进公共体育设施对外开放,保障居民的基本健身需求。顺利完成第12届全国学生运动会各项工作,成功承办全运会女子排球比赛等重大赛事。

7、实事项目全面完成。在确保完成由新区实施的市政府实事项目的同时,新区12大类涉及居民出行、居住、健康、老年人服务等日常生活改善和解决急、难、愁等问题的实事项目全面完成。

六、社会治理水平不断提高

1、进一步加强基层治理。以"两个合法稳定"为导向,狠抓人口综合管理和服务,外来无序流动人口数量明显下降。大力推进基层民主,完善社区代表会议制度和社区共治机制,以居委会自治家园示范点创建为抓手扎实推进居民自治工作。以"一门服务、一口受理、一头管理"为目标,积极推进受理中心标准化建设,进一步规范社区生活服务中心的设置运营和建设管理。

2、促进社会组织健康发展。加大扶持力度,进一步促进社会组织发展,2014年末,新区各类社会组织达1764家。继续推进政府购买服务"供需对接一站式服务平台"建设,累计为59个公益服务项目开展对接服务。强化服务管理,有序开展对四类社会组织进行直接登记,加强社会组织专业培训,提升社工人才综合能力。

七、城市综合环境明显优化

1、基础设施体系进一步完善。轨道交通16号线全线通车,9号线三期、13号线二期工程已启动,10号线二期、14号线已完成部分前期工作。罗山路快速化改建工程竣工,中环线浦东段、东西通道等重大道路工程有序推进。迪士尼、商飞、大型居住社区等配套道路项目按计划实施。加强智慧城市建设统筹规划,城市光网覆盖197万户,百兆家庭宽带接入能力覆盖率达99%,建成4G基站4200个。

2、旧区改造稳步推进。积极落实资金房源,加大工作推进力度,旧区改造受益居民2202户。推进三林、川沙、康桥等8个镇的11个地块列入市"城中村"改造项目,其中三林楔形绿地等项目已经启动。累计完成以"三高"地区为主的"厂中村"改造1013户。

3、生态环保工作力度不断加大。第五轮环保三年行动计划104个项目全面完成。继续推进滨江森林公园二期、开天窗补绿工程和南汇生态专项工程建设,新建公共绿地50公顷。继续推进生活垃圾分类减量各项工作。配合全市完成水价调整工作。加大对重点企业、敏感区域的监管力度,监察企业近1万户次,立案查处275户。加大节能降耗工作力度,出台新能源车购买补贴政策,完成390台锅炉和窑炉的清洁能源替代,实施143栋大型公共建筑的分项计量安装工程,区属单位增加值综合能耗下降率超额完成年度目标。

4、城市管理成效显著。加快街镇网格化平台建设全覆盖,完善六位一体的城市网格化综合管理机制。强力推进"三违"整治,共拆除各类违法建筑432万平方米。强化城市安全管理,生产安全事故数、死亡人数和110报警类警情数量同比均有所下降,全区未发生集体性食物中毒和责任性药害事件。圆满完成亚信峰会等重大活动保障工作。

八、城乡发展一体化有序推进

1、"三农"工作稳步推进。推进落实国家新型城镇化发展规划,以城乡发展一体化为导向,积极推动镇域经济整体发展。2014年,各镇完成固定资产投资612.93亿元。以国家现代农业示范区建设为核心,推进农业产业结构调整,构建新型农业经营体系,提升浦东地产农产品经营效益。发展家庭农场271家,全区20%的粮田由家庭农场经营。在全区22个涉农镇形成52家农业生产投入品供应平台(农资超市),覆盖全区主要农业生产区域。农产品“三品一标”认证覆盖率达到73%。完成村庄改造五年计划，对212个行政村实施村庄改造，惠及20万农户。积极推进美丽乡村建设和创建工作。创新农村综合帮扶工作方式，组建经济薄弱村联合发展平台，采取促进非农就业、涉农补贴政策等多项措施，大力促进农民增收。

2、积极探索城乡发展一体化改革试点。成立地区工作委员会，优化区镇工作机制。调整街镇考核体系，实施分类考核，引导街镇更加关注社会民生和可持续发展。出台鼓励卫生人才向基层和郊区流动的综合激励办法。扩大农村土地承包经营权确权登记试点，有序推进承包土地经营权流转，流转率提高到68%以上。积极开展集体资产产权制度改革，试点范围由39个村扩大到180个村。加强农村基层建设，深化村民自治工作，加强村务公开民主管理，在19个镇、106个村开展“1+1+X”村民自治模式扩大试点工作。

Economic and Social Development of Shanghai Pudong New Area in 2014

In the year of 2014, faced with complicated and changeable external environment, Pudong New Area (PNA) actively implemented the spirit of the Third Plenary Session of the Eighteenth Central Committee, stuck to "innovation-driven development and upgrading economy" under the leadership of PNA Communist Party Committee and PNA Government, and pushed forward "steadying growth, promoting reform, adjusting structure, and benefiting welfare". As a result, economic and social development was stable and orderly, and the implement of yearly plan was overall fine with the completion of all the bounded targets and the majority of the expected targets.

Ⅰ. The transition and the upgrade of the economy have been accelerated.

1. Economic development is overall steady. In 2014, the local added value in PNA reached 711 billion yuan, with an increase of 9.3% over the previous year, a small decline of the increasement, but 2.3% higher than that of the municipality. The quality and efficiency of the economic development have been improved continuously. The local fiscal revenue reached 68.5 billion yuan, an increase of 12.1%. The total social investment on fixed assets reached the highest peak of 176.6 billion yuan with an increase of 5.2%, which overfulfilled the yearly target. Driven by the capital effect of the Free Trade Zone, the contract of foreign investment reached 14.3 billion dollars with an increase of 93.6%, and the registration capital of newly-found domestic enterprises reached 606.2 billion yuan with an increase of 240%.

2. Industrial structure continuously optimized. In 2014, the added value of the tertiary industry reached 476 billion yuan with an increase of 12.7%, occupying 67.0% of the total GDP, an increase of 2.6% over the previous year, which has fulfilled the target of "the Twelfth Five-year Planning" in advance. Among the tertiary industry, modern service industry, such as financial and information service industry, grew with faster speed; and at the same time, newly emerging services, such as e-commerce and internet service also develop rapidly. The structure of the secondary industry has optimized. Among the" three large and the three new" industries, the increase rate of the majority industries is higher than the average of the secondary industry, except that the electronic information manufacturing industry dropped 1.3%, which occupied a relatively small amount of the total added value. The added value of the strategic newly industry grew 8.8%, 3.3% higher than the municipal average, which occupied 32% of the municipal strategic new industry.

3. Construction of major development zone continuously enhanced. Lujiazui, Jinqiao, and Zhangjiang national development zones have speeded up the economy escalation through promoting the concentration of high-end projects. Lingang zone carried out the "two special mechanism" and the "south strategy", and promoted the regional development in high standard. The international tourism zone pushed forward the construction of Disney Land. The Expo zone and the Qiantan Zone has rapidly advanced the outlook building.

Ⅱ. Construction of the nuclear function has advanced.

1. Financial function quickened to improve. At the end of 2014, the deposit and the loan base of the domestic banks grew 9.7% and that of and the foreign banks grew 4.7%. As the business volume of bonds, stocks, and funds in the financial market increased obviously, the turnover of business in Shanghai Stock Exchange increased by 48.1%. The financial institutions have rapided clustered. The headquarter of the BRIC National Development Bank

and the management headquarter of Agriculture Bank of China in Shanghai set up in Pudong. We have introduced 50 regulatory financial institutions, 963 equity investment and management firms, 267 finance leasing firms, 73 independent wealth management firms, and 594 professional financial service institutions. The newly-born financial industry grew rapidly, and relative supporting policy drove the cluster of internet financial institutions, such as the third-party payment and mobile payment firms.

2. Shipping function continuously exploited. In 2014, the cargo handling capacity and container handling capacity respectively achieved an increase of 4.3% and 5.8%. The cargo capacity increased 8.7%, changing the incline trend. The number of internal and international transit containers in Yangshan Port increased by 5.7% and 5.1%, occupying 49.7% and 11%. Earth Shipping Insurance Operation Center, the long-route shipping department of China Foreign Shipping, and five foreign shipping management firms including Shanghai Nanshengbao Shipping Management firm set up in Pudong. Asia Center Classification Society in Shanghai, Sea Damage Settlement of China Trade Promotion Association set up in Pudong.

3. Trade function continuously enhanced. The total sales of commodities achieved 2764 billion yuan, increased by 15.0%. The total retail volume of social consuming goods achieved 174 billion yuan, increased by 8.9%. The total import and export volume achieved USD 267.9 billion in the whole year, an increase of 7.3%. With the steady development on E-business, the trading amount of E-business goods reached 2-digit increasement in the whole year. As the e-trade across the country steadily proceeded, Oriental e-payment, Fast Money, Sheng Payment, and Union Pay have jioned the Free Trade e-payment with the settlement of RMB.

4. Headquarter function continuously strengthened. Both the quantity and the quality of headquarters in Pudong area have contentiously improved. Several headquarters among them served the head function from local area to Asian area. We have brought in 229 multinational corporations in total till the end of 2014, occupying 46.7% in that of the municipality.

Ⅲ. Innovation system continuously improved.

1. Innovation and Venture Environment continuously enhanced. We explored the expanding policy of holding special capital, improved electron industry chain duty-keeping mode, promoted re-manufacturing industry reform trial. We actively promoted the building of incubator base, enhanced the support of incubators, enterprises, and projects, and set up incubators in Nanhui Industry Zone, Lingang Software Zone, and Beicai, Hangtou, Nicheng, etc. The construction of techonology financial service platform was pused forward, and the communication between techonological enterprises and financial institutions was more often. Technology research and self-innovation capability have further improved. The invention patent environment has been further improved.

2. Innovation effect has gradually shown. The number of patent in the whole year reached 10896, the number of invention patent reached 3139, and invention patent per million people over 576. The number of testified high-tech enterprises was over 139, testified high-tech contract was over 2753 with 18 billion yuan transaction. The number of testified national and municipal technology project prize was 160, 12 out of them won naitoanl technology prizes, containing 283 scientists, 148 national and 135 municipal.

Ⅳ. Free trade zone led trial policy, Comprehensive reform further advanced

1. The internal and external coorpration of China (Shanghai) Pilot free trade zone has been approved. According to the strategy of central Party committee, municipal Party committee, and municipal government, we diligently conducted the preparation work of FTZ. We fully carried out the general planning approved by the State Council and actively took part in relevant reform items. The investment management system has been carried out and the Negative-list policy was first tried. Trade supervision system started trail period, and "Open up in front-line, Limited in second-line, free trade within zone" regulation mode. We actively prepared the carry-out of the financial regulation innovation and the settle-up of international energy trade center. Comprehensive supervision system has taken reform. As innovations of the trade function continuously strengthened, we have carried out the first "Front-shop-back-storehouse" operating mode high-end consumption exhibition platform.

2. The transform of government responsibility and administrative approval system have been continuously deepened. We promoted the reform of notice and commitment of major industry projects, and further shortened the take-out of projects. We deepened the reformation of the market-entry area, and promoted the integral registration. Several policies like the integral registration and zero payment of registered capital have been carried out in Lingang area. We also made progress in the mode of "the separation of management and operation" and that of "one-door settlement" in key development areas, and improved the mechanism of "local settlement for local affairs" in key development areas. Last but not the least, we improved the centralization of the social and political management in Lingang area and deeply researched the innovation program of management in Lujiazui Financial City.

Ⅴ. Social construction and people's livelihood continuously improved.

1. Citizen's income and welfare guarantee continuously strengthened. With the steady increase of the earning of the residents, the income of urban and suburban residents reached respectively in the whole year is 49629 and 21814 yuan, an increase of 9.8% and 11.7%, both of which were faster than that of the municipal growth. With further enhancement of the social guarantee, we have increased the average monthly pension for persons with the new rural insurance.

2. The employment and social security work continuously enhanced. We have adopted employment-priority strategy and more active employment policy. Social Gurantee has been strenghtened. The social security work has been strengthened. The average pension has increased and the number of people who gained compensation from displacement and resettlement is 145 thousand people. We have further enhanced social security work system policy, nearly 63 thousand people being helped. There is an increase of 1241 new beds for the aged, providing 6 old people home caring centers, 10 old people dinnering help centers, 266 home reconstruction for old living buildings, 79 standard old people playing hall, helping 58.3 thousand old people for community service and 26.3 thousand old people for home helping service. We started the new project of 2.45 million square meters indemnification housing and completed 1.75 million square meters.

3. Education investment continuously enhanced. As for education, there were 19 new-set kindergardens and primary schools. 15 out of 36 public schools which were urgent in use were under construction, one of them was finished. We actively took cooperation with several famous and extraordinary school building and the first bulding of special high school in Pudong. We further deepened the coorpration between schools and enterprises such as Shangfei Coperation, Ligang Group and Tang Town e-commerce.

4. Medical affairs and healthcare quickly developed. As for healthcare, we have started the operation of the comprehensive building of Punnan Hospital and the expand of Oriental Hospital. The comprehensive building of medical technology in the Seventh Hospital has been actively promoted. Zhuqiao Medical Center, Xinchang Comprehensive medical center has began to set up. Community medical service center has began to built in Huamu, Jinqiao, Gaohang, Nicheng and etc. The International Medical Center began to operate, bringing the medical service in PNA into a new level. We have deepen the reform of public hospital and have improved the overall public hospital appraising system. Based on home doctors, we built up a new mode of resident health management team, improving self-management mode. National comprehensive trial reformation construction was pushed forward. Shanghai important public health service continued to operate for old people above 60.

5. Cultural soft competitive strength gradually improved. As for culture, we have promoted the projects such as Xiezhiliu and Chenpeiqiu Museum, Hangtou big-scale residence cultural center and broadcasting center project. We have successfully held large cultural activities such as Shanghai Summer Music Festival and "Sanlin Tang" Shanghai Folk Cultural Festival. The culture and creative industry quickly developed. The third phase of Zhangjiang National Press Base, Sanlin Old Town Cultural Creative Garden began to build.

6. Sports Affairs steadily promoted. As for sports, we have quickened the construction of projects such as Sanlin Sports Center, and successfully held some large sports events such as Short Track Speed Skating World Championships. We also successfully organized the twelfth national student sport meeting and female volleyball competition

in National Athletic Meeting.

7. Practical projects fully completed. Around the key fields that are closely related to the lives of the people, such as increasing the services for the old, promoting the construction of new villages, quickening the reformation of old buildings, promoting the employment, facilitating the public traffic, and enhancing the service level to the public, we have actively advanced the twelve practical projects both in PNA and the municipality, and fully completed municipal practical projects and practical projects.

Ⅵ. Urban construction and management level continuously advanced.

1. Basic management in town was further strengthened. Based on legal and stable principles, we have further improved the overall population management and service. The number of outcoming household and population dropped in a great amount. We further pushed forward the basic democracy, and improved the community representative meeting system and community self-management standard spot. We served "one spot service, one management bureau" as the target, and actively enhanced the standardlization of the service center and formalized the operation and the management of the community service centers.

2. Social institution healthly grew. We have further enhanced the social support for the development of social instituitions. Till the end of 2014, there were 1764 social institutions in PNA. The governmental purchase "supply-demand one-station service platform" was further pused forward, with 59 public commonweal service projects. We have enhanced the service management and opened the direct registeration of 4 kinds of social instituitions, and improved the integral skill of social workers.

Ⅶ. The city overall environment has been improved.

1. Basic construction system has continously strengthened. Main Construction projects speed up course, such as Line 16 and the third phase of Line 9, the second phase of Line 13, the second phase of Line 10, and Line 14. The speed-up reconstruction of Luoshan Road has been finished. Middle-ring Road Pudong part and east-west tunnel has been advanced. Disney, Shangfei, Big-scale Residence has conducted according to original plan. The city light line has covered 1.97 million households, and the coverage rate of home internet line has reached 99%, and 4200 4G base station has been conpleted.

2. The main construction projects have been speed up. The basic facility net has been carried out during the twelfth planning period. The east part of middle ring road in Pudong area, the Luoshan Road Fast Construction Project, and the east-west tunnel project have been carried out according to previous plan. The project related to other areas in Shanghai also made progress, for example, the Xiayan Road has been completed. Nine projects related to Disney Land project, including Zhoudeng Road, have all been on track. Two projects related to Shangfei project, Keyuan Road and Zhangdong Road, have been completed. Ten road projects, three bus projects, and three water supply and sewage projects have been speed up.

3. Environmental work steadily promoted. The fifth environmental three-year action planed to complete 104 projects. We continously promoted the second phase of Binjiang Forest Park and Nanhui Environmental Construction. We built up 50 public green land. The protection of environment has been improved. The newly built public green land reached 97 arches, and the Liming Resource reuse center has been under operation. We organized the rename of national environmentally friendly town, the construction of beautiful town in Pudong area. The special law supervision of main pollution enterprises was one of the important affair in the last year, with supervision of nearly 10000 enterprises and 275 cases. We carried out 390 new energy replacement in manufacturing enterprises and 143 building reconstruction. The environmental quality data has been better used to improve the daily care of the water, green land, and wet land.

4. The city management has continuously strengthened. The city integral management system innovation made progress, e. g. the set-up of integral leader team in Expo area, "5 + X" platform of city integral management, and the pre-running of city information management center. In central Lujiazui area, we built up the street-oriented operation system with police bureau, market management bureau, and so on. We worked on markets in central streets,

bus stations, schools, and hospitals. We have strengthened the law management, examined, punished and dismantled 4.35 million square meters illegal constructions. Meanwhile, the city safety management has been improved with the decrease of safety production accidents, death persons, and 110 help-calling. There is no large-scale poisoning accident and drug accident caused by drug dealers in the whole district.

Ⅷ. Integration of urban and rural development was steadily promoted.

1. "Three Agricultural" work was steadily promoted. As the agricultural economy operated steadily, the total agricultural output value achieved 6.1 billion yuan in the whole year. We have transformed the villages from which administrative villages and about 271 rural households from 22 towns have been benefited, and completed 52 agricultural system in the countryside, within which 20% were self-operated. We have settled 73% in the capital integration of supporting agriculture basic infrastructure and industrial projects. We have contentiously promoted the increase of rural residential income with new related policies in 212 villiages. We have quickened the construction of five national modern agricultural demonstration bases, almost finished the construction of five town-level comprehensive service centers for agriculture.

2. Integration of urban and rural development revolution was actively tried. The Liming Resource reuse center has been under operation. We organized environmentally friendly town and the construction of beautiful town in Pudong area. The special law supervision of main pollution enterprises was one of the important affairs in the last year, The rate of land transaction reached above 68%. We enlarged the trial group from 39 villiages to 180 ones. We enhanced the rural local construction, operating "1 + 1 + X" trial work in 19 towns and 106 villiages.

第一篇

CHAPTER 1

综 合

GENERAL SURVEY

表 1-1 行政区划
Administrative Regions
(2014)

单位:个 (unit)

地 区 Subdistrict/Town	居民委员会 Neighborhood Committee	村民委员会 Village Committee
街镇总计(36 个) Total (36)	**859**	**371**
街 道(12 个) Subdistricts (12)	**400**	
潍坊新村街道 Weifangxincun Subdistrict	27	
陆家嘴街道 Lujiazui Subdistrict	31	
周家渡街道 Zhoujiadu Subdistrict	32	
塘桥街道 Tangqiao Subdistrict	23	
上钢新村街道 Shanggang xincun Subdistrict	23	
南码头路街道 Nanmatoulu Subdistrict	27	
沪东新村街道 Hudongxincun Subdistrict	33	
金杨新村街道 Jinyangxincun Subdistrict	48	
洋泾街道 Yangjing Subdistrict	38	
浦兴路街道 Puxinglu Subdistrict	40	
东明路街道 Dongminglu Subdistrict	37	
花木街道 Huamu Subdistrict	41	
镇(24 个) Towns (24)	**459**	**371**
川沙新镇 Chuansha New Town	40	43
高桥镇 Gaoqiao Town	28	14
北蔡镇 Beicai Town	51	9
合庆镇 Heqing Town	6	29
唐 镇 Tangzhen Town	10	17
曹路镇 Caolu Town	21	32
金桥镇 Jinqiao Town	11	3
高行镇 Gaohang Town	30	3
高东镇 Gaodong Town	14	12
张江镇 Zhangjiang Town	26	9
三林镇 Sanlin Town	54	16
惠南镇 Huinan Town	24	29
周浦镇 Zhoupu Town	29	10
新场镇 Xinchang Town	7	13
大团镇 Datuan Town	4	16
康桥镇 Kangqiao Town	34	12
航头镇 Hangtou Town	9	13
祝桥镇 Zhuqiao Town	25	40
泥城镇 Nicheng Town	9	11
宣桥镇 Xuanqiao Town	6	12
书院镇 Shuyuan Town	5	13
万祥镇 Wanxiang Town	3	7
老港镇 Laogang Town	2	7
南汇新城镇 Nanhui New Town	11	1

表 1-2　气象概况
Climate
(2014)

月份 Month		气温(℃) Temperature(℃) 平均气温 Average Temperature	平均最高气温 Average Highest Temperature	极端最高气温 Utmost Highest Temperature in Each Month	平均最低气温 Average Lowest Temperature	极端最低气温 Utmost Lowest Temperature in Each Month	35℃以上高温日数(天) >35℃(day)	0℃以下低温日数(天) <0℃(day)
年平均	**Annual Average**	**16.9**	**20.9**	**35.6**	**13.7**	**-4.1**	**4**	**15**
1 月	January	6.7	11.9	19.6	2.6	-4.1		7
2 月	February	6.3	9.2	24.8	3.9	-2.2		4
3 月	March	11.5	15.9	25.7	7.9	1.1		
4 月	April	15.5	19.8	25.5	12.1	4.5		
5 月	May	21.2	25.7	33.6	17.2	8.3		
6 月	June	23.2	26.5	33.3	20.7	18.7		
7 月	July	27.4	31.1	35.6	24.5	20.6	2	
8 月	August	26.3	29.4	35.5	24.0	19.7	2	
9 月	September	24.2	27.6	33.0	21.8	18.3		
10 月	October	20.0	24.3	29.8	16.3	9.5		
11 月	November	14.8	18.6	23.4	11.2	4.4		
12 月	December	6.0	10.4	16.2	2.4	-3.5		4

表 1-2　续表　Continued

月份 Month		日照(小时) Sunshine (hour)	降水 Rainfall 雨量(毫米) Rainfall (mm)	雨日(天) Rainy Day (day)	大雾日(天) Fog Days (day)	霾日(天) Haze Days (day)	平均相对湿度(%) Relative Humidity(%)
全年总计	**Annual Total**	**1 787.0**	**1 541.3**	**137**	**20**	**99**	**75**
1 月	January	178.0	22.5	5	2	8	71
2 月	February	70.8	157.4	16	2	3	79
3 月	March	176.7	67.0	10		2	70
4 月	April	143.1	163.3	15	3	10	77
5 月	May	198.4	66.7	11	1	15	69
6 月	June	102.8	281.1	14	2	11	82
7 月	July	167.4	274.0	15	6	8	82
8 月	August	103.7	225.3	19	1	5	84
9 月	September	118.6	197.4	12		4	81
10 月	October	211.0	38.6	4	1	5	71
11 月	November	139.3	42.5	11	2	9	73
12 月	December	177.2	5.5	5		19	60

注：2014 年极端最高气温 35.6℃，出现在 7 月 12 日；极端最低气温 -4.1℃，出现在 1 月 22 日；初霜日 11 月 19 日，终霜日 3 月 22 日，无霜期 236 天。

Note: In 2014, the utmost highest temperature amounted to35.6℃ on July 6 and the utmost lowest temperature came to -4.1℃ on January 22. The frost season started on November 19 and ended on March 22. There were 236 frost-free days in 2014.

表1-3　主要年份经济发展主要指标
Major Indicators of Economic Development in Main Years

指　标　Indicators		1993	2005	2010	2013	2014
国民经济预算	**Domestic Economic Accounts**					
新区生产总值(亿元)	Gross Domestic Product of PNA (100 million yuan)	164.00	2 108.79	4 707.52	6 448.68	7 109.74
第一产业	Primary Industry	2.12	6.09	31.47	31.28	29.73
第二产业	Secondary Industry	114.45	1 070.96	2 036.58	2 262.39	2 319.38
第三产业	Tertiary Industry	47.43	1 031.74	2 639.47	4 155.01	4 760.63
财　政	**Finance**					
财政收入(亿元)	Financial Revenue (100 million yuan)	11.15	494.94	2 046.17	2 762.84	2 900.77
#一般公共预算收入	Local Financial Revenue	5.53	155.31	428.82	610.59	684.51
一般公共预算支出(亿元)	Local Financial Expenditure (100 million yuan)	9.53	198.79	524.06	738.44	820.36
固定资产投资总额(亿元)	**Total Investment in Fixed Assets(100 million yuan)**	**164.56**	**693.61**	**1 432.30**	**1 679.22**	**1 765.73**
#房地产开发投资	Investment in Real Estate Development		287.92	555.74	826.13	897.87
#城市基础设施投资额	Investment in Urban Infrastructure	54.73	125.95	261.92	267.63	275.25
招商引资	**Business Promotion and Foreign-Fund Attraction**					
外商直接投资合同项目(项)	Projects of Foreigin Direct Investment (unit)	924	1 734	906	1 032	2 185
外商直接投资合同金额(亿美元)	Project Amount of Foreign Direct Investment (USD 100 million)	17.57	56.54	56.25	71.89	143.07
期末内资企业注册数(个)	Number of Registered Domestically-Funded Enterprises at End of Term (unit)			10 961	10 854	13 271
科技创新	**Technological Innovations**					
研发机构数(个)	Number of R&D Institutions (unit)		161	393	508	525
专利申请数(项)	Patent Claiming(item)		3 141	17 587	18 331	19 002
专利授权数(项)	Number of Authorized Patents (Piece)		1 204	12 764	11 073	10 896

注：1. 2005年至2008年,“港口货物吞吐量”和“集装箱吞吐量”为外高桥港区数据;2009年起“港口货物吞吐量”和“集装箱吞吐量”为外高桥港区和洋山深水港区数据。
2. “中外资保险机构原保费收入”与历年年鉴中的“保费收入”统计口径相同,下同。

Note: 1. The items of “Volume of Cargo Handled at Port” and “Container Handling Capacity” are the data at Waigaoqiao Port form 2005 to 2008. These two items are the data at Waigaoqiao Port and Yanghan Deepwater Port since 2009.
2. The items of “Former Premiunm Income of Insurances by Chinese and Foreign Insurance Institutions” has the same statistical approach with that of “Premium Income” of the previous years, hereinafter the same.

表1-3 续表 Continued

指标	Indicators	1993	2005	2010	2013	2014
工业总产值(亿元)	**Gross Output Value of Industry (100 million yuan)**	**604.40**	**4 242.47**	**8 591.50**	**9 375.57**	**9 495.42**
#高技术工业	Industrial Output of High Technologies		1 190.72	2 259.08	2 792.33	2 727.63
国内外贸易	**Domestic and Foreign Trades**					
商品销售总额(亿元)	Aggregate Sales of Commodities (100 million yuan)		2 807.47	8 263.56	24 034.93	27 640.16
社会消费品零售总额(亿元)	Total Retail Sales of Consumer Goods (100 million yuan)	41.92	353.69	1 036.88	1 598.01	1 740.23
外贸进出口总额(亿美元)	Total Imports and Exports (USD 100 million)	25.92	894.75	1 865.62	2 496.08	2 678.71
出口总额	Total Exports	12.02	372.12	738.79	958.25	1 006.10
进口总额	Total Imports	13.90	522.63	1 126.83	1 537.83	1 672.61
功能开发	**Functional Development**					
中外资金融机构数(个)	Number of Chinese and Foreign Financial Institutions (unit)		369	649	794	844
中外资银行本外币存款余额(亿元)	Balance of RMB and Foreign Currencies Deposits in Chinese and Foreign Banks (100 million yuan)		4 244	13 079	17 432	19 130
中外资银行本外币贷款余额(亿元)	Balance of RMB and Foreign Currencies Loans in Chinese and Foreign Banks (100 million yuan)		4 668	10 436	13 457	14 018
期末认定跨国公司地区总部入驻数(户)	Settled Headquarters of Transnational Companies at End of Term (in number)		64	150	214	229
举办展览(博览)(次)	Number of Exhibitions Hosted (time)		114	120	211	220
举办国际性会议(次)	Number of International Conferences Hosted (time)		199	26	2 164	2 068
接待国内外游客总数(万人次)	Foreign and Domestic Tourists Received (10 000 person-times)		1 660	3 215	3 002	3 639
浦东国际机场旅客吞吐量(万人次)	Passenger Capacity at Pudong International Airport (10 000 person-times)		2 358	4 041	4 719	5 169
浦东国际机场货邮吞吐量(万吨)	Volume of Cargo Handled at Pudong International Airport (10 000 tons)		185	322	291	318
港口货物吞吐量(万吨)	Volume of Cargo Handled at Port (10 000 tons)	9 017	10 646	22 470	28 697	29 918
集装箱吞吐量(万标箱)	Container Handling Capacity (10 000 TEUs)		1 272.5	2 509.8	3 058.5	3 236.6

表1-4 主要年份社会发展主要指标
Major Indicators of Social Development in Main Years

指 标	Indicators	1993	2005	2010	2013	2014
人 口	**Population**					
年末常住人口(万人)	Permanent Population at Year end (10 000 persons)		279.19	504.44	540.90	545.12
年末户籍总人口(万人)	Registered Population at Year end (10 000 persons)	143.73	184.81	275.80	283.79	288.44
年末总户数(万户)	Total Households at Year end(10 000 households)	48.63	68.95	106.08	109.87	111.84
自然增长率(‰)	Natural Growth Rate(‰)	-0.08	-0.58	1.06	0.72	1.87
少年人口抚养比(%)	Youth Dependency Ratio(%)				13.83	14.50
老年人口抚养比(%)	Elderly Dependency Ratio(%)				23.04	24.52
劳动就业	**Labor and New Jobs**					
从业人员(万人)	Employed Persons (10 000 persons)	104.40	144.08	235.11	290.59	302.39
第一产业	Primary Industry	4.98	1.99	14.78	13.39	13.63
第二产业	Secondary Industry	66.37	57.07	123.90	155.51	150.33
第三产业	Tertiary Industry	33.05	85.02	96.43	121.70	138.43
职工人数(万人)	Staff and Workers (10 000 persons)	78.88	70.16	85.02	152.84	197.81
新增就业岗位(万人)	Number of New Jobs (10 000 persons)		11.50	14.04	15.10	15.07
期末城镇登记失业人数(万人)	Number of Registered Unemployed Persons in Towns at End of Term (10 000 persons)		4.29	4.35	4.40	4.18
人民生活	**People's Livelihood**					
城镇居民人均年可支配收入(元)	Annual Disposable Income Per Capita of Urban Residents (yuan)		19 089	32 330	45 199	49 629
农村居民人均年可支配收入(元)	Annual Disposable Income Per Capita of Rural Villiage Residents (yuan)		9 779	13 898	19 529	21 814
平均期望寿命(岁)	Life Expectancy (year)	76.10	80.85	82.57	83.03	83.32

表1-4　续表　Continued

指　标　Indicators		1993	2005	2010	2013	2014
教　育	**Education**					
高等学校在校学生数(人)	Student Enrollment of Higher Education (person)	3 776	41 034	167 746	179 866	168 501
中等学校在校学生数(人)	Student Enrollment at High Schools(person)	79 751	149 407	171 968	173 755	166 740
小学在校学生数(人)	Student Enrollment at Primary Schools (person)	131 204	92 062	165 009	195 725	201 261
市实验性、示范性高中和区重点高中就读学生比例(%)	Rate of Students Enrolled in Municipal Experimental and Demonstration High Schools and District-Key High Schools(%)			73.2	80.1	81.1
学龄儿童入学率(%)	Rate of School-age Child Enrollment (%)	99.2	100.0	100.0	100.0	100.0
幼儿园幼儿数(人)	Young Child Enrollment at Kindergartens (person)	42 378	44 554	83 313	108 715	109 807
卫　生	**Health**					
医疗机构数(个)	Healthcare Institutions (unit)	378	630	1 057	1 070	1 044
#医　院	Hospitals	47	57	56	60	64
医院病床(张)	Hospital Bed (bed)	4 840	6 520	15 164	18 993	20 043
卫生技术人员(人)	Healthcare Professionals (person)	7 717	9 794	18 925	26 479	28 341
#执业医生	Medical Practitioners	4 102	4 726	7 644	9 518	10 309
注册护士	Registered Nurses	2 179	3 390	7 448	11 392	12 283
城市建设、环境保护	**Urban Construction and Environmental Protection**					
建成区绿化覆盖率(%)	Coverage of Urban Green Areas in PNA (%)		37.8	36.1	36.0	36.2
城镇污水纳管率(%)	Rate of Sewage Pipe in Towns(%)		70.4	81.9	87.9	89.0
空气质量优良率(%)	Rate of Fine Air Quality (%)		89.3	92.6	68.2	76.7
人均公共绿地(平方米)	Public Green Space Per Capita (sq・m)	3.40	24.42	22.71	24.02	24.00

表1-5 历年社会经济主要指标增长率(以上年为基期)
(1993~2014)

单位:%

指 标	Indicators	1993	1994	1995	1996	1997	1998	1999	2000
年末总户数	Total Households at Year-end		2.6	3.1	3.1	2.8	3.4	3.1	4.1
年末户籍总人口	Registered Population at Year-end	2.2	1.7	1.7	1.7	1.5	1.8	2.5	3.0
男	Male	2.3	1.9	1.8	1.8	1.5	2.0	2.6	3.2
女	Female	2.0	1.6	1.5	1.6	1.5	1.7	2.4	2.8
年末常住人口	Permanent Population at Year-end								
新区生产总值	Gross Output Value of PNA	30.2	28.6	22.0	20.2	18.3	16.8	16.1	16.5
第一产业	Primary Industry	-8.5	5.1	14.2	1.9	5.3	5.9	3.8	4.9
第二产业	Secondary Industry	22.0	21.6	21.9	17.4	16.3	14.0	13.5	15.2
第三产业	Tertiary Industry	46.6	42.8	22.6	30.0	24.3	24.2	22.5	19.6
工业总产值	Gross Domestic Product of Industry	28.7	20.1	19.3	18.2	18.4	15.1	17.3	18.9
财政收入	Financial Revenue		1.2倍(times)	62.9	30.5	21.4	13.0	13.2	30.1
#一般公共预算收入	Local Financial Revenue		1.8倍(times)	51.6	32.1	30.0	10.2	-0.5	27.6
一般公共预算支出	Local Financial Expenditure		1.1倍(times)	93.9	10.1	18.2	10.8	4.8	19.1
固定资产投资总额	Total Investment in Fixed Assets	1.2倍(times)	58.7	9.2	38.6	27.7	15.6	-24.9	-19.9
#房地产开发投资	Investment in Real Estate Development								6.6
城市基础设施投资额	Investment in Urban Infrastructure	1.5倍(times)	43.9	-32.2	84.7	20.9	48.5	-11.7	-65.2
商品销售总额	Aggregate Sales of Commodities			16.7	21.2	28.3	-1.6	93.8	26.9
社会消费品零售总额	Total Retail Sales of Consumer Goods	48.5	97.4	32.9	27.5	15.7	10.3	10.8	8.5
外贸进出口总额	Total Imports and Exports		82.7	52.0	12.2	22.6	21.0	28.2	65.9
出口总额	Total Exports		93.1	70.8	-2.2	18.3	15.1	26.3	43.7
进口总额	Total Imports		73.7	33.9	30.0	26.5	26.1	29.8	82.9

注:凡财政指标均为2004年财税体制改革后的同口径对比数,后续相关指标口径相同。
Note: Every financial indicator is the comparative number with the same approach after reforms of finance and taxation system in 2004, hereinafter the same.

Growth Rate of Major Indicators of Social Economy (the Previous Year as Base)

(%)

2001	2002	2003	2004	2005	2006	2007	2008	2009	2010	2011	2012	2013	2014
2.3	2.4	2.6	2.3	3.3	1.7	1.8	1.3	1.3	2.6	1.2	1.0	1.3	1.8
2.2	2.6	2.2	2.4	2.2	1.5	1.9	1.6	1.4	1.3	1.0	0.9	1.0	1.6
2.3	2.7	2.4	2.4	2.1	1.4	1.8	1.4	1.3	1.2	0.9	0.9	0.9	1.7
2.0	2.5	2.1	2.3	2.2	1.5	2.1	1.9	1.4	1.4	1.0	0.9	1.0	1.6
3.1	3.0	3.0	3.1	3.1	2.2	7.0	0.1	1.7	20.4	2.6	1.7	2.8	0.8
16.1	16.7	17.5	16.4	12.1	13.4	15.2	11.6	10.5	12.4	11.1	10.1	9.7	9.3
6.1	4.9	1.6	-7.3	-4.0	-5.1	-5.4	-5.8	-2.7	-2.7	-0.9	-6.8	-8.8	-4.5
16.3	16.4	19.3	17.2	10.5	12.1	10.1	9.1	6.3	15.3	9.5	3.7	2.4	3.4
16.1	17.1	15.8	15.7	14.0	15.0	20.4	14.0	14.5	10.3	12.4	14.9	14.4	12.7
20.1	21.0	26.4	22.4	11.8	13.3	14.3	9.4	6.7	21.1	11.2	1.1	1.0	1.1
39.1	41.2	46.1	25.7	10.5	18.7	45.4	22.0	5.8	25.4	10.3	4.6	17.0	5.0
47.2	14.6	41.6	20.9	13.0	14.8	46.3	16.0	9.1	12.0	16.7	10.0	11.0	12.1
26.9	36.9	32.6	20.7	2.7	12.0	29.1	28.9	7.1	10.2	17.4	8.4	10.8	11.1
18.5	41.1	2.5	8.3	6.4	-4.8	18.8	11.3	16.2	0.8	0.2	1.4	15.4	5.2
6.5	93.6	13.9	13.7	3.0	-10.5	-4.0	13.1	6.2	28.8	6.1	1.8	37.6	8.7
93.3	62.6	-9.2	-22.1	3.9	23.9	50.3	32.7	33.3	-46.6	3.9	-3.7	2.2	2.8
33.5	77.9	35.5	21.0	-4.3	4.9	22.7	28.6	13.7	39.9	27.1	38.5	12.8	15.0
8.3	22.0	10.2	14.4	13.2	13.1	14.0	15.5	14.4	20.6	16.1	12.1	11.5	8.9
16.9	21.9	57.5	39.0	10.7	19.9	19.3	13.2	-12.9	34.2	21.1	6.1	4.0	7.3
15.0	18.2	55.8	52.8	14.9	19.5	18.8	14.4	-16.9	28.2	20.3	5.7	2.0	5.0
17.9	24.2	58.6	31.1	7.9	20.2	19.7	12.4	-9.8	38.5	21.7	6.4	5.4	8.8

单位:%

表1－5 续表 Continued

指 标	Indicators	1993	1994	1995	1996	1997	1998	1999	2000
浦东国际机场旅客吞吐量	Passenger Capacity at Pudong International Airport								
浦东国际机场货邮吞吐量	Volume of Cargo Handled at Pudong International Airport								
港口货物吞吐量	Volume of Cargo Handled at Port	21.8	-7.8	-27.6	19.7	2.9	-5.8	-1.3	10.1
集装箱吞吐量	Container Handling Capacity				1.9倍 (times)	45.3	48.7	36.2	85.4
外商直接投资合同项目	Projects of Foreigin Direct Investment	63.0	12.0	-19.0	-4.3	-23.2	-9.9	-15.2	47.4
外商直接投资合同金额	Contracted Amount of Foreign Direct Investment	29.9	47.6	25.6	-44.4	-0.5	55.0	-61.5	1.7倍 (times)
中外资银行本外币存款余额	Balance of RMB and Foreign Currencies Deposits in Chinese and Foreign Banks								
中外资银行本外币贷款余额	Balance of RMB and Foreign Currencies Loans in Chinese and Foreign Banks								
城镇居民人均年可支配收入	Annual Disposable Income Per Capita of Urban Residents								
农村居民人均年可支配收入	Annual Disposable Income Per Capita of Rural Residents								
居民储蓄存款年末余额	Residents' Savings Deposit Balance (Year End)	77.1	76.2	56.3	28.9	20.0	13.5	10.6	2.7
高等学校在校学生数	Student Enrollment of Higher Education	26.4	11.3	13.0	6.6	11.9	29.0	21.7	34.4
中等学校在校学生数	Student Enrollment at High Schools	9.6	17.1	15.6	8.2	5.0	5.9	6.2	0.8
小学在校学生数	Student Enrollment at Primary Schools	7.7	0.2	-1.8	-0.1	1.3	-2.7	-6.7	-6.7
幼儿园幼儿数	Young Child Enrollment at Kindergartens		-12.0	-3.5	-9.0	0.5	-0.5	1.0	3.0
医院病床	Hospital Beds	3.1	3.7	4.8	2.8	-1.2	3.4	9.8	2.2
卫生技术人员	Healthcare Professionals	3.4	4.0	2.3	4.4	5.2	3.1	1.2	1.4
#执业医生	Medical Practitioners	6.6	5.1	3.0	6.4	4.5	2.6	1.6	1.5
注册护士	Registered Nurses	3.7	4.9	2.6	3.7	7.6	5.1	2.7	2.6
期末认定跨国公司地区总部入驻数	Settled Headquarters of Transnational Companies at End of Term								

(%)

2001	2002	2003	2004	2005	2006	2007	2008	2009	2010	2011	2012	2013	2014
	64.9	36.3	39.7	12.1	13.1	8.6	-2.8	13.4	26.2	2.5	8.3	5.2	9.5
	79.5	81.8	38.5	-1.1	16.8	16.2	4.8	-2.4	26.8	-3.4	-5.1	-1.4	9.3
20.9	36.9	16.5	36.0	33.2	6.6	15.3	0.4	-4.9	14.3	17.2	3.4	5.4	4.3
56.9	60.2	43.3	42.0	34.9	7.9	13.4	-1.2	-9.7	17.4	14.8	2.5	3.6	5.8
27.0	9.5	73.4	1.0	2.7	-16.6	-13.3	-36.0	-12.1	16.2	9.8	-1.9	5.7	1.1倍
-30.6	33.3	7.8	12.1	75.4	-14.4	2.2	0.9	0.3	1.7	17.3	10.4	-1.3	99.0
				25.3	18.8	25.0	22.2	22.9	24.2	18.9	9.6	2.3	9.7
				21.4	20.2	23.8	12.0	7.6	16.9	11.8	8.1	6.6	4.2
				12.4	12.4	13.2	14.5	9.3	11.0	13.9	11.1	10.5	9.8
				11.4	11.6	12.2	12.5	9.2	12.1	14.1	11.2	10.7	11.7
24.2	35.2	31.9	27.9	30.7	17.1	1.4	34.6	18.2	12.2	14.7	15.1	9.5	3.0
28.0	86.2	21.3	9.6	8.5	5.9	8.2	19.0	4.7	29.5	10.2	-3.7	1.1	-6.3
-1.0	0.2	-1.5	12.3	-2.0	-4.1	-3.8	-3.0	-0.5	-0.7	0.3	-1.2	2.0	-4.0
-6.3	-2.3	-0.6	-11.4	3.3	3.5	3.3	3.1	17.3	3.2	6.9	3.8	6.9	2.8
-1.9	11.0	6.4	7.3	5.4	4.2	9.9	5.5	9.1	10.6	13.7	9.1	5.2	1.0
5.3	6.0	4.6	-0.6	-5.4	17.4	5.6	2.7	2.5	7.8	16.9	2.4	4.6	5.5
0.9	-1.3	-0.1	12.3	0.1	6.5	19.6	10.5	3.2	-1.8	22.1	5.9	8.2	7.0
0.5	-8.4	-0.2	3.7	-0.1	1.4	9.9	9.6	1.8	2.8	16.0	4.1	3.1	8.3
3.9	9.9	0.6	7.4	1.6	18.0	18.2	8.4	8.9	4.4	29.3	7.9	9.6	7.8
					29.7	15.7	19.8	17.4	11.1	14.0	12.9	10.9	7.0

表1-6 社会经济主要指标年均增长速度
Average Annual Growth Rate of Main Social Economic Indicators

单位:% (%)

指标	Indicators	平均每年增长 Annual Growth Rate 1993～2014	1991～1995	1996～2000	2001～2005	2006～2010
年末户籍总人口	Registered Population at Year-end	1.8	2.1	2.1	2.3	1.5
新区生产总值	Gross Domestic Product in PNA	15.8	23.0	17.6	15.7	13.1
第一产业	Primary Industry	-0.6	2.4	4.4	0.1	0.5
第二产业	Secondary Industry	13.2	20.0	15.3	15.9	11.6
第三产业	Tertiary Industry	19.7	29.8	24.1	15.7	14.9
工业总产值	Gross Output Value of Industry	15.1	20.3	17.6	20.3	14.9
*财政收入	Financial Revenue	26.9		21.4	36.8	22.8
* #一般公共预算收入	Local Financial Revenue	25.9		19.2	22.5	18.9
*一般公共预算支出	Local Financial Expenditure	22.6		12.5	23.4	17.1
社会消费品零售总额	Total Retail Sales of Consumer Goods	19.1	50.4	14.4	14.0	16.7
*外贸进出口总额	Total Imports and Exports	23.5		28.8	28.6	15.8
*出口总额	Total Exports	22.4		19.3	31.2	14.7
*进口总额	Total Imports	24.4		37.5	26.9	16.6
中外资银行本外币存款余额	Balance of RMB and Foreign Currencies Deposits in Chinese and Foreign Banks					20.8
中外资银行本外币贷款余额	Balance of RMB and Foreign Currencies Loans in Chinese and Foreign Banks					19.2
居民储蓄存款年末余额	Balance of Residents' Savings Deposits at Year-end	24.0	54.4	14.8	29.9	21.6

注：1. 带"*"指标宾栏第一栏年均增长速度的年份为"1994～2014"。
2. 带"*"指标宾栏第二栏因仅有二年增长速度,故不再计算该指标的年均增长速度。

Note: 1. The year with the annual growth rate in the first horizontal column that is indicated with the symbol of "*" is from 1994 to 2014.
2. Because the second column in the field of indicators with the sign of "*" only has the growth rate of the recent two years, we will not calculate the annual growth rate of this indicator.

表 1-7 社会经济结构主要指标
Main Indicators of Economic and Social Structures

单位:% (%)

指 标	Indicators	2005	2010	2013	2014
第三产业增加值占 GDP 比重	Ratio of Added Value of the Tertiary Industry in GDP	48.9	56.1	64.4	67.0
新区财政收入相当于 GDP 比例	Ratio of PNA Financial Revenue in GDP	23.5	36.1	42.8	40.8
一般公共预算收入相当于 GDP 比例	Ratio of Local Financial Revenue in GDP	7.4	9.0	9.5	9.6
固定资产投资相当于 GDP 比例	Ratio of Fixed Capital Investment in GDP	32.9	30.4	26.0	24.8
外贸进出口总额相当于 GDP 比例	Ratio of Total Volume of Foreign Trade in GDP	342.4	262.5	236.0	230.5
外贸出口总额相当于 GDP 比例	Ratio of Total Exports of Foreign Trade in GDP	142.4	103.9	90.6	86.6
社会消费品零售总额相当于 GDP 比例	Ratio of Total Volume of Retail Sales for Social Consumer Goods in GDP	16.8	22.0	24.8	24.5
六个重点发展行业总产值占工业总产值比重	Ratio of Total Output Value of Six Key Industries in Total Value of Industrial Output	68.1	70.0	69.8	69.7
高技术产业工业总产值占工业总产值比重	Ratio of Total Output Value of High-tech Industries in Total Value of Industrial Output		26.3	29.8	28.7
城市基础设施投资占固定资产投资总额比重	Ratio of Investment for Urban Infrastructure in Gross Investment in Fixed Assets	18.2	18.3	15.9	15.6
房地产开发投资占固定资产投资总额比重	Ratio of Investment for Real Estate Development in Gross Investment in Fixed Assets	41.5	38.8	49.2	50.8
机电产品出口占外贸出口商品总额比重	Ratio of Exports of Machinery and Electrical Equipment in Total Exports of Foreign Trade	61.0	66.4	68.6	68.4
高新技术产品出口占外贸出口商品总额比重	Ratio of Export of High and New Technological Products in Total Export of Foreign Trade	33.4	36.6	42.6	43.1
第三产业实到外资占新区实到外资金额比重	Ratio of Foreign Investment in Place for the Tertiary Industry in Total of Foreign Investment in Place in PNA	71.8	86.8	89.1	93.5
发明专利申请量占专利申请量比重	Ratio of the Number of Applications for Invention Patents in the Volume of Patent Applications	57.1	37.4	52.8	54.1
城镇居民家庭人均食品支出占人均消费支出比重	Ratio of Expenses for Food per Capita of Urban Families in Consumption Expenditure Per Capita	36.2	34.9	36.5	35.3

表1-8 主要年份社会经济部分指标平均每天水平
Daily Average Level of Major Economic and Social Indicators in Main Years

指 标	Indicators	单 位 Unit	2005	2010	2013	2014
新区生产总值	Gross Output Value in PNA	万元 10 000 yuan	57 775	128 973	176 676	194 787
工业总产值	Gross Output Value of Industry	万元 10 000 yuan	116 232	235 384	256 865	260 148
财政收入	Financial Revenue	万元 10 000 yuan	13 560	56 059	75 694	79 473
#一般公共预算收入	Local Financial Revenue	万元 10 000 yuan	4 255	11 748	16 728	18 754
固定资产投资额	Total Investment in Fixed Assets	万元 10 000 yuan	19 003	39 241	46 006	48 376
新增固定资产	Newly Acquired Fixed Assets	万元 10 000 yuan	10 409	17 066	19 496	19 422
商品销售总额	Total Sales of Commodities	万元 10 000 yuan	76 917	226 399	658 491	757 265
社会消费品零售额	Retail Sales of Consumer Goods	万元 10 000 yuan	11 370	28 408	43 781	47 678
外贸出口货物总额	Total Exports Value of Commodities in Foreign Trade	万美元 USD 10 000	10 195	20 241	26 253	27 564
外商直接投资合同项目	Projects of Foreigin Direct Investment	个 unit	4.75	2.48	2.83	5.99
外商直接投资合同金额	Contracted Amount of Foreign Direct Investment	万美元 USD 10 000	1 549	1 541	1 970	3 920
港口货物吞吐量	Volume of Cargo Handled at Port	万吨 10 000 tons	29.17	61.56	78.62	81.97
自来水售水量	Sales of Tap Water	万立方米 10 000 cu. m	114.87	164.62	165.86	166.74
售电量	Electricity Sales	万千瓦·时 10 000 kwh	3 512	6 293	7 224	7 151
管道燃气售气量	Sales of Pipelined Gas	万立方米 10 000 cu·m	121.37	175.89	196.36	205.13
公交车辆乘客人数	Passengers Carried by Public Vehicles	万人次 10 000 person-times	173.12	206.02	167.83	163.66
医院诊疗人数	Outpatients Treated	万人次 10 000 person-times	3.49	8.12	11.37	12.76
出生人数	Birth	人 person	34	61	64	74
死亡人数	Death	人 person	37	53	58	59

表1-9 主要年份社会经济人均指标
Annual Average Level of Major Social and Economi Indicators Per Capita in Main Years

指 标	Indicators	单 位 Unit	2005	2010	2013	2014
工业总产值	Gross Output Value of Industry	元 yuan	154 244	186 066	175 689	174 866
财政收入	Financial Revenue	元 yuan	17 995	44 314	51 773	53 420
#一般公共预算收入	Local Financial Revence	元 yuan	5 647	9 287	11 442	12 606
固定资产投资额	Total Investment in Fixed Assets	元 yuan	25 218	31 019	31 467	32 517
新增固定资产	Newly Acquired Fixed Assets	元 yuan	13 813	13 490	13 335	13 055
社会消费品零售额	Total Retail Sales of Consumer Goods	元 yuan	12 859	22 456	29 945	32 048
外贸出口总额	Total Exports Value of Foreign Trade	美元 USD	13 529	16 000	17 957	18 528
外贸进口总额	Total Imports Value of Foreign Trade	美元 USD	19 001	24 404	28 817	30 803
居民年末储蓄存款余额	Balance of Savings Deposits at Year-end	元 yuan	40 209	63 747	79 717	80 680
职工年平均工资	Annual Average Wage of Staff and Workers	元 yuan	33 186	89 424	100 361	113 668
城镇居民年可支配收入	Annual Disposable Income Per Capita of Urban Residents	元 yuan	19 089	32 330	45 199	49 629
农村居民年可支配收入	Annual Disposable Income Per Capita of Suburban Residents	元 yuan	9 779	13 898	19 529	21 814
公共绿地占有面积	Public Green Area	平方米 sq·m	24.42	22.71	24.02	24.00
邮政订销报刊数	Total Circulation of Newspapers and Magazines	份 in number	43	16	33	33
每万人拥有病床数	Number of Sick-beds per 10 000 Persons	张 bed	23.35	32.84	35.59	36.91
每万人拥有医生数	Number of Doctors per 10 000 Persons	人 person			17.84	18.98
每万名中小学生拥有教职员工数	Number of Teaching Staff per 10 000 Primary and Middle School Students	人 person	882	821	774	799
实有人口万人发案率	Ratio of Criminal Cases per 10 000 Persons	起/万人 in number /10000persons	61.76	50.93	54.44	44.14
每万人拥有律师数	Number of Lawyers per 10 000 Persons	人 person	5.4	6.4	7.2	7.6

注：1. 上述指标除特别注明外，人均水平均采用常住人口计算。
2. 居民年人均可支配收入为住户调查资料。

Note：1. The average level per capita has been calculated in the permanent population except the above-mentioned indicators are otherwise specified.
2. The data of annual disposable income per capita are surveyed from household residents.

表1-10 历年新区生产总值
Gross Domestic Product in PNA
(1990~2014)

单位:亿元 (100 million yuan)

年 份 Year	新区生产总值 Gross Domestic Product of PNA	第一产业 Primary Industry	第二产业 Secondary Industry	#工 业 Industry	第三产业 Tertiary Industry	#金 融 Banking	房地产 Real Estate
1990	60.24	2.22	45.89	43.13	12.13	3.07	
1991	71.54	2.41	53.45	50.46	15.68	4.46	
1992	101.49	1.89	73.72	70.25	25.88	6.96	
1993	164.00	2.12	114.45	108.16	47.43	16.40	
1994	291.20	3.19	197.13	177.45	90.88	23.73	
1995	414.65	4.22	283.92	260.07	126.51	28.59	36.52
1996	496.47	4.57	320.31	286.32	171.59	39.08	40.61
1997	608.22	4.95	376.87	325.38	226.40	69.10	46.20
1998	704.27	5.30	412.82	349.97	286.15	101.31	52.68
1999	801.36	5.47	435.66	388.88	360.23	138.35	47.26
2000	923.51	5.72	488.60	445.43	429.19	159.88	55.36
2001	1 087.53	6.06	560.29	508.62	521.18	170.12	70.39
2002	1 244.00	6.38	635.54	579.86	602.08	166.04	100.51
2003	1 510.32	6.67	767.53	708.98	736.12	183.48	129.12
2004	1 850.13	6.00	952.25	894.13	891.88	218.13	168.25
2005	2 108.79	6.09	1 070.96	1 009.47	1 031.74	249.69	174.48
2006	2 365.33	5.88	1 194.47	1 133.76	1 164.98	313.98	169.24
2007	2 793.39	6.06	1 306.49	1 237.36	1 480.84	474.83	185.38
2008	3 150.99	5.88	1 430.25	1 351.44	1 714.86	553.46	181.49
2009	4 001.39	30.61	1 706.29	1 581.82	2 264.49	708.28	258.94
2010	4 707.52	31.47	2 036.58	1 899.04	2 639.47	825.78	250.08
2011	5 484.35	34.46	2 306.32	2 154.27	3 143.57	991.61	229.71
2012	5 929.91	32.89	2 320.75	2 171.00	3 576.27	1 069.11	269.46
2013	6 448.68	31.28	2 262.39	2 085.15	4 155.01	1 253.67	319.54
2014	7 109.74	29.73	2 319.38	2 135.40	4 760.63	1 503.34	303.56

表1-11　历年新区生产总值结构
Structure of Total Gross Domestic Product in PNA
(1990~2014)

单位:%　　　　　(%)

年 份 Year	新区生产总值 Gross Domestic Product of PNA	第一产业 Primary Industry	第二产业 Secondary Industry	#工 业 Industry	第三产业 Tertiary Industry	#金 融 Banking	房地产 Real Estate
1990	100.0	3.7	76.2	71.6	20.1	5.1	
1991	100.0	3.4	74.7	70.5	21.9	6.2	
1992	100.0	1.9	72.6	69.2	25.5	6.9	
1993	100.0	1.3	69.8	66.0	28.9	10.0	
1994	100.0	1.1	67.7	60.9	31.2	8.1	
1995	100.0	1.0	68.5	62.7	30.5	6.9	8.8
1996	100.0	0.9	64.5	57.7	34.6	7.9	8.2
1997	100.0	0.8	62.0	53.5	37.2	11.4	7.6
1998	100.0	0.7	58.6	49.7	40.7	14.4	7.5
1999	100.0	0.7	54.4	48.6	44.9	17.3	5.9
2000	100.0	0.6	52.9	48.2	46.5	17.3	6.0
2001	100.0	0.6	51.5	46.8	47.9	15.6	6.5
2002	100.0	0.5	51.1	46.6	48.4	13.4	8.1
2003	100.0	0.5	50.8	46.9	48.7	12.1	8.6
2004	100.0	0.3	51.5	48.3	48.2	11.8	9.1
2005	100.0	0.3	50.8	47.9	48.9	11.8	8.3
2006	100.0	0.2	50.5	47.9	49.3	13.3	7.2
2007	100.0	0.2	46.8	44.3	53.0	17.0	6.6
2008	100.0	0.2	45.4	42.9	54.4	17.6	5.7
2009	100.0	0.8	42.6	39.5	56.6	17.7	6.5
2010	100.0	0.7	43.2	40.3	56.1	17.5	5.3
2011	100.0	0.6	42.1	39.3	57.3	18.1	4.2
2012	100.0	0.6	39.1	36.6	60.3	18.0	4.5
2013	100.0	0.5	35.1	32.3	64.4	19.4	5.0
2014	100.0	0.4	32.6	30.0	67.0	21.1	4.3

表1-12 主要年份新区生产总值(新行业分类)

Gross Domestic Product in Main Years(Grouped by New Sectors)

单位:亿元 (100 million yuan)

指 标	Indicators	2005	2010	2013	2014
新区生产总值	**Gross Gross Domestic Production of PNA**	**2 108.79**	**4 707.52**	**6 448.68**	**7 109.74**
第一产业	Primary Industry	6.09	31.47	31.28	29.73
第二产业	Secondary Industry	1 070.96	2 036.58	2 262.39	2 319.38
工 业	Industry	1 009.47	1 899.04	2 085.15	2 135.40
建筑业	Construction	61.49	137.54	177.24	183.98
第三产业	Tertiary Industry	1 031.74	2 639.47	4 155.01	4 760.63
交通运输、仓储业、邮政业	Transportation, Warehousing and Post Service	88.88	170.97	219.76	230.75
信息传输、计算机服务和软件业	Information Transmission, Computer Service and Computer Software	73.34	233.07	420.38	481.36
批发和零售业	Wholesale and Retail	212.05	608.27	1 023.62	1 177.16
住宿和餐饮业	Hotel and Catering	28.13	53.03	63.33	66.50
金融业	Banking	249.69	825.78	1 253.67	1 503.34
房地产业	Real Estate	174.48	250.08	319.54	303.56
其他服务业	Other Services	205.17	498.27	854.71	997.96
构 成(%)	**Composition (%)**	**100.0**	**100.0**	**100.0**	**100.0**
第一产业	Primary Industry	0.3	0.7	0.5	0.4
第二产业	Secondary Industry	50.8	43.2	35.1	32.6
工 业	Industry	47.9	40.3	32.3	30.0
建筑业	Construction	2.9	2.9	2.8	2.6
第三产业	Tertiary Industry	48.9	56.1	64.4	67.0
交通运输、仓储业、邮政业	Transportation, Warehousing and Post Service	4.2	3.6	3.4	3.2
信息传输、计算机服务和软件业	Information Transmission, Computer Service and Computer Software	3.5	5.0	6.5	6.8
批发和零售业	Wholesale and Retail	10.1	12.9	15.9	16.6
住宿和餐饮业	Hotel and Catering	1.3	1.2	1.0	0.9
金融业	Banking	11.8	17.5	19.4	21.1
房地产业	Real Estate	8.3	5.3	5.0	4.3
其他服务业	Other Services	9.7	10.6	13.2	14.0

表1-13　历年新区生产总值指数
Gross Domestic Product Indexes of PNA
(1991～2014)

(以1990年为100)　　(Taking 1990 as 100)

年份 Year	新区生产总值 Gross Domestic Product of PNA	第一产业 Primary Industry	第二产业 Secondary Industry	#工业 Industry	第三产业 Tertiary Industry	#金融 Banking	房地产 Real Estate
1991	113.9	101.2	113.1		119.5	141.0	
1992	138.0	102.3	137.6		143.8	179.1	
1993	179.7	93.6	167.9	121.9	210.7	332.7	
1994	231.1	98.4	204.2	148.0	301.0	408.5	
1995	282.0	112.4	248.9	172.1	369.0	440.0	105.2
1996	339.0	114.5	292.2	199.8	479.7	576.9	111.6
1997	401.0	120.6	339.9	227.4	596.2	856.7	120.8
1998	468.3	127.7	387.4	256.7	740.5	1210.5	132.1
1999	543.8	132.6	439.7	301.4	907.1	1571.2	105.4
2000	633.5	139.1	506.5	352.9	1 084.9	1850.9	127.7
2001	735.5	147.6	589.1	406.2	1 259.6	1937.9	157.4
2002	858.3	154.8	685.7	473.3	1 475.0	1941.7	214.3
2003	1 008.5	157.3	818.0	570.3	1 708.1	2145.6	250.3
2004	1 173.9	145.8	958.7	678.1	1 976.3	2488.9	276.5
2005	1 315.9	140.0	1 059.4	752.0	2 253.0	2854.8	273.5
2006	1 492.2	132.9	1 187.6	849.0	2 591.0	3565.6	261.7
2007	1 719.0	125.7	1 307.5	935.6	3 119.5	4963.3	267.7
2008	1 918.5	118.3	1 426.7	1 019.8	3 555.9	5712.8	257.0
2009	2 119.9	115.1	1 516.6	1 080.9	4 071.6	7369.5	314.1
2010	2 382.8	112.0	1 748.6	1 253.8	4 491.0	7 819.0	282.7
2011	2 647.3	111.0	1 914.7	1 381.8	5 047.8	8 663.5	257.5
2012	2 914.7	103.5	1 985.6	1 435.7	5 799.9	9 694.5	299.3
2013	3 197.4	94.4	2 033.2	1 457.2	6 635.1	11 691.5	311.5
2014	3 494.8	90.2	2 102.3	1 506.7	7 477.8	13 889.5	281.9

注：工业增加值以1992年为100，房地产增加值以1994年为100。
Note: The added industrial value takes the data of 1992 as 100, and the added real estate value takes the data of 1994 as 100.

表 1-14 历年新区生产总值增长速度
Gross Domestic Product Growth Rate of PNA
(1991～2014)

单位:% (%)

年 份 Year	新区生产总值 Gross Domestic Product of PNA	第一产业 Primary Industry	第二产业 Secondary Industry	#工 业 Industry	第三产业 Tertiary Industry	#金 融 Banking	房地产 Real Estate
1991	13.9	1.2	13.1	13.8	19.5	41.0	
1992	21.2	1.1	21.7	20.1	20.3	27.0	
1993	30.2	-8.5	22.0	21.9	46.6	85.8	
1994	28.6	5.1	21.6	21.4	42.8	22.8	
1995	22.0	14.2	21.9	16.3	22.6	7.7	5.2
1996	20.2	1.9	17.4	16.1	30.0	31.1	6.1
1997	18.3	5.3	16.3	13.8	24.3	48.5	8.2
1998	16.8	5.9	14.0	12.9	24.2	41.3	9.4
1999	16.1	3.8	13.5	17.4	22.5	29.8	-20.2
2000	16.5	4.9	15.2	17.1	19.6	17.8	21.1
2001	16.1	6.1	16.3	15.1	16.1	4.7	23.3
2002	16.7	4.9	16.4	16.5	17.1	0.2	36.1
2003	17.5	1.6	19.3	20.5	15.8	10.5	16.8
2004	16.4	-7.3	17.2	18.9	15.7	16.0	10.5
2005	12.1	-4.0	10.5	10.9	14.0	14.7	-1.1
2006	13.4	-5.1	12.1	12.9	15.0	24.9	-4.3
2007	15.2	-5.4	10.1	10.2	20.4	39.2	2.3
2008	11.6	-5.8	9.1	9.0	14.0	15.1	-4.0
2009	10.5	-2.7	6.3	6.0	14.5	29.0	22.2
2010	12.4	-2.7	15.3	16.0	10.3	6.1	-10.0
2011	11.1	-0.9	9.5	10.2	12.4	10.8	-8.9
2012	10.1	-6.8	3.7	3.9	14.9	11.9	16.2
2013	9.7	-8.8	2.4	1.5	14.4	20.6	4.1
2014	9.3	-4.5	3.4	3.4	12.7	18.8	-9.5

表 1-15 历年第三产业增加值增长速度(旧行业分类)

Growth Rate of Value Added in Tertiary Industry(Grouped By Old Sectors) (1991 ~2000)

单位:% (%)

年 份 Year	第三产业增加值 Value Added in Tertiary Industry	#交通、运输、仓储、邮电通讯业 Transportation, Warehousing, Post and Telecommunications	批发和零售贸易、餐饮业 Wholesale, Retail and Catering	金融保险 Banking and Insurance	房地产 Real Estate
1991	19.5	8.8	8.1	41.0	
1992	20.3			27.0	
1993	46.6	37.3	24.8	85.8	
1994	42.8	5.4	54.1	22.8	
1995	22.6	15.2	72.8	7.7	5.2
1996	30.0	28.4	58.9	31.1	6.1
1997	24.3	12.2	18.5	48.5	8.2
1998	24.2	17.0	18.3	41.3	9.4
1999	22.5	22.1	29.1	29.8	-20.2
2000	19.6	17.9	19.1	17.8	21.1

表 1-16 历年第三产业增加值增长速度(新行业分类)

Growth Rate of Value Added in Tertiary Industry(Grouped by New Sectors) (2001 ~2014)

单位:% (%)

年 份 Year	第三产业增加值 Value Added in Tertiary Industry	#交通运输、仓储业、邮政业 Transportation, Warehousing and Post Service	信息传输、计算机服务和软件业 Information Transmission, Computer Service and Computer Software	批发和零售业 Wholesale and Retail	金融业 Banking	房地产业 Real Estate
2001	16.1	27.5	9.4	21.6	4.7	23.3
2002	17.1	27.1	9.7	16.9	0.2	36.1
2003	15.8	15.8	64.3	13.6	10.5	16.8
2004	15.7	22.2	21.4	12.6	16.0	10.5
2005	14.0	18.6	18.3	14.8	14.7	-1.1
2006	15.0	15.2	19.1	12.9	24.9	-4.3
2007	20.4	15.7	16.4	14.7	39.2	2.3
2008	14.0	10.9	20.3	15.4	15.1	-4.0
2009	14.5	-5.3	5.4	14.3	29.0	22.2
2010	10.3	16.5	10.9	20.1	6.1	-10
2011	12.4	12.3	18.4	16.6	10.8	-8.9
2012	14.9	3.4	16.3	18.2	11.9	16.2
2013	14.4	5.5	15.8	12.3	20.6	4.1
2014	12.7	1.0	14.5	14.1	18.8	-9.5

表 1-17 社会经济主要指标占全市比重

The Proportion of Major Economic and Social Indicators in Shanghai

指 标	Indicators	2013			2014		
		浦东新区 PNA	全市 Shanghai	比重(%) Proportion(%)	浦东新区 PNA	全市 Shanghai	比重(%) Proportion(%)
土地面积(平方公里)	Land Area (sq. km)	1 373.82	6 340.50	21.7	1 373.82	6 340.50	21.7
年末常住人口(万人)	Permanent Population at Year-end (10 000 persons)	540.90	2 415.15	22.4	545.12	2 425.68	22.5
年末户籍总人口(万人)	Registered Population at Year-end (10 000 persons)	283.79	1 432.34	19.8	288.44	1 438.69	20.0
从业人员(万人)	Employment (10 000 persons)	290.59	1 368.91	21.2	302.39	1 365.63	22.1
生产总值(亿元)	Gross Domestic Product (100 million yuan)	6 448.68	21 818.15	29.6	7 109.74	23 567.70	30.2
第一产业	Primary Industry	31.28	124.89	25.0	29.73	124.26	23.9
第二产业	Secondary Industry	2 262.39	7 907.81	28.6	2 319.38	8 167.71	28.4
#工 业	Industry	2 085.15	7 139.18	29.2	2 135.40	7 362.84	29.0
第三产业	Tertiary Industry	4 155.01	13 785.45	30.1	4 760.63	15 275.73	31.2
#金 融	Banking	1 253.67	2 823.29	44.4	1 503.34	3 400.41	44.2
房地产	Real Estate	319.54	1 343.77	23.8	303.56	1 530.96	19.8
工业总产值(亿元)	Gross Output Value of Industry (100 million yuan)	9 375.57	33 899.38	27.7	9 495.40	3 4071.19	27.9
固定资产投资总额(亿元)	Total Investment in Fixed Assets (100 million yuan)	1 679.22	5 647.79	29.7	1 765.73	6 016.43	29.3
城市基础设施投资额(亿元)	Investment in Urban Infrastructure (100 million yuan)	267.63	1 043.31	25.7	275.25	1 057.25	26.0
一般公共预算收入(亿元)	Local Government Revenue (100 million yuan)	610.59	4 109.51	14.9	684.51	4 585.55	14.9
一般公共预算支出(亿元)	Local Government Expenditure (100 million yuan)	738.44	4 528.61	16.3	820.36	4 923.44	16.7

表 1-17 续表 Continued

指标 Indicators		2013			2014		
		浦东新区 PNA	全市 Shanghai	比重（%） Proportion（%）	浦东新区 PNA	全市 Shanghai	比重（%） Proportion（%）
商品销售总额（亿元）	Aggregate Sales of Commodities（100 million yuan）	24 034.93	78 744.10	30.5	27 640.16	87 829.31	31.5
社会消费品零售总额（亿元）	Retail Sales of Consumer Goods（100 million yuan）	1 598.01	8 556.96	18.7	1 740.23	9 303.49	18.7
年末居民储蓄存款余额（亿元）	Savings Deposit Balance of Rural and Urban Residents（100 million yuan）	4 254.05	21 185.69	20.1	4 381.03	21 995.54	19.9
外贸进出口商品总额（亿美元）	Total Value of Imports and Exports（USD 100 million）	2 496.08	4 413.98	56.5	2 678.71	4 666.22	57.4
#出口总额	Value of Exports	958.25	2 042.44	46.9	1 006.10	2 102.77	47.8
外商直接投资合同项目（个）	Projects of Foreigin Direct Investment（unit）	1 032	3 842	26.9	2 185	4 697	46.5
外商直接投资合同金额（亿美元）	Contracted Amount of Foreign Direct Investment（USD 100 million）	71.89	246.30	29.2	143.07	316.09	45.3
外商直接投资实际到位金额（亿美元）	Foreign Direct Investment Actually Absorbed（USD 100 million）	50.33	167.80	30.0	44.76	181.66	24.6
港口货物吞吐量（万吨）	Volume of Cargo Handled at Port（10 000 tons）	28 697	77 575	37.0	29 918	75 529	39.6
集装箱吞吐量（万标箱）	Container Handling Capacity（10 000 TEUs）	3 058.5	3 361.7	91.0	3 236.6	3 528.5	91.7
各级各类学校在校学生数（万人）	Student Enrollment by Level and Type of Schools（10 000 persons）	55.01	189.08	29.1	53.65	189.38	28.3
医院病床（张）	Number of Hospital Beds（bed）	18 993	114 314	16.6	20 043	98 261	20.4
专业卫生技术人员（万人）	Medical Technical Personnel（10 000 persons）	2.65	15.64	16.9	2.83	16.40	17.3
#执业医生	Medical Practitioners	0.95	5.81	16.4	1.03	6.13	16.8
申请专利（项）	Patent Claiming（item）	18 331	86 450	21.2	19 002	81 664	23.3

表1-18 财政收支
Fiscal Revenue and Expenditure

单位:万元 (10 000 yuan)

指 标	Indicators	2000	2010	2013	2014
全部财政收入	**Total Financial Revenue**	**1 032 077**	**20 461 744**	**27 628 398**	**29 007 708**
一般公共预算收入	**PNA Government Revenue**	**564 020**	**4 288 216**	**6 105 854**	**6 845 097**
区级财政收入	**PNA Financial Revenue**	**355 863**	**6 866 283**	**9 602 671**	**9 973 518**
#增值税	Value Added Tax	44 293	695 060	1 453 293	1 621 000
营业税	Business Income Tax	122 200	1 478 656	1 303 339	1 296 685
企业所得税	Enterprise Tax	72 712	911 281	1 310 698	1 452 600
个人所得税	Individual Income Tax	77 662	447 612	635 289	732 877
城市维护建设税	Tax on Urban Construction and Maintenance	11 603	64 066	152 615	163 982
房产税	Tax on Real Estate	13 418	78 264	127 008	149 939
印花税	Stamp Tax	3 588	124 409	178 773	211 325
契 税	Contract Tax	7 107	315 205	423 312	404 045
一般公共预算支出	**PNA Government Expenditure**	**695 999**	**5 240 626**	**7 384 418**	**8 203 595**
#一般公共服务	Ordinary Community Services		337 484	407 653	406 499
公共安全	Public Security		217 982	265 907	301 104
教 育	Education		493 988	1 025 495	919 851
科学技术	Technology		239 029	407 344	406 902
文化体育与传媒	Culture, Sports and Media		55 135	97 490	87 792
社会保障和就业	Social Security and Employment		456 319	590 514	690 176
医疗卫生与计划生育	Medical hegienism and Birth Control		260 061	312 571	439 777
节能环保	Lower Power Consumption and Environment Protection		61 191	41 936	39 322
城乡社区事务	Urban and Suburban Community Affairs		1 475 828	1 902 557	1 904 908
农林水事务	Agricultural, Forest and Water Affairs		285 049	348 598	388 434
交通运输	Traffic and Transportation		153 107	312 452	429 758
资源勘探信息等支出	Resource Prospect Information Expend		879 267	1 193 177	1 666 568
商业服务业等支出	Business Services Expend		63 436	83 380	120 673
金融支出	Finanacial Expend		88 000	62 000	76 000

注:1、2007 年财政部进行财税体制改革,起用新科目,2000 及 2005 年口径数据无法提供。
2、2010 年起财政收入数按“十二五”市财税体制改革确定的新体制口径填列。

Note: 1、This table is provided by PNA Financial Bureau. The Financial Department has started the reform of the finance and taxation system since 2007, which began to use the new subject. Data approached in 2000 and those in 2005 are not available.
2. The number of financial revenue are filled in according to the new system approach determined by the municipal financeand system reforms during the “Twelfth-Five-Year Planning” since the year of 2010.

主要统计指标解释

气 温

气温是指空气的温度,一般以摄氏度(℃)为单位表示。气象观测的温度表是放在离地面约 1.5 米处通风良好的百叶箱里测量的,因此,通常说的气温指的是离地面 1.5 米处百叶箱中的温度。其统计计算方法为:

月平均气温是将全月各日的平均气温相加,除以该月的天数而得。

年平均气温是将 12 个月的月平均气温累加后除以 12 而得。

降水量

降水量是指从天空降落到地面的液态或固态(经融化后)水,未经蒸发、渗透、流失而在地面上积聚的深度。其统计计算方法为:

月降水量是将全月各日的降水量累加而得。

年降水量是将 12 个月的月降水量累加而得。

日照时数

日照时数是指太阳实际照射地面的时间。其统计方法与降水量相同。

生产总值(原国内生产总值)

国内生产总值是指按市场价格计算的一个地区所有常住(驻)单位在一定时期内生产活动的最终成果。生产总值有三种表现形态,即价值形态、收入形态和产品形态。从价值形态看,它是所有常驻单位在一定时期内所生产的全部货物和服务价值超过同期投入的全部非固定资产货物和服务价值的差额,即所有常住(驻)单位的增加值之和;从收入形态看,它是所有常住(驻)单位在一定时期内所创造并分配给常住(驻)单位和非常住(驻)单位的初次(分配)收入之和;从产品形态看,它是所有常住单位在一定时期内最终使用的货物和服务减去进口货物和服务。在实际核算中,生产总值有三种计算方法(其三种表现形态体现为三种计算方法),即生产法、收入法和支出法。三种方法分别从不同的方面反映生产总值及其构成。根据国务院和国家统计局有关我国 GDP 核算和数据发布制度的规定,浦东新区国内生产总值自 2004 年起更名为“浦东新区生产总值”,简称“浦东新区 GDP”。

三次产业

根据社会生产活动历史发展的顺序对产业结构的划分,产品直接取自自然界的部门称为第一产业,对初级产品进行再加工的部门称为第二产业,为生产和消费提供各种服务的部门称为第三产业。

第一产业:农林牧渔业(包括农业、林业、畜牧业、渔业和农林牧渔服务业)。

第二产业:包括采矿业、制造业、电力、燃气及水的生产和供应业与建筑业。

第三产业:除第一、第二产业以外的其他各业。

指 数

指数是一种表明社会经济现象动态的相对数。运用指数可以测定不能直接相加和直接对比的社会经济现象的总动态;可以分析社会经济现象总变动中各因素变动的影响程度;可以研究总平均指标变动中各组标志水平和总体结构变动的作用。它是在把各个年份的产值换算成可比价格的基础上,根据定基数等于相应各个环比指数的连乘积这个换算关系计算出来的。

平均每年增长速度

在我国计算平均增长速度有两种方法,一种是习惯上经常使用的“水平法”,又称几何平均法,是各以间隔期最后一年的水平同基期水平对比来计算平均每年增长(或下降)速度。另一种是"累计法",又称代数平均法或方程法,是以间隔期内各年水平的总和同基期水平对比来计算平均每年增长(或下降)速度。

在一般正常情况下,两种方法计算的平均每年增长速度比较接近,但在经济发展不平衡,出现大起大落时,两种方法计算的结果差别较大。

本年鉴内所列的平均每年增长速度,除固定资产投资、直接吸收外资是用“累计法”计算以外,其余均用“水平法”计算。

财政收入

指国家财政参与社会产品分配所取得的收入,是实现国家职能的财力保证。财政收入所包括的内容几经变化,目前主要包括:

(1)各项税收:包括增值税、营业税、消费税、土地增值税、城市维护建设税、资源税、城市土地使用税、企业所得税、个人所得税、关税、证券交易印花税、车辆购置税、农牧业税和耕地占用税等。

(2)专项收入:包括排污费收入、城市水资源费收入、矿产资源补偿费收入、教育费附加收入等。

(3)其他收入:包括利息收入、基本建设贷款归还收入、基本建设收入、捐赠收入等。

(4)国有企业亏损补贴:此项为负收入,冲减财政收入。主要包括对工业企业、商业企业、粮食企业的补贴。

中央财政收入和一般公共预算收入

指按现行分税制财政体制划分的中央本级收入和一般公共预算收入。1994年实行分税制财政体制以后，属于中央财政的收入包括关税、海关代征消费税和增值税，消费税，中央企业所得税，地方银行和外资银行及非银行金融企业所得税，铁道部门、各银行总行、各保险总公司等集中缴纳的营业税、利润和城市维护建设税，车辆购置税，船舶吨税，增值税的75%部分，证券交易税(印花税)94%部分，个人所得税中的利息所得税，利息所得税之外的个人所得税中央分享的部分，海洋石油资源税。属于一般公共预算的收入包括营业税，地方企业所得税，利息所得税之外的个人所得税地方分享的部分，城镇土地使用税，固定资产投资方向调节税，城镇维护建设税，房产税，车船使用税，印花税，屠宰税，农牧业税，农业特产税，耕地占用税，契税，土地增值税、国有土地有偿使用收入，增值税25%部分，证券交易税(印花税)6%部分和除海洋石油资源税以外的其他资源税。

一般公共预算支出

一般公共预算支出指根据政府在经济和社会活动中，按照政府的责权划分确定的支出。地方财政支出主要包括地方行政管理和各项事业费，地方统筹的基本建设、技术改造支出，支援农村生产支出，城市维护和建设经费，价格补贴支出等。

港口货物吞吐量

指经水运进出港区范围，并经过装卸的货物数量，包括邮件及办理托运手续的行李、包裹以及补给运输船舶的燃、物料和淡水。货物吞吐量按货物流向分为进口、出口吞吐量，按货物交流性质分为外贸货物吞吐量和国内贸易货物吞吐量。货物吞吐量的货类构成及其流向，是衡量港口生产能力大小的重要指标。

国际标准集装箱吞吐量

凡经过水运进、出港区范围，并经过装卸的集装箱箱数和重量(含集装箱自重)，通常是按进港和出港分别统计。

TEU是"折合20英尺标准箱"的英文缩写。它是指各种尺寸的国际标准集装箱的自然箱数，按各自的换算比例，折算为20英尺标准箱的换算箱数。其换算比例为：40英尺箱1：2；35英尺箱1：1.75；20英尺箱1：1；10英尺箱1：0.5。

EXPLANATORY NOTES TO MAJOR STATISTICAL INDICATORS

Temperature

Temperature refers to the air temperature. It often uses centigrade as the unit. The thermometry used for weather observation is put in a breezy shutter, which is 1.5 meters high from the ground. Therefore, the commonly used temperature refers to the temperature in the breezy shutter 1.5 meters away from the ground. The calculation method is as follows:

Monthly average temperature is the summation of average daily temperature of one month divided by the actual days of that particular month.

Annual average temperature is the summation of monthly average of a year divided by 12 months.

Volume of Precipitation

Volume of Precipitation refers to the deepness of liquid state or solid state (thawed) water falling from the sky to the ground that has not been evaporated, infiltrated or run off. The calculation method is as follows:

Monthly precipitation is the summation of daily precipitation of a month.

Annual precipitation is the summation of 12 months precipitation of a year.

Sunshine Hours

Sunshine Hours refers to the actual hours of sun irradiating the earth. The calculation method is the same as that of the precipitation.

Gross Domestic Product

Gross Domestic Product refers to the final products at market prices by (of) all resident units of a region during a certain period of time. Gross product is expressed in three different forms, i. e value, income, and products respectively. The form of value added refers to the total value of all products and services produced by all resident units during a certain period of time minus the total value of inputs of non fixed-assets products and services or the summation of the value added of all resident units; the form of income includes all the income items produced by all resident units and distributed primarily to all resident and non-resident units; the form of product refers to all final goods and services minus imports of goods and services. In the practice of national accounting, it is calculated by three approaches, i. e. product approach, income approach, and expenditure approach, respectively, to reflect Gross Product and its composition of different aspects. According to the regulations of GDP national accounting and data release issued by the State Council and National Bureau of Statistics, since 2004 Pudong New Area Gross Domestic Product has been renamed as Pudong New Area Gross Product Value, for short PNA GDP.

Three Industries

Three Industries have been classified according to the historical sequence of development. Primary industry refers to extraction of natural resources; secondary industry involves processing of primary products; and tertiary industry provides services of various kinds for production and consumption.

Primary industry: Agriculture, forestry, animal husbandry and fishery. (including farming, forestry, animal husbandry, fishery industry and service industry for farming, forestry, animal husbandry and fishery).

Secondary industry: Mining, manufacturing, power, steam and water production and supply and construction.

Tertiary industry: All other industries not included in primary or secondary industries.

Index

Index refers to the relative figures indicating social and economic phenomena and developments. Index is used to evaluate the overall development of social and economic phenomena which can not be determined by simple addition or direct comparison. It is also used to analyze the outcome of various changes in the general phenomenon movement of social and economic development, and to study the level of each sub-index in the changes of general average index and the role of the changes of the overall structure. It is calculated at the comparable prices conversed from the output value of each year, using the formula of index number with fixed base period equal to the continuous product of its relative chain index.

Average Annual Growth Rate

Two methods for calculating Average Annual Growth Rate are applied in China, one is often called "level approach" or geometry average, which is derived by comparing the growth rate for the last year of the interval with that of the beginning year; the other is called "accumulating approach" or algebraic average or equation method, which is calculated by comparing the total growth rate of each year for the interval with that of base year.

Usually the results calculated by the two methods are fairly close, but they differ sharply when imbalance occurred in economic development with striking fluctuations in growth.

The Average Annual Growth Rates listed in this statistical yearbook are calculated by "level approach" except for the growth rate of investment in fixed assets and foreign capital absorbed.

Government Revenue

Government Revenue refers to the revenue of the government finance by means of participating in the distribution of the social products, which is the financial resources for ensuring the government to function. The contents of government revenue have been changed several times. Now it includes the following main items:

(1) Various tax revenues, including value added tax, business tax, consumption tax, land value added tax, tax on city maintenance and construction, resources tax, tax on use of urban land, enterprise income tax, personal income tax, tariff, stamp tax on security transactions, tax on purchase of motor vehicles, tax on agriculture and animal husbandry and tax on occupancy of cultivated land, etc.

(2) Special revenues, including revenues from the fee on sewage treatment, fee on urban water resources, fee for the compensation of mineral resources and extra-charges for education, etc.

(3) Other revenues, including revenue from interest, revenue from the repayment of capital construction loan, revenue from capital construction projects, and donations and grants.

(4) Subsidies for the losses of the state-owned enterprises. This is an item of negative revenue, consisting of subsidies to industrial, commercial and grain purchasing and supply enterprises.

Revenue of the Central Government and Revenue of the Local Government

Revenue of the central government and revenue of the local governments: refers to the revenue of the central government and that of the local governments as defined by the decentralized taxation system starting from 1994. In accordance with this system, the revenue of the central government includes tariff, consumption tax and value added tax levied by the customs, consumption tax, income tax of the enterprises subordinate to the central government, income taxes of the local banks, foreign-funded banks and non-bank financial institutions, business tax and profits of railways, head offices of banks, head office of insurance company , which are handed over to the government in a centralized way, tax on city maintenance and construction, tax on purchasing motor vehicles, tonnage tax of ships, 75% of the value added tax, 94% of the tax on stock dealing (stamp tax), interest income tax in the personal income tax, proportion of the personal income tax (other that interest income tax) to be shared by the central government, and tax on ocean petroleum resources. The revenue of the local governments includes business tax, income tax of the enterprises subordinate to the local government, proportion of the personal income tax (other that interest income tax) to be shared by the central government, tax on the use of urban land, tax on the adjustment of the investment in fixed assets, tax on town maintenance and construction, tax on real estates, tax on the use of vehicles and ships, stamp tax, slaughter tax, tax on agriculture and animal husbandry, tax on special agricultural products, tax on the occupancy of cultivated land, contract tax, value-added tax on land, income from charges on use of state-owned land, 25% of the value added tax, 6% of the tax on stock dealing (stamp tax) and tax on resources other than the ocean petroleum resources.

Expenditure of the Local Government

Expenditure of the local government includes mainly the administrative expenses and various operating expenses at the level of local governments, the expenditure for capital construction and technological innovation with the funds raised by the local government, expenditure for supporting rural production, expenditure for city maintenance and construction and expenditure for price subsidies, etc.

Volume of Freight Handled in Ports

Volume of Freight Handled in Ports refers to the volume of cargo passing in and out the harbor area of the ports and having been loaded and unloaded. The volume includes that of the postal matters, registered luggage and fuels, materials and fresh water as supplies of the ships. The volume of freight handled may be classified by direction of flow as freight for import and freight for export, or by nature of cargo as freight for domestic trade and freight for foreign trade. As an important indicator, the volume of freight handled by type of cargo and by main flow direction reflects the production capacity of ports.

International Container Throughput Capacity

International Container Throughput Capacity refers to number and weight of containers which are loaded or unloaded within port area via water carriage. It is often calculated by entering and leaving port, respectively. TEU was the abbreviation of twenty foot equivalent unit, which refers to converted number of all kinds of containers. The conversion method is based on respective conversion ratio and the number of all kinds of container is converted to the standard number of twenty foot equivalent unit. The conversion ratio is: 40 feet container 1 : 2, 35 feet container 1 : 1.75, 20 feet container 1 : 1, 10 feet container 1 : 0.5.

第二篇

CHAPTER 2

人口

POPULATION

表 2－1　历年常住人口、户籍人口、流动人口情况
(1990～2014)

单位:万人

年　份 Year	年末常住人口 Permanent Population at Year-end	常住人口密度 (人/平方公里) Density of Permanent Population (Persons/sq·km)	年末户籍人口 Registered Population at Year-end	按户籍 Grouped by Types of 非农业 Non-agriculture
1990			133.94	81.67
1991			137.34	85.45
1992			140.67	89.65
1993			143.73	97.78
1994			146.20	104.63
1995			148.63	109.73
1996			151.11	113.84
1997			153.40	119.20
1998			156.18	123.70
1999			160.08	128.51
2000	240.23	4 503	164.87	134.57
2001	247.56	4 641	168.45	139.85
2002	255.11	4 782	172.82	146.25
2003	262.89	4 616	176.69	153.46
2004	270.91	4 756	180.90	160.13
2005	279.19	4 902	184.81	170.17
2006	285.30	5 009	187.56	175.24
2007	305.35	5 361	191.16	179.90
2008	305.70	5 367	194.29	183.62
2009	419.05	3 462	272.28	240.32
2010	504.44	3 908	275.80	245.06
2011	517.50	4 007	278.53	248.63
2012	526.39	3 832	281.12	252.24
2013	540.90	3 937	283.79	255.37
2014	545.12	3 968	288.44	260.87

Permanent Population, Household Registered Population and Migrating Population

(10 000 Persons)

性质分 Residence Registration	按性别分 Grouped by Sex		户籍人口密度 (人/平方公里) Density of Registered Population (persons/sq. km)	期末登记流动人口数 Number of Registered Migrating Population
农 业 Agriculture	男 Male	女 Female		
52.27	66.41	67.53	2 584	
51.89	68.22	69.12	2 650	
51.02	69.96	70.71	2 714	
45.95	71.59	72.14	2 749	
41.57	72.92	73.28	2 797	
38.90	74.23	74.40	2 843	
37.27	75.53	75.58	2 891	
34.20	76.70	76.70	2 934	
32.48	78.21	77.97	2 988	
31.57	80.22	79.86	3 001	
30.30	82.75	82.12	3 091	
28.60	84.66	83.79	3 158	
26.57	86.97	85.85	3 240	67.94
23.23	89.03	87.66	3 102	80.16
20.77	91.20	89.70	3 176	82.58
14.64	93.12	91.69	3 245	93.73
12.32	94.45	93.11	3 293	119.75
11.26	96.13	95.03	3 356	130.97
10.67	97.48	96.81	3 411	127.30
31.96	136.00	136.28	2 249	169.53
30.74	137.60	138.20	2 137	218.33
29.90	138.87	139.65	2 156	206.50
28.88	140.18	140.94	2 046	238.32
28.42	141.49	142.30	2 066	266.81
27.57	143.86	144.59	2 100	252.11

表2-2 土地面积、户数、人口、人口密度及人口迁移情况
(2014年底)

单位:人

地 区 Subdistrict/Town		土地面积(平方公里) Land Area (sq. km)	户 数(户) Household (household)	年末人口 Population Year-end	按户籍性质分 Grouped by Types of Residence Registration	
					非农业 Non-agriculture	农 业 Agriculture
总 计	**Total**	**1 373.82**	**1 118 356**	**2 884 440**	**2 608 666**	**275 774**
街道小计	**Subdistrict Tot**	**85.69**	**441 634**	**1 165 228**	**1 165 178**	**50**
潍坊新村街道	Weifangxincun Subdistrict	3.74	31 757	91 437	91 437	
陆家嘴街道	Lujiazui Subdistrict	6.89	38 133	117 667	117 667	
周家渡街道	Zhoujiadu Subdistrict	5.52	43 234	113 174	113 174	
塘桥街道	Tangqiao Subdistrict	3.86	21 875	57 686	57 683	3
上钢新村街道	Shanggangxincun Subdistrict	7.54	36 606	101 329	101 329	
南码头路街道	Nanmatoulu Subdistrict	4.25	30 115	80 546	80 545	1
沪东新村街道	Hudongxincun Subdistrict	5.39	28 764	73 018	73 018	
金杨新村街道	Jinyangxincun Subdistrict	8.02	52 766	131 853	131 853	
洋泾街道	Yangjing Subdistrict	7.38	40 281	107 607	107 606	1
浦兴路街道	Puxinglu Subdistrict	6.25	42 106	103 457	103 457	
东明路街道	Dongminglu Subdistrict	5.95	27 960	67 320	67 284	36
花木街道	Huamu Subdistrict	20.90	48 037	120 134	120 125	9
镇小计	**Town Tot**	**1 288.13**	**676 722**	**1 719 212**	**1 443 488**	**275 724**
川沙新镇	Chuansha New Town	96.70	57 126	153 994	119 742	34 252
高桥镇	Gaoqiao Town	39.00	34 719	89 670	85 198	4 472
北蔡镇	Beicai Town	23.71	51 459	131 571	128 024	3 547
合庆镇	Heqing Town	41.86	22 939	57 553	37 858	19 695
唐 镇	Tangzhen Town	32.30	17 467	44 628	42 081	2 547
曹路镇	Caolu Town	45.40	25 907	75 628	64 825	10 803
金桥镇	Jinqiao Town	25.20	11 059	29 247	28 753	494
高行镇	Gaohang Town	22.80	21 561	55 157	55 117	40
高东镇	Gaodong Town	35.10	14 237	36 796	32 959	3 837
张江镇	Zhangjiang Town	45.00	27 883	78 918	78 904	14
三林镇	Sanlin Town	34.19	53 358	133 771	127 114	6 657
惠南镇	Huinan Town	65.38	46 577	115 466	101 202	14 264
周浦镇	Zhoupu Town	42.68	32 753	79 856	73 666	6 190
新场镇	Xinchang Town	53.44	22 326	53 659	35 378	18 281
大团镇	Datuan Town	50.57	29 070	66 979	35 557	31 422
康桥镇	Kangqiao Town	41.55	27 561	70 154	68 967	1 187
航头镇	Hangtou Town	59.51	26 474	64 175	48 730	15 445
祝桥镇	Zhuqiao Town	160.19	54 662	138 080	105 303	32 777
泥城镇	Nicheng Town	59.27	25 028	57 784	43 192	14 592
宣桥镇	Xuanqiao Town	45.81	19 009	43 353	35 027	8 326
书院镇	Shuyuan Town	54.20	22 722	52 194	28 454	23 740
万祥镇	Wanxiang Town	23.14	10 024	24 852	16 630	8 222
老港镇	Laogang Town	38.90	13 429	33 809	18 895	14 914
南汇新城镇	Nanhui New Town	152.23	9 372	31 918	31 912	6

注：南汇新城镇集体户口居多,因此不计算他的户规模。
Note: As the nubmer of collective households in Nanhui New Town is much more than that of urban households, we do not calculate its scale of households.

Land Area, Households, Population, Density of Population and Migration of Population (End of 2014)

(person)

按性别分 Grouped by Sex		平均每户人口 Average Persons Per Household	人口密度 (人/平方公里) Population Density (persons/sq·km)	人口迁移情况 Population Mobility		
男 Male	女 Female			迁入 Population Moved-in	迁出 Population Moved-out	净迁入 Net Mobility
1 438 574	**1 445 866**	**2.58**	**2 100**	**25 031**	**9 741**	**15 290**
582 017	**583 211**	**2.64**	**13 598**	**9 583**	**1 401**	**8 182**
45 159	46 278	2.88	24 448	605	67	538
57 782	59 885	3.09	17 078	965	425	540
55 973	57 201	2.62	20 503	802	86	716
28 501	29 185	2.64	14 945	327	41	286
50 382	50 947	2.77	13 439	389	47	342
39 766	40 780	2.67	18 952	417	43	374
37 326	35 692	2.54	13 547	638	72	566
66 067	65 786	2.50	16 441	950	110	840
53 881	53 726	2.67	14 581	1 189	284	905
53 008	50 449	2.46	16 553	1 252	96	1 156
34 361	32 959	2.41	11 314	665	33	632
59 811	60 323	2.50	5 748	1 384	97	1 287
856 557	**862 655**	**2.54**	**1 335**	**15 448**	**8 340**	**7 108**
76 387	77 607	2.70	1 592	776	81	695
44 736	44 934	2.58	2 299	505	75	430
66 246	65 325	2.56	5 549	1 231	255	976
28 309	29 244	2.51	1 375	217	35	182
22 294	22 334	2.55	1 382	555	56	499
37 582	38 046	2.92	1 666	1 791	1 996	-205
14 762	14 485	2.64	1 161	264	40	224
27 953	27 204	2.56	2 419	828	62	766
18 362	18 434	2.58	1 048	211	34	177
40 055	38 863	2.83	1 754	1 739	739	1 000
66 400	67 371	2.51	3 913	1 029	61	968
56 908	58 558	2.48	1 766	408	445	-37
39 757	40 099	2.44	1 871	675	263	412
26 601	27 058	2.40	1 004	172	24	148
33 346	33 633	2.30	1 324	66	28	38
35 419	34 735	2.55	1 688	1 284	878	406
31 850	32 325	2.42	1 078	329	25	304
68 220	69 860	2.53	862	318	60	258
28 587	29 197	2.31	975	116	31	85
21 459	21 894	2.28	946	187	23	164
25 799	26 395	2.30	963	93	17	76
12 351	12 501	2.48	1 074	22	6	16
16 761	17 048	2.52	869	49	10	39
16 413	15 505		210	2 583	3 096	-513

表2-3 各街镇户籍人口自然变动
Natural Change of Registered Population in Subdistricts and Towns
(2014)

单位:人 (person)

指 标	Indication	出生人口 Birth Population			死亡人口 Death Population			自然增加人口 Natural Growth		
		合 计 Total	男 Man	女 Female	合 计 Total	男 Man	女 Female	合 计 Total	男 Man	女 Female
总 计	**Total**	**26 980**	**13 974**	**13 006**	**21 582**	**11 488**	**10 094**	**5 398**	**2 486**	**2 912**
街道小计	**Subdistrict Tot**	**10 995**	**5 697**	**5 298**	**9 389**	**5 039**	**4 350**	**1 606**	**658**	**948**
潍坊新村街道	Weifangxincun Subdistrict	787	427	360	760	413	347	27	14	13
陆家嘴街道	Lujiazui Subdistrict	1 087	586	501	959	510	449	128	76	52
周家渡街道	Zhoujiadu Subdistrict	880	442	438	1 089	581	508	-209	-139	-70
塘桥街道	Tangqiao Subdistrict	551	277	274	482	261	221	69	16	53
上钢新村街道	Shanggangxincun Subdistrict	681	353	328	1 047	568	479	-366	-215	-151
南码头路街道	Nanmatoulu Subdistrict	654	337	317	736	375	361	-82	-38	-44
沪东新村街道	Hudongxincun Subdistrict	696	333	363	606	323	283	90	10	80
金杨新村街道	Jinyangxincun Subdistrict	1 129	619	510	1 040	567	473	89	52	37
洋泾街道	Yangjing Subdistrict	1 095	570	525	703	403	300	392	167	225
浦兴路街道	Puxinglu Subdistrict	1 113	566	547	751	418	333	362	148	214
东明路街道	Dongminglu Subdistrict	711	369	342	625	311	314	86	58	28
花木街道	Huamu Subdistrict	1 611	818	793	591	309	282	1 020	509	511
镇小计	**Town Tot**	**15 985**	**8 277**	**7 708**	**12 193**	**6 449**	**5 744**	**3 792**	**1 828**	**1 964**
川沙新镇	Chuansha New Town	1 465	759	706	1030	543	487	435	216	219
高桥镇	Gaoqiao Town	690	373	317	721	377	344	-31	-4	-27
北蔡镇	Beicai Town	1 409	743	666	1 109	583	526	300	160	140
合庆镇	Heqing Town	426	217	209	431	216	215	-5	1	-6
唐 镇	Tangzhen Town	582	308	274	289	157	132	293	151	142
曹路镇	Caolu Town	696	357	339	462	248	214	234	109	125
金桥镇	Jinqiao Town	257	126	131	207	117	90	50	9	41
高行镇	Gaohang Town	678	341	337	412	230	182	266	111	155
高东镇	Gaodong Town	267	135	132	293	145	148	-26	-10	-16
张江镇	Zhangjiang Town	1 078	569	509	437	227	210	641	342	299
三林镇	Sanlin Town	1 377	720	657	997	527	470	380	193	187
惠南镇	Huinan Town	950	485	465	762	402	360	188	83	105
周浦镇	Zhoupu Town	901	456	445	554	316	238	347	140	207
新场镇	Xinchang Town	503	266	237	414	228	186	89	38	51
大团镇	Datuan Town	394	220	174	534	276	258	-140	-56	-84
康桥镇	Kangqiao Town	936	497	439	467	232	235	469	265	204
航头镇	Hangtou Town	537	274	263	479	243	236	58	31	27
祝桥镇	Zhuqiao Town	1 032	505	527	1 072	568	504	-40	-63	23
泥城镇	Nicheng Town	382	197	185	386	192	194	-4	5	-9
宣桥镇	Xuanqiao Town	357	171	186	280	142	138	77	29	48
书院镇	Shuyuan Town	387	198	189	346	199	147	41	-1	42
万祥镇	Wanxiang Town	172	92	80	163	75	88	9	17	-8
老港镇	Laogang Town	248	138	110	242	152	90	6	-14	20
南汇新城镇	Nanhui New Town	261	130	131	106	54	52	155	76	79

表2-4 主要年份户籍人口变动
Change of Registered Population in Main Years

单位:人 (person)

指 标	Indicators	1990	1993	2000	2005	2010	2013	2014
人口自然变动	**Natural Changes in Population**							
出生人口	Birth	13 459	9 785	8 229	12 363	22 337	23 201	26 980
出生率(‰)	Birth Rate (‰)	10.20	6.88	5.07	6.76	8.10	8.18	9.35
死亡人口	Death	8 711	9 899	11 007	13 423	19 415	21 169	21 582
死亡率(‰)	Death Rate (‰)	6.60	6.96	6.78	7.34	7.04	7.46	7.48
自然增长人口	Natural Growth	4 748	-114	-2 778	-1 060	2 922	2 032	5 398
自然增长率(‰)	Natural Growth Rate (‰)	3.60	-0.08	-1.71	-0.58	1.06	0.72	1.87
人口迁移变动	**Population Mobility**							
迁入人口	Population Moved-in from Other Provinces and Chongming	18 079	59 214	160 975	128 476	27 440	23 945	25 031
#市外迁入	Non-Shanghai Population Moved-in	8 102	10 469	18 522	18 346	26 845	23 125	24 158
迁出人口	Population Moved-out to Other Provinces and Chongming	15 820	32 457	103 486	88 315	9 119	11 129	9 741
#迁出市外	Population Moved Out of Shanghai	5 843	3 356	5 734	2 612	8 434	10 577	9 143
移入人口	Population Moved-in from other districts in Shanghai			70 435	51 427	38 696	39 996	52 290
移出人口	Population Moved-out to other districts in Shanghai			33 274	27 544	24 737	27 689	26 341

表2－5　年末流动人口登记情况
Registered Migrating Population at Year-end

单位:人　　　　(person)

指　标	Indicators	2005	2010	2013	2014
总　计	**Total**	**937 331**	**2 183 277**	**2 668 090**	**2 521 103**
潍坊新村街道	Weifangxincun Subdistrict	10 975	30 057	33 090	30 867
陆家嘴街道	Lujiazui Subdistrict	17 538	53 091	55 980	51 685
周家渡街道	Zhoujiadu Subdistrict	13 614	28 984	26 520	25 847
塘桥街道	Tangqiao Subdistrict	7 319	19 797	25 028	22 917
上钢新村街道	Shanggangxincun Subdistrict	9 998	17 907	18 590	17 995
南码头路街道	Nanmantoulu Subdistrict	9 295	19 957	28 978	27 222
沪东新村街道	Hudongxincun Subdistrict	11 559	23 289	26 335	23 120
金杨新村街道	Jinyangxincun Subdistrict	27 016	42 152	55 021	46 739
洋泾街道	Yangjing Subdistrict	19 041	50 032	48 357	43 153
浦兴路街道	Puxinglu Subdistrict	15 898	38 169	53 962	51 548
东明路街道	Dongminglu Subdistrict	14 981	26 787	30 741	29 439
花木街道	Huamu Subdistrict	36 626	60 266	73 372	71 046
申港街道	Shengang Subdistrict		11 759		
水上派出所	Boat Police Station	333			
世博园区	Shibo Park		14	5 163	14 491
外高桥保税区	Waigaoqiao Free Trade Zone	3 036	3 443	2 483	7 890
川沙新镇	Chuansha New Town	123 566	173 882	162 110	156 903
高 桥 镇	Gaoqiao Town	51 477	84 918	106 050	99 415
北 蔡 镇	Beicai Town	75 586	140 747	166 922	159 041
合 庆 镇	Heqing Town	40 144	72 050	87 166	85 393
唐　 镇	Tangzhen Town	49 296	79 778	103 180	94 847
曹 路 镇	Caolu Town	55 245	96 229	130 426	118 033
金 桥 镇	Jinqiao Town	69 312	65 756	57 732	52 747
高 行 镇	Gaohang Town	45 035	63 057	88 199	80 057
高 东 镇	Gaodong Town	59 380	71 851	76 797	74 219
张 江 镇	Zhangjiang Town	51 157	124 278	139 640	129 512
三 林 镇	Sanlin Town	119 904	196 584	222 168	211 042
惠 南 镇	Huinan Town		92 325	127 626	122 836
周 浦 镇	Zhoupu Town		67 239	102 729	100 347
新 场 镇	Xinchang Town		42 297	49 757	48 222
大 团 镇	Datuan Town		13 800	17 085	16 562
芦潮港镇	Luchaogang Town		12 406		
康 桥 镇	Kangqiao Town		152 304	210 907	184 907
航 头 镇	Hangtou Town		59 749	80 192	76 572
六 灶 镇	Liuzao Town		18 292		
祝 桥 镇	Zhuqiao Town		46 462	119 621	114 549
泥 城 镇	Nicheng Town		21 397	27 920	28 045
宣 桥 镇	Xuanqiao Town		26 775	37 228	32 426
书 院 镇	Shuyuan Town		19 569	23 427	23 145
万 祥 镇	Wanxiang Town		3 440	6 754	6 736
老 港 镇	Laogang Town		12 388	11 594	11 041
南汇新城镇	Nanhui New Town			29 240	30 547

表2-6　户籍人口年龄结构
Age Structure of Registered Population

单位:万人　　　　(10 000 persons)

指　标　Indicators		年末人口数 Population at the End of the Year		比重(%) Percentage	
		2013	2014	2013	2014
户籍人口年龄构成	**Age Structure of Registered Population**				
合　计	**Total**	**283.79**	**288.44**	**100.0**	**100.0**
17岁及以下	17 and below	33.60	34.98	11.8	12.1
18~34岁	18~34	62.03	61.25	21.9	21.2
35~59岁	35~59	115.44	114.31	40.7	39.6
60岁及以上	60 and below	72.72	77.90	25.6	27.0
户籍老年人口年龄构成	**Age Structure of Registered Aging Population**				
合　计	**Total**	**72.72**	**77.90**	**100.0**	**100.0**
60~64岁	60~64	24.92	27.03	34.3	34.7
65~79岁	65~79	35.18	37.38	48.4	48.0
80岁及以上	80 and above	12.61	13.49	17.3	17.3

表2-7　主要年份婚姻登记和计划生育情况
Marriage Registration and Family Planning in Main Years

单位:人　　　　(person)

指　标	Indicators	1993	2000	2005	2010	2013	2014
婚姻登记	**Marriage Registration**						
准予登记结婚(对)	Registered Marriage (couple)	7 362	11 083	14 602	23 831	29 322	28 853
离婚登记(对)	Registered Divorce (couple)	489	2 102	4 402	7 511	13 699	12 065
计划生育	**Planned Birth**						
出　生	**Birth**						
出生人数	Number of Births	9 785	9 958	12 363	22 337	23 201	26 980
第一孩	First Child	9 309	9 669	11 928	20 893	20 812	23 120
第二孩	Second Child	471	285	424	1 423	2 357	3 811
多　孩	≥ Third Child	5	4	11	21	32	49
符合计划生育人数	Planned Parenthood	9 760	9 903	12 323	22 273	23 132	26 919
计划生育率(%)	Rate of Planned Birth (%)	99.74	99.45	99.68	99.71	99.70	99.80
节　育	**Birth Control**						
已婚育龄妇女人数(万人)	Married Women at Child-bearing Age (10 000 persons)	31.69	32.34	29.33	45.08	45.22	45.14
已领独生子女证人数(万人)	Persons Who Have Applied for One-child Certificate (10 000 persons)	22.66	15.48	10.84	13.80	14.96	13.72
独生子女领证率(%)	Rate of One-child Certificate (%)	71.50	47.86	36.98	30.60	33.10	30.40
晚　婚	**Late Marriage**						
女性初婚人数	Number of First Marriage of Female	5 712	7 564	11 594	12 054	14 856	13 784
#23岁以上	≥ 23 Years Old	2 115	4 217	8 941	10 289	13 184	12 811
晚婚率(%)	Rate of Belated Marriage (%)	37.03	55.75	77.12	85.36	88.75	92.94

主要统计指标解释

人口数

为每年12月31日的年末总人口。根据统计口径的不同,分为户籍人口和常住人口。户籍人口是指在公安部门办理了户籍登记的人口。常住人口是指实际上经常居住在一个地方(住所)的人口,一般都以在其住所居住半年以上者为常住人口。年鉴中除特别注明是常住人口、实有人口等统计口径外,其他均为户籍人口数。

农业人口、非农业人口

是人口按经济特征分组的主要指标。农业人口指依靠从事农业(包括种植业、林业、牧业、渔业)维持生活的全部人口,即包括从事农、林、牧、渔业生产的人口以及由他们抚养的人口。非农业人口指依靠从事农业以外职业的人口以及由他们抚养的人口。但长期来在户籍管理上,往往把在农村中就业并按工资形式获得劳动报酬及由其抚养的人口统计为非农业人口;在农村劳动并参加农村合作经济收益分配的人,及由其抚养的人口作为农业人口统计。

出生率(又称粗出生率)

指在一定时期内(通常为一年)一定地区的出生人数与同期平均人数(或期中人数)之比,一般用千分率表示。计算公式:

$$出生率 = \frac{年出生人数}{年平均人数} \times 1000‰$$

出生人数是指活产婴儿,即胎儿脱离母体时(不管怀孕月数),有过呼吸或其他生命现象。年平均人数是年初、年底人口数的平均数,也可用年中人口数代替。

死亡率(又称粗死亡率)

指在一定时期内(通常为一年)一定地区的死亡人数与同期平均人数(或期中人数)之比,一般用千分率表示。计算公式:

$$死亡率 = \frac{年死亡人数}{年平均人数} \times 1000‰$$

人口自然增长率

指在一定时期内(通常为一年)人口自然增加数(出生人数减死亡人数)与该时期内平均人数(或期中人数)之比,一般用千分率表示。计算公式:

人口自然增长率 =

$$\frac{本年出生人数 - 本年死亡人数}{年平均人数} \times 1000‰$$

人口自然增长率 = 人口出生率 - 人口死亡率

EXPLANATORY NOTES TO MAJOR STATISTICAL INDICATORS

Population

Population refers to the total population by December 31 every year. According to different statistical approaches, there are two definitions of population named as population with registered residence and population with permanent residence. The former refers to the population with registration in the police while the latter refers to the population that actually reside in a place (residence) permanently ,usually longer than half a year. Unless the statistical approaches are specified as permanent population and present population, the others are the number of registered population in this Yearbook.

Agricultural Population, Non-agricultural Population

Agricultural Population, Non-agricultural Population are main indicators of population grouped by economic features. Agricultural Population refers to the total number of people who live on agriculture, including farming, forestry, husbandry and fishery, and their dependents. Non-agricultural Population refers to the number of people who live on non-agricultural jobs and their dependents. According to the resident registering control system, however, the people who are employed in rural area, receive income, and their dependents are actually registered as non-agricultural population. The people who work in rural area and receive their income from agricultural collective units and their dependents are statistically defined as agricultural population.

Birth Rate

Birth Rate (or gross birth rate) means the ratio of the number of births in a certain period (usually a year) to the average population in the same period (or mid-year figure). It is usually calculated in terms of permillage and its calculating formula is:

$$\text{Birth Rate} = \frac{\text{Number of Births}}{\text{Average Number of Popualtion}} \times 1000‰$$

Number of Births refers to live births, when babies have showed any vital phenomena regardless of the length of pregnancy.

Average Number of Population is the average of the number of population at the beginning of the year and that at the end of the year, sometimes substituted for with mid-year population.

Death Rate

Death Rate (or Gross Death Rate) refers to the ratio of number of deaths to the average population (or mid-year population) during a certain period of time (usually a year), which is often presented as permillage. Its calculating formula is :

$$\text{Death Rate} = \frac{\text{Number of Deaths}}{\text{Average Number of Population}} \times 1000‰$$

Natural Growth Rate of Population

Natural Growth Rate of Population refers to the ratio of natural increase in population (number of births minus number of deaths) in a certain period of time (usually a year) to the average population (or mid-year population) of the same period, which is often presented as permillage. The following formula are applied:

Natural Growth Rate of Population =

$$\frac{\text{Number of Births-Number of Deaths}}{\text{Average Number of Population}} \times 1000‰$$

Natural Growth Rate of Population = Birth Rate-Death Rate

第三篇

CHAPTER 3

固定资产投资

INVESTMENT IN FIXED ASSETS

表3－1　固定资产投资主要指标
(2014)

指　标	Indicators	合　计 Total	内　资 Domestic Investment	国　有 State-owned	集　体 Collective-owned
本年完成投资额(亿元)	**Completed Investment in This Year (100 million yuan)**	**1 765.73**	**1 364.72**	**438.47**	**5.91**
按构成分	**By Composition**				
建筑安装工程	Construction and Installation	998.77	805.96	264.03	4.62
设备工具器具购置	Purchase of Equipment and Instrument	178.40	84.81	47.47	
其他费用	Others	588.56	473.95	126.98	1.29
按建设性质分	**By Type of Construction**				
#新　建	New Construction	652.53	502.09	371.34	2.15
改　建	Reconstruction	93.91	51.82	32.37	0.98
扩　建	Expansion	35.59	25.76	19.55	0.10
按三次产业分	**By Industry**				
第一产业	Primary Industry	5.48	5.48	0.32	1.52
第二产业	Secondary Industry	303.80	165.54	81.60	0.10
第三产业	Tertiary Industry	1 456.45	1 193.70	356.55	4.29
按主要行业分	**By Main Sector**				
#工　业	Industry	303.80	165.54	81.60	0.10
交通运输、仓储和邮政业	Transportation, Warehousing and Post Service	122.03	113.84	91.29	1.39
信息传输、计算机服务和软件业	Information Transmission, Computer Service and Computer Software	15.58	15.19	9.46	
批发和零售业	Wholesale and Retail	7.41	7.41	3.13	
住宿和餐饮业	Hotel and Catering	16.87	2.09		
金融业	Banking	18.38	18.38	14.70	
新增固定资产	**Newly-increased Fixed Assets**	**708.92**	**548.94**	**113.76**	**3.43**
固定资产交付使用率(%)	Application Rate of Fixed Assets (%)	40.10	40.20	25.90	58.10
房屋建筑面积(万平方米)	**Floor Area of Buildings (10 000 sq. m)**				
施工面积	Floor Area Under Construction	4 470.67	3 995.78	338.75	43.86
#住　宅	Residential Housing	2 222.93	2 085.42	38.85	22.04
竣工面积	Floor Area Completed	797.31	764.44	73.71	0.27
#住　宅	Residential Housing	474.53	467.10	25.09	

注：按建设性质分不含房地产开发投资

Note: The field of "By Type of Construction" does not include the investment in real estate development.

Major Indicators of Investment in Fixed Assets

联 营 Jointly Operated	有限责任公司 Companies with Limited Liability	股份有限公司 Companies Limited by Shares	私营及个 体 Private/ Individual	其 他 Others	港澳台商投资 Hong Kong/ Macao/Taiwan Funded	#独资企业 Solely Foreigner Funded Enterprises	外商投资 FIE	#独资企业 Solely Foreigner Funded Enterprises
1.72	**577.33**	**55.95**	**266.90**	**18.44**	**104.67**	**71.12**	**296.34**	**87.71**
1.15	307.90	38.23	179.34	10.68	38.38	22.32	154.43	34.75
0.56	11.25	10.82	14.52	0.19	7.41	3.38	86.18	47.49
0.01	258.17	6.90	73.04	7.57	58.88	45.43	55.73	5.48
1.50	65.16	18.26	43.68		3.05	2.94	147.39	27.16
0.08	14.62	1.24	2.35	0.19	9.87	6.17	32.22	4.96
0.14	1.98	1.94	2.05		2.17	0.10	7.66	5.01
0.08	1.26		2.30					
0.70	27.69	13.06	42.20	0.19	13.09	7.03	125.17	68.89
0.94	548.38	42.89	222.40	18.25	91.58	64.09	171.17	18.82
0.70	27.69	13.06	42.20	0.19	13.09	7.03	125.17	68.89
0.14	5.48	12.76	2.78		0.75	0.62	7.44	2.66
	2.75	2.13	0.85				0.38	0.38
	1.01		3.27					
	2.09						14.78	0.44
	2.39	1.29						
2.15	268.72	26.15	134.73		38.99	3.33	120.99	70.32
125.00	46.50	46.70	50.50		37.30	4.70	40.80	80.20
	2 403.35	160.21	1 049.61		225.06	94.45	249.83	124.68
	1 548.41	19.53	456.58		46.11	36.82	91.40	23.66
	446.46	28.63	215.37		14.12	1.38	18.75	12.91
	292.76	8.06	141.19		6.56		0.87	

表3-2　历年固定资产投资总额
Total Investment in Fixed Assets
(1990～2014)

单位:亿元　　(100 million yuan)

年　份 Year	投资总额 Total Investment	#城市基础设施 Investment in Urban Infrastructure	#房地产开发 Real Estate Development	#工　业 Industry
1990	14.15	7.50		
1991	28.95	5.42		
1992	75.00	21.84		
1993	164.56	54.73		
1994	261.13	78.76		
1995	285.07	53.42	18.26	
1996	395.04	98.68	95.45	112.55
1997	504.36	119.32	125.00	140.95
1998	583.22	177.24	134.87	209.11
1999	438.20	156.54	103.88	135.50
2000	351.06	54.51	110.74	140.65
2001	416.18	105.36	111.66	161.48
2002	587.20	171.36	215.80	192.87
2003	602.16	155.63	245.81	191.00
2004	651.94	121.21	279.49	200.29
2005	693.61	125.95	287.92	144.61
2006	659.97	156.04	257.81	139.56
2007	784.10	234.54	247.46	224.59
2008	872.68	311.30	279.97	158.59
2009	1 420.77	490.77	431.36	298.71
2010	1 432.30	261.92	555.74	336.72
2011	1 435.39	272.02	589.45	361.03
2012	1 454.98	261.86	600.30	356.55
2013	1 679.22	267.63	826.13	329.40
2014	1 765.73	275.25	897.87	303.80
1990～2014年累计 Accumulated from 1990 to 2014	17 556.97	4 038.80	6 414.97	4 137.96

表3-3 各行业固定资产投资情况
Investment in Fixed Assets by Sector
(2014)

指 标	Indicators	施工项目(个) Projects Under Construction (unit)	竣工项目(个) Projects Completed (unit)	本年完成投资额(亿元) Investment (100 million yuan)	新增固定资产(亿元) Newly Increased Fixed Assets (100 million yuan)
总 计	**Total**	**1 192**	**334**	**1 765.73**	**708.92**
农、林、牧、渔业	Agriculture, Forest, Animal Husbandry and Fishery	21	16	5.49	4.42
工 业	Industry	415	148	303.80	160.99
#制造业	Manufacturing	343	110	267.74	131.07
电力、热力、燃气及水生产和供应业	Production and Supply of Electricity, Thermal Power, Gas and Water	72	38	36.06	29.92
建筑业	Construction				
批发和零售业	Wholesale and Retail	7	2	122.03	22.75
交通运输、仓储和邮政业	Transportation, Warehousing and Postal Service	77	22	15.58	5.14
住宿和餐饮业	Hotel and Catering	5		7.4	13.98
信息传输、软件和信息技术服务业	Information Transmission, Computer Services and Software	21	4	16.87	0.44
金融业	Banking	8	3	18.38	9.43
房地产业	Real Estate	348	77	901.80	444.54
租赁和商务服务业	Leasing and Commercial Services	21	3	58.37	1.77
科学研究和技术服务业	Scientific Research and Technology Services	37	13	25.61	13.03
水利、环境和公共设施管理业	Water Conservancy, Environment and Public Facilities Management	161	34	142.11	17.64
居民服务、修理和其他服务业	Residents' Services, Repair and Other Services	1		0.37	
教 育	Education	32	7	54.74	5.22
卫生和社会工作	Healthcare and Social Work	16	1	4.32	7.28
文化、体育和娱乐业	Culture, Sports and Entertainment	14	1	88.03	1.17
公共管理、社会保障和社会组织	Public Management, Social Guarantee and Social Organizations	8	3	0.83	1.12

表3-4 固定资产投资房屋建筑面积
Floor Space of Housing and Buildings in Fixed Assets Investment

单位:万平方米 (10 000 sq · m)

指 标 Indicators		2005	2010	2013	2014	1990～2014 年累计 Accumulated Investment (1990～2014)
房屋施工面积	**Floor Area Under Construction**					
合 计	**Total**	**2 483.56**	**4 322.59**	**4 454.42**	**4 470.67**	
住 宅	Residential Housing	1 510.04	2 086.26	2 185.66	2 222.93	
厂房仓库	Factory Building and Warehouse	120.52	308.28	396.26	450.56	
商业营业用房	Commerce	276.76	491.29	385.94	404.39	
办公楼	Offices	196.68	601.15	583.26	475.54	
教育用房	Education	20.35	48.36	54.85	66.70	
医疗用房	Healthcare	7.39	9.20	13.47	15.23	
其 他	Others	351.82	778.05	834.98	835.32	
房屋竣工面积	**Floor Area Completed**					
合 计	**Total**	**615.37**	**646.98**	**672.55**	**797.31**	**14 191.66**
住 宅	Residential Housing	408.44	297.89	350.37	474.53	8 488.99
厂房仓库	Factory Building and Warehouse	43.89	55.50	55.37	68.76	1 519.19
商业营业用房	Commerce	85.64	61.83	32.37	71.08	935.83
办公楼	Office	54.08	93.82	72.45	41.39	1 269.17
教育用房	Education	8.37	10.06	16.34	19.85	281.83
医疗用房	Healthcare		4.56	6.17	8.73	93.08
其 他	Others	14.95	123.32	139.48	112.97	1 603.57

表3-5 历年新增固定资产
Newly Increased Fixed Assets
(1994 ~2014)

指 标 Indicators		1994	1995	1996	1997	1998	1999	2000
新增固定资产（亿元）	Newly Increased Fixed Assets (100 million yuan)	141.03	150.76	260.75	329.84	331.79	396.22	379.60
固定资产交付使用率(%)	Rate of Fixed Assets Transferred in Use (%)	54.0	52.9	66.8	65.4	56.9	90.4	108.1

表3-5 续表1 Continued

指 标 Indicators		2001	2002	2003	2004	2005	2005	2006
新增固定资产（亿元）	Newly Increased Fixed Assets (100 million yuan)	261.82	279.79	407.66	633.37	379.92	522.56	380.96
固定资产交付使用率(%)	Rate of Fixed Assets Transferred in Use (%)	62.9	47.6	67.7	97.2	54.8	79.2	48.6

表3-5 续表2 Continued

指 标 Indicators		2007	2008	2009	2010	2011	2012	2013	2014
新增固定资产（亿元）	Newly Increased Fixed Assets (100 million yuan)	638.70	656.15	622.89	789.74	663.74	711.60	711.60	708.92
固定资产交付使用率(%)	Rate of Fixed Assets Transferred in Use (%)	73.2	46.2	43.5	55.0	45.6	42.4	42.4	40.1

表3-6 主要年份固定资产投资资金来源
Capital Resources of Investment in Fixed Assets in Main Years

单位:亿元 (100 million yuan)

指 标 Indicators		2010	2013	2014
资金来源合计	**Total Capital Resources**	**2 045.60**	**2 679.00**	**2 891.75**
上年末结余资金	Balance at End of Previous Year	363.69	709.16	828.04
本年资金来源小计	Sub-total of Capital Resources in this Year	1 681.91	1 969.84	2 063.71
国家预算内资金	State Budgetary Funds	23.97	86.22	97.52
国内贷款	Domestic Loans	381.47	412.63	571.27
债 券	Bonds	8.00		
利用外资	Foreign Investment	79.00	86.19	90.95
#外商直接投资	Foreign Direct Investment	42.14	56.24	87.30
自筹资金	Self-Financed Capital	872.50	821.86	864.48
#企事业自有资金	Self-Financed by Enterprises and Institutions	515.87	382.28	535.58
其他资金	Other Capitals	316.97	562.94	439.49
#集 资	Raised Funds	2.86		
本年各项应付投资款	Investment Due to Pay in this Year	196.79	130.87	297.96
#工程款	Project Funds	85.70	84.54	172.66

表3-7　城市基础设施投资额
Investment in Urban Infrastructure

指　标	Indicators	2010	2013	2014	1990~2014年累计 Accumulated Investment (1990~2014)
投资额总计(亿元)	**Total Investment (100 million yuan)**	**261.92**	**267.63**	**275.25**	**4 038.80**
电力建设	Electricity	24.38	7.66	28.69	442.08
运输邮电	Transportation, Post and Telecommunications	116.85	88.37	107.21	1 768.39
#市内公共交通	Urban Public Transportation	31.48	20.97	51.42	547.35
公用设施	Public Facilities	120.69	171.60	139.35	1 828.33
公用事业	Public Utilities	3.85	1.97	2.88	149.95
自来水	Tap Water	2.56	1.03	0.99	74.68
燃　气	Gas	1.29	0.94	1.89	75.27
市政建设	Civic Construction	116.85	169.63	136.47	1 678.38
市政工程	Civic Projects	100.51	154.73	119.37	1 518.69
园林绿化	Garden/Park	14.08	11.99	14.26	120.26
环境卫生	Environmental Sanitation	2.10	0.10	2.84	30.26
其　他	Others	0.17	2.81		9.17
构　成(%)	**Composition(%)**				
投资额总计	**Total Investment**	**100.0**	**100.0**	**100.0**	**100.0**
电力建设	Electricity	9.3	2.9	10.4	10.9
运输邮电	Transportation, Post and Telecommunications	44.6	33.0	39.0	43.8
#市内公共交通	Urban Public Transportation	12.0	7.8	18.7	13.6
公用设施	Public Facilities	46.1	64.1	50.6	45.3
公用事业	Public Utilities	1.5	0.7	1.0	3.7
自来水	Tap Water	1.0	0.4	0.4	1.8
燃　气	Gas	0.5	0.4	0.7	1.9
市政建设	Civic Construction	44.6	63.4	49.6	41.6
市政工程	Civic Projects	38.3	57.8	43.4	37.6
园林绿化	Garden/Park	5.4	4.5	5.2	3.0
环境卫生	Environmental Sanitation	0.8	…	1.0	0.7
其　他	Others	0.1	1.0		0.2

表3-8 工业各行业投资主要指标
Main Indicators of Investment by Industrial Sectors
(2014)

指　标	Indicators	施工项目(个) Projects Under Construction (unit)	全部建成投产项目(个) Projects Completed and Put into Production (unit)	建成投产率(%) Rate of Projects Completed and Put into Use(%)	工业本年完成投资额(亿元) Completed Investment in Industry in This Year (100 million yuan)
总　计	**Total**	**339**	**125**	**36.9**	**303.80**
#制造业	**Manufacturing**	**267**	**87**	**32.6**	**267.74**
农副食品加工业	Processing of Agricultural Side-line Food	3	1	33.3	0.89
食品制造业	Food Manufacturing	4	1	25.0	1.34
酒、饮料和精制茶制造业	Alcohol, Beverage, and tea Manufacturing	1	1	100.0	1.40
烟草制品业	Tobacco Manufacturing	1			3.63
纺织业	Textile Industry	1	1	100.0	0.48
纺织服装、服饰业	Textile Clothes and Accessories	3	2	66.7	0.16
造纸和纸制品业	Paper-making and Paper Products	1	1	100.0	0.19
印刷业和记录媒介复制业	Manufacturing of Printing and Record Medium Reproduction	11	6	54.5	2.93
石油加工、炼焦和核燃料加工业	Petroleum Processing, Coking and Processing of Nuclear Fuels	18	8	44.4	5.08
化学原料和化学制品制造业	Chemical Materials and Chemical Products	17	11	64.7	4.82
医药制造业	Medicine Manufacturing	27	6	22.2	31.33
橡胶和塑料制品业	Manufacturing of Rubber and Plastic Products	2	2	100.0	2.30
非金属矿物制品业	Manufacturing of Non-metal Mineral Products	2	1	50.0	0.65
黑色金属冶炼和压延加工业	Manufacturing of Smelting and Processing of Ferrous Metals				0.13
有色金属冶炼和压延加工业	Manufacturing of Smelting and Processing of Non-ferrous Metals	1	1	100.0	0.27
金属制品业	Manufacturing of Metal Products	12	3	25.0	5.59
通用设备制造业	Manufacturing of General-use Equipment	24	6	25.0	14.11
专用设备制造业	Manufacturing of Special Equipment	27	3	11.1	23.24
汽车制造业	Manufacturing of Automobiles	41	16	39.0	53.29
铁路、船舶、航空航天和其他运输设备制造业	Manufacturing of Railway, Ship, Aviation and Aerospace, and Other Transportation Equipment	12			24.14
电气机械和器材制造业	Manufacturing of Electric Machinery and Apparatus	15	3	20.0	8.22
计算机、通信和其他电子设备制造业	Manufacturing of Computer, Telecommunications and Other Electronic Equipment	24	9	37.5	65.46
仪器仪表制造业	Manufacturing of Instrument and Meter	4			2.46
其他制造业	Other Manufacturings	15	5	33.3	13.03
废弃资源综合利用业	Comprehensive Recycling of Discarded Resources	1			2.59
电力、热力、燃气及水生产和供应业	**Production and Supply of Electricity, Thermal Power, Gas and Water**	**72**	**38**	**52.8**	**36.06**
电力、热力生产和供应业	Production and Supply of Electricity and Thermal Power	63	32	50.8	33.17
燃气生产和供应业	Production and Supply of Gas	5	5	100.0	1.89
水的生产和供应业	Production and Supply of Tap Water	4	1	25.0	0.99

表3-9　主要年份建设改造投资主要指标
Major Indicators of Investment on Constructions and Transformations

指　标	Indicators	2013	2014
投资总额(亿元)	**Total Investment (100 million yuan)**	**853.09**	**867.86**
按建设性质分	**Grouped by Type of Construction**		
#新　建	New Construction	560.31	652.53
改建和技改	Reconstruction and Technologic Reforms	160.48	93.91
扩　建	Expansion	42.98	35.59
按产业分	**Grouped by Type of Industry**		
第一产业	Primary Industry	7.58	5.49
第二产业	Secondary Industry	334.80	303.80
第三产业	Tertiary Industry	510.71	558.57
按行业分	**Grouped by Sectors**		
农、林、牧、渔业	Farming, Forestry, Animal Husbandry and Fishery	7.58	5.49
工　业	Industry	329.40	303.80
建筑业	Construction	4.90	
批发和零售业	Wholesale and Retail	114.63	122.03
交通运输、仓储和邮政业	Transportation, Storage and Post Service	10.21	15.58
住宿和餐饮业	Hotel and Catering	17.93	7.41
信息传输、软件和信息技术服务业	Information Transmission, Software and Information Technology Services	6.29	16.87
金融业	Financial Industry	13.64	18.38
房地产业	Real Estate Industry	1.69	3.92
租赁和商务服务业	Leasing and Business Service	49.92	58.37
科学研究和技术服务业	Scientific Research andTechnology Service	19.90	25.61
水利、环境和公共设施管理业	Water Conservancy, Environment and Public Facilities Management	173.98	142.11
居民服务、修理和其他服务业	Residents´Services, Repair and Other Services	1.28	0.37
教　育	Education	22.95	54.74
卫生和社会工作	Healthcare and Social Work	16.76	4.32
文化、体育和娱乐业	Culture, Sports and Entertainment	55.88	88.03
公共管理、社会保障和社会组织	Public Management, Social Guarantee and Social Organizations	6.15	0.83
新增固定资产	**Newly Increased Fixed Assets**		
固定资产交付使用率(%)	Application Rate of Fixed Assets(%)	35.5	30.5
房屋建筑面积(万平方米)	**Floor Area of Buildings (10 000 sq. m)**		
施工面积	Floor Space Under Construction	882.22	731.45
#住　宅	Residential Housing	0.25	
竣工面积	Floor Space Completed	102.32	92.45
#住　宅	Residential Housing	0.02	0.02

表3-10 主要年份住宅投资(按经济类型分)
Investment in Residential Housing in Main Years (by Ownership)

单位:亿元 (100 million yuan)

指 标	Indicators	2010	2013	2014
住宅投资额总计	**Total Investment in Residential Housing**	**343.57**	**441.62**	**518.60**
占固定资产投资额比重(%)	Percentage of Investment in Fixed Assets (%)	23.8	25.1	29.4
内 资	Domestic Investment	309.32	366.58	412.01
国 有	State-owned	48.69	46.65	4.74
集 体	Collective-owned	30.06	7.55	1.52
联 营	Jointly-operated	26.31	18.56	
有限责任公司	Companies with Limited Liability	115.45	216.87	286.53
股份有限公司	Companies Limited by Shares	0.92	2.41	4.67
私 营	Private	87.88	74.54	114.55
港澳台商投资	Hong Kong/Macao/Taiwan Invested	12.16	22.92	50.27
#港澳台商独资	Solely Hong Kong/Macao/Taiwan Funded	6.18	20.40	48.42
外商投资	FIE	22.09	52.12	56.32
#外商独资	Solely Foreigner Funded	21.37	42.68	6.57

表3-11　主要重大项目(浦东部分)投资完成额
Amount of Completed Investment in Key Civic Projects in PNA (2014)

单位:亿元　　(100 million yuan)

序号 No.	指标	Indication	计划总投资 Total Planned Investment	累计完成投资 Accumulated Investment	#2014年完成投资 Investment Completed in 2014
1	上海迪士尼乐园项目	Shanghai Disneyland Park Project	293.70	154.09	77.89
2	轨道交通十一号线南段工程	Porject of Southern Part in Line 11	160.84	178.12	15.00
3	上海轨道交通11号线北段工程二期(华山路中间风井~罗山路)	The Second Phase of Northern Part Project in Line 11	129.65	127.41	6.90
4	中环线浦东段(军工路隧道-高科中路)	Pudong Area of Shanghai Middle Ring Road (Jugong Road Tunnel-Gaoke Middle Road)	122.55	71.65	23.04
5	上海轨道交通9号线三期东段工程	The Third Phase of Eastern Part Project in Line 9	102.82	12.54	11.00
6	通用汽车设计与工程技术中心金桥基地暨金桥扩能项目	Design and Engineering Tech Center of Shanghai GM and Jinqiao Expansion Project	78.00	25.64	14.82
7	东西通道	East and West Channel	71.95	54.71	2.96
8	C919大型客机研制保障条件能力建设项目	Research and Maintenance Capability Project for C919 Large Airplane of Shanghai Airplane Manufacturing Co., Ltd	69.85	52.66	5.24
9	中航商用航空发动机有限责任公司临港基地项目	Lingang Base Project of China Commercial Aircraft	66.01	30.65	12.00
10	浦东新区环城绿带开天窗补绿工程	The Green Project of Pudong Green Belt around the City	64.50	44.89	4.64
11	上海世博会地区B02、B03地块地下空间工程	The Underground Project of B02, B03 in Shanghai Expo Area	61.13	36.44	16.04
12	上海烟草浦东科技创新园区建设项目	Pudong Technology Innovation Construction of Shanghai Cigaratte	58.90	13.53	3.63
13	上海通用汽车增资生产新一代中级、中高级轿车项目	New-generation Middle and High Grade Car Project with Newly-increased Investment of Shanghai GM	52.00	40.63	1.51
14	上海迪士尼乐园配套项目	Relevant Supportive Project of Shanghai Disneyland Park	45.26	24.96	14.34
15	上海浦东国际机场第五跑道工程	The Fifth Runway of Shanghai Pudong International Airport	43.59	34.75	1.55
16	轨道交通11号线北段(罗山路—迪士尼乐园)工程	Project of Northern Part in Line 11 (Lushan Road-Disney Park)	40.63	22.74	14.74
17	上海汽车临港基地自主品牌新产品技术改造项目	Technology Update of New Product Lingang Base of SAIC	36.72	36.71	1.94
18	上海科技大学新校区一期工程	Shanghai Stock Exchange Project in Shanghai International Financial Center	35.03	21.53	17.00
19	上海国际金融中心上交所项目	Shanghai International Financial Center and Shanghai Security Exchange Project	35.00	20.16	3.41
20	中国商飞总部基地	Shanghai Commerical Aircraft Center Base	34.49	24.54	4.97
21	国家电网世博园区办公楼项目	The Office Building of State Grid in Expo Area	33.28	21.86	2.16
22	滨江大道及绿化工程	Foreshore Binjiang Avenue and Green Project	30.23	20.40	13.81
23	南汇生态专项	Nanhui Speicial Eco-project	30.09	31.14	5.34
24	上海浦东国际机场第四跑道工程	The Fourth Runway Project of Shanghai Pudong International Airport	26.28	22.15	3.47
25	华能上海大厦	Huaneng Shanghai Mansion	24.39	13.12	13.12

表3-12　当年建成部分大项目一览表
Major Projects Completed in Current Year (2014)

单位:亿元　　(100 million yuan)

序号 No.	指　标	Indication	计　划 总投资 Total Planned Investment	累计完 成投资 Accumulated Investment	#2014年完成投资 Investment Completed in 2014
1	长泰国际广场	Changtai International Plaza	40.00	32.06	17.60
2	保利御樽苑	Baoli Yuzun Garden	24.70	22.65	1.48
3	上海通用汽车新一代大型直立四缸发动机项目	Shanghai GM New-generation Large Verticle Four-cylinder Engine Project	26.93	20.04	0.16
4	新城碧翠园	Xincheng Green Garden	21.00	20.66	2.61
5	象屿鼎城	Xiangyu Ding City	19.95	19.59	1.43
6	陆家嘴金融贸易区 X3—2 地块	Lujiazui Financial Trade Zone X3 - 2	19.85	20.18	1.96
7	罗山路(龙东大道—S20)	Luoshan Road (Longdong Avenue S20)	18.64	22.51	4.96
8	临港新城滴水湖站交通枢纽工程(含配套地下空间)	Lingang New City Dishui Lake Station Traffic Project (including underground space)	16.00	14.41	0.97
9	上海意得商城二期	Shanghai Yide Shopping Mall Second Phase	15.28	15.28	0.64
10	金谊河畔三期	Jinyi Riverside Third Phase	13.25	14.37	1.88
11	世博轴综合利用改建工程	Shibo Center Comprehensive Reconstruction Project	13.76	13.76	3.13
12	小上海新城	Petite Shanghai New City	13.00	11.98	0.63
13	世和商务中心	Shihe Business Center	11.00	10.77	0.25
14	昌硕添置生产测试设备	Changshuo Production Test Equipment	10.00	10.00	8.15
15	中国金融信息大厦	China Finance Information Building	8.72	8.72	2.35
16	丽都华庭	Lidu Beautiful Garden	8.70	8.66	1.26
17	绿地崴廉公寓	Green Land William Apartment	8.25	8.25	1.03
18	森兰外高桥中块商业中心	Senlan Waigaoqiao Middle Land Business Center	7.89	7.27	3.97
19	中科院蛋白质科学研究(上海)设施国家重大科技基础设施	China Academy of Sciences Protein Science Research (Shanghai) Equipment and National Important Technology Basic Equipment	7.58	7.58	4.48
20	南六公路(S1—S32)	Nanliu Road (S1 - S32)	7.42	14.23	4.00
21	锦绣17#地块一期	Jinxiu No.17 Land Phase 1	7.00	6.63	1.31
22	张家浜楔形绿地住宅三期	Zhangjiabang	6.65	6.68	1.12
23	浦东新区森兰外高桥 D4 - 5 地块	Pudong New Zone Senlan Waigaoqiao D4 - 5 Land	6.30	6.29	4.20
24	金潼苑住宅小区	Jintong Garden	4.20	4.20	0.95
25	亿凯商城	Yikai Shopping Mall	4.00	4.00	1.03

主要统计指标解释

全社会固定资产投资

固定资产投资是国民经济再生产活动的一个重要部分。固定资产投资额是以货币形式表现的在一定时期内建造和购置固定资产的工作量以及与此有关的费用总称。它是反映固定资产投资规模、结构和发展速度的综合性指标。按照现行国家统计制度，全社会固定资产投资包括建设改造、房地产开发、城乡集体经济单位、城乡私人建房和其他经济单位投资。

从2011年起，固定资产投资统计起点为500万元（含500万元）以上项目。

房地产开发投资

指各种登记注册类型的房地产开发公司、商品房建设公司及其他房地产开发法人单位和附属于其他法人单位实际从事房地产开发或经营活动的单位统一开发的包括统代建、拆迁还建的住宅、厂房、仓库、饭店、宾馆、度假村、写字楼、办公楼等房屋建筑物和配套的服务设施，土地开发工程（如道路、给水、排水、供电、供热、通讯、平整场地等基础设施工程）的投资；不包括单纯的土地交易活动。

固定资产投资按国民经济行业分

固定资产投资按国民经济行业分是根据建设项目建成投产后的主要产品或主要用途及社会经济活动性质来确定国民经济行业。一般情况下，一个建设项目或一个企业、事业单位只能属于一种国民经济行业。

固定资产投资按构成分

（1）建筑工程（建筑工作量）包括：

①各种房屋如厂房、仓库、办公室、住宅、商店、学校、医院、俱乐部、食堂、招待所等工程，包括列入房屋工程预算内的暖气、卫生、通风、照明、煤气等设备的价值及装饰油饰工程，列入建筑工程预算内的各种管道（如蒸汽、压缩空气、石油、给排水等管道）、电力、电讯电缆导线的敷设工程。

②设备基础、支柱、操作平台、梯子、烟囱、凉水塔、水池、灰塔等建筑工程；炼焦炉、蒸汽炉等各种窖炉的砌筑工程及金属结构工程。

③为施工而进行的建筑场地的布置、工程地质勘探，原有建筑物和障碍物的拆除，平整土地、施工临时用水、电、气、道路工程，以及完工后建筑场地的清理、环境绿化美化工作等。

④矿井的开凿，井巷掘进延伸，露天矿的剥离，石油、天然气钻井工程和铁路、公路、港口、桥梁等工程。

⑤水利工程，如水库、堤坝、灌溉以及河道整治等工程。

⑥防空、地下建筑等特殊工程。

（2）安装工程（安装工作量）包括：

①生产、动力、起重、运输、传动和医疗、实验等各种需要安装设备的装配和安装，与设备相连的工作台、梯子、栏杆等装设工程，附属于被安装设备的管线敷设工程，被安装设备的绝缘、防腐、保温、油漆等工作。

②为测定安装工程质量，对单个设备、系统设备进行单机试运，系统联动无负荷试运工作（投料试运工作不包括在内）。在安装工程中，不得包括被安装设备本身价值。

（3）设备、工具、器具购置：是指把工业生产的产品转为固定资产的购置活动，包括建设单位或在企、事业单位购置或自制达到固定资产标准的设备、工具、器具的价值。固定资产的标准按财务部门规定。新建单位及扩建单位的新建车间，按照设计和计划要求购置或自制的全部设备、工具、器具，不论是否达到固定资产标准均计入“设备、工具、器具购置”中。

①设备：指各种生产设备、传导设备、动力设备、运输设备等。分为需要安装的设备和不需要安装的设备两种。

需要安装的设备（简称“需安设备”）：是指必须将其整体或几个部位装配起来，安装在基础上或建筑物支架上才能使用的设备。如轧钢机、发电机、蒸汽锅炉、变压器、塔、换热器、各种泵、机床等。有的设备虽不要基础，但必须进行组装工作，并在一定范围内使用，如生产用电铲、塔吊、门吊、皮带运输机等也作为需要安装的设备统计。

不需要安装的设备（简称“不需安设备”）：指不必固定在一定位置或支架上就可以使用的各种设备，如电焊机、叉车、汽车、机车、飞机、船舶以及生产上流动使用的空压机、泵等。

②工具、器具：是指具有独立用途的各种生产用具、工作工具和仪器。如生产和维修用的切削工具、压延工具、铆焊工具、模压器、铸型、风镐等，检验、实验测量用的各种计量、分析、化验仪器，以及达到固定资产标准的包装容器等。

购置旧设备：是指从外单位购入的，已经使用过的各种设备。不包括从国外购进的旧设备。旧设备一般是指在国内其他单位作为固定资产使用过的设备（单纯购置旧设备不纳入固定资产投资统计）。

用于更新的设备：是指为更换陈旧设备而购置的投资。用于更新的设备与原有设备在台数和价值上不一定相等。购置的设备如不是用于更换原有设备，而是用于新增或扩大生产能力的，不能作为用于“更新的设备”统计。

（4）其他费用：指不属于上述几项的投资完成额。包括计入固定资产的费用（如农林建设单位牲畜购置费、各种经济林木营造费、办公和生活用家具、器具购置费、建设单位管理费、土地、青苗补偿和安置补偿费、勘察设计费、研究试验费、负荷联合试运费、引进技术和进口设备项目的其他费用）。

固定资产投资按建设性质分

按建设项目情况填写。

(1)新建:指从无到有"平地起家"开始建设的项目。现有企业、事业、行政单位投资的项目一般不属于新建。但如有的单位原有基础很小,经过建设后新增的固定资产价值超过该企业、事业、行政单位原有固定资产价值(原值)三倍以上的,也应作为新建。

(2)扩建:是指企(事)业单位在厂内或其他地点,为扩大原有产品的生产能力(或效益)或增加新的产品生产能力,而增建主要生产车间(或主要工程)独立的生产线、分厂等。行政、事业单位在原单位增建业务用房(如学校增建的教学用房、医院增建门诊部、病房)也作为扩建。

现有企、事业单位为扩大原有主要产品生产能力或增加新的产品生产能力,增建一个或几个主要生产车间(或主要工程)、总厂之下的分厂,如同时进行一些更新改造工程的建设,则也应作为扩建。

(3)改建和技术改造:是指现有企业、事业单位对原有设施进行技术改造或更新(包括相应配套的辅助性生产、生活福利设施)的建设项目。改建项目包括现有企业、事业单位为适应市场变化的需要,而改变企业的主要产品种类(如军工企业转民产品等)的建设项目,原有产品生产作业线由于各工序(车间)之间能力不平衡,为填平补齐充分发挥原有生产能力而增建不增加本企业主要产品设计能力的车间的建设项目。技术改造是指企业、事业单位在现有基础上,用先进的技术代替落后的技术,用先进的工艺和装备代替落后的工艺和装备,以改变企业落后的技术经济面貌,实现以内涵为主的扩大再生产,达到提高产品质量、促进产品更新换代、节约能源、降低消耗、扩大生产规模、全面提高社会经济效益的目的。技术改造具体包括以下内容:机器设备和工具的更新改造;生产工艺改革、节约能源和原材料的改造;厂房建筑和公共设施的改造;保护环境进行的"三废"治理改造;劳动条件和生产环境的改造等。

(4)单纯建造生活设施:是指企(事)业及行政单位在不扩建、改建生产性工程和业务用房的情况下,单纯建造职工住宅、托儿所、子弟学校、医务室、浴室、食堂等生活福利设施。

(5)迁建:指为改变生产能力布局或由于城市环境保护和安全生产的需要等原因搬迁到另地建设的企、事业单位。在搬迁另地建设过程中,不论是维持原来规模还是扩大规模都按迁建统计。

(6)恢复:是指因自然灾害、战争等原因,使原有固定资产全部或部分报废,以后又投资恢复建设的单位。不论是按原规模恢复还是在恢复的同时进行扩建的都按恢复项目统计。尚未建成投产的基本建设项目,因自然灾害而损坏重建的,仍按原有建设性质划分。

(7)单纯购置:是指现有企、事业、行政单位单纯购置不需要安装的设备、工具、器具而不进行工程建设的单位。有些单位当年虽然只从事一些购置活动,但其设计中规定有建筑安装活动,应根据设计文件的内容来确定建设性质,不得作为单纯购置统计。

新增固定资产

新增固定资产又称交付使用的固定资产,是指已经完成建造和购置过程,并已交付生产或使用单位的固定资产价值。新增固定资产是表示固定资产投资成果的价值量指标,也是反映建设进度、计算固定资产投资效果的必要数据。

固定资产交付使用率

固定资产交付使用率又称固定资产运用系数,是指一定时期新增固定资产与同期完成投资额的比率。它反映各个时期固定资产动用速度,衡量建设过程中宏观投资效果的综合性指标。

施工项目

施工项目指报告期内进行过建筑或安装施工活动的项目。凡是报告期内施过工的建设项目,不论施工时间长短,均作为施工项目统计。施工项目个数可以反映一定时期固定资产投资的实际规模,与同期建成投产的建设项目个数相比,可以从建设速度的角度反映固定资产投资的效果。根据建设项目施工活动的不同性质,施工项目又分为:本年正式施工项目、本年收尾项目和以前年度全部停缓建项目。

全部投产项目

工业项目指设计文件规定形成生产能力的主体工程及其相应配套的辅助设施全部建成,经负荷试运转,证明具备生产设计规定合格产品的条件,并经过验收鉴定合格或达到竣工验收标准,与生产性工程配套的生活福利设施可以满足近期正常生产的需要,正式移交生产的建设项目。非工业项目指设计文件规定的主体工程和相应的配套工程全部建成,能够发挥设计规定的全部效益,经验收鉴定合格或达到竣工验收标准,正式移交使用的建设项目。

EXPLANATORY NOTES TO MAJOR STATISTICAL INDICATORS

Total Investment in Fixed Assets

Investment in Fixed Assets constitutes an important portion of the national economic reproduction. Fixed assets investment is a general term for both the work volume of production and purchase of fixed assets and relevant expenditure, in the form of currency, during a certain period. It is a comprehensive indicator of scale, structure and development speed of fixed assets investment. As stipulated in the current national statistics regulations, the social fixed assets investment includes the investment into infrastructure and reformation, real estate development, urban and rural collective economic bodies, private house construction in urban and rural areas and other economic bodies.

Since the year of 2011, the fixed assets items have only include those with an investment of 5 million yuan and above.

Investment in Real Estate Development

Investment in Real Estate Development refers to the investment by the real estate development companies, commercial buildings construction companies and other real estate development units of various types of ownership in the construction of house buildings, such as residential buildings, factory buildings, warehouses, hotels, guesthouses, holiday villages, office buildings, and the complementary service facilities and land development projects, such as roads, water supply, water drainage, power supply, heating, telecommunications, land leveling and other projects of infrastructure. It excludes the activities in pure land transactions.

Investment in Fixed Assets by Sector

Investment in Fixed Assets by Sector refers to determining the classification of construction projects by the major products or the purpose of the projects when they are put into production or use, and by the nature of their social economic activities. In general, one project or one enterprise or institution can only be classified into one sector.

Investment in Fixed Assets by Composition

(1) Construction Projects (work volume of construction) include:

① Various kinds of houses and buildings such as workshops, warehouses, offices, residential buildings, shops, schools, hospitals, clubs, canteens and hostels, including the value of equipment such as heating, sanitation, lighting, and gas that are covered by the budget of housing projects and some decoration and polishing projects, various kinds of pipelines such as steam, compressed air, petroleum, tap water and sewage that are covered by the budget of construction projects and the pavement for cable conductors of electricity and telecommunications.

② Construction projects such as equipment foundations, pillars, operating platforms, ladders, chimneys, cooling towers, pools and gray towers, the masonry of various kinds of kilns and stoves for coke and stream ovens, and the metal structure work.

③ Site layout and geological explorations for the construction, demolition of the old buildings and barriers, site leveling, projects of temporary tap water, electricity , gas and road for the construction, and clearing up and green environment after the construction.

④ The mine excavation, the excavation and extension of roadway, the stripping of open pits, drilling engineering works for petroleum and natural gas, and the projects of railway, highway, ports and bridges.

⑤ Projects of water conservancy, such as reservoirs, dams, irrigation and river regulation.

⑥ Special projects such as air-raid shelters and underground constructions.

(2) Installation Projects (work volume of installation) include:

① Various assembly and installations that need equipment for installation, such as production, power, lifting, transportation, transmission and medical experiments, decoration projects that are connected with the equipment, such as tables, ladders and railings, pipeline laying works that are attached with the installed equipment, and works such as isolation, anti-corrosion and painting for the installed projects.

② In order to determine the quality of the installation project, the system equipment will be operated on trial separately and the system will be connected without any load (excluding the trial with feeding). The installation project will not include the value of the installed equipment itself.

(3) Purchase of equipment, tools and instruments refers to the total value of equipment, tools, and instruments purchased or self-produced which come up to standards for fixed assets by the construction units or the enterprises or institutions. The standards for fixed assets are specified by the financial departments. All of the equipment, tools and instruments purchased or self-produced for new workshops by newly established or expanded units are categorized as "purchase of equipment, tools and instruments" no matter whether they come up to the standards for fixed assets.

① Equipment refers to various kinds of equipment for production, transmission, power and transportation. It is divided into two categories: one that need installation and the other that need not be installed.

Equipment that need installation refers to the equipment that must be assembled in whole or in several parts, and mounted on the base or on the brackets of the building for normal operation, such as rolling machines, generators, steam boilers, transformers, towers, heat exchangers, pumps and machine tools. Although some equipment need not a base, they need the job for assembly and can only be used in a certain scope, such as shovels, cranes, gantry cranes and belt conveyors for production.

Equipment that need not be installed refers to various kinds of equipment that are not necessarily installed at a certain place or bracket and can be put into use, such as welding machines, forklifts, cars, motorcycles, planes, ships, and air compressors and pumps that are used in a non-fixed place during the production.

② Tools and instruments refer to various production supplies, working tools and instruments with their independent uses, such as cutting, rolling and riveting tools, molded devices and picks for production and repair, various measurement, analysis, laboratory equipment for inspection and experiment, and containers that can meet the standards of fixed assets.

Purchase of old equipment refers to various kinds of used equipment that have been bought from other units, which exclude used equipment purchased from foreign countries. Old equipment generally refers to the equipment that other domestic units have used as fixed assets (Simple purchasing of old equipment will not be covered in the statistical investment of fixed assets).

Equipment for updating refers to the investment that is purchased for updating the old equipment. Equipment for updating does not necessarily have the same number and value as those of the original equipment. If the purchased equipment is not used to replace the old equipment but to increase or enlarge its production capability, it can not be identified as "Equipment for updating".

(4) Other Expenses refer to the completed investment that are other than those mentioned above, which include expenses that are covered by fixed assets, such as purchasing livestock, planting economic trees, furniture and appliances for office and living, manage-

ment, land, compensation for young crops, resettlement compensation, survey and design, research and test, joint trial for load and combination, introduction of foreign technology and imported equipment by construction units of agriculture and forest.

Investment in Fixed Assets by Property of Construction

It is filled out according to the specific construction project.

(1) New construction refers to completely new construction from scratch. Projects of the existing enterprises, institutions or administrative units are not considered as new construction. In case the assets of the existing unit are quite small, and the value of newly added fixed assets exceeds the original value of assets by three times, the expansion will also be considered as new construction.

(2) Expansion refers to construction of new major production workshop, branch factory or independent production line within a factory or in other locations, for the purpose of increasing the production capacity (or improving efficiency) of the original products. Newly constructed houses for the operation of institutions and administrative organizations (such as the newly constructed buildings for teaching in schools, buildings for clinics or wards in hospitals, etc.) are also classified as expansion.

Also included in the expansion are investments by existing enterprises or institutions in building major production line (s) or branch factory(ies) along with some work on innovation, for the purpose of expending the production capacity of original products or producing new products.

(3) Reconstruction and technological reforms refers to construction projects by existing enterprises or institutions in innovation or technical transformation of the old facilities (including auxiliary production equipment and welfare facilities). Also considered as reconstruction is the construction of new workshops by the existing enterprises or institutions to change the variety of products to meet the market demand (such as the production of civil products by defense industries), or to bring the designed production capacity into full play through a more balanced production process on production lines. Technological reforms refer to the fact that enterprises and institutions, on an ongoing basis, replace outdated technology with advanced technology and replace backward process and equipment with advance ones, in order to change the outdated technology of the enterprises and improve the economic benefits while lowering the consumption of the energy. Technological reforms include the following contents: renovation of the machinery and tools, reform of production process, saving energy and raw materials, reform of plant buildings and public facilities, protection of the environment, and reform of the working conditions and environment.

(4) Simple construction of living facilities refers to facilities for living and welfare, such as residential buildings, nurseries, schools, medical rooms, bathrooms and canteens for the staff and workers, simply built by enterprises and institutions without expanding or reconstructing production projects or business buildings.

(5) Relocation: Enterprises and institutions relocate their plants to other places because of the change of production layout or for reasons of protecting the urban environment and safe production. During the construction of relocation to other places, the original or expanded scale of construction will be covered in the statistics.

(6) Restoration: Enterprises and institutions restore the construction with investment after all or part of their original fixed assets has been scrapped due to natural disasters and wars. Restoration to their original scale or any expansion will be covered as restored projects.

(7) Simple purchase: Existing enterprises, institutions and administrative units simply purchase equipment, tools and instruments that need not be installed or any construction. Although some units purchased some equipment in the previous year, there are some construction and installation in their design. These constructions should be determined to the contents of the design files, not being covered as simple purchase.

Newly Increased Fixed Assets

Newly Increased Fixed Assets, also called fixed assets put into operation, refers to the value of fixed assets that has been put into production or handed over to the production units after the completion of the process of construction and purchase. The newly increased fixed asset is a value indicator of the result of investment. It is also the necessary data for reflecting the construction process and the result of investment in fixed assets.

Rate of Fixed Assets Completed and Put into Operation

Rate of Fixed Assets Completed and Put into Operation, also called the fixed assets operation ratio, refers to ratio of newly increased fixed assets to total investment completed in the same period, which is a comprehensive indicator, reflecting the development of fixed assets investment and investment efficiency.

Projects under Construction

Projects under Construction refer to projects with construction and installation activities undertaken in the reference period. All projects that have construction activities undertaken during the reference period are reported as projects under construction irrespective of the length of construction work. The number of projects under construction can reflect the actual size of investment in fixed assets during a given period, and when compared with the number of projects completed and put into use during the same period, it demonstrates the results of investment in fixed assets. Depending on the nature of construction activities, projects under construction can also be classified into projects under construction in current year, winding-up projects in current year and stopped or suspended projects in previous years.

Projects Completely Put into Use

Industrial projects refer to the major projects and accessory facilities completed which result in forming production capacity and have been checked and accepted while the living and welfare facilities have been completed and can ensure normal production and formally put into production. Non-industrial projects refer to the major projects and accessory facilities completed which possess the designed capacity and have been checked, accepted and formally put into production.

第四篇

CHAPTER 4

招商引资

BUSINESS PROMOTION AND
FOREIGN-FUND ATTRACTION

表 4 - 1　历年外商直接投资情况
(1990 ~ 2014)

年　份 Year	外商直接投资合同项目(项) Contracted Projects of Foreign Direct Investment(unit)	#中外合资 Joint-venture	中外合作 Sino-foreign Cooperative	外商独资 Solely Foreigner Funded
1990	28	22	2	4
1991	92	79	4	9
1992	567	467	38	56
1993	924	610	38	275
1994	1 035	547	51	432
1995	838	340	41	455
1996	802	285	38	479
1997	615	132	36	447
1998	554	88	30	435
1999	470	71	18	380
2000	693	109	21	563
2001	880	110	10	758
2002	964	119	14	829
2003	1 563	175	15	1 370
2004	1 688	188	9	1 489
2005	1 734	149	8	1 574
2006	1 446	143	7	1 292
2007	1 254	112	3	1 138
2008	803	90	3	710
2009	780	100	4	676
2010	906	140	1	765
2011	995	181	2	809
2012	976	207	2	763
2013	1 032	274	1	757
2014	2 185	262	4	1 551

注：从 2004 年起，外商直接投资实际到位金额中不包含间接吸收外资。
Note：The actual paid amount of foreign direct investment will not include the indirectly-attracted foreign capital after the year of 2004.

Foreign Direct Investment

外商直接投资合同金额(亿美元) Contracted Value of Foreign Direct Investment (USD 100 million)	#中外合资 Joint-venture	中外合作 Sino-foreign Cooperative	外商独资 Solely Foreigner Funded	外商直接投资实际到位金额(亿美元) Capital in Place of Foreign Direct Investment (USD 100 million)
0.34	0.29	0.01	0.05	0.13
1.01	0.92	0.03	0.06	0.68
13.53	7.28	0.82	2.77	2.49
17.57	13.08	1.53	2.78	4.29
25.93	14.14	4.10	7.32	6.85
32.56	10.47	2.56	17.43	12.81
18.09	5.04	5.84	7.21	14.25
18.00	13.39	0.82	3.79	10.13
27.90	13.77	0.63	2.90	15.37
10.73	2.95	0.55	6.91	5.92
28.84	2.73	0.47	25.63	8.85
20.02	4.51	1.12	14.16	23.04
26.68	5.72	1.36	17.22	18.47
28.75	6.47	0.12	21.19	18.01
32.24	5.05	0.56	26.08	23.78
56.54	7.84	0.38	42.20	31.11
48.42	7.67	0.32	39.46	32.20
49.49	5.08	0.39	41.30	33.06
49.92	5.87	0.12	43.12	34.35
55.29	4.80	1.22	47.13	39.08
56.25	8.57	0.01	45.35	38.56
65.97	9.31	0.59	55.00	52.97
72.86	4.21	2.17	62.09	48.30
73.89	9.36	0.04	61.62	50.33
143.07	34.09	2.00	103.83	44.76

表4－2　外商直接投资合同项目
Number of Contracted Projects of Foreign Direct Investment

单位:个　(unit)

指　标	Indicators	2005	2010	2013	2014	至2014年末累计 Accumulated by the End of 2014
总　计	**Total**	**1 734**	**906**	**1 032**	**2 185**	**23 841**
按投资方式分	**By Way of Investment**					
中外合资	Joint-venture	149	140	274	262	5 051
中外合作	Sino-foreign Cooperative	8	1	1	4	407
外商独资	Solely Foreigner Funded	1 574	765	757	1 551	17 925
外商投资股份制	Foreign investment shareholding system	3			4	44
按投资行业分	**By Sector**					
#第二产业	Secondary Industry	209	52	16	13	4 061
#工　业	Industry	188	46	12	11	3 442
第三产业	Tertiary Industry	1 524	854	1 015	2 170	19 752
#批发零售业	Wholesale and Retail	672	476	526	1 151	10 802
交通运输、仓储和邮政业	Transportation, Warehousing, Post and Telecommunications	18	20	21	19	811
房地产业	Real Estate	25	3	12	8	360
租赁和商务服务业	Leasing and Commercial Services	295	216	291	630	4 127
按投资国别、地区分	**By Country/Region**					
#中国香港	Hong Kong, China	307	301	430	890	7 213
中国澳门	Macao, China	2			9	74
中国台湾	Taiwan, China	82	62	73	214	1 541
日　本	Japan	270	101	63	88	2 878
新加坡	Singapore	107	52	62	99	1 384
韩　国	Republic of Korea	80	29	29	75	694
英　国	United Kingdom	35	15	18	45	437
德　国	Germany	52	27	40	56	674
法　国	France	26	10	10	34	237
荷　兰	the Netherlands	24	10	17	17	267
瑞　士	Switzerland	14	8	7	12	204
美　国	United States of America	146	87	75	183	2 594
加拿大	Canada	19	10	15	64	391
澳大利亚	Australia	22	8	14	56	369
海外中资集团	Overseas Chinese Group Companies					72

表4-3　外商直接投资合同金额
Contract Value of Foreign Direct Investment

单位:万美元　　　　(USD 10 000)

指　标	Indicators	2005	2010	2013	2014	至2014年末累计 Accumulated by the End of 2014
总　计	**Total**	**565 369**	**562 487**	**718 878**	**1 430 736**	**9 218 656**
按投资方式分	**By Way of Investment**					
中外合资	Joint-venture	78 437	85 679	93 585	340 876	1 806 802
中外合作	Sino-foreign Cooperative	3 771	122	383	20 028	195 766
外商独资	Solely Foreigner Funded	421 985	453 504	616 240	1 052 927	6 821 739
外商投资股份制	Foreign investment shareholding system	61 176	23 182	8 670	16 905	394 349
按投资行业分	**By Sector**					
第二产业	Secondary Industry	172 056	98 697	37 786	21 701	2 110 875
#工　业	Industry	162 312	95 872	37 080	21 029	1 632 044
第三产业	Tertiary Industry	393 242	463 790	680 820	1 408 388	7 104 824
#批发零售业	Wholesale and Retail	61 919	90 922	25 518	324 744	527 384
交通运输、仓储和邮政业	Transportation, Warehousing, Post and Telecommunications	114 776	18 896	159 860	20 477	578 675
房地产业	Real Estate	49 390	100 310	92 880	26 269	168 545
租赁和商务服务业	Leasing and Business Service	114 149	163 058	180 335	352 719	787 766
按投资国别、地区分	**By Country/Region**					
#中国香港	Hong Kong, China	68 253	200 809	372 544	880 058	3 083 111
中国澳门	Macao, China	68	19	9 487	18 008	
中国台湾	Taiwan, China	2 795	2 936	6 083	35 160	118 492
日　本	Japan	69 789	49 831	52 118	39 496	878 622
新加坡	Singapore	18 363	30 632	33 140	98 513	573 217
韩　国	Republic of Korea	5 438	4 463	4 097	4 636	97 587
英　国	United Kingdom	6 245	10 809	3 059	3 628	120 065
德　国	Germany	54 020	9 016	1 970	13 031	224 036
法　国	France	2 531	21 750	3 759	34 366	166 136
荷　兰	the Netherlands	8 424	9 744	17 764	13 770	250 711
瑞　士	Switzerland	1 340	1 037	3 647	1 889	59 021
美　国	United States of America	41 169	21 172	56 689	76 684	818 174
加拿大	Canada	1 101	-92	808	7 416	32 960
澳大利亚	Australia	787	1 024	369	10 796	33 101
海外中资集团	Overseas Chinese Group Companies					20 657

表4-4　当年签约投资5000万美元以上的外商投资企业

FIEs with Current Year Contracted Investment Over USD 50 Million (2014)

单位：万美元　　(USD 10 000)

序号 No.	指 标 Indicators		国别(地区) Country/Region	总投资 Total Investment	外商合同投资 Contracted Foreign Investment
1	历峰商业有限公司	Lifeng Business Co., Ltd	香港 Hong Kong	48 720	42 256
2	惠而浦(中国)投资有限公司	Whirlpool (China) Investment Co., Ltd	卢森堡 Luxemburg	40 000	30 000
3	普新投资(上海)有限公司	Puxin Investment (Shanghai) Co.,Ltd	新加坡 Singapore	30 000	30 000
4	上海璞能融资租赁有限公司	Shanghai Puneng Leasing Co.,Ltd	香港 Hong Kong	29 900	29 900
5	上海永盛融资租赁有限公司	Shanghai Yongsheng Leasing Co., Ltd	香港 Hong Kong	29 900	29 900
6	液化空气(中国)投资有限公司	Air Liquid (China) Investment Co., Ltd	法国 France	26 237	26 237
7	上海复星冶金投资管理有限公司	Shanghai Fuxing Metallurgy Investmnet Management Co., Ltd	香港 Hong Kong	22 970	22 970
8	绿巨人能源有限公司	Green Giant Energy Co., Ltd.	香港 Hong Kong	29 900	20 000
9	蒙牛(中国)投资有限公司	Mengniu Dairy (China) Investment Co., Ltd	开曼群岛 Cayman Islands	20 000	20 000
10	平安国际融资租赁有限公司	Pingan International Leasing Co.,Ltd	香港 Hong Kong	26 206	18 387
11	上海国际主题乐园有限公司	Shanghai International Theme Park Co.,Ltd	美国 USA	80 056	17 212
12	上海幂宙实业有限公司	Shanghai Miyu Real Estate Co., Ltd	香港 Hong Kong	49 114	16 371
13	凯德管理(上海)有限公司	Kaide Management (Shanghai) Co., Ltd	新加坡 Singapore	21 592	16 234
14	国投融资租赁有限公司	Country Investment Leasing Co., Ltd	香港 Hong Kong	15 000	15 000
15	霖园置业(上海)有限公司	Linyuan Real Estate (Shanghai) Co., Ltd	台湾省 Taiwan	11 393	11 393
16	上海合茂房地产发展有限公司	Shanghai Hemao Real Estate Development Co., Ltd	香港 Hong Kong	20 508	10 254
17	埃培克塑料制品(上海)有限公司	Epec Plastic Products (Shanghai) Co., Ltd	泰国 Thailand	10 000	10 000
18	大势融资租赁(上海)有限公司	General Trend Financing Lease (Shanghai) Co., Ltd	香港 Hong Kong	10 000	10 000
19	上海鼎融融资租赁有限公司	Shanghai Dingrong Leasing Co., Ltd	香港 Hong Kong	10 000	10 000
20	中海集装箱运输股份有限公司	China Shipping Container Lines Incorporated Corporation	香港 Hong Kong	29 509	9 474
21	远东新世纪(中国)投资有限公司	Far East New Century (China) Investment Co.,Ltd	百慕大 Bermuda	9 209	9 209
22	纽海信息技术(上海)有限公司	New Information Technology (Shanghai) Co., Ltd.	香港 Hong Kong	9 000	9 000
23	宏润(上海)融资租赁有限公司	Hongrun (Shanghai) Leasing Co., Ltd	香港 Hong Kong	7 294	8 927
24	上海库博投资管理有限公司	Shanghai Kubo Investment Management Co.,Ltd	香港 Hong Kong	8 186	8 186
25	天鼎融资租赁有限公司	Tianding Leasing Co., Ltd	香港 Hong Kong	8 127	8 127

单位:万美元　　表4－4　续表　Continued　　(USD 10 000)

序号 No.	指　标 Indicators		国别(地区) Country/Region	总投资 Total Investment	外商合同投资 Contracted Foreign Investment
26	光大幸福国际租赁有限公司	Guangda Happiness Leasing Co. , Ltd	香港 Hong Kong	16 221	8 111
27	远鼎实业(上海)有限公司	Yuanding Real Estate (Shanghai) Co. , Ltd	投资性公司投资 Investment Companies	16 175	8 087
28	福特汽车金融(中国)有限公司	Ford Car Financing (China) Co. , Ltd	美国 USA	7 964	7 964
29	宝矿贸易(上海)有限公司	Baokuang Trading (Shanghai) Co. , Ltd	香港 Hong Kong	24 000	7 600
30	龙源电力集团(上海)投资有限公司	Longyuan Electric Group (Shanghai) Investment Co. , Ltd	香港 Hong Kong	10 000	7 500
31	中交建融租赁有限公司	China Communications Construction Leasing Co. ,Ltd	日本 Japan	29 232	7 308
32	上海易航仓储服务有限公司	Shanghai Yihang Storage Service Co. , Ltd	香港 Hong Kong	21 000	7 000
33	美铝中电投铝业投资有限公司	Alcoa and CPI Investment Co. , Ltd	美国 USA	10 600	6 936
34	土信置业(上海)有限公司	Tuxin Real Estate (Shanghai) Co. , Ltd	香港 Hong Kong	7 002	6 500
35	上海智廊置业有限公司	Shanghai Zhilang Real Estate Co. , Ltd	新加坡 Singapore	11 666	6 298
36	宜家(中国)投资有限公司	IKEA (China) Investment Co. , Ltd	荷兰 Holland	6 200	6 200
37	美西国际融资租赁有限公司	Meixi International Leasing Co. , Ltd	香港 Hong Kong	6 000	6 000
38	中新能融资租赁有限公司	Zhongxinneng Leasing Co. ,Ltd	澳门 Macao	10 000	6 000
39	东航国际融资租赁有限公司	China East	香港 Hong Kong	16 221	5 677
40	倍思得(上海)投资管理有限公司	Best (Shanghai) Investment Management Co. , Ltd	台湾省 Taiwan	14 000	5 000
41	光大融资租赁(上海)有限公司	Guangda Leasing (Shanghai) Co. , Ltd	香港 Hong Kong	5 000	5 000
42	兰亭商业发展(上海)有限公司	Lanting Business Development (Shanghai) Co. , Ltd	新加坡 Singapore	7 100	5 000
43	农宝(上海)投资管理有限公司	Nongbao (Shanghai) Investment Management Co. , Ltd	塞舌尔 Seychelles	5 000	5 000
44	上海景元融资租赁有限公司	Shanghai Jingyuan Leasing Co. , Ltd	香港 Hong Kong	5 000	5 000
45	上海市卓然商业保理有限公司	Shanghai Zhuoran Commercial Factoring Co. ,Ltd	香港 Hong Kong	5 000	5 000
46	上海星懋实业有限公司	Shanghai Xingmao Real Estate Co. ,Ltd	香港 Hong Kong	5 000	5 000
47	上海邮乐网络技术有限公司	Shanghai Youle Internet Technology Co. ,Ltd	香港 Hong Kong	5 000	5 000
48	尚隽商业保理(上海)有限公司	Shangjuan Commercial Factoring (Shanghai) Co. , Ltd	香港 Hong Kong	5 000	5 000
49	盛泽融资租赁有限公司	Shengze Leasing Co. , Ltd	香港 Hong Kong	5 000	5 000

表4-5 外商直接投资实际到位金额
Capital in Place of Foreign Direct Investment

单位:万美元 (USD 10 000)

指 标	Indicators	2010	2013	2014
总 计	**Total**	**385 567**	**503 300**	**447 577**
按投资方式分	**By Way of Investment**			
#中外合资	Joint-venture	59 492	48 317	63 768
中外合作	Sino-foreign Cooperative	836	32 179	72 683
外商独资	Solely Foreigner Funded	325 239	422 804	310 144
按投资行业分	**By Sector**			
#第二产业	Secondary Industry	50 926	54 643	29 143
#工 业	Industry	48 603	52 873	28 692
第三产业	Tertiary Industry	334 516	448 657	418 436
#批发和零售业餐饮业	Wholesale and Retail Catering	64 727	123 667	59 825
房地产业	Real Estate	64 706	51 160	57 573
租赁和商务服务业	Leasing and Business Service	118 916	135 376	90 105
按投资国别、地区分	**By Country/Region**			
#中国香港	Hong Kong, China	116 495	206 603	185 321
日 本	Japan	37 506	46 262	27 903
新加坡	Singapore	61 672	31 492	20 133
英 国	United Kingdom	4 632	1 518	1 811
德 国	Germany	8 738	4 969	12 740
法 国	France	14 871	10 090	5 454
荷 兰	the Netherlands	27 020	11 414	7 829
开曼群岛	Cayman Islands	12 702	22 741	982
英属维尔京群岛	British Virgin Islands	17 901	11 721	39 742
美 国	United States of America	21 956	59 874	94 518
萨摩亚	Samoa	1 358	2 055	2 795

表4-6 内资企业工商注册情况
Registered Domestic Enterprises

指 标	Indicators	单 位 Unit	2013	2014
期末实有注册企业	**Actual Registered Enterprises at End of Term**	**个 unit**	**10 854**	**13 271**
第一产业	Primary Industry	个 unit	141	146
第二产业	Secondary Industry	个 unit	2 375	2 361
# 制造业	Manufacturing	个 unit	1 886	1 861
建筑业	Construction	个 unit	429	442
第三产业	Tertiary Industry	个 unit	8 338	10 764
# 交通运输、仓储和邮政业	Transportation, Warehousing and Post Service	个 unit	510	580
批发和零售业	Wholesale and Retail	个 unit	2 908	3 676
金融业	Banking	个 unit	205	417
房地产业	Real Estate	个 unit	888	926
期末实际注册资金总额	**Total of Actual Registered Capital at End of Term**	**亿元（100 million yuan）**	**9 300.90**	**12 614.66**
第一产业	Primary Industry	亿元(100 million yuan)	18.37	27.16
第二产业	Secondary Industry	亿元(100 million yuan)	2 312.50	2 485.07
# 制造业	Manufacturing	亿元(100 million yuan)	1 446.30	1 516.15
建筑业	Construction	亿元(100 million yuan)	604.01	716.84
第三产业	Tertiary Industry	亿元(100 million yuan)	6 970.03	10 102.43
# 交通运输、仓储和邮政业	Transportation, Warehousing and Post Service	亿元（100 million yuan）	923.95	1 052.98
批发和零售业	Wholesale and Retail	亿元（100 million yuan）	761.50	1 147.76
金融业	Banking	亿元（100 million yuan）	687.49	1 121.62
房地产业	Real Estate	亿元（100 million yuan）	1 122.97	1 204.57

注：内资注册数和注册资本含市局登记，不含分支机构。

Note: The number of domestic registered enterprises and that of registered capital included those registered in Shanghai municipal bureaus and excluded those registered in branch bureaus.

表 4-7　私营企业基本情况
Statistics of Private Enterprises

指　标	Indicators	户　数（户）Number of Enterprises (unit)		注册资金（亿元）Registered Capital (100 million yuan)	
		2013	2014	2013	2014
总　计	**Total**	**106 740**	**142 104**	**6 891.93**	**12 880.02**
农、林、牧、渔业	Farming, Forestry, Animal Husbandry and Fishery	763	827	10.18	17.64
采掘业	Mining and Quarrying	4	4	1.31	1.31
制造业	Manufacturing	16 816	17 164	348.56	433.29
建筑业	Construction	3 670	4 820	166.03	297.20
交通运输业、仓储和邮政业	Transportation, Warehousing and Post Service	4 114	5 066	169.73	243.20
信息传输、计算机服务	Information Transmission and Computer Service	3 219	4 908	163.31	282.67
批发零售贸易业	Wholesale and Retail	38 601	52 711	1 148.12	2 224.72
住宿和餐饮业	Accommodation and Catering	1 889	2 066	15.15	18.02
居民服务和其他服务业	Resident Service and Other Services	2 886	3 101	37.72	47.23
房地产	Real Estate	2 561	2 814	457.39	563.48
其　他	Others	32 217	48 623	4 374.43	8 751.26

表4-8 个体工商户基本情况
Self-employment Business

指 标	Indicators	户 数（户）Number of Enterprises (unit)		注册资金（万元）Registered Capital (10 000 yuan)	
		2013	2014	2013	2014
总 计	**Total**	**68 944**	**75 727**	**188 422**	**214 253**
农、林、牧、渔	Farming, Forestry, Animal Husbandry and Fishery	476	517	2 933	3 170
制造业	Manufacturing	1 646	1 737	4 741	5 365
建筑业	Construction	74	91	201	345
交通运输业、仓储业	Transportation and Warehousing	540	569	3 546	3 928
批发零售贸易业、住宿和餐饮业	Wholesale, Retail and Catering Businesses	58 317	64 374	154 466	175 542
批发零售贸易业	Wholesale and Retail	54 754	60 558	141 171	160 015
住宿和 餐饮业	Accommodation and Catering	3 563	3 816	13 295	15 527
居民服务和其他服务业	Resident Service and Other Services	6 933	7 388	19 030	21 859
其 他	Others	958	1 051	3 505	4 044

主要统计指标解释

外商直接投资

外商直接投资是指外国企业和经济组织或个人(包括华侨、港澳台胞以及我国在境外注册的企业)按我国有关政策、法规,用现汇、实物、技术等在我国境内开办外商独资企业、与我国境内的企业或经济组织共同举办中外合资经营企业、合作经营企业或合作开发资源的投资(包括外商投资收益的再投资)以及企业投资总额内直接投资者对企业的贷款,即外方股东贷款(需在报告期内将相应合同及贷款协议报商务部备案核查)。

合同投资额

是指经有关部门批准的我方与外商正式签订的合同规定的可使用的贷款额、外商投资额和中方对外发行债券、股票总值,以及"补偿贸易"外商提供的设备价款,"国际租赁"境外出租人提供的设备等价款总值。

外商实际投资额

是指按合同(章程)规定,外商以现金、实物及专有技术等工业产权计价的全部实缴资本额,包括经有关部门批准,外商用于扩大再生产、发展企业规模或补充基本建设资金不足而投入的追加资金。外商的实缴资本额一律折成美元计算。

EXPLANATORY NOTES TO MAJOR STATISTICAL INDICATORS

Foreign Direct Investment

Foreign Direct Investment refers to the investments made inside China by foreign enterprises and economic organizations or individuals (including overseas Chinese, compatriots in Hong Kong, Macao and Chinese enterprises registered abroad), in line with the relevant policies and laws of China, for the establishment of wholly foreign-owned enterprises, and joint ventures or development projects launched in China (including re-investment of profits from foreign businesses), and the funds that enterprises borrow from abroad in the total investment of projects which are approved by the relevant departments of the governments and the loans from the direct investors within the total investment of the projects, i. e. foreign shareholders' loans. (The related contracts and loans agreements in the report period should be filed with the Ministry of Commerce.)

Agreed (Contracted) Investment

Agreed (Contracted) Investment includes usable loans which are approved by government departments and with contracts signed formally by Chinese units and foreign investors, investment of foreigners, total value of bonds and stocks issued in international market by Chinese units, the value of equipment provided by foreign investors for compensation trade, the value of equipment which are leased from foreign firms, etc.

Actual Investment of Foreign Investors

Actual Investment of Foreign Investors refers to all foreign investors paid-in capital, in cash, in kind or in special technique, based on contracts, which includes the additional funds used for extensional reproduction, expanding enterprise scale or complements to capital construction. All the foreigners paid-in capital is measured by or converted to US dollars.

第五篇

CHAPTER 5

农 业

AGRICULTURE

表5-1 主要年份农村户数、人口和劳动力
Rural Households, Population and Workforce in Main Years

指 标	Indicators	单 位 Unit	1990	2000	2005	2010	2013	2014
户 数	Household	万户 10 000 households	15.74	13.67	12.67	32.90	30.70	31.20
人 口	Population	万人 10 000 persons	47.00	36.82	35.57	82.96	76.71	75.61
劳动力使用	Workforce	万人 10 000 persons	27.70	19.86	19.66	48.70	46.32	45.30
第一产业	Primary Industry	万人 10 000 persons	6.83	4.04	1.67	10.62	9.04	8.68
第二产业	Secondary Industry	万人 10 000 persons	14.91	8.98	11.53	25.95	27.60	26.72
第三产业	Tertiary Industry	万人 10 000 persons	5.96	6.83	6.46	12.13	9.69	9.90
外省市流入劳动力	Migrant Workforce from Other Provinces	万人 10 000 persons	1.53	9.13	26.52	65.32	70.19	67.75
第一产业	Primary Industry	万人 10 000 persons	0.28	1.47	1.65	4.08	4.11	3.91
第二产业	Secondary Industry	万人 10 000 persons	1.18	5.27	18.44	43.32	44.13	42.75
第三产业	Tertiary Industry	万人 10 000 persons	0.06	2.38	6.43	17.92	21.95	21.09

注：表中涉及的户数、人口和劳动力是指居住在农村地区的本市户籍常住户数和人口。
Note: The numbers of households, population and labor force involved in this table are referred to those that live in the rural area of Shanghai.

表5-2 各镇耕地面积
Cultivated Area by Town

单位:公顷 (hectare)

镇	Town	2013年末耕地面积 Cultivated Area (End of 2013)	2014年净减少耕地面积 Net Decrease in Cultivated Area in 2014	2014年末耕地面积 Cultivated Area (End of 2014)	水田 Paddy Field	水浇地 Irrigated Land
川沙新镇	Chuansha New Town	1 826.9	77.0	1 749.9	1 655.4	94.5
高桥镇	Gaoqiao Town	430.4		430.4	16.6	413.8
北蔡镇	Beicai Town	146.0		146.0		146.0
合庆镇	Heqing Town	801.1	2.2	798.9	729.7	69.2
唐镇	Tangzhen Town	191.8	16.5	175.3	10.5	164.8
曹路镇	Caolu Town	524.8	0.7	524.1	524.1	
金桥镇	Jinqiao Town	24.8		24.8	24.8	
高行镇	Gaohang Town	4.6	2.3	2.3		2.3
高东镇	Gaodong Town	255.0	3.6	251.4	229.7	21.7
张江镇	Zhangjiang Town	211.0		211.0	211.0	
三林镇	Sanlin Town	249.0	2.0	247.0		247.0
惠南镇	Huinan Town	1 707.4	145.2	1 562.2	1 562.2	
周浦镇	Zhoupu Town	595.4	23.6	571.8	487.7	84.1
新场镇	Xinchang Town	2 275.9	5.9	2 270.0	1 182.3	1 087.7
大团镇	Datuan Town	1 317.9	-16.3	1 334.2	1 155.0	179.2
康桥镇	Kangqiao Town	245.2	15.5	229.7	68.0	161.7
航头镇	Hangtou Town	1 798.4	43.0	1 755.4	1 080.2	675.2
祝桥镇	Zhuqiao Town	2 720.5	23.5	2 697.0	1 402.0	1 295.0
泥城镇	Nicheng Town	1 861.6		1 861.6	1 421.6	440.0
宣桥镇	Xuanqiao Town	1 888.4	-9.8	1 898.2	1 082.7	815.5
书院镇	Shuyuan Town	2 646.9	193.5	2 453.4	2 293.4	160.0
万祥镇	Wanxiang Town	921.1	-1.4	922.5	846.2	76.3
老港镇	Laogang Town	1 746.3	1.1	1 745.2	571.4	1 173.8
南汇新城镇	Nanhui New Town	2 533.3		2 533.3	1 627.6	905.7
农场	Farm	26.1		26.1	26.1	
棉种场	Cotton Farm	23.5		23.5	23.5	

注：2013年始批准数指标取消，现各镇反映的数据均为实际经营数。后续相关指标口径相同。
Note: Since 2013, the authorized indicators of cultivated area are cancelled, so the numbers of each town all represent the real operating ones. The same principle goes on in this book.

表5-3　主要年份耕地面积增减情况
Increase and Decrease of Cultivated Land in Main Years

单位:公顷　　　　(hectare)

指　标	Indicators	2005	2010	2013	2014
年初耕地面积	Cultivated Area (Year Beginning)	9 483	44 001	21 238	21 415
当年减少	Decrease in Current Year	634	450	-177	528
年末耕地面积	Cultivated Area (Year End)	8 849	43 551	21 415	20 887

注：2013 年起批准数指标取消，为实际经营数。
Note: Since 2013, the authorized indicators of cultivated area are cancelled, so the numbers all represent the real operating ones.

表5-4　主要年份农业总产值
Gross Output Value of Agriculture in Main Years

单位:万元　　　　(10 000 yuan)

指　标	Indicators	1990	2000	2005	2010	2013	2014
按当年价格计算	**Calculated in Current Year**						
总　计	**Total**	**55 318**	**125 732**	**116 248**	**698 552**	**689 814**	**650 962**
种植业	Planting	24 015	59 584	66 809	396 127	412 650	372 813
林　业	Forestry	234	1 279	25 424	10 420	18 398	19 609
牧　业	Animal Husbandry	29 528	60 837	19 488	183 084	137 209	139 810
渔　业	Fishery	1 541	4 032	4 527	70 921	78 285	77 650
农、林、牧、渔服务业	Agriculture, forestry, animal husbandry and fishery			38 000	38 500	43 272	41 080
构　成(%)	**Composition (%)**						
总　计	**Total**	**100.0**	**100.0**	**100.0**	**100.0**	**100.0**	**100.0**
种植业	Planting	43.4	47.4	57.5	56.7	59.8	57.3
林　业	Forestry	0.4	1.0	21.9	1.5	2.6	3.0
牧　业	Animal Husbandry	53.4	48.4	16.8	26.2	20.0	21.5
渔　业	Fishery	2.8	3.2	3.8	10.2	11.3	11.9
农、林、牧、渔服务业	Agriculture, forestry, animal husbandry and fishery				5.4	6.3	6.3

表5-5 各镇农业总产值
Gross Output Value of Agriculture by Town
(2014)

单位:万元 (10 000 yuan)

指 标	Indicators	农业总产值（按现行价格计算）Gross Output Value of Agriculture (at Current Price)	#种植业 Planting	林 业 Forestry	牧 业 Animal Husbandry	渔 业 Fishery
总 计	**Total**	**650 962**	**372 813**	**19 609**	**139 810**	**77 650**
川沙新镇	Chuansha New Town	49 337	27 463	5 178	12 301	1 895
高 桥 镇	Gaoqiao Town	1 911	1 860			51
北 蔡 镇	Beicai Town	461	371			90
合 庆 镇	Heqing Town	9 609	6 317		2 990	302
唐 镇	Tangzhen Town	1 067	875			88
曹 路 镇	Caolu Town	31 134	13 871	612	16 431	170
金 桥 镇	Jinqiao Town	36		36		
高 行 镇	Gaohang Town					
高 东 镇	Gaodong Town	2 104	2 046			58
张 江 镇	Zhangjiang Town	5 838	5 598	111		129
三 林 镇	Sanlin Town	3 530	1 298	250		140
惠 南 镇	Huinan Town	30 313	20 194		7 881	2 238
周 浦 镇	Zhoupu Town	15 094	12 076		2 453	565
新 场 镇	Xinchang Town	60 799	47 123		9 343	4 333
大 团 镇	Datuan Town	45 008	26 235		16 335	2 438
康 桥 镇	Kangqiao Town	3 684	3 575		109	
航 头 镇	Hangtou Town	46 833	24 833	2 141	17 664	2 195
祝 桥 镇	Zhuqiao Town	56 269	38 049	230	12 058	5 932
泥 城 镇	Nicheng Town	41 284	29 012	1 012	1 323	9 667
宣 桥 镇	Xuanqiao Town	24 016	9 642		13 250	1 124
书 院 镇	Shuyuan Town	34 019	21 888	5	7 968	4 158
万 祥 镇	Wanxiang Town	14 248	9 155		2 675	2 418
老 港 镇	Laogang Town	42 182	26 342		12 837	3 003
南汇新城镇	Nanhui New Town	30 217	23 436	47	218	6 516
其 他	Others	101 969	21 554	9 987	3 974	30 140

表5-6　各镇粮食和蔬菜作物播种面积和产量
Sown Area and Output of Grain Crops and Vegetables by Town (2014)

指　标 Indicators		粮食播种面积（公顷）Sown Area（hectare）	粮食总产量（吨）Total Output of Grain Crops（ton）			粮食单位面积产量（千克/公顷）Yield Per Unit（kg/hectare）	蔬菜播种面积（公顷）Sown Area of Vegetables（hectare）	蔬菜总产量（吨）Total Output of Vegetables（ton）
				夏　粮 Summer Harvested	秋　粮 Autumn Harvested			
总　计	**Total**	**18 762.5**	**132 657**	**24 321**	**108 336**	**7 070**	**24 705.0**	**777 032**
川沙新镇	Chuansha New Town	479.8	3 654	679	2 975	7 616	2 365.4	73 881
高桥镇	Gaoqiao Town						280.2	6 135
北蔡镇	Beicai Town						147.3	1 801
合庆镇	Heqing Town	170.8	1 205	243	962	7 055	479.9	17 645
唐　镇	Tangzhen Town	19.5	121	32	89	6 205	85.5	1 773
曹路镇	Caolu Town	96.8	885	25	860	9 143	1 066.7	29 993
金桥镇	Jinqiao Town						5.8	
高行镇	Gaohang Town						0.6	
高东镇	Gaodong Town						210.0	3 424
张江镇	Zhangjiang Town	106.0	740	220	520	6 981	147.5	3 984
三林镇	Sanlin Town						123.6	3 072
惠南镇	Huinan Town	936.6	6 969	1 635	5 334	7 441	1 135.4	31 122
周浦镇	Zhoupu Town	416.1	2 873	743	2 130	6 905	1 112.9	27 028
新场镇	Xinchang Town	1 090.1	7 369	1 005	6 364	6 760	2 702.6	76 472
大团镇	Datuan Town	1 365.8	9 312	1 563	7 749	6 818	762.1	32 297
康桥镇	Kangqiao Town	148.6	969	325	644	6 521	388.6	13 075
航头镇	Hangtou Town	525.6	3 853	746	3 107	7 331	2 407.0	97 258
祝桥镇	Zhuqiao Town	1 840.7	12 300	2 903	9 397	6 682	3 926.7	159 489
泥城镇	Nicheng Town	1 248.8	9 489	2 202	7 287	7 598	2 113.4	56 503
宣桥镇	Xuanqiao Town	310.8	2 382	428	1 954	7 664	2 017.1	48 710
书院镇	Shuyuan Town	1 961.8	13 834	3 176	10 658	7 052	1 153.6	39 025
万祥镇	Wanxiang Town	1 023.7	7 451	1 554	5 897	7 278	544.4	15 052
老港镇	Laogang Town	3 282.3	23 900	2 682	21 218	7 281	817.1	26 373
南汇新城镇	Nanhui New Town	3 738.7	25 351	4 160	21 191	6 781	711.6	12 920

表5-7 主要农产品产量
Output of Main Farm Products

指 标 Indicators		单 位 Unit	2005	2010	2013	2014
粮食作物	Grain Crops	吨 ton	13 671	148 707	141 489	132 657
夏熟作物	Summer Harvested	吨 ton	1 303	27 147	29 971	24 321
#小 麦	Wheat	吨 ton	1 064	20 291	20 231	17 059
秋熟作物	Autumn Harvested	吨 ton	12 368	121 560	111 518	108 336
#单季晚稻	Single-season Late Harvested Rice	吨 ton	10 580	116 437	109 929	105 299
油菜籽	Rapeseed	吨 ton	89	2 315	2 363	2 042
蔬 菜	Vegetables	万吨 10 000 tons	30	81	77	80
西甜瓜	Watermelons	万吨 10 000 tons	2	23	14	10
水果产量	Output of Fruits	吨 ton	4 219	108 714	67 180	76 068
#柑 桔	Mandarin Oranges	吨 ton	607	56 543	17 294	19 023
生 梨	Pears	吨 ton	274	7 829	10 339	9 961
葡 萄	Grapes	吨 ton	727	4 304	7 338	9 243
桃 子	Peaches	吨 ton		39 153	31 263	36 578
生猪饲养数	Stock of Hogs	万头 10 000 in number	16.72	96.61	90.00	90.96
生猪出栏数	Hogs on Market	万头 10 000 in number	8.80	56.36	47.28	51.71
猪肉产量	Pork Output	万吨 10 000 tons	0.77	3.66	3.91	4.42
牛奶产量	Milk Output	万吨 10 000 tons	1.27	4.43	4.64	3.70
家禽出栏数	Poultry on Market	万羽 10 000 in number	24.28	1 913.32	733.99	679.09
鲜蛋产量	Output of Fresh Eggs	万吨 10 000 tons	0.17	2.26	1.63	1.82
水产品产量	Output of Aquatic Products	万吨 10 000 tons	0.23	2.16	2.26	2.14
海水产品	Sea Products	万吨 10 000 tons		0.32	0.11	0.10
淡水产品	Fresh Water Products	万吨 10 000 tons	0.23	1.84	2.15	2.04

表5-8　种源农业生产、销售情况
Seed Agriculture Production and Sales
(2014)

指　标	Indicators	单　位　Unit	生　产 Production	自产自用 For Self-use	销　售 Sales
总　计	**Total**	**万元 10 000 yuan**	**19 679**	**14 180**	**5 499**
农业(种植业)	**Agriculture(Crop Farming)**	**万元 10 000 yuan**	**953**	**111**	**842**
#粮食种籽	Grain Seed	吨 ton	887	618	269
金　额	Amount	万元 10 000 yuan	136	52	84
蔬菜种籽	Vegetable Seed	公斤 kilogram	23 443	7 017	16 426
金　额	Amount	万元 10 000 yuan	564	9	555
食用菌种	Eatable Mushroom Seed	万元 10 000 yuan	27	9	18
西甜瓜种籽	West Muskmelon Seed	吨 ton			
金　额	Amount	万元 10 000 yuan			
花卉种苗	Flower Seed	万枝 10 000 unit	1 500	333	1 167
金　额	Amount	万元 10 000 yuan	225	40	185
林　业	**Forestry**	**万元 10 000 yuan**	**661**	**56**	**605**
#树　苗	Sapling	百棵 100 unit	14 710	1 553	13 157
金　额	Amount	万元 10 000 yuan	561	47	514
畜牧业	**Animal Husbandry**	**万元 10 000 yuan**	**16 870**	**13 449**	**3 421**
#苗　猪	Procreating Boar	只 unit	231 743	199 303	32 440
金　额	Amount	万元 10 000 yuan	15 205	12 040	3 165
苗　禽	Procreating Bird	万只 10 000 unit	551	498	53
金　额	Amount	万元 10 000 yuan	1 055	902	153
种　蛋	Procreating Egg	万只 10 000 unit	552	540	12
金　额	Amount	万元 10 000 yuan	546	462	84
羊　羔	Procreating Sheep	只 unit	2 032	1 092	940
金　额	Amount	万元 10 000 yuan	62	43	19
渔　业	**Fishing**	**万元 10 000 yuan**	**1 195**	**564**	**631**
#鱼　苗	Procreating Fish	万尾 10 000 unit	138	82	56
金　额	Amount	万元 10 000 yuan	107	64	43
鳗　苗	Procreating Eel	万尾 10 000 unit	33		33
金　额	Amount	万元 10 000 yuan	338		338

表5-9 浦东新区特色农业发展情况
The Development of Characteristic Agriculture in Pudong New Area

指 标 Indicators		单 位 Unit	2013	2014
农业组织化	**Organised Agriculture**			
农业产业化龙头企业	Top Enterprises of Agriculture Industrialization	个 in number	69	53
家庭农场	Home Farming	个 in number		271
农业品牌	**Famous Brand in Agriculture**			
中国驰名商标	Famous Brand in China	个 in number	1	1
市名牌产品	Famous Municipal Products	个 in number	18	16
市著名商标	Famous Municipal Brand	个 in number	13	21
农业科技	**Agro-technology**			
国家级项目	National Project	个 in number	4	17
市级项目	Municipal Project	个 in number	11	34
农业设施化、标准化	**Agriculture Standardlization**			
设施粮田面积	Facilitated Grain Land Area	公顷 hectare	5 509.8	5 509.8
设施菜地面积	Facilitated Vegetable Land Area	公顷 hectare	4500	4650
设施果园面积	Facilitated Fruit Land Area	公顷 hectare	700	723.7
标准化畜禽养殖场	Standardlized Livestock Farm	个 in number	42	41
标准化水产养殖场	Standardlized Fishing Lake	个 in number	22	22
农产品认证	**Agricultural product certification**			
"三品一标"认证覆盖率	The Coverage of Harmless Agro-product, Green Food, Organic Agro-product, and Agro-product with Geographical Indications	%	66.6	73.4
无公害农产品认证企业数	Enterprises with Identified Harmless Agro-product	个 in number	312	400
绿色食品认证企业数	Enterprises with Identified Green Food	个 in number	16	19
有机农产品认证企业数	Enterprises with Identified Organic Agro-product	个 in number	13	9
农业旅游	**Agro-tourism**			
旅游景点	Travel Spot	个 in number	41	42
接待人次	Number of Tourists	万人 10 thousand	480	420

表5-10　农业机械拥有量
Farm Machinery Holding

指　标	Indicators	单　位 Unit	2010	2013	2014
农业机械总动力	**Total Power of Farm Machinery**	**千瓦 kw**	**112 420**	**118 524**	**144 525**
耕作机械动力合计	Total Power of Farm Machinery	千瓦 kw	46 605	51 603	60 822
大、中型拖拉机	Large/Medium Tractors	台 set	925	1 124	1 319
小型拖拉机	Walking Tractors	台 set	938	583	583
排灌机械动力	Total Power of Drainage and Irrigation Machinery	千瓦 kw	15 603	14 408	18 506
种植机械动力	Total Power of Cultivation	千瓦 kw	2 897	4 137	5 200
植物保护机械动力	Total Power of Crop Protection Machinery	千瓦 kw	6 141	8 033	8 410
#机动喷雾器	Motorized Sprayers	台 set 千瓦 kw	2 043 6 052	2 626 8 027	2 826 8 410
收获机械动力合计	Total Power of Harvest Machinery	千瓦 kw	14 293	17 063	19 671
#联合收割机	Combines	台/千瓦 set/kw	383/10 176	338/14 498	376/17 008
农产品加工机械动力	Power of Farm Processing Machinery	千瓦 kw	6 468	3 893	3 893
积肥机械动力	Power of Manure - Collecting Machinery	千瓦 kw	1 629	1 011	1 011
畜牧机械动力	Power of Animal Husbandry Machinery	千瓦 kw	2 831	2 938	3 011
渔业机械动力	Total Power of Fishery Machinery	千瓦 kw	9 673	10 946	19 303
园艺机械动力	Total Power of Horticultural Machinery	千瓦 kw	492	1 269	1 363
其他农业机械动力	Total Power of Other Agricultural Machineries	千瓦 kw	5 788	3 223	3 335
#农用载重汽车	Trucks for Agricultural Use	辆 in number	75	27	27
机动运输船	Transport Ships with Mechanical Power	艘 in number	43	25	25
每公顷耕地拥有动力	Power Per Hectare	千瓦 kw	5	6	7
每万公顷耕地拥有拖拉机	Tractors Per 10 000 Hectare	台 set	842	797	911

表5-11 农田水利建设情况
Construction of Farmland Water Conservancy

指 标 Indicators		单 位 Unit	2010	2013	2014
有效灌溉面积	Effectively Irrigated Area	公顷 hectare	18 510	16 209	16 188
本年实灌面积	Actually Irrigated Area (Current Year)	公顷 hectare	11 939	12 405	11 924
当年新增改善灌溉面积	Increased and Improved Irrigated Area (Current Year)	公顷 hectare	242	43	1 331
旱涝保收面积	Ensured Area from Drought and Flood	公顷 hectare	11 939	12 405	11 924
易涝面积	Area Subjected to Flood	公顷 hectare		3 259	286
水 闸	Dams	座 nit	11	16	16
堤 防	Dikes	公里 km	180.59	183.12	183.12
#郊区海塘	Rural/Suburban Sea Wall	公里 km	115.28	117.81	117.81
江 堤	Embankment	公里 km	65.31	65.31	65.31
围垦面积	Enclosed Tideland for Cultivation	公顷 hectare			
小机口新增	Newly Increased Small Machinery	座/台套/千瓦 unit /set /kw	29/29/316.5	6/8/120	41/84/1 086
新增排涝泵站	Newly Built Pump Houses for Draining Water-logging Fields	座/台套/千瓦 unit /set /kw	1/3/10		2/4/30
新建排涝涵洞	Newly Built Culvert for Draining Water-logging Fields	座/米 unit /meter	57/2 681		2/146
改造地下渠道	Underground Irrigation Ditch Reformed	公里 km	101.74	39.45	286.50
改造渡槽倒虹吸	Siphon Aqueduct Transformed	条/米 unit/meter	192/3 851	113/2 261	162/8 099

表5-12 历年农田水利工程投资
Investment in Farmland Water Conservancy Projects (1990~2014)

单位:万元 (10 000 yuan)

年 份 Year	合 计 Total	国家投资 State-invested	乡村自筹 Funded by Villages	乡村自筹所占比重(%) Percentage of Investment Funded by Villages(%)
1990	1 363.74	668.75	694.99	51.0
1991	906.70	354.80	551.90	60.9
1992	826.30	311.90	514.40	62.3
1993	1 517.22	357.80	1 159.42	76.4
1994	2 673.15	1 253.61	1 419.54	53.1
1995	2 426.99	1 262.82	1 164.17	48.0
1996	3 357.97	1 766.90	1 591.07	47.4
1997	4 203.64	2 154.13	2 049.51	48.8
1998	4 849.08	2 419.01	2 430.07	50.1
1999	4 907.60	2 152.70	2 754.90	56.1
2000	6 321.21	2 333.20	3 988.01	63.1
2001	5 627.80	2 787.75	2 840.05	50.5
2002	7 975.97	3 423.95	4 552.02	57.1
2003	7 259.27	3 281.75	3 977.52	54.8
2004	7 137.29	3 583.26	3 554.03	49.8
2005	10 131.48	4 403.23	5 728.25	56.5
2006	15 053.70	6 661.95	8 391.75	55.7
2007	14 859.89	7 510.40	7 349.49	49.5
2008	43 846.67	21 908.07	21 938.60	50.0
2009	37 513.48	15 601.77	21 911.71	58.4
2010	68 474.03	52 745.21	15 728.82	23.0
2011	59 262.87	41 412.45	17 850.42	30.1
2012	89 338.99	66 015.05	23 323.94	26.1
2013	79 466.92	67 345.18	12 121.74	15.3
2014	91 098.12	73 759.35	17 338.77	19.0

表5-13 农村实用人才基本情况(至2014年末)
The Basic Information of the Applied Personnel in Rural Area(at the end of 2014)

单位:人 (persons)

指 标	Indicators	合 计 In total	按人才类型分 By type of personnel				
			生产型 in Production	经营型 in Operation	技能服务型 in Skill Service	技能带动型 in Skill Driven	社会服务型 in Social Service
合 计	**In total**	**12 479**	**3 386**	**2 456**	**865**	**931**	**4 841**
按学历分	**By Educational Background**						
研究生及以上	Master Degree and Above	33		9	15		9
大学本科	Bachelor Degree	718	11	83	148	1	475
高等专科	Junior College	1 875	43	223	175	7	1 427
高中(含中专)	High School	2 791	293	725	206	70	1 497
初中及以下	Junior High School and below	7 062	3 039	1 416	321	853	1 433
按专业技术职称分	**By Technical Title**						
高 级	Senior	50	5	14	23		8
中 级	Medium	502	35	92	136	11	228
初 级	Junior	1 008	55	86	123	28	716
按职业资格分	**By Vocational Qualification**						
高级技师	Senior Technicians	105	10	13	17	9	56
技 师	Technicians	30	3	6	11		10
高级工	Senior Workers	123	5	21	43	2	52
中级工	Medium Workers	237	9	49	60	4	115
初级工	Junior Workers	825	117	146	100	25	437
专业技能提升渠道	**By Technical Skill Training**						
国家级层面培训	National Training	700	271	91	60	15	263
市级培训	Municipal Training	113	4	12	52	1	44
区县级培训	County Training	1 001	34	73	303	6	585
街镇级培训	Street Training	940	108	71	92	3	666
本单位培训	Training of Own Company	3 612	764	844	128	297	1 579

主要统计指标解释

农村从业人员

指乡村人口中16岁以上实际参加生产经营活动并取得实物或货币收入的人员，既包括劳动年龄内实际参加劳动人员，也包括超过劳动年龄但实际参加劳动的人员，但不包括户口在家的在外学生、现役军人和丧失劳动能力的人，也不包括待业人员和家务劳动者。劳动者年龄为16岁以上。

农业总产值

农业总产值是以货币表现的农、林、牧、渔业全部产品的总量和对农林牧渔生产活动进行的各种支持性服务活动的价值。它反映一定时期内农业生产的总规模和总成果。

农、林、牧、渔业的统计范围是：

（1）农业　包括农作物种植业和其他农业。

农作物种植业包括谷物、豆类、薯类、棉、油料、糖料、麻类、烟叶、蔬菜、药材、瓜类和其他农作物的种植，以及茶园、桑园、果园的生产经营。

其他农业包括采集野生植物的果实、纤维、树胶、树脂、油料以及柴草、野生药材、菌类等及农民家庭兼营的商品性工业。

（2）林业　包括林木的栽培（不包括茶园、桑园和果园的栽培、管理和收获等活动）、林产品的采集和村及村以下合作经济组织和农户的竹木采伐。

（3）牧业　包括除渔业养殖以外的一切动物饲养和放牧，以及野生动物的捕猎和饲养。

（4）渔业　包括水生动物和海藻类植物的养殖和捕捞。

（5）农林牧渔服务业　包括农林牧渔业生产活动进行的各种支持性服务活动。但不包括各种科学技术和专业技术服务活动。

从所有制看，包括国有经济的各种专业农（农、林、牧、渔）场以及国家各级机关团体学校、科研机构、部队经营的农业；集体所有制的乡镇村各级办农场；农村各种经济组织经营的农、林、牧、渔业以及工矿企业家属集体经营的农业；农民家庭自营的农林牧渔业及兼营商品性工业等。

农业总产值的计算方法通常是按农林牧渔业产品及其副产品的产量分别乘以各自单位产品价格求得，少数生产周期较长、当年没有产品或产品产量不易统计的，则采用间接方法匡算其产值，然后将四业产品产值和服务业产值相加即为农业总产值。

1957年以前的农业总产值中包括了厩肥和农民自给性手工业（如农民自制衣服、鞋、袜，自己从事粮食初步加工等）。1958年及以后的农业总产值，林业中增加了村及村以下竹木采伐产值；牧业中取消了厩肥产值；副业中取消了农民自给性手工业产值，增加了村及村以下办的工业产值；渔业中增加了海洋捕捞水产品产值。1980年及以后的农业总产值，在副业中增加了农民家庭兼营工业商品部分的产值。从1984年起村及村以下办工业产值划归工业。从1993年起，取消副业。将野生动物的捕猎划入牧业，野生植物采集和农民家庭兼营商品性工业划归农业。从2003年起，农业总产值中包括了农林牧渔服务业产值。

当年价格

当年价格（或现行价格）是指报告期的实际价格，如工业品的出厂价格、农产品的收购价格、商品零售价格等。用当年价格计算的一些以货币表现的物量指标或劳务总量指标，如国内生产总值、工农业总产值、社会商品零售额等，反映当年的实际情况，使国民经济各项指标互相衔接，便于考察当年社会经济效益，便于对生产和流通、生产和分配、生产和消费之间进行经济核算和综合平衡。

按当年价格计算的以货币表现的指标，在不同年份之间进行对比时，因包含各年间价格变动的因素，不能确切地反映实物量的增减变动，必须消除价格变动的因素后，才能真实反映经济发展动态。因此，在计算增长速度时都使用按可比价格计算的数字。

可比价格

可比价格指在对不同时期的价值指标对比时，扣除了价格变动的因素，以确切反映物量的变化。按可比价格计算有两种方法，一种是直接按产品产量乘其某一年的不变价格计算；另一种是用价格指数换算。

不变价格

指以同类产品某年的平均价格作为固定价格，用于计算各年的产品价值。按不变价格计算的产品价值消除了价格变动因素，不同时期对比可以反映生产的发展速度。新中国成立后，随着工农业产品价格水平的变化，国家统计局先后五次制定了全国统一的工业产品不变价格和农业产品不变价格。从1952年到1957年使用1952年工（农）业产品不变价格，从1957年到1970年使用1957年不变价格，从1971年到1980年使用1970年不变价格，从1981年到1990年使用1980年不变价格，从1991年到2000年使用1990年不变价格，从2001年开始使用2000年不变价格。

年末耕地面积

年末耕地面积指能够种植农作物，经常进行耕锄的田地。包括熟地、当年新开荒地、新开垦围垦地、连续撂荒未满三年的耕地和当年休闲地（轮歇地）。以种植农作物为主并附带种植桑树、茶树、果树和其他林木的土地，以及沿海、沿湖地区已围垦利用的“海涂”、“湖田”等也应包括在内，但不包括专业性桑园、茶园、果园、果木苗圃、林地、芦苇地、天然草原等。小于一米宽的渠、路、田埂,包括在耕地中。

农作物播种面积

农作物播种面积指报告期内收获农产品的作物的实际播种或移植有农作物的面积。凡是实际种植农作物的面积,不论种植在耕地上还是种植在非耕地上,均包括在农作物播种面积中。在播种季节基本结束后,因遭灾而重新改种和补种的农作物面积,也包括在内。

粮食产量

指全社会的产量。包括国有经济经营的、集体统一经营的和农民家庭经营的粮食产量,还包括工矿企业办的农场和其他生产单位的产量。粮食除包括稻谷、小麦、玉米、高粱、谷子及其他杂粮外,还包括薯类和豆类。其产量计算方法,豆类按去豆荚后的干豆计算;薯类(包括甘薯和马铃薯,不包括芋头和木薯)1963 年以前按每 4 公斤鲜薯折 1 公斤粮食计算,从 1964 年开始改为按 5 公斤鲜薯折 1 公斤粮食计算。城市郊区作为蔬菜的薯类(如马铃薯等)按鲜品计算,并且不作粮食统计。其他粮食一律按脱粒后的原粮计算。1989 年以前全国粮食产量数据主要靠全面报表取得,1989 年开始使用抽样调查数据。

水产品产量

指人工养殖的水产品和天然生长的水产品的捕捞量。包括海水的鱼类、虾蟹类、贝类和藻类以及内陆水域的鱼类、虾蟹类和贝类,不包括淡水生植物。水产品产量是通过各级水产和统计部门逐级上报取得数据。1995 年及以前,贝类中牡蛎按鲜肉计算;蚶、蛤、蛏按 5 斤鲜品折 1 斤计算。1996 年以后则统一按鲜品计算。

猪、牛、羊肉产量

指当年出栏并已屠宰、除去头蹄下水后带骨肉(即胴体重)的重量。包括全社会范围内的产量。1996 年前为各级逐级上报数据。1996 年第一次农业普查以后,由于畜牧业产品年报数据与普查数据之间存在一定的差距,国家统计局农调总队对畜牧业年报数据与普查数据进行衔接。1999 年以后,国家统计局开展了猪、牛、羊、禽等主要畜禽品种的抽样调查,并用抽样数据作为国家定案数据使用。未开展抽样调查的品种,仍使用各级统计部门逐级上报数据。

种源农产品

指农业生产中,农作物的种籽、种苗、菌种;林业生产中的种籽、树苗;畜禽生产中的种畜、种畜精液、仔畜、种禽、种蛋、苗禽;渔业生产中的种鱼、鱼苗、虾蟹苗。

种源农产品生产

指报告期内生产的种源农产品的数量和金额。

种源农产品自产自用

指调查单位和农户自己生产(包括报告期外生产的)的农产品在报告期内进行再生产自用。

种源农产品出售

指报告期内出售自己生产(包括指报告期外生产的)的种源农产品数量和金额。金额按实际成交价格计算。

农业机械总动力

农业机械总动力指用于农、林、牧、渔业生产的各种动力机械的动力总和。动力机械包括耕作、排灌、种植、植物保护、收获、农产品加工、运输、畜牧、渔业、农田水利等各种机械。不包括专门用于乡办工业、基本建设、非农业运输、科学试验和教学等非农业生产方面用的动力机械与作业机械的数量。

EXPLANATORY NOTES TO MAJOR STATISTICAL INDICATORS

Personnel Employed in Rural Areas

Personnel Employed in Rural Areas refers to people in rural areas who are older than 16 years and engaged in production and business activities that generate incomes in cash or in practicality. It includes all working laborers, no matter whether they are within the working age or not, whereas students studying outside but with their registered residence at home, active serviceman, people who lost their ability to work, unemployed people, and those engaged in housework are not included. The working age is defined as older than 16 years.

Gross Output Value of Agriculture

Gross Output Value of Agriculture refers to the total volume of products of farming, forestry, animal husbandry and fishery expressed in the monetary terms and output value of all kinds of service activities that support farming, forestry, animal husbandry and fishery production. It reflects the overall scale and achievements of agricultural production during a given period of time.

The scope of statistics on farming, forestry, animal husbandry, and fishery are as follows:

(1) Farming includes cultivation of farm crops and other agricultural activities.

Cultivation of farm crops include cultivation of grain crops, legume crops, tuber-crops, cotton, oil-bearing crops, sugar crops, bastfiber plants, tobacco, vegetables, medicinal herbs, melon crops, and cultivation and management of tea plantations, mulberry fields and orchards.

Other agricultural activities include harvesting wild fruits, fiber, tree gum, resin, oil-bearing plants, firewood, wild medicinal herbs, fungus, and rural-household commodity industries.

(2) Forestry refers to planting trees of various kinds (excluding tea plantations, mulberry fields and orchards), collection of forestry products and cutting and felling of bamboo and trees by villages and other cooperative organizations under village level.

(3) Animal husbandry refers to raising and grazing of all kinds of farm animals except fishing and aquatic cultivating, and hunting and rising of wild animals.

(4) Fishery refers to cultivation and catching of fish and other aquatic products and cultivation and collection of seaweed and other aquatic plants.

(5) Service Industry for Farming, Forestry, Animal Husbandry and Fishery refers to all kinds of service activities that support farming, forestry, animal husbandry and fishery production, whereas activities of science, technology and professional service are not included.

In terms of ownership, China's agriculture includes specialized state farms (for farming, forestry, animal husbandry, fishery), farms managed by various government agencies, organizations, schools, research institutions, and army; farms managed by rural collective organizations at levels of the township, town, and village; farming, forestry, animal husbandry, fishery run by various rural collective organizations and farming run by collective family members' organizations of mining and industrial enterprises; farming, forestry, animal husbandry and fishery and some commodity industries run by individual farmers.

Gross output value of agriculture is obtained by first multiplying the output of products or by-products by their unit price. For a small number of products, annual output of which is not available or difficult to get due to the long production/growing process involved, the output value will be estimated through an indirect approach. The sum of output value of all products of farming, forestry, animal husbandry and fishery and output value of service activities will then and together to form gross output value of agriculture.

Before 1957, China's gross agricultural output value included the value of barnyard manure and handicraft products for self-consumption (clothes, shoes, stockings, and initial grain processing under-taken by peasants). After 1958, the output value of cutting and felling of bamboo and trees by villages and other cooperative organizations under villages have been included in forestry; value of barnyard manure has been excluded from animal husbandry; the value of self-consumed handicrafts has been excluded from sideline occupations, while output value of industries run by villages and cooperative organizations under village level has been included in sideline occupations and output value of fish catches by motor fishing boats has been added to fishery. Since 1980, the output value of handicraft products made for sale by farmer households has been added to sideline occupations, From 1984, industries run by villages and cooperative organizations under village level have been included in the sector of industry. After 1993, the category of sideline occupations has been canceled and hunting of wild animals has been classified into husbandry, and harvesting of wild vegetation and commodity industry run by rural households have been grouped into the category of agriculture. Since 2003, the output value of service industry for farming, forestry, animal husbandry and fishery is included in the gross output value of agriculture.

Current Prices

Current prices refer to the actual prices in the report period, for example, industrial producers prices, procurement prices of agricultural products, retail prices, and so on. Goods and services measured by the current prices, such as gross national product, gross output value of industry and agriculture, total retail sales, reflect the current-year actual activities. The various national economic indicators, such as current-year social economic efficiency, production, exchange, distribution and consumption could be understood and compared directly if they are measured by the current prices.

The indicators measured by the current prices can not exactly reflect the real change over different years, if the price level changes during the period of time. The comparable prices would be used in measuring growth rates, in order to deflate the price change.

Comparable Prices

Comparable Prices are applied when comparing indicators over time to reflect accurately the changes in real term. Two methods are used for calculating comparable prices: 1. output by constant price of certain year; 2. output in current prices divided by relevant price index.

Constant Price

Constant Price refers to the average price of a given product in certain year, which is used for comparison of output value over time. As the output value at constant prices removes the factor of price changes, it reflects the trend of production development over time. Since 1949, with the changes in general price level, National Bureau of Statistics has issued nationally unified constant prices five times: the 1952 constant prices for 1949 – 1957; the 1957 constant prices for 1957 – 1971; the 1970 constant prices for 1971 – 1981; the 1980 constant prices for 1981 – 1990; the 1990 constant prices for 1991 – 2000; and the 2000 constant prices have been used since 2001.

The Actual Area of Plowland at Year End

The Area of Plowland at Year End refers to the area of arable land and frequently-tended farm-fields at the beginning of a year. It includes cultivated land, the newly-reclaimed wasteland and inning land in the year, the farmland which has been laid idle for no more than three consecutive years, and land on fallow that year. It shall also include farmland with mulberry, tea, fruit and other trees but used mainly for growing crops as well as the reclaimed "beach-land" and "lake-land" along the sea coasts and the lake banks. However, it shall not include the land devoted especially for mulberry and the tea gardens, orchards, nurseries, woodlands, reed marches and natural grasslands. Ditches, pathways and ridges of field which are less than one meter wide are included in plowland.

Sown Area of Crops

Sown Area of Crops refers to area of land sown or transplanted with crops that have been harvested during report period, regardless of being in cultivated area or non-cultivated area. Area of land re-sown due to natural disasters is also included.

Grain Output

Grain Output refers to the total output in the whole country including grains produced by state farms, collective units, rural households, as well as by farms affiliated to industrial and mining enterprises and other production units. Grain includes rice, wheat, corn, sorghum, millet and other miscellaneous grains as well as tubers and bean. Output of beans refers to dry beans without pods. The output of tubers (sweet potatoes and potatoes, not including taros and cassava) was converted into that of grain at the ratio 4 : 1, i. e. 4 kilograms of fresh tubers was equivalent to 1 kilogram of grain up to 1963. Since 1964 the ratio for conversion has been 5 : 1. Tubers supplied as vegetables (such as potatoes) in cities and suburbs are calculated as fresh vegetables and their output is not included in the output of grain. Output of all other grains refers to husked grain. Data on grain production before 1989 were obtained through Comprehensive Statistical Reporting System. Since 1989, data from sample surveys are used.

Output of Aquatic Products

Output of Aquatic Products refers to catches of both artificially cultured and naturally grown aquatic products, including fish, shrimps, crabs and shellfish in sea and inland water as well as seaweed. Freshwater plants are not included. Data on output of aquatic products are reported by aquatic product and statistical agencies level by level. Before 1995, among the shellfish, the oyster was counted as fresh meat; 5 kilograms of ark shell, clams and frogs are equivalent to 1 kilogram of fresh aquatic products; they are all counted as fresh aquatic products since 1996.

Output of Pork, Beef, and Mutton

Output of Pork, Beef, and Mutton refers to the meat of slaughtered hogs, cattle, sheep and goats with head, feet, and offal taken away. Data refers to the production of the whole country. The first agriculture census of China in 1996 revealed some discrepancy between the production of animal products from the annual reports and that from the census. Efforts were made by the Rural Socio-economic Survey Organization of NBS to adjust the output value of animal husbandry to make the figures from the annual reports consistent with the census data. Since 1999, NBS conducted sample survey for the major animal husbandry products, such as hogs, cattle, sheep and goats and fowls, and the data from sample surveys are used as national finalized data. Those products, which are not covered by the sample survey, are still reported by statistical agencies level by level.

Seed Agriculture

Seed agriculture includes four aspects, respectively, the seeds, plants, and strains of crops in farm production; the seeds and plants in forestry production; livestocks and poultry breedings, poultries, sperm, eggs, and procreating birds in livestock production; fish, shrimp, and crab seedlings in fishery production.

Seed Agriculture Production

Seed agriculture production refers to the number and amount of seed agriculture products.

Seed Agriculture Products for Self-use

Seed agriculture products for self – use refers to the farming products that are used for self-use or re-production (including those produced not in the reporting period).

Seed Agriculture Products for Selling

Seed agriculture products for selling refers to the number and amount of the seed agriculture products that are used for selling. The amount is calculated by the real settlement price.

Total Power of Farm Machinery

Total Power of Farm Machinery refers to the total mechanical power of machinery used in farming, forestry animal husbandry and fishery, including machines used for ploughing, irrigation and drainage, crop growing, plant protection, harvesting, farm product processing, transport, stock breeding, fishery and water conservancy. Machinery employed for non-agricultural purposes such as township industry, capital construction, non-agricultural transport, scientific experiments and for teaching is excluded.

第六篇

CHAPTER 6

工业

INDUSTRY

表6-1 主要年份工业总产值及其构成

单位:亿元

指 标	Indicators	1990	1995	1999	2000	2001	2002	2003
总 计	**Total**	**176.85**	**968.03**	**1 450.81**	**1 625.77**	**1 888.74**	**2 193.82**	**2 856.68**
按隶属关系分	**By Subordination**							
中央工业	Central	42.48	225.99	323.62	381.41	386.40	431.13	549.05
市属工业	Municipal	88.44	491.63	610.35	599.57	779.48	805.98	1 082.55
非中央、市属工业	Local	45.93	250.41	516.84	644.79	722.86	956.71	1 225.08
按登记注册类型分	**By Type of Registration**							
国 有	State-owned	110.18	449.57	309.87	275.85	344.02	241.56	290.97
集 体	Collective-owned	49.09	122.54	90.04	70.91	57.02	49.57	46.02
港澳台及外商投资	Overseas Invested	7.07	231.94	851.48	1 012.34	1 242.91	1 522.31	1 985.30
其 他	Others	10.51	163.98	199.42	266.67	244.79	380.38	534.39
按轻、重工业分	**By Light/Heavy Industry**							
轻工业	Light Industry	72.08	424.42	533.52	514.58	535.06	541.28	647.92
重工业	Heavy Industry	104.77	543.61	917.29	1 111.19	1 353.68	1 652.54	2 208.76
按企业规模分	**By Scale of Enterprises**							
大型企业	Large	81.32	632.35	988.53	1 138.11	1 294.24	1 564.20	1 229.85
中型企业	Medium	21.40	96.37	163.48	187.00	239.26	209.92	862.86
小型企业	Small	74.13	239.31	298.80	300.66	355.24	419.70	763.97
构 成(%)	**Composition (%)**							
总 计	**Total**	**100.0**	**100.0**	**100.0**	**100.0**	**100.0**	**100.0**	**100.0**
按隶属关系分	**By Subordination**							
中央工业	Central	24.0	23.3	22.3	23.5	20.4	19.7	19.2
市属工业	Municipal	50.0	50.8	42.1	36.9	41.3	36.7	37.9
非中央、市属工业	Local	26.0	25.9	35.6	39.6	38.3	43.6	42.9
按登记注册类型分	**By Type of Registration**							
国 有	State-owned	62.3	46.4	21.4	17.0	18.2	11.0	10.2
集 体	Collective-owned	27.8	12.7	6.2	4.3	3.0	2.3	1.6
港澳台及外商投资	Overseas Invested	4.0	24.0	58.7	62.3	65.8	69.4	69.5
其 他	Others	5.9	16.9	13.7	16.4	13.0	17.3	18.7
按轻、重工业分	**By Light/Heavy Industry**							
轻工业	Light Industry	40.8	43.8	36.8	31.7	28.3	24.7	22.7
重工业	Heavy Industry	59.2	56.2	63.2	68.3	71.7	75.3	77.3
按企业规模分	**By Scale of Enterprises**							
大型企业	Large	46.0	65.3	68.1	70.0	68.5	71.3	43.1
中型企业	Medium	12.1	10.0	11.3	11.5	12.7	9.6	30.2
小型企业	Small	41.9	24.7	20.6	18.5	18.8	19.1	26.7

注：本篇从6－2表至6－11表,数据均为年主营业务收入2000万元及以上企业。
Note: In this chapter, form table 6－2 to table 6－11, date refer to the enterprises with revenue over 20 million yuan.

Gross Output Value of Industry and its Composition in Main Years

(100 million yuan)

2004	2005	2006	2007	2008	2009	2010	2011	2012	2013	2014
3 519.71	**4 242.47**	**4 758.76**	**5 188.12**	**5 649.22**	**7 141.55**	**8 591.50**	**9 553.79**	**9 424.67**	**9 375.57**	**9 495.42**
677.04	1 321.05	1 538.42	1 663.26	1 999.48	1 653.93	2 216.69	2 278.33	2 235.91	2 299.88	2 213.84
1 254.17	1 135.29	1 249.74	1 373.81	1 289.49	2 010.76	2 043.34	2 284.38	1 986.87	1 983.98	2 061.92
1 588.50	1 786.13	1 970.60	2 151.05	2 360.25	3 476.86	4 331.47	4 991.08	5 201.89	5 091.71	5 219.67
358.04	550.18	573.84	662.21	679.71	729.56	885.71	927.97	960.60	834.91	838.06
49.09	38.67	36.87	34.89	31.60	47.87	34.70	34.67	33.63	23.72	30.39
2 461.66	2 632.70	2 980.46	3 001.98	3 088.54	4 008.58	5 047.75	5 899.02	5 846.88	5 834.32	5 981.89
650.92	1 020.92	1 167.59	1 489.04	1 849.37	2 355.54	2 623.34	2 692.13	2 583.56	2 682.62	2 645.09
764.94	825.40	878.66	952.26	1 070.62	1 402.71	1 535.63	1 677.47	1 638.43	1 687.97	1 752.95
2 754.77	3 417.07	3 880.10	4 235.86	4 578.60	5 738.84	7 055.87	7 876.32	7 786.24	7 687.60	7 742.47
1 426.29	1 989.45	1 976.08	2 309.39	2 731.96	3 318.52	4 097.63	6 154.87	6 105.36	5 854.97	5 895.29
1 083.29	1 173.99	1 725.62	1 841.13	1 822.86	2 022.62	2 593.18	1 477.88	1 580.14	1 688.82	1 637.61
1 010.13	1 079.03	1 057.06	1 037.60	1 094.40	1 800.41	1 900.69	1 921.04	1 739.17	1 831.78	1 962.52
100.0	**100.0**	**100.0**	**100.0**	**100.0**	**100.0**	**100.0**	**100.0**	**100.0**	**100.0**	**100.0**
19.3	31.1	32.3	32.0	35.4	23.2	25.8	23.8	23.7	24.5	23.3
35.6	26.8	26.3	26.5	22.8	28.1	23.8	23.9	21.1	21.2	21.7
45.1	42.1	41.4	41.5	41.8	48.7	50.4	52.3	55.2	54.3	55.0
10.2	13.0	12.1	12.8	12.0	10.2	10.3	9.7	10.2	8.9	8.8
1.4	0.9	0.8	0.7	0.6	0.7	0.4	0.4	0.4	0.3	0.3
69.9	62.0	62.6	57.8	54.7	56.1	58.8	61.7	62.0	62.2	63.0
18.5	24.1	24.5	28.7	32.7	33.0	30.5	28.2	27.4	28.6	27.9
21.7	19.5	18.5	18.4	19.0	19.6	17.9	17.6	17.4	18.0	18.5
78.3	80.5	81.5	81.6	81.0	80.4	82.1	82.4	82.6	82.0	81.5
40.5	46.9	41.5	44.5	48.3	46.5	47.7	64.4	64.8	62.4	62.1
30.8	27.7	36.3	35.5	32.3	28.3	30.2	15.5	16.8	18.0	17.2
28.7	25.4	22.2	20.0	19.4	25.2	22.1	20.1	18.5	19.6	20.7

表6-2　工业总产值、销售产值和出口交货值
(2014)

单位:亿元

指　标　Indicators		工业总产值（按现行价格计算）Gross Output Value of Industry (at Current Price)
总　计	**Total**	**9 197.19**
按隶属关系分	**By Subordination**	
中央工业	Central	2 213.00
市属工业	Municipal	2 060.42
非中央、市属工业	Local	4 923.78
按登记注册类型分	**By Type of Registration**	
内　资	Domestic Funded	3 253.69
国　有	State-owned	837.44
集　体	Collective-owned	25.28
股份合作制	Share-holding	4.32
联　营	Jointly-operated	4.56
有限责任公司	Companies with Limited Liability	1 036.60
股份有限公司	Companies Limited by Shares	672.58
私　营	Private	672.91
其　他	Others	
港澳台商投资	Hong Kong/Macao/Taiwan Invested	835.77
#港澳台商独资	Solely Hong Kong/Macao/Taiwan Funded	537.77
外商投资	Foreigner Invested	5 107.74
#外商独资	Solely Foreigner Funded	2 620.95
按轻、重工业分	**By Light/Heavy Industry**	
轻工业	Light Industry	1 633.12
重工业	Heavy Industry	7 564.07
按企业规模分	**By Scale of Enterprises**	
大型企业	Large	5 895.29
中型企业	Medium	1 636.20
小型企业	Small	1 665.70

Gross Output Value, Sales Value and Export Delivery Value

(100 million yuan)

#镇及镇以上 Town and Above	工业销售产值 Sales Value of Industry	#镇及镇以上 Town and Above	出口交货值 Export Delivery Value	#镇及镇以上 Town and Above
4 601.99	**9 099.25**	**4 530.53**	**2 518.11**	**570.46**
2 213.00	2 190.22	2 190.22	355.64	355.64
2 060.42	2 013.53	2 013.53	192.95	192.95
328.58	4 895.50	326.77	1 969.52	21.87
2 318.21	3 203.52	2 283.48	295.64	208.04
831.70	836.92	831.24	5.81	4.51
12.38	25.09	11.86	1.35	0.92
1.00	4.43	1.00	0.10	
1.29	4.55	1.29		
875.84	1 015.71	858.52	164.20	153.64
596.00	655.21	579.58	51.95	48.97
	661.60		72.24	
125.46	837.80	127.08	368.98	17.38
	540.06		248.20	
2 158.32	5 057.93	2 119.96	1 853.50	345.03
	2 615.81		1 414.19	
617.32	1 588.89	597.78	337.44	129.57
3 984.67	7 510.36	3 932.74	2 180.67	440.89
3 757.08	5 845.20	3 705.75	1 901.81	489.30
511.69	1 598.59	492.49	351.72	54.18
333.22	1 655.46	332.29	264.59	26.98

表6-3 主要工业产品生产和销售量
Output and Sales Volume of Major Industrial Products
(2014)

产品名称	Products	单 位 Unit	生产量 Output	销售量 Sales Volume	生产量占全市比重(%) PNA/ Shanghai(%)
汽 油	Gasoline	万吨 10 000 tons	184.54	184.37	39.1
柴 油	Diesel Oil	万吨 10 000 tons	278.59	274.27	40.7
化学纤维	Chemical Fiber	万吨 10 000 tons	11.26	11.55	24.8
合成纤维聚合物	Synthetic Polymer	万吨 10 000 tons	58.99	59.29	50.1
化学药品原药	Original Chemical Drug	吨 ton	3 102.17	3 038.00	9.4
钢 材	Steel	万吨 10 000 tons	43.93	43.19	1.9
家用洗衣机	Household Washing Machine	万台 10 000 sets	164.75	164.69	90.6
房间空气调节器	Household Air-conditioner	万台 10 000 sets	167.72	165.36	41.6
数字程控交换机	Program-controlled Exchange	万线 10 000 lines	153.97	153.97	100.0
电话单机	Telephone Set	万部 10 000 sets	181.63	171.67	100.0
笔记本计算机	Including Notebooks	万台 10 000 sets	1 450.00	1 543.16	32.4
移动通信手持机(手机)	Mobile Phone	万台 10 000 sets	4 682.63	4 704.95	85.4
液晶(LCD)电视机	Color TV Set	万部 10 000 sets	143.16	142.50	92.2
气体压缩机	Gas Compressor	万台 10 000 sets	1 239.42	1 212.96	65.3
轿 车	Car	万辆 10 000 vehicles	71.29	71.36	33.3
#新能源汽车	in which new-energy-fueled car	辆 vehicle	3 285.00	2 997.00	14.2
集成电路	Integrated Circuit	亿块 100 million pieces	112.12	112.27	50.2
集成电路圆片	IC Wafer	万片 10 000 pieces	305.95	299.00	74.3

表6-3　续表　Continued

产品名称 Products		单　位 Unit	生产量 Output	销售量 Sales Volume	生产量占全市比重(%) PNA/Shanghai(%)
起重机	Crane	万吨 10 000 tons	43.14	40.14	91.1
微波炉	Microwave Oven	万台 10 000 sets	358.02	355.68	100.0
发电量	Electricity	亿千瓦时 100 mil. kwh	242.50	303.01	30.6
电子元件	Electronic Component	亿只 100 million pieces	158.26	168.08	37.5
光电子器件	Optoelectronic Device	亿只 100 million units	15.68	49.51	90.5
电饭锅	Electric Rice Cooker	万个 10 000 units	15.17	29.93	4.4
原电池(折 R20 标准只)	Size D Battery (R20 standard)	亿只 100 million units	11.91	12.20	69.0
塑料制品	Plastic Product	万吨 10 000 tons	27.89	27.64	14.0
合成橡胶	Synthetic Rubber	万吨 10 000 tons	20.42	22.64	91.7
初级形态的塑料	Plastics in Primary Form	万吨 10 000 tons	60.88	59.04	16.8
涂　料	Paint	万吨 10 000 tons	64.13	53.67	34.3
化学农药原药	Original Chemicals of Chemical Pesticide	吨 ton	1 194.11	1 042.54	9.2
服　装	Garment	亿件 100 million units	0.81	0.70	16.2
印染布	Printing & Dyeing Cloth	万米 10 000 meters	156.10	112.10	4.2
布	Cloth	万米 10 000 meters	638.80	758.10	4.8
乳制品	Dairy Products	万吨 10 000 tons	1.01	1.02	1.9
商品混凝土	Commercial Concrete	万立方米 10 000 cu. m	800.95	788.33	22.5

表6-4 按行业分的工业总产值、销售产值和出口交货值
Gross Output Value, Sales Value and Export Delivery Value by Sector (2014)

单位:亿元 (100 million yuan)

指 标	Indicators	工业总产值(按现行价格计算) Gross Output Value of Industry (at Current Price)	工业销售产值 Sales Value of Industry	出口交货值 Export Delivery Value
总 计	**Total**	**9 197.19**	**9 099.25**	**2 518.11**
#农副食品加工业	Processing of Agricultural Side-line Food	126.78	127.33	0.21
食品制造业	Food Manufacturing	42.41	41.29	1.93
酒、饮料和精制茶制造业	Manufacturing of Liquor, Beverage and Refined Tea	37.05	38.27	4.53
烟草制品业	Tobacco Products	4.86	4.86	0.04
纺织业	Textile Industry	36.40	36.29	13.53
纺织服装、服饰业	Textile Clothes and Accessories	110.82	111.66	20.60
皮革、毛皮、羽毛及其制品和制鞋业	Leather, Fur, Feather and their Products and Shoe-making	8.27	8.22	1.72
木材加工及木、竹、藤、棕、草制品业	Timber-processing, Bamboo, Cane, Palm Fiber and Straw Products	4.94	5.02	0.02
家具制造业	Furniture Manufacturing	97.36	91.53	17.35
造纸及纸制品业	Paper-making and Paper Products	51.26	49.69	10.16
印刷业和记录媒介复制业	Printing and Record Pressing	47.98	48.44	5.04
文教、工美、体育和娱乐用品制造业	Manufacturing of Cultural, Educational, Arts, Sports and Leisure Products	33.90	32.54	5.47
石油加工、炼焦及核燃料加工业	Petroleum Processing, Coke Products and Processing of Nuclear Fuel	544.67	527.60	43.66
化学原料和化学制品制造业	Raw Chemical Materials and Chemical Products	542.22	537.28	91.04
医药制造业	Medicine Manufacturing	306.67	281.75	17.03

单位:亿元 表 6－4 续表 Continued (100 million yuan)

指 标 Indicators		工业总产值(按现行价格计算) Gross Output Value of Industry (at Current Price)	工业销售产 值 Sales Value of Industry	出口交货值 Export Delivery Value
化学纤维制造业	Chemical Fiber Manufacturing	3.19	2.98	0.21
橡胶和塑料制品业	Rubber and Plastic Products	123.12	123.41	25.72
非金属矿物制品业	Nonmetal Mineral Products	109.04	107.24	14.62
黑色金属冶炼及压延加工业	Smelting and Pressing of Ferrous Metal	53.58	53.41	3.09
有色金属冶炼及压延加工业	Smelting and Pressing of Nonferrous Metal	62.42	62.80	8.22
金属制品业	Metal Products	156.66	155.34	43.83
通用设备制造业	General Purpose Equipment Manufacturing	669.61	665.92	217.08
专用设备制造业	Special Purpose Equipment Manufacturing	317.64	315.68	64.44
汽车制造业	Automobile Manunfacturing	1 550.16	1 524.59	78.90
铁路、船舶、航空航天和其他运输设备制造业	Manufacturing of Railway, Ships, Aeronautics & Astronautics, and Other Transportation Equipment	366.82	355.11	118.79
电气机械及器材制造业	Electric Equipment and Machinery	484.35	480.18	139.25
计算机、通信和其他电子设备制造业	Manufacturing of Computers, Telecommunications and Other Electronic Equipment	2 223.52	2 230.23	1 517.36
仪器仪表制造业	Manufacturing of Instruments and Apparatuses	111.00	112.14	49.80
其他制造业	Other Manufacturing	24.89	25.49	2.00
废弃资源综合利用业	Comprehensive Reutilization of Discarded Resources	1.24	1.00	
金属制品、机械和设备修理业	Repairing of Metal Products, Machineries and Equipment	22.33	22.03	2.49
电力、热力的生产和供应业	Production and Supply of Electricity and Heating Power	880.62	880.56	
燃气生产和供应业	Production and Supply of Gas	23.70	23.82	
水的生产和供应业	Production and Supply of Tap Water	17.72	15.52	

表6-5　工业重点发展行业主要指标
(2014)

单位:万元

指　标	Indicators	企业单位数（个）Enterprises (unit)	从业人数（人）Employed Persons (person)	工业总产值 Gross Output Value of Industry
总　计	**Total**	**855**	**419 435**	**66 222 542**
按登记注册类型分	**By Type of Registration**			
内　资	Domestic Funded	413	120 373	17 482 755
国　有	State-owned	4	3 326	449 219
集　体	Collective-owned	7	1 330	102 867
股份合作制	Share-holding	2	213	9 105
联　营	Jointly-operated	1	121	10 478
有限责任公司	Companies with Limited Liability	95	51 080	7 399 754
股份有限公司	Companies Limited by Shares	18	18 273	5 972 134
私　营	Private	286	46 030	3 539 198
港澳台商投资	Hong Kong/Macao/Taiwan Invested	96	42 040	6 425 433
#港澳台商独资	Solely Hong Kong/Macao/Taiwan Funded	63	26 989	4 823 038
外商投资	Foreigner Invested	346	257 022	42 314 354
#外商独资	Solely Foreigner Funded	244	178 335	21 444 469
按轻、重工业分	**By Light/Heavy Industry**			
轻工业	Light Industry	135	45 811	6 852 358
重工业	Heavy Industry	720	373 624	59 370 184
按企业规模分	**By Scale of Enterprises**			
大型企业	Large	61	257 144	46 236 677
中型企业	Medium	164	88 399	11 491 741
小型企业	Small	630	73 892	8 494 124
按行业分	**By Industry**			
电子信息产品制造业	Manufacturing of Electronic and Information Technology Products	229	198 298	24 399 275
汽车制造业	Auto Manufacturing	129	74 931	15 501 583
石油化工及精细化工制造业	Manufacturing of Petrochemical and Fine Chemicals	104	25 466	10 394 683
精品钢材制造业	Manufacturing of High Quality Steel Products	16	2 074	460 207
成套设备制造业	Manufacturing of Complete Equipment	288	86 744	11 536 658
生物医药制造业	Manufacturing of Biological Medicine	89	31 922	3 930 138

Major Indicators of Pillar Industries

(10 000 yuan)

工业销售产值 Sales Value of Industry	固定资产原价 Original Value of Fixed Assets	资产总计 Total Assets	负债总计 Total Liabilities	实收资本 Paid-in Capital	主营业务收入 Revenue of Primary Operations	税金 Tax	利润总额 Total Profits
65 427 691	**28 637 222**	**79 737 209**	**38 950 071**	**15 579 722**	**81 714 968**	**2 571 433**	**7 439 381**
17 018 071	8 714 734	36 184 739	13 005 456	6 184 828	18 986 437	1 152 126	2 946 256
448 720	422 600	700 312	144 792	582 571	442 174	9 595	32 916
102 465	16 914	61 412	38 466	12 446	101 731	5 834	1 762
9 082	5 120	9 904	7 386	758	8 957	162	68
10 426	1 574	1 485	415	773	10 426	139	44
7 179 680	4 668 241	13 032 529	7 784 507	3 097 580	7 955 088	155 465	342 744
5 801 070	2 683 273	18 532 340	2 995 387	1 845 913	6 953 355	877 547	2 310 887
3 466 629	917 012	3 846 757	2 034 503	644 788	3 514 707	103 384	257 836
6 452 273	4 007 064	6 981 064	3 690 837	1 577 610	7 780 005	69 640	425 844
4 855 730	3 498 285	4 984 326	3 006 960	1 188 090	6 092 108	32 667	285 489
41 957 347	15 915 424	36 571 406	22 253 778	7 817 283	54 948 526	1 349 667	4 067 282
21 487 243	7 827 611	14 702 565	8 494 557	3 932 602	23 762 115	214 162	1 141 391
6 525 900	1 956 651	6 834 869	3 232 124	1 431 431	6 632 175	299 633	707 203
58 901 791	26 680 571	72 902 339	35 717 947	14 148 291	75 082 793	2 271 800	6 732 178
45 810 977	21 848 286	57 710 669	27 287 928	10 553 648	59 909 394	2 008 543	5 809 880
11 159 597	4 067 883	13 068 202	7 366 966	2 678 724	13 053 564	263 180	835 456
8 457 118	2 721 054	8 958 338	4 295 176	2 347 350	8 752 010	299 711	794 045
24 449 765	11 867 686	21 131 944	12 768 847	6 024 922	28 408 755	138 813	848 228
15 245 863	5 318 871	28 327 146	8 776 567	2 987 211	26 536 990	1 153 480	5 212 070
10 166 258	3 805 969	5 965 423	2 710 698	1 786 199	10 631 758	859 361	276 688
464 236	315 851	367 810	235 824	363 484	483 329	7 361	- 4 857
11 429 072	6 030 898	19 076 176	12 087 430	3 381 327	11 906 849	220 942	650 093
3 672 496	1 297 948	4 868 711	2 370 705	1 036 579	3 747 287	191 476	457 159

表6-6 高技术工业主要指标
(2014)

单位:万元

指 标	Indicators	企业单位数(个) Enterprises (unit)	从业人数(人) Employed Persons (person)	工业总产值 Gross Output Value of Industry
总 计	**Total**	**241**	**218 197**	**27 276 339**
按登记注册类型分	**By Type of Registration**			
内 资	Domestic Funded	81	29 503	2 228 868
国 有	State-owned			
集 体	Collective-owned			
股份合作制	Share-holding			
联 营	Jointly-operated	1	121	10 478
有限责任公司	Companies with Limited Liability	28	16 760	1 383 834
股份有限公司	Companies Limited by Shares	6	2 638	199 196
私 营	Private	46	9 984	635 360
港澳台商投资	Hong Kong/Macao/Taiwan Invested	41	26 527	4 369 318
#港澳台商独资	Solely Hong Kong/Macao/Taiwan Funded	28	17 863	3 410 698
外商投资	Foreigner Invested	119	162 167	20 678 154
#外商独资	Solely Foreigner Funded	92	141 333	15 772 466
按轻、重工业分	**By Light/Heavy Industry**			
轻工业	Light Industry	90	36 287	5 174 975
重工业	Heavy Industry	151	181 910	22 101 363
按企业规模分	**By Scale of Enterprises**			
大型企业	Large	35	166 775	20 625 330
中型企业	Medium	56	32 697	4 558 401
小型企业	Small	150	18 725	2 092 607
按工业行业分	**By Sector**			
信息化学品制造	Manufacturing of Information Chemicals	1	70	6 770
医药制造业	Manufacturing of Medicine	58	23 739	3 066 734
航空航天器制造	Manufacturing of Aviation and Space Vehicles	4	872	86 539
电子及通信设备制造业	Manufacturing of Electronics and Telecommunications Equipment	97	89 545	10 034 907
电子计算机及办公设备制造业	Manufacturing of Electronic Computers and Office Equipment	17	86 282	12 399 740
医疗设备及仪器仪表制造业	Manufacturing of Medical Equipment and Instrument	64	17 689	1 681 650

Major Indicators of High-tech Industrial Enterprises

(10 000 yuan)

工业销售产值 Sales Value of Industry	固定资产原价 Original Value of Fixed Assets	资产总计 Total Assets	负债总计 Total Liabilities	实收资本 Paid-in Capital	主营业务收入 Revenue of of Floating Assets	税金 Tax	利润总额 Total Profits
27 117 079	**12 684 484**	**24 876 538**	**14 404 141**	**6 861 341**	**31 094 209**	**283 639**	**1 318 272**
2 137 602	2 017 909	4 367 796	2 088 106	1 518 816	2 273 444	86 253	191 778
10 426	1 574	1 485	415	773	10 426	139	44
1 309 181	1 752 532	3 223 460	1 560 000	1 301 091	1 414 314	47 194	107 417
201 320	78 288	406 572	149 010	87 881	201 500	11 050	27 239
616 675	185 514	736 279	378 681	129 072	647 204	27 870	57 078
4 384 783	3 154 261	5 116 209	2 721 647	1 104 805	5 555 397	35 739	299 343
3 429 373	2 855 161	3 760 543	2 396 025	831 906	4 574 807	17 384	206 451
20 594 694	7 512 315	15 392 533	9 594 389	4 237 720	23 265 368	161 647	827 151
15 828 841	6 184 355	9 931 283	6 004 324	2 899 470	17 937 076	79 891	585 357
4 889 989	1 414 982	5 403 899	2 682 214	1 148 745	4 957 789	204 607	514 069
22 227 090	11 269 502	19 472 639	11 721 927	5 712 595	26 136 420	79 032	804 203
20 604 068	10 769 420	17 207 785	10 253 176	5 382 385	23 232 779	121 636	700 589
4 466 451	1 144 591	5 161 838	3 062 775	737 381	5 739 803	76 411	402 883
2 046 559	770 474	2 506 915	1 088 190	741 575	2 121 627	85 592	214 800
7 943	995	3 298	545	800	7 943	148	363
2 817 478	1 021 240	3 939 816	2 088 243	860 062	2 878 748	162 117	321 173
86 539	74 414	106 105	59 441	109 430	86 533	2 145	11 706
9 946 084	10 558 131	13 040 475	6 509 681	5 178 149	10 795 864	79 299	527 553
12 576 354	599 286	6 027 409	5 164 325	363 807	15 608 276	11 498	231 396
1 682 682	430 420	1 759 435	581 906	349 093	1 716 845	28 432	226 081

表6-7 独立核算工业企业主要财务指标
(2014)

单位:万元

指 标	Indicators	企业单位数(个) Enterprises (unit)	从业人数(人) Employed Persons (person)	工业总产值 Gross Output Value of Industry
总 计	**Total**	**1 788**	**644 497**	**91 971 923**
按隶属关系分	**By Subordination**			
中央工业	Central	43	71 990	22 129 992
市属工业	Municipal	92	91 577	20 604 168
非中央、市属工业	Local	1 653	480 930	49 237 764
按登记注册类型分	**By Type of Registration**			
内 资	Domestic Funded	986	226 806	32 536 863
国 有	State-owned	13	20 203	8 374 380
集 体	Collective-owned	17	2 288	252 823
股份合作制	Share-holding	9	1 141	43 209
联 营	Jointly-operated	4	239	45 569
有限责任公司	Companies with Limited Liability	199	76 028	10 365 955
股份有限公司	Companies Limited by Shares	29	22 051	6 725 808
私 营	Private	715	104 856	6 729 121
港澳台商投资	Hong Kong/Macao/Taiwan Invested	186	68 147	8 357 662
#港澳台商独资	Solely Hong Kong/Macao/Taiwan Funded	111	34 670	5 377 652
外商投资	Foreigner Invested	616	349 544	51 077 398
#外商独资	Solely Foreigner Funded	431	234 008	26 209 548
按轻、重工业分	**By Light/Heavy Industry**			
轻工业	Light Industry	559	166 121	16 331 243
重工业	Heavy Industry	1 229	478 376	75 640 681
按企业规模分	**By Scale of Entrerprises**			
大型企业	Large	90	329 636	58 952 920
中型企业	Medium	273	149 576	16 361 994
小型企业	Small	1 425	165 285	16 657 010

Major Indicators of Industrial Enterprises with Independent Accounting Systems

(10 000 yuan)

工业销售产值 Sales Value of Industry	实收资本 Paid-in Capital	资产总计 Total Assets	流动资产合计 Total Circulating Assets	固定资产合计 Total Fixed Assets	固定资产原价 Original Value of Fixed Assets
90 992 521	**21 936 780**	**117 017 122**	**60 970 577**	**30 188 849**	**63 337 822**
21 902 181	5 509 466	36 931 614	13 456 393	16 470 953	32 599 846
20 135 344	5 907 584	35 601 698	16 999 052	5 236 382	10 861 770
48 954 996	10 519 729	44 483 809	30 515 131	8 481 514	19 876 207
32 035 170	9 727 816	62 837 362	25 003 252	19 662 906	38 307 425
8 369 204	1 358 963	17 195 061	1 754 325	12 421 007	24 653 640
250 888	16 854	162 895	145 780	15 446	46 818
44 340	6 056	47 058	33 552	11 713	23 621
45 533	5 547	12 416	10 955	1 395	5 047
10 157 051	5 195 883	18 950 208	10 551 470	5 111 794	8 818 778
6 552 112	2 040 063	19 646 688	7 826 927	902 339	2 831 657
6 616 043	1 104 450	6 823 036	4 680 244	1 199 213	1 927 864
8 378 021	2 237 651	9 248 721	6 152 789	1 930 706	5 157 741
5 400 590	1 464 668	5 662 469	4 094 317	1 308 653	3 977 696
50 579 330	9 971 313	44 931 039	29 814 535	8 595 238	19 872 656
26 158 110	4 947 793	19 143 321	13 475 853	3 795 324	9 672 907
15 888 887	3 647 249	16 154 961	10 571 476	3 202 881	6 143 903
75 103 634	18 289 530	100 862 161	50 399 101	26 985 969	57 193 919
58 452 025	12 262 852	78 587 733	35 245 623	22 219 727	48 065 218
15 985 882	4 863 725	20 025 699	13 375 637	3 742 751	7 440 984
16 554 614	4 810 203	18 403 690	12 349 316	4 226 372	7 831 620

单位:万元 表 6-7 续表 Continued

指 标	Indicators	本年折旧 Depreciation of the Current Year	负债合计 Total Liabilities	所有者权益 Owner's Equity
总 计	**Total**	**3 479 348**	**54 453 607**	**62 505 335**
按隶属关系分	**By Subordination**			
中央工业	Central	1 694 175	17 090 170	19 815 201
市属工业	Municipal	621 332	13 070 799	22 530 898
非中央、市属工业	Local	1 163 841	24 292 638	20 159 236
按登记注册类型分	**By Type of Registration**			
内 资	Domestic Funded	2 071 879	22 695 551	40 116 597
国 有	State-owned	1 331 456	4 423 407	12 771 654
集 体	Collective-owned	2 397	116 255	46 640
股份合作制	Share-holding	1 327	21 646	25 411
联 营	Jointly-operated	164	5 206	7 210
有限责任公司	Companies with Limited Liability	460 422	10 892 476	8 036 324
股份有限公司	Companies Limited by Shares	153 191	3 540 590	16 104 266
私 营	Private	122 923	3 695 971	3 125 092
港澳台商投资	Hong Kong/Macao/Taiwan Invested	180 932	4 941 607	4 304 440
#港澳台商独资	Solely Hong Kong/Macao/Taiwan Funded	125 109	3 320 469	2 339 464
外商投资	Foreigner Invested	1 226 537	26 816 448	18 084 298
#外商独资	Solely Foreigner Funded	657 204	11 005 548	8 142 978
按轻、重工业分	**By Light/Heavy Industry**			
轻工业	Light Industry	336 963	8 397 857	7 733 847
重工业	Heavy Industry	3 142 385	46 055 750	54 771 488
按企业规模分	**By Scale of Enterprises**			
大型企业	Large	2 652 558	34 101 127	44 452 481
中型企业	Medium	405 118	10 759 952	9 275 931
小型企业	Small	421 671	9 592 528	8 776 924

(10 000 yuan)

主营业务收入 Revenue of Primary Operations	税金 Tax	#本年应交增值税 Current Year Value-added Tax Payable	营业利润 Operation Profits	利润总额 Total Profits	应付职工薪酬 Wage/Fringe Benefits
108 643 321	**3 432 452**	**2 153 000**	**8 459 545**	**8 911 728**	**6 567 606**
23 031 300	1 210 047	567 199	347 580	428 695	1 297 263
31 796 955	1 313 566	797 372	5 318 400	5 505 148	1 483 114
53 815 066	908 839	788 430	2 793 565	2 977 885	3 787 229
34 509 535	1 733 145	1 023 235	3 337 217	3 678 283	2 447 248
8 473 948	343 210	314 959	350 146	356 497	493 256
257 724	7 614	6 952	3 976	3 428	11 746
44 415	1 851	1 706		1 550	4 571
45 533	987	908	874	892	1 147
11 108 976	292 306	242 785	395 979	573 552	1 005 539
7 702 495	885 547	279 614	2 211 165	2 311 818	379 176
6 876 446	201 632	176 311	375 092	430 545	551 812
9 622 599	108 476	95 189	572 086	604 148	599 998
6 637 666	42 615	36 604	273 624	287 974	346 491
64 511 187	1 590 830	1 034 577	4 550 242	4 629 297	3 520 360
28 831 798	347 899	300 509	1 354 654	1 380 301	2 002 174
16 649 124	565 278	487 356	1 203 863	1 265 181	1 417 166
91 994 197	2 867 174	1 665 645	7 255 682	7 646 547	5 150 440
72 651 628	2 435 140	1 282 814	6 107 991	6 392 498	3 799 543
18 472 767	452 967	387 626	1 142 652	1 218 384	1 497 055
17 518 926	544 345	482 561	1 208 903	1 300 846	1 271 008

表6-8 独立核算大中型工业企业主要指标
(2014)

单位:万元

指 标	Indicators	企业单位数(个) Enterprises (unit)	从业人数(人) Average Number of Employed Persons (person)	工业总产值 Gross Output Value of Industry
总 计	**Total**	**363**	**474 519**	**75 314 913**
按隶属关系分	**By Subordination**			
中央工业	Central	27	70 047	21 870 647
市属工业	Municipal	52	84 774	18 584 426
非中央、市属工业	Local	284	319 698	34 859 840
按登记注册类型分	**Type of Registration**			
内 资	Domstic Funded	131	130 603	24 732 554
国 有	State-owned	8	19 388	8 347 886
集 体	Collective-owned	1	518	51 682
股份合作制	Share-holding			
联 营	Jointly-operated			
有限责任公司	Companies with Limited Liability	54	54 340	7 665 467
股份有限公司	Companies Limited by Shares	14	19 823	6 397 664
私 营	Private	54	36 534	2 269 855
其他内资	Other Domestic Investment			
港澳台商投资	Hong Kong/Macao/Taiwan Invested	57	51 310	6 699 596
#港澳台商独资	Solely Hong Kong/Macao/Taiwan Funded	27	24 619	4 201 029
外商投资	Foreigner Invested	175	292 606	43 882 763
#外商独资	Solely Foreigner Funded	110	191 181	21 240 743
按轻、重工业分	**By Light/Heavy Industry**			
轻工业	Light Industry	112	105 739	11 280 576
重工业	Heavy Industry	251	368 780	64 034 337
按从业人数分	**By Number of Employees**			
5 000 人及以上	≥5 000 persons	12	163 329	34 784 938
3 000～4 999 人	3 000～4 999 persons	17	66 589	11 066 444
1 000～2 999 人	1 000～2 999 persons	66	106 545	13 223 648
999 及以下	≤ 999 persons	268	138 056	16 239 882
按工业总产值分	**By Gross Output Value of Industry**			
5 亿元及以上	≥500 million yuan	173	376 274	70 723 355
10000～49999 万元	100～499.99 million yuan	161	87 367	4 378 689
5 000～9 999 万元	50～99.99 million yuan	25	9 594	196 369
5 000 万元以下	<50 million yuan	4	1 284	16 500
按固定资产原价分	**By Original Value of Fixed Assets**			
5 亿元及以上	≥500 million yuan	90	274 503	56 041 467
1 0000～49999 万元	100～499.99 million yuan	144	132 123	13 613 893
1 000～9 999 万元	50～99.99 million yuan	119	61 993	5 513 547
1 000 万元以下	<10 million yuan	10	5 900	146 007
按利税总额分	**By Profits and Taxes**			
1 亿元及以上	≥100 million yuan	103	280 788	60 137 784
5 000～9 999 万元	50～99.99 milion yuan	54	47 657	4 881 963
1 000～4 999 万元	10～49.99 milion yuan	113	78 628	6 232 578
1 000 万元以下	<10 million yuan	93	67 446	4 062 588

Major Indicators of Large and Medium Industrial Enterprises with Independent Accounting Systems

(10 000 yuan)

工业销售产值 Sales Value of Industry	固定资产原价 Original Value of Fixed Assets	资产总计 Total Assets	#固定资产合计 Total Fixed Assets	#流动资产合计 Total Floating Assets	主营业务收入 Revenue of of Floating Assets	利润总额 Total Profits
74 437 906	**55 506 202**	**98 613 432**	**25 962 478**	**48 621 260**	**91 124 395**	**7 610 882**
21 641 418	32 454 840	36 642 300	16 433 387	13 222 324	22 760 133	414 145
18 107 751	8 308 516	32 889 418	3 711 398	15 917 389	29 715 834	5 217 867
34 688 738	14 742 846	29 081 714	5 817 693	19 481 548	38 648 429	1 978 870
24 297 380	33 723 377	53 362 921	16 959 195	19 416 351	26 401 133	3 161 249
8 343 174	24 642 226	17 169 505	12 415 330	1 734 668	8 447 025	356 053
51 670	6 332	17 935	1 757	16 163	51 441	4 907
7 462 726	5 824 654	15 066 148	3 361 239	8 794 159	8 312 288	324 169
6 234 248	2 721 105	19 026 303	846 526	7 448 153	7 382 656	2 285 678
2 205 563	529 061	2 083 029	334 343	1 423 208	2 207 724	190 443
6 720 761	4 353 086	7 289 877	1 515 321	4 832 475	7 909 792	486 390
4 225 756	3 432 710	4 395 782	1 008 297	3 206 026	5 426 708	206 519
43 419 765	17 429 739	37 960 635	7 487 962	24 372 434	56 813 469	3 963 243
21 216 247	8 016 884	14 306 702	3 026 667	9 678 035	23 645 702	972 103
10 922 375	4 186 814	10 726 321	2 152 505	6 773 267	11 276 564	904 948
63 515 531	51 319 387	87 887 111	23 809 973	41 847 994	79 847 831	6 705 934
34 646 076	35 642 790	58 339 286	16 935 687	23 879 516	47 795 993	5 135 762
10 879 102	6 747 948	8 193 212	2 309 889	4 377 296	11 519 977	346 288
13 043 978	5 742 700	12 465 948	3 017 084	7 182 434	13 454 816	912 308
15 868 750	7 372 765	19 614 987	3 699 817	13 182 014	18 353 608	1 216 524
69 864 376	52 356 509	90 256 550	24 290 464	43 831 237	86 013 610	7 365 854
4 357 403	3 006 536	8 076 753	1 612 778	4 590 082	4 883 194	245 762
196 807	118 847	250 617	50 577	180 028	203 664	4 609
19 320	24 309	29 512	8 659	19 913	23 927	-5 343
55 509 202	51 484 445	81 259 582	23 901 149	35 736 804	69 154 753	6 232 152
13 216 192	3 363 503	12 265 598	1 758 366	8 516 398	14 957 302	1 091 983
5 566 615	653 165	5 004 587	299 774	4 294 000	6 870 371	281 893
145 898	5 088	83 666	3 189	74 060	141 970	4 854
59 531 765	47 282 746	80 096 266	21 579 936	37 634 688	74 595 872	7 346 636
4 839 528	2 521 503	4 733 141	1 131 845	3 044 535	5 154 676	297 319
6 176 238	2 249 341	5 911 331	1 184 114	3 921 196	7 247 148	200 279
3 890 375	3 452 612	7 872 694	2 066 583	4 020 842	4 126 700	-233 351

表6-9 港澳台及外商投资工业企业主要指标 (2014)

单位:万元

指 标	Indicators	企业单位数(个) Enterprises (unit)	从业人数(人) Employed Persons (person)	工业总产值 Gross Output Value of Industry
总 计	**Total**	**802**	**412 149**	**59 435 060**
按登记注册类型分	**By Type of Registration**			
与港澳台商合资经营企业	China-Hong Kong/Macao/Taiwan Joint Venture	66	25 224	2 144 349
与港澳台商合作经营企业	China-Hong Kong/Macao/Taiwan Cooperative	6	1 124	69 872
港澳台商独资企业	Solely Hong Kong/Macao/Taiwan Funded	111	35 172	5 377 652
港澳台商投资股份有限公司	Hong Kong/Macao/Taiwan Investment Companies Limited by Shares	3	5 546	765 789
其他港澳台商投资	Other HongKong/Macao/Taiwan Investment			
中外合资经营企业	Sino-Foreign Jointly-operated	169	84 817	20 224 087
中外合作经营企业	Sino-Foreign Cooperative	10	6 547	569 759
外商独资企业	Solely Foreigner Funded	431	229 549	26 209 548
外商投资股份有限公司	Foreign Investment Company Limited by Shares	6	24 170	4 074 004
按行业分	**By Sector**			
农副食品加工业	Processing of Agricultural Side-line Food	11	1 799	839 371
食品制造业	Food Manufacturing	7	3 886	342 316
酒、饮料和精制茶制造业	Manufacturing of Liquor, Beverage and Refined Tea	5	4 551	309 753
烟草制品业	Tobacco Products			
纺织业	Textile Industry	13	2 240	170 797
纺织服装、服饰业	Textile Clothes and Accessories	26	10 984	317 124
皮革、毛皮、羽毛及其制品和制鞋业	Leather, Fur, Feather and their Products and Shoe-making	5	854	24 608
木材加工及木、竹、藤、棕、草制品业	Timber-Processing, Bamboo, Cane, Palm Fiber and Straw Products	2	220	10 431
家具制造业	Furniture Manufacturing	9	9 498	938 199
造纸及纸制品业	Paper-making and Paper Products	14	3 628	352 529

Major Indicators of HK/Macao/Taiwan & Overseas Invested Industrial Enterprises

(10 000 yuan)

工业销售产值 Sales Value of Industry	固定资产原价 Original Value of Fixed Assets	资产总计 Total Assets	负债总计 Total Liabilities	实收资本 Paid-in Capital	主营业务收入 Revenue of of Floating Assets	税金 Tax	利润总额 Total Profits
58 957 351	**25 030 397**	**54 179 760**	**31 758 055**	**12 208 964**	**74 133 786**	**1 699 307**	**5 233 445**
2 146 019	939 967	2 673 856	1 357 171	609 586	2 129 631	55 730	271 936
68 721	75 998	90 744	79 572	37 371	64 587	2 580	-1 906
5 400 590	3 977 696	5 662 469	3 320 469	1 464 668	6 637 666	42 615	287 974
762 691	164 080	821 652	184 396	126 026	790 716	7 552	46 143
19 783 354	6 646 403	16 396 680	9 438 458	3 531 657	30 107 418	1 189 126	3 142 555
581 827	336 873	556 989	306 997	205 481	685 728	30 570	21 701
26 158 110	9 672 907	19 143 321	11 005 548	4 947 793	28 831 798	347 899	1 380 301
4 056 039	3 216 472	8 834 050	6 065 445	1 286 383	4 886 243	23 235	84 740
831 388	114 547	707 302	407 915	81 520	1 169 741	12 920	45 890
330 988	167 391	215 031	256 255	108 900	335 513	15 770	-56 559
325 861	299 457	254 106	221 648	180 219	376 790	18 294	1 103
170 042	64 985	184 178	111 759	47 643	168 422	2 066	4 806
331 236	59 087	276 517	216 268	46 053	328 537	13 993	-13 421
23 839	6 156	10 770	7 247	6 672	23 839	875	-619
11 275	667	4 831	3 151	1 094	10 122	737	-166
879 641	146 088	854 929	546 566	106 010	833 669	10 658	183 399
337 186	348 520	441 226	219 687	197 559	346 481	8 252	-9 067

单位:万元

表6－9　续表　Continued

指　标	Indicators	企业单位数（个） Enterprises (unit)	从业人数（人） Employed Persons (person)	工业总产值 Gross Output Value of Industry
印刷业、记录媒介的复制	Printing and Record Medium Reproduction	8	2 073	111 951
文教、工美、体育和娱乐用品制造业	Manufacturing of Cultural, Educational, Arts, Sports and Leisure Products	11	1 739	69 505
石油加工、炼焦及核燃料加工业	Petroleum Processing, Coke Products and Processing of Nuclear Fuel	5	726	183 934
化学原料及化学制品制造业	Raw Chemical Materials and Chemical Products	66	15 145	4 318 011
医药制造业	Medicine Manufacturing	28	12 905	1 949 891
化学纤维制造业	Chemical Fiber	1	101	3 983
橡胶和塑料制品业	Rubber and Plastic Products	48	11 664	616 592
非金属矿物制品业	Nonmetal Mineral Products	28	6 114	547 965
黑色金属冶炼及压延加工业	Smelting and Pressing of Ferrous Metal	5	1 565	393 925
有色金属冶炼及压延加工业	Smelting and Pressing of Nonferrous Metal	6	1 072	316 453
金属制品业	Metal Products	38	8 873	758 542
通用设备制造业	General Purpose Equipment Manufacturing	130	43 655	5 668 002
专用设备制造业	Specialized Equipment Manufacturing	73	19 678	2 561 026
汽车制造业	Automobile Manufacturing	61	42 486	12 615 978
铁路、船舶、航空航天和其他运输设备制造业	Manufacturing of Railway, Ships, Aeronautics &Astronautics, and Other Transportation Equipment	17	3 294	249 088
电气机械及器材制造业	Electric Equipment and Machinery	59	27 356	3 044 107
计算机、通信和其他电子设备制造业	Manufacturing of Computers, Telecommunication and other Electronic Equipment	81	159 215	21 244 199
仪器仪表制造业	Manufacturing of Instrument and Apparatus	32	10 712	1 031 749
其他制造业	Other Manufacturing	6	3 932	237 858
金属制品、机械和设备修理业	Repairing of Metal Products, Machine and Equipment	3	809	83 304
电力、热力生产和供应业	Production and Supply of Electricity and Heating Power	3	247	24 166
水的生产和供应业	Production and Supply of Tap Water	1	1 128	99 704

(10 000 yuan)

工业销售产值 Sales Value of Industry	固定资产原价 Original Value of Fixed Assets	资产总计 Total Assets	负债总计 Total Liabilities	实收资本 Paid-in Capital	主营业务收入 Revenue of of Floating Assets	税金 Tax	利润总额 Total Profits
117 395	107 884	140 855	70 878	33 698	117 964	6 586	8 526
64 300	22 406	57 456	27 847	16 537	72 528	995	2 743
190 877	37 987	95 611	30 033	32 612	215 146	7 357	12 352
4 275 921	1 626 375	3 457 513	1 486 919	923 380	4 360 555	111 485	394 103
1 755 193	655 901	2 357 826	1 419 428	447 459	1 794 684	97 199	204 104
3 983	1 388	5 195	1 029	2 700	3 983	16	847
610 751	307 708	526 540	210 823	167 572	605 908	11 429	30 492
540 019	581 690	945 265	323 320	390 144	620 741	23 895	75 747
395 461	283 348	285 480	186 718	339 673	413 803	8 681	846
315 796	141 899	379 663	279 751	87 752	332 588	4 119	6 855
740 055	368 196	766 106	361 786	229 941	782 594	19 627	58 240
5 653 018	3 582 665	9 152 872	6 134 753	1 271 025	6 303 261	122 371	272 969
2 557 613	739 524	2 536 734	1 333 248	481 209	2 651 747	62 523	256 491
12 403 083	3 675 676	9 849 418	5 670 076	1 394 823	22 255 699	966 850	2 634 567
241 145	94 475	260 572	125 066	60 326	249 085	2 934	19 733
3 024 220	783 320	2 152 497	1 111 362	465 557	3 124 091	55 186	270 963
21 347 150	9 574 109	16 299 428	10 223 103	4 528 790	25 121 120	77 434	623 366
1 044 118	212 962	970 699	361 490	191 221	1 068 090	7 924	127 221
243 984	266 607	305 184	62 103	70 841	243 986	19 444	28 596
83 304	74 232	103 931	58 177	109 033	83 298	2 136	11 300
24 166	110 021	113 924	10 618	37 000	33 906	1 389	14 178
84 343	575 130	468 101	279 033	152 000	85 895	6 164	23 841

表6-10　私营工业企业主要指标
(2014)

单位:万元

指　标	Indicators	企业单位数(个) Enterprises (unit)	从业人数(人) Average Number of Employed Persons (person)	工业总产值 Gross Output Value of Industry
总　计	**Total**	**715**	**103 755**	**6 729 121**
按轻、重工业分	**By Light/Heavy Industry**			
轻工业	Light Industry	243	35 535	1 967 801
重工业	Heavy Industry	472	68 220	4 761 320
按主要工业行业分	**By Main Sector**			
#农副食品加工业	Processing of Agricultural Side-line Food	7	3 922	197 364
食品制造业	Food Producing	7	606	29 002
酒、饮料和精制茶制造业	Manufacturing of Liquor, Beverage and Refined Tea	1	196	45 123
纺织业	Textile Industry	14	1 593	81 777
纺织服装、服饰业	Manufacturing of Textile Clothes, Shoes and Hats	54	7 279	291 587
皮革、毛皮、羽毛及其制品和制鞋业	Leather, Fur, Feather and their Products and Shoe-making	11	1 885	46 633
木材加工及木、竹、藤、棕、草制品业	Timber-processing, Bamboo, Cane, Palm Fiber and Straw Products	4	451	36 337
家具制造业	Furniture Making	9	927	32 380
造纸及纸制品业	Paper-making and Paper Products	20	2 406	121 466
印刷业和记录媒介的复制	Printing and Record Medium Reproduction	22	3 514	181 381
文教、工美、体育和娱乐用品制造业	Manufacturing of Cultural, Educational, Arts, Sports and Leisure Products	10	1 462	230 583
石油加工、炼焦及核燃料加工业	Petroleum Processing, Coke Products and Processing of Nuclear Fuel	5	298	39 075
化学原料及化学制品制造业	Raw Chemical Material and Chemical Products	37	3 378	359 515
医药制造业	Medicine Manufacturing	15	2 615	273 711
化学纤维制造业	Chemical Fiber Manufacturing	3	284	27 882
橡胶和塑料制品业	Rubber and Plastic Products	69	7 629	407 695
非金属矿物制品业	Nonmetal Mineral Products	30	2 332	162 144
黑色金属冶炼及压延加工业	Smelting and Pressing of Ferrous Metal	15	1 500	111 023
有色金属冶炼及压延加工业	Smelting and Pressing of Nonferrous Metal	14	429	122 021
金属制品业	Metal Products	72	9 839	548 816
通用设备制造业	Manufacturing of General Purpose Equipment	84	11 757	702 412
专用设备制造业	Manufacturing of Specialized Equipment	38	5 245	328 101
汽车制造业	Automobile Manufacturing	43	11 632	763 792
铁路、船舶、航空航天和其他运输设备制造业	Manufacturing of Railway, Ship, Aviation and Aerospace, and other Transportation Equipment	16	2 109	108 528
电气机械及器材制造业	Manufacturing of Electrical Machinery and Equipment	85	11 275	1 107 658
计算机、通信和其他电子设备制造业	Manufacturing of Computers, Telecommunications and Other Electronic Equipment	17	5 694	280 886
仪器仪表制造业	Manufacturing of Instrument and Meters	7	862	46 656
其他制造业	Other Manufacturings	2	277	10 993
废弃资源综合利用业	Comprehensive Utilization of Waste Resource	1	103	9 523
金属制品、机械和设备修理业	Repairing of Metal Products, Machineries and Equipment	3	2 256	25 056

Major Indicators of Private Industrial Enterprises

(10 000 yuan)

工业销售产值 Sales Value of Industry	固定资产原价 Original Value of Fixed Assets	资产总计 Total Assets	负债总计 Total Liabilities	实收资本 Paid-in Capital	主营业务收入 Revenue of of Floating Assets	税金 Tax	利润总额 Total Profits
6 616 043	**1 927 864**	**6 823 036**	**3 695 971**	**1 104 450**	**6 876 446**	**201 632**	**430 545**
1 929 077	641 241	1 883 148	1 006 574	293 355	1 986 444	72 847	136 621
4 686 966	1 286 623	4 939 888	2 689 397	811 095	4 890 002	128 785	293 924
197 403	44 523	123 383	71 506	16 023	193 050	3 148	8 808
28 964	7 120	31 617	19 701	7 410	29 202	1 022	924
40 813	907	36 112	14 639	12 000	40 813	7 033	16 128
82 112	26 319	76 827	33 948	15 608	79 146	2 872	2 796
287 754	74 629	231 949	171 113	32 507	317 832	7 427	1 329
46 862	6 752	29 676	24 606	2 938	49 506	1 585	91
36 313	1 633	13 345	7 477	3 000	36 368	790	1 268
32 604	12 200	38 473	25 682	4 353	32 620	702	750
118 105	66 942	107 272	62 718	13 941	126 068	4 005	2 411
180 272	89 626	167 892	71 447	26 499	178 313	8 098	19 372
222 915	19 347	207 288	111 310	26 960	224 293	1 430	16 983
36 129	13 917	44 949	22 144	12 130	38 983	786	663
359 246	109 012	385 438	153 057	79 710	359 267	12 868	28 790
265 393	71 741	345 302	175 082	50 474	287 678	16 604	35 706
25 771	4 852	15 831	6 944	3 870	25 771	951	3 136
407 322	148 876	384 720	187 881	57 911	407 471	12 152	24 341
160 464	63 645	207 012	146 969	34 470	166 193	6 024	5 002
107 037	50 858	116 845	66 901	27 739	107 768	2 153	1 522
124 836	10 484	71 704	57 235	12 801	295 264	385	
544 218	182 203	521 192	303 164	60 463	541 699	18 781	24 698
693 481	262 866	818 098	415 792	128 308	699 551	24 783	58 413
317 431	83 041	482 574	288 870	65 999	334 063	11 241	23 643
718 126	174 412	636 551	321 935	79 748	710 888	16 156	77 246
109 977	49 646	196 142	122 578	26 773	122 115	4 866	2 760
1 106 489	261 415	1 159 277	612 119	247 183	1 102 737	22 774	51 172
276 671	66 537	232 964	126 133	32 115	278 353	7 721	18 705
46 208	11 748	94 705	44 152	20 659	48 358	1 894	3 476
10 953	3 857	10 525	9 230	1 600	10 958	294	-466
7 121	6 045	18 952	9 977	760	6 681	4	559
25 056	2 711	16 422	11 664	500	25 438	3 083	511

表6-11 工业企业单位数和从业人员平均人数的各种分组
Classification of Industrial Enterprises and Average Employees

指 标	Indicators	企业单位数(个) Enterprises (unit)		从业人员平均人数(人) Average Number of Persons Employed (person)	
		2013	2014	2013	2014
总 计	**Total**	**1 860**	**1 788**	**660 137**	**644 497**
按隶属关系分	**By Subordination**				
中央工业	Central	46	43	63 742	71 990
市属工业	Municipal	103	92	96 518	91 577
非中央、市属工业	Local	1 711	1 653	499 877	480 930
按登记注册类型分	**By Type of Registration**				
内 资	Domestic Funded	1 031	986	237 175	226 806
国 有	State-owned	19	13	23 183	20 203
集 体	Collective-owned	21	17	2 031	2 288
股份合作	Share-holding	11	9	1 521	1 141
联 营	Jointly Operated	5	4	316	239
有限责任公司	Companies with Limited Liabilities	211	199	78 135	76 028
股份有限公司	Companies Limited by Shares	30	29	23 730	22 051
私 营	Private	734	715	108 259	104 856
港澳台商投资	HK/Macao/Taiwan Invested	197	186	69 100	68 147
#港澳台商独资	Solely HK/Macao/Taiwan Funded	116	111	33 424	34 670
外商投资	Foreigner Invested	632	616	353 862	349 544
#外商独资	Solely Foreigner Funded	439	431	250 229	234 008
按轻、重工业分	**By Light/Heavy Industry**				
轻工业	Light Industry	582	559	173 802	166 121
重工业	Heavy Industry	1 278	1 229	486 335	478 376
按企业规模分	**By Scale of Enterprises**				
大型企业	Large	106	90	355 610	329 636
中型企业	Medium	271	273	138 258	149 576
小型企业	Small	1 483	1 425	166 269	165 285

表6-12 工业企业分行业能源消费情况
Energy Consumption of Industrial Enterprises by Sector
(2014)

指标	Indicators	企业单位数（个） Enterprises (in Number)	综合能源消费量（吨标准煤） Comprehensive Energy Consumption (tons of standard coal)	产值能耗（吨标准煤/万元） Energy Consumption of Production Value (tons of standard coal/10 000 yuan
总计	**Total**	**1 768**	**8 281 997**	**0.103**
农副食品加工业	Processing of Agricultural Side-line Food	21	108 175	0.085
食品制造业	Food Manufacturing	18	26 372	0.064
酒、饮料和精制茶制造业	Manufacturing of Liquor, Beverage and Refined Tea	7	30 170	0.081
烟草制品业	Tobacco Products	1	3 642	0.075
纺织业	Textile Industry	35	39 937	0.147
纺织服装、服饰业	Textile Clothes and Accessories	81	16 073	0.015
皮革、毛皮、羽毛及其制品和制鞋业	Leather, Fur, Feather and their Products and Shoe-making	19	3 954	0.048
木材加工及木、竹、藤、棕、草制品业	Timber-processing, Bamboo, Cane, Palm Fiber and Straw Products	7	1 107	0.026
家具制造业	Furniture Manufacturing	16	21 497	0.022
造纸及纸制品业	Paper-making and Paper Products	37	175 310	0.340
印刷业和记录媒介复制业	Printing and Record Pressing	39	36 517	0.080
文教、工美、体育和娱乐用品制造业	Manufacturing of Cultural, Educational, Arts, Sports and Leisure Products	26	6 798	0.020
石油加工、炼焦及核燃料加工业	Petroleum Processing, Coke Products and Processing of Nuclear Fuel	13	2 013 469	0.370
化学原料和化学制品制造业	Raw Chemical Materials and Chemical Products	118	639 412	0.119
医药制造业	Medicine Manufacturing	59	129 489	0.042
化学纤维制造业	Chemical Fiber Manufacturing	4	4 970	0.156
橡胶和塑料制品业	Rubber and Plastic Products	132	155 822	0.128
非金属矿物制品业	Nonmetal Mineral Products	77	184 230	0.170
黑色金属冶炼及压延加工业	Smelting and Pressing of Ferrous Metal	27	98 635	0.187
有色金属冶炼及压延加工业	Smelting and Pressing of Nonferrous Metal	29	52 638	0.084
金属制品业	Metal Products	130	108 466	0.070
通用设备制造业	Manufacturing of General Purpose Equipment	221	215 506	0.033
专用设备制造业	Manufacturing of Special Purpose Equipment	121	73 839	0.024
汽车制造业	Automobile Manunfacturing	127	461 505	0.030
铁路、船舶、航空航天和其他运输设备制造业	Manufacturing of Railway, Ships, Aviation and Aerospace, and Other Transportation Equipment	46	63 870	0.085
电气机械及器材制造业	Manufacturing of Electric Machinery and Equipment	164	150 004	0.032
计算机、通信和其他电子设备制造业	Manufacturing of Computers, Telecommunications and Other Electronic Equipment	116	782 331	0.035
仪器仪表制造业	Manufacturing of Instruments and Apparatuses	39	20 067	0.019
其他制造业	Other Manufacturings	8	27 501	0.111
废弃资源综合利用业	Comprehensive Reutilization of Discarded Resources	2	236	0.019
金属制品、机械和设备修理业	Repairing of Metal Products, Machineries and Equipment	12	14 229	0.062
电力、热力的生产和供应业	Production and Supply of Electricity and Thermal Power	9	2 531 830	0.288
燃气生产和供应业	Production and Supply of Gas	2	22 250	0.094
水的生产和供应业	Production and Supply of Tap Water	5	62 145	0.3603

表6-13 工业企业分行业主要能源品种消费情况
(2014)

指标	Indicators	原 煤(吨) Raw Coal (tons)	洗精煤(吨) Cleaned Coal (tons)	其他洗煤 (吨) Other Washed Coals(tons)
总 计	**Total**	**10 079 805**	**17 259**	**14 956**
# 农副食品加工业	Processing of Agricultural Side-line Food	40 082	229	
食品制造业	Food Manufacturing	8 430		
酒、饮料和精制茶制造业	Manufacturing of Liquor, Beverage and Refined Tea			
烟草制品业	Tobacco Products			
纺织业	Textile Industry	24 298		
纺织服装、服饰业	Textile Clothes and Accessories	591		
皮革、毛皮、羽毛及其制品和制鞋业	Leather, Fur, Feather and their Products and Shoe-making	1 047		23
木材加工及木、竹、藤、棕、草制品业	Timber-processing, Bamboo, Cane, Palm Fiber and Straw Products	24		
家具制造业	Furniture Manufacturing	420		
造纸及纸制品业	Paper-making and Paper Products	168 591	2 534	2 444
印刷业和记录媒介复制业	Printing and Record Pressing	702		
文教、工美、体育和娱乐用品制造业	Manufacturing of Cultural, Educational, Arts, Sports and Leisure Products			
石油加工、炼焦及核燃料加工业	Petroleum Processing, Coke Products and Processing of Nuclear Fuel			
化学原料和化学制品制造业	Raw Chemical Materials and Chemical Products	933 371		406
医药制造业	Medicine Manufacturing	29 671		
化学纤维制造业	Chemical Fiber Manufacturing			
橡胶和塑料制品业	Rubber and Plastic Products	15 300	11 570	12 083
非金属矿物制品业	Nonmetal Mineral Products	6 642		
黑色金属冶炼及压延加工业	Smelting and Pressing of Ferrous Metal	7 588	370	
有色金属冶炼及压延加工业	Smelting and Pressing of Nonferrous Metal	1 025		
金属制品业	Metal Products	5 923	2 252	
通用设备制造业	Manufacturing of General Purpose Equipment	43	89	
专用设备制造业	Manufacturing of Special Purpose Equipment	1 223	200	
汽车制造业	Automobile Manunfacturing	2 010	15	
铁路、船舶、航空航天和其他运输设备制造业	Manufacturing of Railway, Ships, Aviation and Aerospace, and Other Transportation Equipment			
电气机械及器材制造业	Electric Equipment and Machinery	4 437		
计算机、通信和其他电子设备制造业	Manufacturing of Computers, Telecommunications and Other Electronic Equipment			
仪器仪表制造业	Manufacturing of Instruments and Apparatuses	12		
其他制造业	Other Manufacturings	2 825		
废弃资源综合利用业	Comprehensive Reutilization of Discarded Resources			
金属制品、机械和设备修理业	Repairing of Metal Products, Machineries and Equipment			
电力、热力的生产和供应业	Production and Supply of Electricity and Thermal Power	8 825 549		
燃气生产和供应业	Production and Supply of Gas			
水的生产和供应业	Production and Supply of Tap Water			

Consumption of Main Kinds of Engery in Industrial Enterprises by Sector

煤制品(吨) Coal Products (tons)	焦 炭(吨) Coke (tons)	发生炉煤气(万立方米) Generator Gas (10 000 cu · m)	天然气(气态)(万立方米) Natural Gas (gas state) (10 000 cu · m)	液化天然气(液态)(吨) LNG(liquid state) (tons)	天然原油(吨) Crude Oil (tons)	汽油(吨) Gasoline (tons)
87 844	**3 891**	**5**	**79 883**	**2 271**	**8 235 103**	**37 490**
			295			313
			139			228
			5			53
			4			13
			267			473
			27	1		1 246
			1	2		233
						96
	38		79			147
			265			669
			62			894
						276
			6 388		8 235 103	861
84 860			1 538			2 092
			374	26		943
						94
			6			2 080
			3 648			829
379	2 013		2 324			419
2 605	1 574					306
	137		1 130			1 987
	129		431	1 815		3 379
			227			1 306
			3 116	388		8 508
			627	39		887
			727			2 653
		5	2 140			1 574
			14			320
			344			63
						11
			30			283
			47 783			3 611
			7 891			441
						203

表6－13　续表1　Continued

指标　Indicators		煤油(吨) Kerosene (tons)	柴油(吨) Diesel Oil (tons)
总　计	**Total**	**3 453**	**48 780**
#农副食品加工业	Processing of Agricultural Side-line Food		3 023
食品制造业	Food Manufacturing		1 132
酒、饮料和精制茶制造业	Manufacturing of Liquor, Beverage and Refined Tea		1 280
烟草制品业	Tobacco Products		6
纺织业	Textile Industry		273
纺织服装、服饰业	Textile Clothes and Accessories		1 003
皮革、毛皮、羽毛及其制品和制鞋业	Leather, Fur, Feather and their Products and Shoe-making		21
木材加工及木、竹、藤、棕、草制品业	Timber-processing, Bamboo, Cane, Palm Fiber and Straw Products	4	45
家具制造业	Furniture Manufacturing		179
造纸及纸制品业	Paper-making and Paper Products	2	1 361
印刷业和记录媒介复制业	Printing and Record Pressing	1	1 465
文教、工美、体育和娱乐用品制造业	Manufacturing of Cultural, Educational, Arts, Sports and Leisure Products		78
石油加工、炼焦及核燃料加工业	Petroleum Processing, Coke Products and Processing of Nuclear Fuel		166
化学原料和化学制品制造业	Raw Chemical Materials and Chemical Products	2 514	4 388
医药制造业	Medicine Manufacturing		1 085
化学纤维制造业	Chemical Fiber Manufacturing	191	3
橡胶和塑料制品业	Rubber and Plastic Products		1 862
非金属矿物制品业	Nonmetal Mineral Products		5 264
黑色金属冶炼及压延加工业	Smelting and Pressing of Ferrous Metal	1	479
有色金属冶炼及压延加工业	Smelting and Pressing of Nonferrous Metal	397	1 422
金属制品业	Metal Products	56	3 350
通用设备制造业	Manufacturing of General Purpose Equipment	159	10 272
专用设备制造业	Manufacturing of Special Purpose Equipment	30	697
汽车制造业	Automobile Manunfacturing	71	1 876
铁路、船舶、航空航天和其他运输设备制造业	Manufacturing of Railway, Ships, Aviation and Aerospace, and Other Transportation Equipment	6	1 027
电气机械及器材制造业	Electric Equipment and Machinery	22	1 664
计算机、通信和其他电子设备制造业	Manufacturing of Computers, Telecommunications and Other Electronic Equipment		318
仪器仪表制造业	Manufacturing of Instruments and Apparatuses		56
其他制造业	Other Manufacturings		200
废弃资源综合利用业	Comprehensive Reutilization of Discarded Resources		
金属制品、机械和设备修理业	Repairing of Metal Products, Machineries and Equipment		348
电力、热力的生产和供应业	Production and Supply of Electricity and Thermal Power		4 420
燃气生产和供应业	Production and Supply of Gas		
水的生产和供应业	Production and Supply of Tap Water		19

燃料油 （吨） Fuel Oil （tons）	液化石油气 （吨） LPG （tons）	炼厂干气 （吨） Dry Gas from Refineries （tons）	石脑油 （吨） Naphtha （tons）	润滑油 （吨） Lude （tons）	石 蜡 （吨） Ceresin Wax （tons）
25 623	**28 341**	**262 022**	**1**	**11 536**	**38**
369	7				
	18				
1 039	195				
	3				
19	16				
	3				
	48			1	
75	47				
475	145				
	6				
12 466	4 647	255 594			
1 852	20 780	6 428		245	9
	1 047				
222	43			20	21
207	6				
1 298			1		
632	424				
139	78			880	
	7			160	8
	207			10 091	
	49			11	
	377			57	
	184				
	1				
6 830				71	
	2				

表 6－13 续表 2 Continued

指标	Indicators	溶剂油（吨）Solvent Naphtha (tons)	其他石油制品（吨）Other Petroleum Products (tons)
总 计	**Total**	**11 660**	**922 837**
#农副食品加工业	Processing of Agricultural Side-line Food		805
食品制造业	Food Manufacturing		
酒、饮料和精制茶制造业	Manufacturing of Liquor, Beverage and Refined Tea		
烟草制品业	Tobacco Products		
纺织业	Textile Industry		
纺织服装、服饰业	Textile Clothes and Accessories		
皮革、毛皮、羽毛及其制品和制鞋业	Leather, Fur, Feather and their Products and Shoe-making	37	
木材加工及木、竹、藤、棕、草制品业	Timber-processing, Bamboo, Cane, Palm Fiber and Straw Products		
家具制造业	Furniture Manufacturing		
造纸及纸制品业	Paper-making and Paper Products		
印刷业和记录媒介复制业	Printing and Record Pressing		
文教、工美、体育和娱乐用品制造业	Manufacturing of Cultural, Educational, Arts, Sports and Leisure Products		
石油加工、炼焦及核燃料加工业	Petroleum Processing, Coke Products and Processing of Nuclear Fuel	7 241	902 698
化学原料和化学制品制造业	Raw Chemical Materials and Chemical Products	4 285	18 476
医药制造业	Medicine Manufacturing		
化学纤维制造业	Chemical Fiber Manufacturing	37	
橡胶和塑料制品业	Rubber and Plastic Products	29	39
非金属矿物制品业	Nonmetal Mineral Products		
黑色金属冶炼及压延加工业	Smelting and Pressing of Ferrous Metal		
有色金属冶炼及压延加工业	Smelting and Pressing of Nonferrous Metal		
金属制品业	Metal Products		148
通用设备制造业	Manufacturing of General Purpose Equipment	24	48
专用设备制造业	Manufacturing of Special Purpose Equipment	7	
汽车制造业	Automobile Manunfacturing		495
铁路、船舶、航空航天和其他运输设备制造业	Manufacturing of Railway, Ships, Aviation and Aerospace, and Other Transportation Equipment		
电气机械及器材制造业	Electric Equipment and Machinery		47
计算机、通信和其他电子设备制造业	Manufacturing of Computers, Telecommunications and Other Electronic Equipment	1	3
仪器仪表制造业	Manufacturing of Instruments and Apparatuses		69
其他制造业	Other Manufacturings		7
废弃资源综合利用业	Comprehensive Reutilization of Discarded Resources		
金属制品、机械和设备修理业	Repairing of Metal Products, Machineries and Equipment		1
电力、热力的生产和供应业	Production and Supply of Electricity and Thermal Power		
燃气生产和供应业	Production and Supply of Gas		
水的生产和供应业	Production and Supply of Tap Water		

热　力 （百万千焦） Heating Power （1 million KJ）	电　力 （万千瓦时） Electric Power （10 000 KWH）	城市生活 垃圾用于燃料 （吨） City Life Garbage for Fuel（tons）	生物质废料 用于燃料 （吨） Biology Waste for Fuel（tons）	其他工业 废料用于燃料 （吨） Other Industry Waste for Fuel（tons）	其他燃料 （吨标准煤） Other Fuels （tons/standard coal）
15 543 600	**1 861 124**	**406 394**	**2 863**	**7 602**	**49**
973 827	11 870				
34 414	5 117				
63 643	8 057				
30 652	840				
1 980	5 893		410		
6 000	3 861	51	300		
	914				
	292				
	5 435		18	7 602	
54 551	12 949				
71 944	9 461				
	2 089				
9 090 273	92 064				
2 785 429	125 954				
637 543	26 213				
	1 497				
18 348	40 023				
5 500	40 780				
	19 026				
	14 922		1 300		
21 193	25 484		835		
53 855	60 914				49
18 263	21 991				
559 082	123 044				
10 302	17 463				
24 331	43 122				
515 531	244 605				
	6 409				
	6 873				
	73				
	4 304				
208 895	856 901	406 343			
358 043	2 078				
	20 605				

表6-14　工业企业能源消费分组情况
Energy Consumption of Industrial Enterprises by Group
(2014)

指标　Indicators		综合能源消费量（吨标准煤）Comprehensive Energy Consumption (tons of standard coal)	单位产值能耗（吨标准煤/万元）Energy Consumption of Production Value (tons of standard coal/10 000 yuan)
按轻、重工业分	**By Light/Heavy Industry**		
轻工业	Light Industry	896 325	0.056
重工业	Heavy Industry	7 385 673	0.102
按企业规模分	**By Scale of Enterprises**		
大型企业	Large	5 768 531	0.103
中型企业	Medium	1 097 378	0.070
小型企业	Small	1 416 089	0.087
按高载能行业分	**By High Engery Bearing**		
石油加工、炼焦及核燃料加工业	Petroleum Processing, Coke Products and Processing of Nuclear Fuel	2 013 469	0.370
非金属矿物制品业	Nonmetal Mineral Products	184 230	0.170
化学原料及化学制品制造业	Raw Chemical Materials and Chemical Products	639 412	0.119
黑色金属冶炼及压延加工业	Smelting and Pressing of Ferrous Metal	98 635	0.187
电力、热力的生产和供应业	Production and Supply of Electricity and Thermal Power	2 531 830	0.288
按重点行业分	**By Key Industry**		
电子信息产品制造业	Manufacturing of Electronic and Information Products	917 210	0.037
汽车制造业	Automobile Industry	469 200	0.030
石油化工及精细化工制造业	Petrochemical and Refining Industry	2 572 500	0.249
精品钢材制造业	Manufacturing of Refined Steel Products	74 737	0.167
成套设备制造业	Manufacturing of Complete Equipment	276 644	0.033
生物医药制造业	Manufacturing of Biological Medicine	160 834	0.039
按高技术行业分	**By High-tech Industry**		
信息化学品制造	Manufacturing of Information Chemicals	155	0.023
医药制造业	Manufacturing of Medicines	129 489	0.042
航空航天器制造	Manufacturing of Aviation and Space Vehicles	3 009	0.025
电子及通信设备制造业	Manufacuring of Electronic and Communication Equipment	693 797	0.069
电子计算机及办公设备制造业	Manufacturing of Electronic Computer and Office Equipment	89 541	0.007
医疗设备及仪器仪表制造业	Manufacturing of Medical Equipment, Instrument and Meters	35 544	0.022

主要统计指标解释

工　业

指从事自然资源的开采,对采掘品和农产品进行加工和再加工的物质生产部门。具体包括:(1)对自然资源的开采,如采矿、晒盐等(但不包括禽兽捕猎和水产捕捞);(2)对农副产品的加工、再加工,如粮油加工、食品加工、缫丝、纺织、制革等;(3)对采掘品的加工、再加工,如炼铁、炼钢、化工生产、石油加工、机器制造、木材加工等,以及电力、自来水、煤气的生产和供应等;(4)对工业品的修理、翻新,如机器设备的修理、交通运输工具(包括小卧车)的修理等。

1984 年以前农村的村及村以下办工业归属农业,1984 年以后划归工业。

工业统计调查单位为独立核算法人工业企业。

独立核算法人工业企业指从事工业生产经营活动的单位。独立核算法人工业企业应同时具备以下条件:①依法成立,有自己的名称、组织机构和场所,能够承担民事责任;②独立拥有和使用资产,承担负债,有权与其他单位签订合同;③独立核算盈亏,并能够编制资产负债表。

轻工业

指主要提供生活消费品和制作手工工具的工业。按其所使用的原料不同,可分为两大类:(1)以农产品为原料的轻工业,是指直接或间接以农产品为基本原料的轻工业。主要包括食品制造、饮料制造、烟草加工、纺织、缝纫、皮革和毛皮制作、造纸以及印刷等工业;(2)以非农产品为原料的轻工业,是指以工业品为原料的轻工业。主要包括文教体育用品、化学药品制造、合成纤维制造、日用化学制品、日用玻璃制品、日用金属制品、手工工具制造、医疗器械制造、文化和办公用机械制造等工业。

重工业

指为国民经济各部门提供物质技术基础的主要生产资料的工业。按其生产性质和产品用途,可以分为下列三类:(1)采掘(伐)工业,是指对自然资源的开采,包括石油开采、煤炭开采、金属矿开采、非金属矿开采等工业;(2)原材料工业,指向国民经济各部门提供基本材料、动力和燃料的工业。包括金属冶炼及加工、炼焦及焦炭、化学、化工原料、水泥、人造板以及电力、石油和煤炭加工等工业;(3)加工工业,是指对工业原材料进行再加工制造的工业。包括装备国民经济各部门的机械设备制造工业、金属结构、水泥制品等工业,以及为农业提供的生产资料如化肥、农药等工业。

根据上述划分原则,修理业中以重工业产品为修理作业对象的划为重工业,反之划为轻工业。

工业总产值

(1) 定义:工业总产值是以货币形式表现的,工业企业在一定时期内生产的工业最终产品或提供工业性劳务活动的总价值量。它反映一定时间内工业生产的总规模和总水平。

(2) 计算原则:工业生产的原则,即凡是企业在报告期生产的经检验合格的产品,不管是否在报告期销售,均包括在内。

最终产品的原则,即凡是计入工业总产值的产品,必须是本企业生产的经检验合格的,不需要再进行任何加工的最终产品。如果企业有中间产品(半成品)对外销售,则对外销售的中间产品应视为企业的最终产品。

工厂法原则,即工业总产值是以工业企业作为基本计算(核算)单位,即按企业的最终产品计算工业总产值。按这种方法计算的工业总产值,不允许同一产品价值在企业内部重复计算,不能把企业内部各个车间(分厂)生产的成果相加,但允许企业间的重复计算。

(3) 内容及计算方法:1995 年全国工业普查对工业总产值(原规定)的内容及计算原则和方法做了某些修订,修订后的工业总产值(新规定)包括三项内容:即本期生产成品价值、对外加工费收入、在制品半成品期末期初差额价值三部分。

本期生产成品价值:指企业本期生产,并在报告期内不再进行加工,经检验、包装入库的全部工业成品(半产品)价值合计,包括企业生产的自制设备及提供给本企业在建工程、其他非工业部门和福利部门等单位使用的成品价值。本期生产成品价值为按自备原材料生产的产品的数量乘以本期不含增值税(销项税额)的产品实际销售平均单价计算;会计核算中按成本价格转帐的自制设备和自产自用的成品,按成本价格计算生产成品价值。生产成品价值中不包括用定货者来料加工的成品(半产品)价值。

对外加工费收入:指企业在报告期内完成的对外承接的工业品加工(包括用定货者来料加工产品)的加工费收入和对外工业修理作业所取得的加工费收入。对外加工费收入按不含增值税(销项税额)的价格计算,可根据会计“产品销售收入”科目的有关资料取得。

对于本企业对内非工业部门提供的加工修理、设备安装的劳务收入,如果企业会计核算基础较好,能取得这部分资料,而且这部分价值所占比重较大,应包括在对外加工费收入中。

自制半成品在制品期末期初差额价值:指企业报告期在制品期末减期初的差额价值,本指标一般可以从会计核算资料中取得。如果会计产品成本核算中不计算半成品、在制品的成本,则总产值中也不包括这部分价值,反之则包括。

(4) 工业总产值统计范围变化和计算方法修订情况:1984 年以前工业总产值不包括村办工业,村办工业总产值划归农业。1984 年以后工业总产值包括村办工业。

1995 年工业普查对工业总产值计算方法做了修订,即从 1995 年始按新修订(新规定)方法计算工业总产值。新规定与原规定的区别如下:

全价与加工费的计算原则不同:新规定为凡自备原材料,不论其生产繁简程度如何,一律按全价计算工业总产值;凡来料加工,允许按加工费计算工业总产值。原规定则视生产加工的繁简程度不同,规定哪些行业按全价,哪些行业按加工费计算工业总产值。

自制半成品、在产品期末期初差额价值的计算原则不同:新规定要求,凡会计产品成本核算时计算了成本的差额价值,总产值中就应包括,否则可不包括;原规定则按生产周期六个月的界限区分,凡生产周期六个月以上的企业,总产值计算中应包括这部分差额价值,否则可不包括。

计算价格不同:新规定按不含增值税(销项税额)的价格计算;原规定则按含增值税(销项税额)的价格计算。

工业销售产值

是以货币表现的工业企业在一定时期内销售的、本企业生产的工业产品总量。包括已销售的成品、半成品价值,对外提供的工业性作业价值和对本单位基本建设部门、生活福利部门等提供的产品和工业性作业及自制设备的价值。工业销售产值依循的是以产品所有权转移为计算原则,因此,已销售的成品、半成品不论是本期生产的、还是上期生产的,只要是本期销售出去的均包括在内。对外提供的工业性作业是指企业按合同对外提供的工业性劳务。

工业销售产值的计算范围、计算价格和计算方法与工业总产值一致,但两者计算的基础不同,工业销售产值计算的基础是产品销售总量,工业总产值计算的基础是工业产品生产总量。

出口交货值

是指工业企业交给外贸部门或自营(委托)出口(包括销往香港、澳门地区、台湾省)的产品价值;批量销于国内或在过境批量出口等但用外汇价格结算的产品价值;外商来样、来料加工,来件装配和补偿贸易等生产,分别参照计算总产值的规定要求按全价或加工费计算的价值。

大、中、小型企业

根据工业和信息化部、国家统计局、国家发展改革委、财政部《关于印发中小企业划型标准规定的通知》(工信部联企业【2011】300号),依据从业人员、营业收入、资产总额等指标或替代指标,将我国的企业划分为大型、中型、小型、微型等四种类型,原划分办法废止。工业企业划型标准见下表:

指标名称	计量单位	大　型	中　型	小　型	微　型
从业人员(X)	人	X≥1000	300≤X<1000	20≤X<300	X<20
主营业务收入(Y)	万元	Y≥40000	2000≤Y<40000	300≤Y<2000	Y<300

说明:大型、中型和小型企业必须同时满足所列指标下限,否则下划一档;微型企业只须满足所列指标中的一项即可。

独立核算工业企业、非独立核算工业生产单位

工业企业按其行政和财务是否独立,分为独立核算工业企业和非独立核算工业生产单位。

独立核算工业企业应同时具备下列三个条件:(1)行政上有独立的组织形式;(2)经济上独立核算,自负盈亏,编制独立的资金平衡表(或资产负债表);(3)有权与其他单位签订合同,并在银行设有独立帐户。独立核算工业企业不论是单一性生产或联合性生产的企业,均以整个企业作为一个基层单位进行统计,而不按分厂、车间统计。

非独立核算工业生产单位是指不同时具备独立核算工业企业三个条件,附设于其他企业、事业、机关、团体、学校、科研机构、部队等单位的工业生产单位。非独立核算工业生产单位必须同时具备下列三个条件,才可列入工业统计范围,即:(1)有固定的生产场所和生产设备;(2)有固定的生产工人和学徒在10人以上;(3)一般单位常年生产,季节性生产的单位全年开工时间在三个月以上。

资产总计

资产是指企业拥有或者控制的能以货币计量的经济资源,包括各种财产、债权和其他权利。资产按其流动性(即资产的变现能力和支付能力)划分为:流动资产、长期投资、固定资产、无形资产、递延资产和其他资产。该指标根据企业会计"资产负债表"中"资产总计"项目的期末数增列。

流动资产合计

指可以在一年或者超过一年的一个营业周期内变现或者耗用的资产,包括现金及各种存款、短期投资、应收及预付货款、存款等。

流动资产平均余额

指企业在报告期内全部流动资产的平均余额。

固定资产净值年平均余额

指固定资产净值在报告期内余额的平均数。计算公式为:

固定资产净值年平均余额 = 1 至 12 月各月月初、月末固定资产净值之和/24

该指标根据"资产负债表"中"固定资产原价"、"累计折旧"指标的期初、期末数计算填列。

固定资产净值指固定资产原价减去历年已提折旧额后的净额。计算公式为:

固定资产净值 = 固定资产原价 - 累计折旧

负债合计

负债合计是指企业所承担的能以货币计量,将以资产或劳务偿付的债务总计。负债一般按偿还期长短分为流动负债和长期负债。流动负债合计是指企业在一年内或超过一年的一个营业周期内偿还的债务;长期负债合计是指偿还期在一年以上或者超过一年的一个营业周期内偿还债

务。

所有者权益

指企业投资人对企业净资产的所有权。企业净资产等于企业全部资产减去全部负债后的余额,包括企业投资人对企业的最初投入的实际到位的资产及资本公积金、盈余公积金和未分配利润。所有者权益合计数小于零,表示企业资不抵债。

利润总额

指企业生产经营活动的最终成果,是企业在一定时期内实现的盈亏相抵后的利润总额(亏损以" - "号表示),它等于营业利润加上补贴收入加上投资收益加上营业外净收入再加上以前年度损益调整。

EXPLANATORY NOTES TO MAJOR STATISTICAL INDICATORS

Industry

Industry refers to the material production sector which is engaged in extraction of natural resources and processing and reprocessing of minerals and agricultural products, including (1) extraction of natural resources, such as mining, salt production (but not including hunting and fishing); (2) processing and reprocessing of farm and sideline produces, such as rice husking, flour milling, wine making, oil pressing, silk reeling, spinning and weaving, and leather making; (3) manufacture of industrial products, such as steel making, iron smelting, chemicals manufacturing, petroleum processing, machine building, timber processing; water and gas production and electricity generation and supply; (4) repairing of industrial products such as the repairing of machinery and means of transport (including cars).

Prior to 1984, the rural industry run by villages and cooperative organizations under village was classified into agriculture. Since 1984, it has been grouped into industry.

Units of industrial statistics survey corporate industrial enterprises with independent accounting system.

Corporate industrial enterprises with independent accounting system refer to enterprises engaging in industrial production activities, which meet the following requirements: ①They are established legally, having their own names, organizations, location, able to take civil liability; ②They possess and use their assets independently, assume liabilities, and are entitled to sign contracts with other units; ③They are financially independent and compile their own balance sheets.

Light Industry

refers to the industry that produces consumer goods and hand tools. It consists of two categories, depending on the materials used:

(1) Industries using farm products as raw materials. These are branches of light industry which directly or indirectly use farm products as basic raw materials, including the manufacture of food and beverages, tobacco processing, textile, clothing, fur and leather manufacturing, paper making, printing, etc.

(2) Industries using non farm products as raw materials. These are branches of light industry which use manufactured goods as raw materials, including the manufacture of cultural, educational articles and sports goods, chemicals, synthetic fiber, chemical products for daily use, glass products for daily use, metal products for daily use, hand tools, medical apparatus and instruments, and the manufacture of cultural and clerical machinery.

Heavy Industry

refers to the industry which produces capital goods, and provides various sectors of the national economy with necessary material and technical basis. It consists of the following three branches according to the purpose of production or the use of products:

(1) Mining, quarrying and logging industry refers to the industry that extracts natural resources, including extraction of petroleum, coal, metal and non-metal ores.

(2) Raw materials industry refers to the industry that provides various sectors of the national economy with raw materials, fuels and power. It includes smelting and processing of metals, coking and coke chemistry, chemical materials and building materials such as cement, plywood, and power, petroleum refining and coal dressing.

(3) Manufacturing industry refers to the industry that processes raw materials. It includes machine building industry which equips sectors of the national economy, industries of metal structure and cement products, industries producing means of agricultural production, such as chemical fertilizers and pesticides. According to the above principle of classification, the repairing trades which are engaged primarily in repairing products of heavy industry are classified into heavy industry while these engaged in repairing products of light industry are classified into light industry.

Gross Output Value of Industry

(1) Definition: Gross industrial output value is the total volume of final industrial products produced and industrial services provided during a given period. It reflects the total achievements and overall scale of industrial production during a given period.

(2) Principles for calculation: Statistics on industrial production follow the principle that all products produced by the enterprises and accepted during the reference period are to be included no matter whether they are sold or not during the reference period.

Determination of final products follow the principle that all products that are included in the calculation of grow industrial output value are the final products of the enterprise which have been accepted through quality check and require no further processing. If an enterprise has intermediate (semi-finished) products to sell, these intermediate products are considered as the final products of the enterprise.

Gross industrial output value is calculated following the principle of factory approach, i. e. industrial enterprise is used as the basic accounting unit in calculating the gross industrial output value. By this approach, value of the same product is not to be double counted, and the output value of different workshops (branch factories) should not be added. However, this approach does not exclude the possibility of double counting between enterprises.

(3) Content and calculation method: The old definition of gross industrial output value was modified duringthe national industrial census in 1995. The revised (new) definition of gross industrial output value consists of 3 components: value of the finished products during the reference period, income from external processing, and value of change in semi-finished products at the end and at the beginning of the reference period.

Value of the finished products during the reference period: refers to the value of all finished (semi-finished) industrial products that are produced during the reference period without the need for further processing, checked for acceptance, packed and put into the warehouse of the enterprise, including the value of own-produced equipment and the value of products provided to the projects under construction of the enterprise, and to other non-industrial or welfare units. Value of finished products during the reference period is calculated by the quantity of products produced using own materials multiplied by the average unit prices at which products are sold (excluding value-added tax). Own-produced equipment and products produced for own use are value at cost prices as in the case of enterprise accounting. Value of finished products does not include the value of finished products (semi-finished products) that are produced using the materials from the clients who make the orders.

Income from external processing: refers to income from contracted external processing of industrial products (including processing of industrial products using materials from the clients), and the income from industrial repairing work provided to other units. Income from external processing is calculated using information from the item "products sales income" in the enterprise accounting at the prices excluding value-added tax.

For income from services such as processing, repairing and installation of equipment provided to non-industrial units within the enterprise, if the accounting work of the enterprise is good enough to separate it from other records, and the share of such services is significant, it should also be included in the income from external processing.

Value of change in semi-finished products at the end and at the beginning of the reference period: refers to the value of change in semi-finished products at the end and at the beginning of the reference period, which generally can be obtained from accounting records of enterprises. If the enterprise accounting excludes the cost of semi-finished products, then it should not be included in the gross industrial output value, and vice versa.

(4) Changes in the coverage and method of calculation of gross industrial output value: Prior to 1984, the value of rural industry run by villages was classified into agriculture instead of industry. Since 1984, it has been included in the gross industrial output value.

Method of calculation for the gross industrial output value was modified in the industrial census in 1995. The difference in the new method as compared with the old one is outlined below:

Principle in using full value vs. processing fee: The new method stipulates that all products produced using own materials are to be calculated with full value in reporting the gross industrial output value irrespective of sophistication of production, and for external processing, it allows calculation using processing fee. In the old method, however, the use of full value or processing fee was determined by the degree of sophistication of production in different branches of industries.

Principle in determining the value of change in semi-finished products: The new method requires that value of the change in semi-finished products should be included in the gross industrial output value if it is included in the accounting record of the enterprise, otherwise it should not be included. By the old method, it is determined by the type of enterprises in terms of production cycle. If the production cycle is over 6 months, the value of change in semi-finished products is included in the gross industrial output value, otherwise it is excluded.

Difference in prices: The new method uses prices excluding value-added tax in the calculation of gross industrial output value, while the old method used prices including value-added tax.

Sales Output Value of Industry

refers to total sales value of products produced by industrial enterprises during a given period, including sales of finished goods, value of semi-products, value of industrial services provided to other units, value of products provided for capital construction sector, welfare sector and value of industrial services provided and self produced equipment within enterprises. Sales of finished goods and-semi-products in current period are taken into account regardless of their production period.

The coverage, pricing, and calculation method for sales output value of industry are the same as for gross output value of industry except that the former is based on sales of products and the latter is based on the output of products.

Export Delivery Value of Industry

refers to the product value which industrial enterprises deliver to Foreign Trade Department, or value of products which are exported directly from producers (including the sales to Hong Kong, Macao and Taiwan) ; the product value, (at foreign exchange rate,) of domestic batch sale or transit batch export; full price or processing fee of the production with design, materials, assembling parts supplied by foreign businessmen and compensation trade.

Large, Medium and Small Enterprises

According to the Notice of the Ministry of Industry and Information Technology, National Bureau of Statistics, National Development and Reform Commission and the Ministry of Finance on printing and distributing the classification standard for middle and small enterprises (<2011> No. 300), we will divide our national enterprises into four kinds that are large, middle, small and mini in accordance with the indicators or substitute indicators such as employed persons, operation income and total assets. The former method for classification will be discarded. The classification standard for industrial enterprises are shown as followed.

Indicators	Unit	Large	Middle	Small	Mini
Employed Persons(X)	Persons	$X \geq 1000$	$300 \leq X < 1000$	$20 \leq X < 300$	$X < 20$
Main Operation Income(Y)	10 000 yuan	$Y \geq 40000$	$2000 \leq Y < 40000$	$300 \leq Y < 2000$	$Y < 300$

Note: Large, middle and small enterprises must meet all of the lowest limit of the listed indicators, or they will be classified into the lower kind, respectively. Mini enterprises can meet only one of the listed indicators.

Industrial Enterprises with Independent Accounting

Systems and Industrial Production Units with Non-Independent Accounting Systems.

Depending on whether they have independent administration and accounting, industrial enterprises can be divided into industrial enterprises with independent accounting system and industrial production units with non-independent accounting system. An industrial enterprise with independent accounting system shall operate simultaneously under the following three conditions: (1) having an independent organization in terms of administration; (2) economically having independent accounting, taking care of its own profits and losses, and filing independent balance sheets; and (3) enjoying the right to sign contracts with other units and to open independent bank accounts. An industrial enterprise with independent accounting system, no matter under a unitary management or cooperative operation, shall be counted as single grassroots unit in statistics and its branch factories and workshops shall not be calculated separately.

An industrial production unit with non-independent accounting system is an industrial production unit which does not operate simultaneously under the above mentioned three conditions of industrial enterprises with independent accounting systems and is attached to an enterprise, institution, government department, organization, school, scientific research institution, or army unit. An industrial production with non-independent accounting system unit can be included into the industrial statistics only when it operates simultaneously under the following three conditions: (1) having fixed production sites and production equipment; (2) having more than 10 permanent workers and apprentices; and (3) operating all year round if it's a normal production unit or operating more than three months a year if it's a seasonal production unit.

Aggregate Assets

Total Assets refer to all economic resources, in monetary terms, that is owned or controlled by enterprises, including properties, creditors equity and other economic rights of all forms. Classified by the degree of equitability, total assets include circulating assets, long-term investment, fixed assets, intangible assets and deferred assets, and other assets. Data on this indicator can be obtained by the year-end figures of total assets in the Assets and Liability Table of accounting records of enterprises.

Total of Working Capitals

Total of Working Capitals refer to capitals which can be cashed in or spent or consumed in an operating cycle of one year or over one year, including cash, all kinds of deposits, short term investment, receivable and payable payment for goods or deposits.

Average Value of Working Capitals

Average Value of Working Capitals refers to the average value of all working capitals of the enterprise during the reference period.

Annual Average of Net Value of Fixed Assets

refer to average of the net value of fixed assets during the reference period, calculated with the following formula:

Annual Average of Net Value of Fixed Assets = sum of net value of fixed assets at the beginning and at the end of each month from January to December / 24.

Information on this indicator can be obtained from the beginning and ending figures of the original value of fixed assets and cumulative depreciation from the Assets and Liability Table of enterprises.

Net value of fixed assets refers to the original value of fixed assets minus depreciation over the years, i. e. :

Net value of fixed assets = original value of fixed assets-cumulative depreciation

Aggregate Liabilities

Aggregate liabilities refer to the total debts of an enterprise which can be calculated in monetary term and will be repaid in the forms of assets or service. Usually, the debts are divided into liquid liability and long-term debt according to the length of the payback period. The liquid liability is the debt that an enterprise will pay back during an operation cycle which is either shorter or longer than a year. The long-term debt refers to a debt whose payback period is longer than a year or which will be repaid during an operation cycle that is longer than a year.

Creditors' Equity

Creditors' Equity refers to investors ownership of net assets of the enterprise, which is equal to the total assets of the enterprise minus its total liabilities, including the primary input actually received at the enterprise from investors, capital accumulation fund, surplus accumulation fund and undistributed profit. When the total of creditors' equity is less than zero, that indicates the liability of the enterprise is larger that its assets.

Total Profits

Total Profits refer to the final achievements of production and operation of the enterprises, represented by the total profits after deducting losses (loss is expressed by the negative figure). It is the sum of profits from operation, income from subsidies, investment earnings, net income from activities other than operation, and adjustment of profits and losses of previous years.

Ratio of Profits, Taxes and Interests to Average Assets

Ratio of Profits, Taxes and Interests to Average Assets reflects the profit-making capability of all assets of the enterprise and is a key indicator manifesting the performance and management and evaluating the profit-making potential of the enterprise. It is calculated as follows:

Ratio of Profits, Taxes and Interests to Average Assets (%) = [(total profits + total taxes + interest payment) / average assets] ×100%

In the above formula, total taxes is the sum of tax and extra charges on the sales of products and value-added tax payable; and average assets is the arithmetic mean of the sum of beginning assets and ending assets.

第七篇

CHAPTER 7

建筑业

CONSTRUCTION

表7-1　主要年份建筑业企业主要指标

指　标	Indicators	单　位　Unit	1995
施工企业单位数	Number of Construction Enterprises	个 unit	243
年末从业人员数	Employed Persons (Year End)	人 person	125 627
全年从业人员平均数	Annual Average Employed Persons	人 person	140 994
建筑业总产值	Gross Output Value of Construction	万元 10 000yuan	1 045 601
#建筑工程	Construction Projects	万元 10 000 yuan	905 848
安装工程	Installation Projects	万元 10 000 yuan	110 763
竣工产值	Output Value of Construction Projects Completed	万元 10 000 yuan	446 202
房屋建筑面积	Floor Space of Buildings		
施工面积	Floor Space Under Construction	万平方米 10 000sq · m	1 042.05
#本年新开工	New Start in Current Year	万平方米 10 000sq · m	285.02
竣工面积	Floor Space Completed	万平方米 10 000sq · m	290.25
#住　宅	Housing	万平方米 10 000sq · m	150.63
全员劳动生产率	Overall Labor Productivity	元/人 yuan/person	74 159
房屋建筑面积竣工率	Ratio of Floor Space Completed over That under Construction	%	27.9
平均每个职工竣工房屋面积	Floor Space Completed Per Staff Member	平方米/人 sq. m/person	20.59

注：建筑业总产值为建筑业企业自行完成的施工产值。
Note：Gross output value of construction refers to the output value of construction completed by construction enterprises themselves.

Major Indicators of Construction Industry in Main Years

2000	2005	2010	2011	2012	2013	2014
367	398	699	720	651	593	586
93 753	159 099	253 822	259 056	268 981	181 421	172 806
116 722	208 807	361 140	424 530	358 747	277 915	315 666
935 731	3 353 790	9 801 257	11 353 474	12 231 885	12 936 456	12 923 297
886 356	2 599 981	8 001 415	9 746 424	10 415 352	11 366 000	11 526 916
115 164	643 346	1 526 037	1 440 514	1 602 576	1 383 923	1 213 571
786 808	2 322 347	6 858 981	5 650 019	6 128 065	7 805 169	7 012 587
1 149.25	3 009.91	6 886.55	8 451.28	9 976.65	11 285.84	12 627.52
426.18	1 291.18	2 501.17	2 675.90	3 040.28	3 578.08	3 322.24
520.61	903.45	1 641.86	1 520.70	1 619.20	1 824.35	1 947.10
350.65	523.94	695.52	677.63	843.41	878.72	999.28
80 167	160 617	271 398	267 436	340 961	465 482	409 398
45.3	30.0	23.8	18.0	16.2	16.2	15.4
44.60	43.27	45.46	35.82	45.13	65.64	61.68

表7-2 建筑业企业主要指标
(2014)

指 标 Indicators		企业单位数(个) Number of Enterprises (unit)	年末从业人员数(人) Employed Persons at Year-end (person)	年从业人员平均数(人) Annual Average Employed Persons (person)	建筑业总产值(万元) Gross Output Value of Construction (10 000 yuan)	竣工产值(万元) Output Value of Completed Construction Projects (10 000 yuan)
合 计	**Total**	**586**	**172 806**	**315 666**	**12 923 297**	**7 012 587**
按登记注册类型分	**By Type of Registration**					
内 资	Domestic Investment	555	167 109	300 024	12 184 167	6 517 290
国 有	State-owned	1	189	146	2 479	2 479
集 体	Collective-owned	6	479	1 257	37 760	27 062
股份合作	Share-holding	1	33	45	1 151	1 151
联 营	Jointly Operated	2	180	364	5 558	7 583
国有独资公司	Wholly state-owned Companies	15	24 252	30 551	1 472 175	1 277 005
有限责任公司	Companies with Limited Liabilities	86	42 996	142 684	6 850 100	3 427 023
股份有限公司	Companies Limited by Shares	6	1 935	6 428	226 618	40 395
私 营	Private	438	97 045	118 549	3 588 326	1 734 592
港澳台商投资	HK/Macao/Taiwan Invested	12	2 854	3 463	219 014	12 041
外商投资	Foreigner Invested	19	2 933	12 179	520 116	483 256
按行业分	**By Sector**					
房屋建筑业	Housing Construction	169	101 657	209 130	8 449 383	4 969 842
土木工程建筑业	Civil Engineering Construction	157	33 426	56 109	2 355 312	1 053 215
建筑安装业	Installation	121	12 405	18 758	840 428	432 683
建筑装饰和其他建筑业	Other Constructions	139	25 318	31 669	1 278 174	556 847
按资质标准分	**By Qualification Standard**					
#特 级	Special Grade	2	16 101	100 306	5 174 943	2 819 940
一 级	Grade Ⅰ	73	68 903	100 738	4 297 769	2 164 580
二 级	Grade Ⅱ	186	54 718	698 742	2 146 964	1 291 692
三 级	Grade Ⅲ	318	32 154	40 343	1 133 708	703 107

注：1. 建筑业总产值为建筑业企业自行完成的施工产值;建筑业资质等级为新标准资质。
2. 本表数据不包括外省市在沪建筑业企业。

Note: 1. Gross Output Value of Construction refers to the output value of construction completed by construction enterprises themselves. Qualification of construction industry refers to the qualification under new standards.
2. The numbers in this form does not include the construction enterprises that operate in Shanghai, but are registered in other provinces.

Major Indicators of Construction Enterprises

房屋建筑施工面积（万平方米） Floor Space Under Construction (10 000 sq・m)	#本年新开工 New Start in Current Year	房屋竣工面积（万平方米） Floor Space Completed (10 000 sq・m)	#住宅 Residential Housing	全员劳动生产率（元/人） Overall Labor Productivity (yuan/person)	平均每个职工竣工房屋面积（平方米/人） Floor Space Completed Per Staff Member (sq・m/person)	房屋建筑面积竣工率（%） Ratio of Floor Space Completed (%)
12 627.52	**3 322.24**	**1 947.10**	**999.28**	**409 398**	**61.68**	**15.4**
12 511.97	3 245.62	1 895.64	999.28	406 106	63.18	15.2
3.66	2.12	2.56	0.82	169 795	175.34	69.9
9.06	1.72	1.72		300 398	13.68	19.0
				255 778		
14.70	14.70			152 692		
267.86	58.53	99.19	88.70	481 875	32.47	37.0
10 599.94	2 460.77	1 394.34	780.19	480 089	97.72	13.2
52.29				352 548		
1 564.46	707.78	397.83	129.57	302 687	33.56	25.4
				632 440		
115.55	76.62	51.46		427 060	42.25	44.5
12 469.84	3 261.43	1 890.80	992.54	404 025	90.41	15.2
96.56	48.52	35.54	6.74	419 774	6.33	36.8
54.37	10.40	15.63		448 037	8.33	28.7
6.75	1.89	5.13		403 604	1.62	76.0
10 246.57	2 329.46	1 249.86	709.51	515 916	124.60	12.2
1 234.28	511.15	322.01	195.90	426 628	31.97	26.1
885.60	315.20	274.27	66.94	30 726	3.93	31.0
261.06	166.43	100.96	26.93	281 017	25.03	38.7

表 7－3　建筑业财务报表
（2014）

单位：万元

指　标	Indicators	合　计 Total	内　资 Domestic Investment
企业单位数（个）	**Number of Enterprises（unit）**	**586**	**555**
年末资产负债	**Balance Sheet at Year-end**		
资产总计	Total Assets	17 225 996	15 124 427
#流动资产	Floating Assets	13 104 480	11 173 342
固定资产	Fixed Assets	1 228 735	1 081 563
固定资产原价	Initial Value of Fixed Assets	1 917 245	1 736 024
累计折旧	Accumulated Depreciation	789 296	755 248
#本年折旧	Depreciation This Year	101 707	94 412
负债总计	Total Liabilities	12 710 318	10 952 482
流动负债	Current Liabilities	12 003 430	10 279 716
非流动负债	Non-current Liabilities	706 888	672 766
所有者权益总计	Total Rights and Interests of Owners	4 515 678	4 171 945
损益及分配	**Profit and Loss and Their Distribution**		
主营业务收入	Income of Main Operations	15 733 671	14 337 592
主营业务成本	Cost of Main Operations	14 183 213	12 962 370
主营业务税金及附加	Taxes and Additional Taxes of Main Operations	431 180	415 096
管理费用	Administrative Expenses	529 025	437 936
#税　金	Taxes	8 947	8 589
财务费用	Financial Expenses	89 857	87 556
营业利润	Operation Profits	389 937	328 249
利润总额	Total Profits	428 949	367 121

注：以上财务数据不包括外省市在沪建筑业企业。
Note：The above-mentioned financial data exclude construction enterprises from other provinces and cities that enter the construction market in Shanghai.

Financial Statements of Construction Industry

(10 000yuan)

国 有 State-owned	集 体 Collective-owned	股份合作 Share-holding	联 营 Jointly-operated	国有独资公司 Wholly state-owned company	责任有限公司 Companies with Limited Liability	股份有限公司 Companies Limited by Shares	私 营 Private	港澳台商投资 Hong kong/ Macao/ Taiwan Investment	外商投资 FIE
1	6	1	2	15	86	6	438	12	19
7 014	36 219	930	9 618	2 197 025	7 839 061	1 113 840	3 920 720	959 777	1 141 792
7 011	33 710	925	8 433	1 452 076	5 849 799	387 464	3 433 924	805 224	1 125 914
3	1 589	5	1 185	476 078	312 037	45 220	245 446	140 518	6 654
351	5 595	107	1 448	781 076	449 784	59 371	438 292	162 843	18 378
348	4 196	102	266	322 379	195 595	20 450	211 912	22 325	11 723
1	248	…	3	37 767	29 053	2 469	24 871	5 953	1 342
4 793	22 779	196	3 969	1 447 272	6 367 218	613 269	2 492 986	814 232	943 604
4 793	22 523	196	3 969	1 313 585	6 028 490	513 777	2 392 383	781 282	942 432
	256			133 687	338 728	99 492	100 603	32 950	1 172
2 221	13 440	734	5 649	749 753	1 471 843	500 571	1 427 734	145 545	198 188
826	40 667	1 151	15 499	1 691 496	8 679 515	281 734	3 626 704	773 847	622 232
499	36 139	1 029	14 617	1 309 406	8 089 900	239 310	3 271 470	700 703	520 140
26	1 151	32	383	44 794	254 412	7 409	106 889	6 074	10 010
13	3 991	67	235	59 432	198 118	18 807	157 273	45 245	45 844
…	45	10	4	369	4 138	70	3 953	217	141
…	-30	-5	-6	7 765	40 867	15 966	22 999	4 212	-1 911
288	-51	28	224	97 315	131 154	49 700	49 591	15 600	46 088
288	-2	41	400	104 221	148 925	51 203	62 045	16 403	45 425

主要统计指标解释

建筑业总产值

建筑业总产值是以货币形式表现的建筑业企业在一定时期内生产的建筑业产品和提供的服务的总和。建筑业总产值包括：

(1)建筑工程产值：指列入建筑工程预算内的各种工程价值。

(2)安装工程产值：指设备安装工程价值,不包括被安装设备本身价值。

(3)其他产值:建筑业总产值中除建筑工程、安装工程以外的产值。包括房屋构筑物修理产值、非标准设备制造产值、总包企业向分包企业收取的管理费以及不能明确划分的施工活动所完成的产值。

a. 房屋构筑物修理产值:指房屋和构筑物修理所完成的产值,但不包括被修理房屋、构筑物本身价值和生产设备的修理产值。

b. 非标准设备制造产值:指加工制造没有定型的非标准生产设备的加工费和原材料价值(如化工厂、炼油厂用的各种罐、槽,矿井生产统一使用的各种漏斗、三角槽、阀门等)以及附属加工厂为本企业承建工程制作的非标准设备的价值。

房屋建筑施工面积

房屋建筑施工面积指在报告期内施过工的全部房屋建筑面积,包括本期新开工的房屋面积、上期施工跨入本期继续施工的房屋面积、上期停缓建在本期恢复施工的房屋面积、本期竣工的房屋面积及本期施工后又停缓建的房屋面积。

房屋建筑竣工面积

房屋建筑竣工面积 指在报告期内房屋建筑按照设计要求全部完工,达到了使用条件,经验收鉴定合格的房屋建筑面积。

房屋建筑面积竣工率

指一定时期内房屋竣工面积占同期房屋施工面积的比率。该指标从房屋建筑施工速度的角度反映投资效果的指标。

EXPLANATORY NOTES TO MAJOR STATISTICAL INDICATORS

Gross Output Value of Construction

Gross Output Value of Construction refers to total of construction products and services, expressed in money terms, produced or rendered by (completed by) construction enterprises during a given period of time. It includes:

(1) Output value of construction projects, that is the value of projects covered by the project budgets;

(2) Output value of installation projects, that is the value of the installation of equipment, (excluding the value of the equipment to be installed);

(3) Output value of other projects refers to other output value of gross output value of construction industry besides construction and installation projects. It includes the output value of building repairing, nonstandard equipment manufacturing, the management fees going from subcontractor to original contractor and other construction output value which can not be measure off definitely.

a. Output value of repair of buildings and structures, that is the value created through the repairs of buildings or structures, but does not include the value of buildings or structures being repaired and the value of the repair of production equipment;

b. Output value of manufactured non – standard equipment that is the value of non – standard production equipment (including raw materials and manufacturing cost) made for the construction project, irrespective of whether the equipment is manufactured on the construction site or by subsidiary workshops.

Floor Space of Buildings under Construction

Floor Space of Buildings under Construction refers to floor space of buildings under construction during the reference period, including newly started buildings, buildings started earlier and continued during the reference period, and buildings suspended earlier but restarted during the reference period, buildings completed during the reference period, and buildings under construction and then suspended during the reference period.

Floor Space of Buildings Completed

Floor Space of Buildings Completed refers to the floor space of buildings that are completed in the reference period in accordance with the requirements of the design, up to the standard for putting them into use, and have been checked and accepted by concerned departments as qualified ones.

Completion Rate of Floor Space of Buildings

Completion Rate of Floor Space of Buildings refers to the ratio of the floor space of buildings completed in certain period of time to the floor space of buildings under construction in the same period. This indicator reflects the investment result from the perspective of the speed of construction.

第八篇

CHAPTER 8

金融业及要素市场

FINANCIAL INDUSTRY
AND FACTOR MARKETS

表8-1　各类金融机构数
Statistics of all Kinds of Financial Institutions

单位:个　　　　(unit)

指　标	Indicators	2010	2013	2014
总　计	**Total**	**649**	**794**	**844**
银行类机构合计	**Subtotal of Banks**	**211**	**233**	**240**
中资银行	Chinese Banks	29	36	48
外资银行法人行	Foreign Banks and Corporate Banks	18	18	18
外资银行分行	Branches of Foreign Banks	57	62	55
外资银行代表处	Representative Offices of Foreign Banks	60	68	67
银行营运中心及业务分部	Bank Operation Centers and Sectors	23	24	24
非银行金融机构	Non-banking Financial Institutions	24	25	28
证券类机构合计	**Subtotal of Securities Institutions**	**261**	**325**	**358**
中资证券(包括中介机构)	Chinese Securities Institutions (including intermediary organs)	68	86	94
外资证券(包括代表处)	Foreign Securities Institutions (including representative offices)	53	55	55
基金公司(包括第三方销售)	Fund Companies (including third-party sales agency)	46	66	87
期货公司	Futures Companies	81	99	103
非证券金融机构	Non-securities Financial Institutions	13	19	19
保险机构合计	**Subtotal of Insurance Companies**	**177**	**236**	**246**
中资保险(集团)	Chinese Insurance Companies (Groups)	46	54	57
外资保险	Foreign Insurance Companies	27	32	34
外资保险代表处	Representative Offices of Foreign Insurance Companies	23	31	31
保险中介	Agencies of Insurance Companies	76	107	109
保险营运中心	Insurance Operation Centers	5	12	15

表8-2 主要年份中资银行人民币存贷款年末余额
Chinese Banks' Year-end RMB Balance of Deposits and Loans in Main Years

单位:亿元 (100 million yuan)

指 标	Indicators	1990	2000	2005	2010	2013	2014
存款余额合计	**Total Deposit Balance**	**36.48**	**1 046.81**	**2 915.41**	**8 848.87**	**11 167.20**	**12 781.72**
# 企业存款	Enterprise Deposits	9.67	644.79	1 530.99	5 239.12	5 967.39	7 304.44
居民储蓄存款	Resident Savings Deposits	20.62	360.99	1 105.96	2 943.49	4 254.05	4 381.03
其他存款	Others	1.66	10.61	166.38	427.38	578.26	661.24
贷款余额合计	**Total Loan Balance**	**28.19**	**891.59**	**2 674.76**	**6 434.95**	**8 174.52**	**8 857.93**
# 企业贷款	Enterprise Loans			2 014.23	5 343.68	6 529.71	6 955.50
# 短期贷款	Short Term Loans			716.01	1 504.28	1 977.19	2 012.17
中长期贷款	Medium and Long Term Loans			1 298.22	3 839.40	4 552.52	4 943.33
票据融资	Securities Financing			193.73	82.59	216.22	373.61
个人贷款	Individual Loans			464.40	1 007.62	1 413.30	1 519.35
# 住房按揭贷款	Housing Mortgage Loans			431.28	888.58	1 098.43	1 198.72
汽车消费贷款	Car Loans			4.08	14.76	41.74	33.60

表8-3　外资银行主要指标
(2014)

指　标　Indicators		单位数(个) Enterprises (unit)	从业人数(人) Employed Persons (person)	普通贷款(亿美元) Ordinary Loans (USD 100 million)
总　计	**Total**	**68**	**19 439**	**247.55**
按各大洲分	**By Continent**			
亚洲地区	Asia	36	14 011	161.17
欧洲地区	Europe	21	3 190	38.41
美洲地区	America	6	1 875	29.69
其他地区	Others	5	363	18.28
按进驻各大厦分	**By Mansion Where Enterprises Handle Their Businesses**			
环球金融中心大厦	Shanghai World Financial Center	10	2 386	43.79
汇亚大厦	Azia Center	8	2 037	43.46
金茂大厦	Jinmao Building	6	430	16.55
恒生银行大厦	Hangseng Bank Tower	4	432	17.49
花旗大厦	Citigroup Mansion	3	2 196	11.54
船舶大厦	Marine Tower	3	124	5.64
东亚银行大厦	Global Financial Tower	3	1 405	5.72
国金中心	Shanghai International Financial Center	8	3 354	41.77
其他大厦	Others	23	7 075	61.59
按普通贷款分	**By Regular Loans**			
7 亿美元以上	> USD 700 million	11	7 631	164.81
5 ~ 7 亿美元	USD 500 ~ 700 million	2	257	11.75
3 ~ 5 亿美元	USD 300 ~ 500 million	7	2 143	31.10
1 ~ 3 亿美元	USD 100 ~ 300 million	16	1 051	31.06
1 亿美元以下	< USD 100 million	32	8 357	8.83
按普通存款分	**By Regular Deposit**			
10 亿美元以上	> USD 1 0000 million	6	5 715	102.34
3 ~ 10 亿美元	USD 300 ~ 1 0000 million	6	2 972	51.80
1 ~ 3 亿美元	USD 100 ~ 300 million	9	1 766	29.65
1 千万 ~ 1 亿美元	USD 10 ~ 100 million	17	984	38.66
1 千万美元以下	< USD 10 million	30	8 002	25.10
按资产总额分	**By Total Assets**			
10 亿美元以上	> USD 1 0000 million	24	14 970	189.91
5 ~ 10 亿美元	USD 500 ~ 1 0000 million	15	2 910	35.31
3 ~ 5 亿美元	USD 300 ~ 500 million	9	469	9.67
1 ~ 3 亿美元	USD 100 ~ 300 million	16	813	11.22
1 亿美元以下	< USD 100 million	4	277	1.44
按税金分	**By Tax**			
2000 万元以上	≥20 million yuan	23	13 921	197.92
500 ~ 2000 万元	5 ~ 20 million yuan	26	3 567	40.26
100 ~ 500 万元	1 ~ 5 million yuan	13	475	9.08
100 万元以下	< 1 million yuan	6	1 476	0.29

Major Indicators of Foreign Banks

普通存款（亿美元）Ordinary Deposits (USD 100 million)	人民币贷款（亿元）RMB Loans (100 million yuan)	人民币存款（亿元）RMB Deposits (100 million yuan)	资产总额（亿美元）Total Assets (USD 100 million)	利润总额（亿元）Operation Profit (100 million yuan)	拆放同业（亿元）Banker Call Loans (100 million yuan)
169.93	**2 311.73**	**4 502.57**	**13 410.53**	**84.58**	**963.76**
109.71	1 427.41	2 795.10	8 149.13	13.35	494.54
31.09	565.27	993.09	1 691.84	45.37	311.54
22.83	274.33	601.85	167.35	18.06	126.58
6.30	44.72	112.53	3 402.21	7.80	31.10
36.69	301.39	547.52	6 886.63	29.77	169.02
26.92	221.96	518.04	144.68	8.72	186.36
2.33	84.05	71.70	71.09	5.55	61.87
6.38	121.52	245.49	38.63	5.46	97.21
18.14	232.39	432.26	257.28	4.99	27.36
4.40	34.02	18.60	16.53	1.86	3.50
2.35	172.40	225.61	45.72	2.80	36.26
32.90	422.58	1 053.57	391.97	29.67	114.90
39.82	721.42	1 389.78	5 558.00	-4.24	267.28
125.12	1 413.39	3 059.24	11 102.61	69.47	475.41
2.19	77.96	97.67	14.03	4.27	4.68
20.87	408.11	841.58	238.54	25.35	175.12
10.06	205.17	281.71	1 552.26	22.34	123.05
11.69	207.10	222.37	503.09	-36.85	185.50
105.11	1 020.19	2 384.33	5 689.25	46.37	265.44
38.28	571.30	1 125.54	3 642.45	44.15	289.90
18.20	321.81	599.09	3 317.38	20.87	97.98
7.88	241.60	315.28	252.91	15.77	176.09
0.46	156.83	78.33	508.54	-42.58	134.35
151.10	1 836.68	3 798.21	13 233.93	75.47	752.33
7.97	307.40	475.94	106.07	1.32	143.43
5.28	62.81	87.73	34.57	7.08	29.38
4.72	79.41	102.87	33.57	-0.03	24.62
0.86	25.43	37.82	2.39	0.74	14.00
155.64	2 034.92	4 168.28	13 005.29	104.79	794.96
8.00	237.89	262.52	338.47	-7.42	128.94
1.84	32.51	43.20	32.16	-1.06	31.27
4.45	6.41	28.57	34.61	-11.73	8.59

表8-4 外资银行存贷款年末余额
Foreign Banks' Year-end Balance of Deposits and Loans

指 标	Indicators	单 位 Unit	2013	2014
外汇存贷款	**Deposits and Loans of Foreign Exchange**			
客户存款	Deposits of Customers	亿美元 USD 100 million	176.66	169.93
#单 位	Corporations	亿美元 USD 100 million	143.24	144.68
同业存款	Inter-bank Deposits	亿美元 USD 100 million	41.36	42.16
存放同业	Due from Banks	亿美元 USD 100 million	108.31	137.06
有价证券及投资	Securities Assets and Investments	亿美元 USD 100 million	1.54	1.37
贷 款	Total Loans	亿美元 USD 100 million	249.88	247.55
#短 期	Short-term Loans	亿美元 USD 100 million	114.78	100.31
#贸易融资	Trade Financing	亿美元 USD 100 million	21.56	18.10
拆放同业	Deposits to Other Banks	亿美元 USD 100 million	94.27	201.09
人民币存贷款	**RMB Deposits and Loans**			
客户存款	Deposits of Customers	亿元 100 million yuan	4 552.98	4 502.57
同业存款	Inter-bank Deposits	亿元 100 million yuan	2 101.18	2 401.98
同业拆借	Inter-bank Lending	亿元 100 million yuan	201.66	322.51
贷 款	Total Loans	亿元 100 million yuan	2 325.52	2 311.73
证券资产	Securities Assets	亿元 100 million yuan	800.21	965.09
拆放同业	Deposits to Other Banks	亿元 100 million yuan	1 109.84	963.76

表8-5 历年中资保险机构原保险保费收入和赔款支出
Original Premium Income and Indemnity Expenditure of Chinese Insurance Business (1992~2014)

单位:亿元 (100 million yuan)

年份 Year	原保险保费收入 Original Premium Income	财产险 Property Insurance	人身险 Life Insurance	原保险赔款支出 Former Indemnity Expenditure	财产险 Property Insurance	人身险 Life Insurance	赔款率(%) Rate of Indemnity(%)	财产险 Property Insurance	人身险 Life Insurance
1992	1.13	0.75	0.38	0.69	0.20	0.49	61.1	26.7	128.9
1993	2.51	1.42	1.09	0.30	0.06	0.24	12.0	4.2	25.9
1994	5.37	3.30	2.07	1.77	1.63	0.14	33.0	49.4	6.8
1995	13.63	10.42	3.21	3.12	2.97	0.15	22.9	28.5	4.7
1996	22.02	7.70	14.32	3.83	3.41	0.42	17.4	44.3	2.9
1997	38.34	9.19	29.15	4.91	4.71	0.20	12.8	51.3	0.7
1998	44.09	9.93	34.16	6.28	4.48	1.80	14.2	45.1	5.3
1999	51.42	10.84	40.58	7.76	5.71	2.05	15.1	52.7	5.1
2000	63.31	13.40	49.91	7.06	3.87	3.19	11.2	28.9	6.4
2001	99.36	13.73	85.63	9.08	4.92	4.16	9.1	35.8	4.9
2002	118.31	16.55	101.76	10.12	7.17	2.95	8.6	43.3	2.9
2003	129.83	21.88	107.95	20.73	9.04	11.69	16.0	41.3	10.8
2004	118.09	29.52	88.57	19.59	11.62	7.97	16.6	39.4	9.0
2005	140.63	40.03	100.60	23.16	20.09	3.07	16.5	50.2	3.1
2006	171.47	45.51	125.96	26.17	22.16	4.01	15.3	48.7	3.2
2007	182.33	52.47	129.86	29.29	24.54	4.75	16.1	46.8	3.7
2008	230.84	55.25	175.59	37.01	30.99	6.02	16.0	56.1	3.4
2009	221.20	68.75	152.45	43.54	36.26	7.28	19.7	52.7	4.8
2010	329.82	100.41	229.41	45.65	39.93	5.72	13.8	39.8	2.5
2011	295.18	120.53	174.65	61.74	56.19	5.52	20.9	46.6	3.2
2012	319.56	130.38	189.18	80.74	72.11	8.63	25.3	55.3	4.6
2013	371.92	204.10	167.82	126.71	117.86	8.85	34.1	57.7	5.3
2014	426.93	233.59	193.34	139.10	125.90	13.20	32.6	53.9	6.8

表8-6　中资保险机构主要险种的原保险保费收入和赔款支出
Original Premium Income and Indemnity Expenditure of Major Types of Chinese Funded Insurance Business
(2014)

单位:亿元　(100 million yuan)

指　标	Indicators	原保险保费收入 Original Premium Income	原保险赔款支出 Original Indemnity Expenditure	赔款率(%) Rate of Indemnity(%)
总　计	**Total**	**426.93**	**139.10**	**32.6**
财产险小计	Subtotal of Property Insurance	233.59	125.90	53.9
#企业财产险	Enterprise Property Insurance	15.27	7.16	46.9
机动车辆险	Motor Vehicle Insurance	191.06	106.23	55.6
货运险	Cargo Transportation Insurance	9.22	3.96	43.0
责任保险	Liability Insurance	10.64	3.37	31.7
人身险小计	Subtotal of Life Insurance	193.34	13.20	6.8

表8-7　外资保险机构主要险种的原保险保费收入和赔款支出
Original Premium Income and Indemnity Expenditure of Major Types of Foreign Funded Insurance Business
(2014)

单位:亿元　(100 million yuan)

指　标	Indicators	原保险保费收入 Original Premium Income	原保险赔款支出 Original Indemnity Expenditure	赔款率(%) Rate of Indemnity(%)
总　计	**Total**	**216.91**	**11.31**	**5.2**
财产保险小计	Subtotal of Property Insurance	19.11	6.24	32.7
#企业财产险	Enterprise Property Insurance	4.36	1.38	31.7
货运险	Cargo Transportation Insurance	3.46	1.30	37.6
家财险	Household Property Insurance	0.13	0.04	30.8
责任保险	Liability Insurance	4.86	1.27	26.1
人身险小计	Subtotal of Life Insurance	197.80	5.07	2.6

表8-8 上海证券交易所市场交易主要指标
Statistics of Shanghai Stock Exchange

指 标	Indicators	单 位 Unit	2014
交易天数	**Trading Days**	**天 day**	**245**
上市证券数	**Number of Securities Traded**	**个 unit**	**3 758**
股 票	Stocks	个 unit	1 039
A 股	A Share	个 unit	986
B 股	B Share	个 unit	53
优先股	Preferred Stocks	个 unit	5
债 券	Bonds	个 unit	2 646
政府债	Government Bonds	个 unit	267
公司债	Corporate Bonds	个 unit	2 336
回 购	Repurchase	个 unit	43
基 金	Funds	个 unit	68
股票市价总值	**Total Value of Stock Price**	**亿元 100 million yuan**	**243 974.02**
成交金额	**Turnover Value**	**亿元 100 million yuan**	**1 281 497.98**
股 票	Stocks	亿元 100 million yuan	377 162.12
A 股	A Share	亿元 100 million yuan	375 149.95
B 股	B Share	亿元 100 million yuan	484.45
股票回购	Repurchase	亿元 100 million yuan	1 527.72
优先股	Preferred Stocks	亿元 100 million yuan	4.27
债 券	Bonds	亿元 100 million yuan	866 848.59
政府债	Government Bonds	亿元 100 million yuan	1 247.47
公司债	Corporate Bonds	亿元 100 million yuan	24 198.95
债券回购	Repurchase	亿元 100 million yuan	841 402.17
基 金	Funds	亿元 100 million yuan	37 479.25
其 他	Others	亿元 100 million yuan	3.75
成交数量	**Volume Turnover**	**亿手 100 million yuan**	**48 354.15**
股 票	Stocks	亿手 100 million yuan	42 938.82
A 股	A Share	亿手 100 million yuan	42 471.35
B 股	B Share	亿手 100 million contracts	96.01
股票回购	Repurchase	亿手 100 million contracts	371.46
优先股	Preferred Stocks	亿手 100 million contracts	0.04
债 券	Bonds	亿手 100million contracts	865.65
政府债	Government Bonds	亿手 100 million contracts	1.25
公司债	Corporate Bonds	亿手 100 million contracts	22.99
债券回购	Repurchase	亿手 100 million contracts	841.41
基 金	Funds	亿手 100 million contracts	4 549.64
其 他	Others	亿手 100 million contracts	…

注：2010年起，上交所统计口径有调整，原表中"国债现货"和"地方政府债"数据，现合并为"政府债"；原表中"公司债"和"可转债"数据，现合并统称为"公司债"。

Note: Shanghai Stock Exchange has changed its statistical approach for its data since 2010. The data in the fields of "National Debts on Spots" and "Local Government Bonds" in the former table have been merged as those of "Government Bonds" and the fields of "Corporate Debts" and "Convertible Bonds" have been merged as "Corporate Bonds".

表8-9　上海证券交易所市盈率和换手率
P/E Ratio & Turnover Rate of Shanghai Stock Exchange

指　标	Indicators	2005	2010	2013	2014
市盈率(%)	**P/E Rate**	**16.3**	**21.6**	**11.0**	**16.0**
A　股	A Share	16.4	21.6	11.0	16.0
B　股	B Share	12.4	23.9	11.6	15.8
换手率(%)	**Turnover Rate**	**274.4**	**198.5**	**123.6**	**173.8**
A　股	A Share	290.7	199.3	123.8	174.4
B　股	B Share	58.5	119.0	89.4	64.6

表8-10　上海证券交易所市场筹集资金
Capital Raising of Shanghai Stock Exchang

单位:亿元　　(100 million yuan)

指　标	Indicators	2005	2010	2013	2014
A股小计	**Subtotal of A Shares**	**308.75**	**5 532.14**	**2 515.72**	**3 962.59**
A股首次发行	IPO of A Shares	28.55	1 891.51		311.77
A股再次发行	Second Issuing of A Shares	280.20	3 640.62	2 515.72	3 650.82
#A股增发	Additional Issuing of A Shares	278.78	2 102.90	1 980.09	2 819.40
A股配股	Rights Issuing of A Shares	1.42	1 415.73	383.42	107.61
A股行权	Rights Claiming of A Shares		84.28		
优先股	**Preferred Stocks**				**1 030.00**

表8-11　浦东新区上市公司分行业汇总情况
Listed Companies in PNA by Sector
(2014)

指　标	Indicators	单　位　Unit	地产类 Real Estate	工业类 Industry	公用事业类 Public Utilities	商业类 Commerce	综合类 Comprehens-ive
发行股数	Number of Stocks Issued	亿股 100 million in number	82.07	212.86	416.35	37.79	850.06
流通股数	Number of Stocks Circulated	亿股 100 million in number	80.82	202.10	392.44	33.64	693.48
成交额	Volume	亿元 100 million yuan	2 803.17	7 224.89	3 839.90	1 452.90	13 428.43
成交股数	Number of Stock Transacted	亿股 100 million in number	229.16	615.21	566.66	128.41	1 528.92
市盈率	P/E Ratio	%	42.4	48.3	26.1	53.6	9.8
换手率	Turnover Rate	%	286.7	305.4	147.9	385.0	221.6
市价总值	Total Market Value	亿元 100 million yuan	1 487.79	2 484.40	2 974.56	551.05	8 175.02
流通市值	Circulating Market Value	亿元 100 million yuan	1 447.47	2 335.56	2 702.89	463.38	6 674.69

注：1. 浦东新区上市公司指公司注册地含"浦东"的公司。
2. 数据包含A股和B股。
3. "成交额"、"成交股数"、"换手率"为2014年整年数据。
4. "发行股数"、"流通股数"、"市盈率"、"市值总值"、"流通市值"为2014年12月31日数据。

Note: 1. Public listed companies in PNA refer to those companies that have been registered in Pudong.
2. The data include both A shares and B shares.
3. The items of Business Volume, Number of Stocks Transacted and Turnover Rate are data in the whole year of 2014.
4. The items of Number of Stocks Issued, Number of Stocks Circulated, P/E Ratio, Total Market Value and Circulating Market Value are data of December 31, 2014.

表8-12 上海期货交易所市场交易主要指标
Major Indicators of Shanghai Futures Exchange

指 标 Indicators		单 位 Unit	2005	2010	2013	2014
会员单位	**Membership**	**户 unit**	**215**	**209**	**206**	**203**
经纪单位	Broking	户 unit	175	164	157	151
非经纪单位	Non-Broking	户 unit	40	45	49	52
交易天数	Business Days in the Year	天 day	242	242	238	245
上市交易品种	Business Lines	个 unit	4	8	11	12
成交量	**Total Volume of Business**	**万手 10 000 contracts**	**6 757.95**	**124 379.64**	**128 494.79**	**168 458.84**
铜	Copper	万手 10 000 contracts	2 470.41	10 157.71	12 859.17	14 102.06
铝	Aluminum	万手 10 000 contracts	425.00	3 452.40	661.12	2 785.26
锌	Zinc	万手 10 000 contracts		29 317.87	2 416.63	8 085.87
铅	Lead	万手 10 000 contracts			34.55	291.56
黄 金	Gold	万手 10 000 contracts		679.41	4 017.56	4 773.08
白 银	Silver	万手 10 000 contracts			34 644.52	17 726.32
天然橡胶	Natural Rubber	万手 10 000 contracts	1 900.63	33 482.98	14 487.61	38 697.53
燃料油	Fuel Oil	万手 10 000 contracts	1 961.91	2 136.44	0.21	0.29
石油沥青	Bitumen	万手 10 000 contracts			626.86	130.03
螺纹钢	Rebar	万手 10 000 contracts		45 122.48	58 745.79	81 615.62
线 材	Wire Rod	万手 10 000 contracts		30.35	0.77	0.13
热轧卷板	Hot Rolled Coils	万手 10 000 contracts				251.09
成交金额	**Total Value of Business**	**亿元 100 million yuan**	**65 402.03**	**1 234 794.76**	**1 208 335.47**	**1 264 706.51**
铜	Copper	亿元 100 million yuan	40 463.23	296 437.54	334 647.25	337 457.53
铝	Aluminum	亿元 100 million yuan	3 714.46	28 342.48	4 814.63	19 256.90
锌	Zinc	亿元 100 million yuan		255 725.62	18 081.85	66 571.36
铅	Lead	亿元 100 million yuan			492.56	2 072.87
黄 金	Gold	亿元 100 million yuan		18 291.92	107 090.62	119 826.28
白 银	Silver	亿元 100 million yuan			231 109.73	255 570.06
天然橡胶	Natural Rubber	亿元 100 million yuan	15 601.79	426 464.81	290 535.56	230 182.98
燃料油	Fuel Oil	亿元 100 million yuan	5 622.55	9 886.37	5.02	4.96
石油沥青	Bitumen	亿元 100 million yuan			2 741.07	553.71
螺纹钢	Rebar	亿元 100 million yuan		199 517.15	218 814.26	232 408.06
线 材	Wire Rod	亿元 100 million yuan		128.87	2.92	0.44
热轧卷板	Hot Rolled Coils	亿元 100 million yuan				801.36
年末持仓量	**Year End Contracts**	**万手 10 000 contracts**	**30.95**	**206.46**	**418.78**	**478.68**
铜	Copper	万手 10 000 contracts	10.58	37.31	51.86	67.93
铝	Aluminum	万手 10 000 contracts	7.89	23.73	21.60	34.27
锌	Zinc	万手 10 000 contracts		40.24	22.96	25.74
铅	Lead	万手 10 000 contracts			2.60	4.42
黄 金	Gold	万手 10 000 contracts		7.88	17.10	19.48
白 银	Silver	万手 10 000 contracts			67.02	40.69
天然橡胶	Natural Rubber	万手 10 000 contracts	5.70	21.46	29.19	31.13
燃料油	Fuel Oil	万手 10 000 contracts	6.78	10.44		0.01
石油沥青	Bitumen	万手 10 000 contracts			4.42	0.02

表 8－12 续表　Continued

指　标　Indicators		单　位　Unit	2005	2010	2013	2014
螺纹钢	Rebar	万手 10 000 contracts		65.40	202.03	252.50
线　材	Wire Rod	万手 10 000 contracts		0.01		
热轧卷板	Hot Rolled Coils	万手 10 000 contracts				2.49
交割量	**Volume of Transaction**	**万手 10 000 contracts**	**8.73**	**37.69**	**28.58**	**33.07**
铜	Copper	万手 10 000 contracts	3.07	3.84	5.16	4.66
铝	Aluminum	万手 10 000 contracts	2.18	11.52	8.19	14.51
锌	Zinc	万手 10 000 contracts		6.15	3.74	3.89
铅	Lead	万手 10 000 contracts			1.96	2.92
黄　金	Gold	万手 10 000 contracts		0.05	0.28	0.37
白　银	Silver	万手 10 000 contracts			5.78	1.77
天然橡胶	Natural Rubber	万手 10 000 contracts	1.52	2.57	1.46	2.51
燃料油	Fuel Oil	万手 10 000 contracts	1.96	6.90	0.01	
石油沥青	Bitumen	万手 10 000 contracts				1.35
螺纹钢	Rebar	万手 10 000 contracts		6.00	2.00	1.07
线　材	Wire Rod	万手 10 000 contracts		0.66		
热轧卷板	Hot Rolled Coils	万手 10 000 contracts				0.02
交割金额	**Value of Transaction**	**亿元 100 million yuan**	**88.29**	**349.06**	**345.96**	**320.64**
铜	Copper	亿元 100 million yuan	54.54	113.40	139.26	114.43
铝	Aluminum	亿元 100 million yuan	18.07	90.41	59.81	96.96
锌	Zinc	亿元 100 million yuan		53.77	27.77	31.28
铅	Lead	亿元 100 million yuan			32.48	20.03
黄　金	Gold	亿元 100 million yuan		1.46	7.54	9.00
白　银	Silver	亿元 100 million yuan			42.48	24.62
天然橡胶	Natural Rubber	亿元 100 million yuan	10.79	32.21	29.22	15.40
燃料油	Fuel Oil	亿元 100 million yuan	4.89	30.28	0.18	0.03
石油沥青	Bitumen	亿元 100 million yuan				5.74
螺纹钢	Rebar	亿元 100 million yuan		24.89	7.22	3.09
线　材	Wire Rod	亿元 100 million yuan		2.64		
热轧卷板	Hot Rolled Coils	亿元 100 million yuan				0.06
交割率	**Rate of Transaction**					
铜	Copper	%	0.2	0.1	0.1	0.1
铝	Aluminum	%	1.0	0.7	2.4	1.2
锌	Zinc	%		0.1	0.3	0.1
铅	Lead	%			17.1	2.3
黄　金	Gold	%		…	…	…
白　银	Silver	%			…	…
天然橡胶	Natural Rubber	%	0.3	…	…	…
燃料油	Fuel Oil	%	0.2	0.5	3.6	2.1
石油沥青	Bitumen	%				0.4
螺纹钢	Rebar	%		…	…	…
线　材	Wire Rod	%		2.0		
热轧卷板	Hot Rolled Coils	%				…

表8-13 上海钻石交易所市场交易主要指标
Major Indicators of Shanghai Diamond Exchange

指 标	Indicators	单 位 Unit	2010	2013	2014
会员单位	**Membership**	**户 Unit**	**283**	**364**	**369**
外资会员	Foreign Member	户 Unit	193	238	233
中资会员	Chinese Member	户 Unit	90	126	136
成交量	**Total Volume of Business**	**万克拉 10 000 carat**	**19 762.53**	**8 022.96**	**11 094.94**
钻石进境量	Volume of Diamond Coming in Border	万克拉 10 000 carat	92.60	251.22	172.25
钻石出境量	Volume of Diamond Leaving our Country	万克拉 10 000 carat	24.03	34.28	47.40
钻石进口量	Volume of Imports	万克拉 10 000 carat	118.53	151.84	178.60
钻石出口量	Volume of Exports	万克拉 10 000 carat	19 518.03	7 575.01	10 345.32
钻石保税交易量	Volume of Bonded Transactions	万克拉 10 000 carat	7.54	9.69	350.46
钻石加工贸易量	Volume of Processing Trade	万克拉 10 000 carat	1.80	0.92	0.91
成交金额	**Total Value of Transactions**	**亿美元 100 million USD**	**28.86**	**43.27**	**51.31**
钻石进境额	Amount of Diamond Coming in Border	亿美元 100 million USD	10.46	16.70	18.55
钻石出境额	Amount of Diamond Leaving our Country	亿美元 100 million USD	3.80	7.55	6.45
钻石进口额	Amount of Imports	亿美元 100 million USD	13.11	17.30	22.55
钻石出口额	Amount of Exports	亿美元 100 million USD	0.13	0.17	0.62
钻石保税交易额	Amount of Bonded Transactions	亿美元 100 million USD	1.30	1.50	3.09
钻石加工贸易额	Amount of Processing Trade	亿美元 100 million USD	0.05	0.05	0.05

表8－14　区属人才交流市场基本情况

Basic Statistics of PNA Professional Resources Market(PPRM)

指　标　Indicators		单　位　Unit	2005	2010	2013	2014
全年举办交流活动	Number of Exchange Activites in the Year	场 in number	133	193	208	208
参与人才招聘单位	Number of Participating Organizations	个 unit	3 859	7 462	6 623	6 678
接待咨询服务人次	Job-seeking Visitors Received	万人次 10 000 person-times	19.67	37.00	39.20	30.10
办理择业登记人数	Job-seeking Visitors Registered	人次 person-time	90 452	211 000	178 000	143 000
达成意向人数	Number of Job-seekers Who Have Signed Letters of Intent	人 person	37 302	39 949	31 320	26 828
获得上海市居住证人数	Number of Persons Who Have Obtained Shanghai Residence Permits	人 person	7 158	30 985	38 490	71 134
后续服务	**Follow-up Services**					
档案保管	File-keeping	件 file	5 691	13 489	15 314	16 680
户籍挂靠(迁入)	Domiciling(immigration)	户 unit	1 605	1 175	2 208	4 334

主要统计指标解释

存 款

是企业、机关、团体或居民等根据资金必须收回的原则,把货币资金存入银行或其他信用机构保管并取得一定利息的一种信用活动形式。根据存款对象的不同可划分为企业存款、财政存款、机关团体存款、储蓄存款等科目。它是银行信贷资金的主要来源。

贷 款

是银行或其他信用机构根据资金必须归还的原则,按一定利率,为企业、个人等提供资金的一种信用活动形式。我国银行贷款分为短期贷款、中期流动资金贷款、中长期贷款、信托贷款以及工业贷款、商业贷款等科目。

居民储蓄存款年末余额

居民和农民个人在银行、信用社等金融机构储蓄存款年末余额。不包括居民的手存现金和企事业单位、部队、机关团体等的集体存款。

保险金额

指保险人承担赔偿或者给付保险金责任的最高限额。

保险费

保险费是指投保人根据保险合同的有关规定,为保险受益人取得因保险事故发生所造成的经济损失予以补偿(或给付)权利,付给保险人的代价。包括财产险和人身险储金类支出。

保险赔款及给付

保险赔款及给付指保险事故发生后,经查证确属保险责任范围以内的保险标的损失,保险人根据保险合同的规定履行赔偿义务,给予被保险人(或投保人指定的受益人)的款项。

市价总值

市价总值即全部股份乘上市场价格。

流通市值

流通市值指在某特定时间内当时可交易的流通股股数乘以当时股价得出的流通股票总价值。

市盈率

市盈率是某种股票每股市价与每股盈利的比率。

市盈率 = 普通股每股市场价格 ÷ 普通股每年每股盈利

换手率

换手率是指在一定时间内市场中股票转手买卖的频率。

金融债券

金融债券,是指银行和非银行金融机构为筹集资金而发行的债券。其债务人为发行债券的金融机构。

企业债券

企业债券通常又称为公司债券,是企业依照法定程序发行,约定在一定期限内还本付息的债券。企业债券代表着发债企业和投资者之间的一种债权债务关系。债券持有人是企业的债权人,不是所有者,无权参与或干涉企业经营管理,但债券持有人有权按期收回本息。企业债券与股票一样,同属有价证券,可以自由转让。

可转换债券

可转换债券,又译可换股债券,是债券的一种,它可以转换为债券发行公司的股票,其转换比率一般会在发行时确定。可转换债券通常具有较低的票面利率,因为可以转换成股票的权利是对债券持有人的一种补偿。另外,将可转换债券转换为普通股时,所换得的股票价值一般远大于原债券价值。可转换债券是在发行公司债券的基础上,附加了一份期权,并允许购买人在规定的时间范围内将其购买的债券转换成指定公司的股票。

持仓量

持仓量指的是在交易所市场上未平仓的期权合约的数量,也指某一种类或系列中未平仓的期权合约的数量。

成交量

成交量指当天成交的股票数量。

交 割

交割概念来源于期货,分为:实物交割和现金交割。

实物交割,是指期货合约的买卖双方于合约到期时,根据交易所制订的规则和程序,通过期货合约标的物的所有权转移,将到期未平仓合约进行了结的行为。商品期货交易一般采用实物交割的方式。

现金交割,是指到期未平仓期货合约进行交割时,用结算价格来计算未平仓合约的盈亏,以现金支付的方式最终了结期货合约的交割方式。这种交割方式主要用于金融期货等期货标的物无法进行实物交割的期货合约。

EXPLANATORY NOTES TO MAJOR STATISTICAL INDICATORS

Deposits

Deposits are a form of credit by which enterprises, institutions, organizations or residents put money into banks and other credit institutions for safekeeping and earn interests under the principle of free withdrawal. According to different depositors, deposits are divided into enterprise deposits, treasury deposits, deposits of institutions and organizations, urban savings deposits and other deposits. Deposits constitute a major source of bank credit funds.

Loans

Loans are a form of credit by which banks and other credit institutions provide funds with a specified interest to enterprises and individuals under the principle of free repayment. Loans from Chinese banks include short term loans, medium term circulating capital loans, long term loans, trust loans, industrial loans and commercial loans.

Savings Deposit Balance of Urban and Rural Residents

Refers to year-end savings deposit balance of urban residents and farmers at banks, credit unions and other financial institutions, excluding cash held by residents and collective savings of enterprises, institutions, military units and government agencies.

Amount Insured

Amount Insured refers to the maximum that the insurant will get for the claim of the case insured .

Premium

Premium is the fee paid by the insurant to the insurer to obtain the obligation of compensation from the insurance within the agreed terms. It includes saving payment for property and life insurance.

Insurance Indemnity

Insurance Indemnity is the compensation paid by the insurer to the insurant or the beneficiary, when an accident has happened to the insured property or life and the loss has been investigated and verified to be within the insurance obligation.

Total Market Value

Total Market Value means all of the stock shares multiplied by their relevant market price.

Circulation Value on the Market

Circulation Value on the Market means the tradable circulation shares multiplied by their relevant share prices during a certain period of time.

P/E Ratio

P/E Ratio refers to the ratio between the price of a certain share and its earnings per year. The P/E ratio is the price of a traded common share divided by its annual earnings.

Exchange Rate

Exchange Rate means the trading frequency of certain stock shares on the market during a certain period of time.

Financial Bonds

Financial Bonds refer to those that banks and non-banking financial institutions issue to raise funds. Their debtors are the financial institutions that issue the bonds.

Corporate Bonds

Corporate Bonds usually refer to business bonds, which will be issued in accordance with the statutory procedures of the business and repay the original investment plus agreed interest within a certain period of time. Corporate bonds represent a kind of debtor-creditor relationship between the issuing enterprises and the investors. Bondholders are creditors of the certain enterprise, not the owners, and they do not have the right to participate or interfere with the business management. However, the bondholders have the right to claim the principal and interest on time. Like the stock shares, corporate bonds belong to marketable securities and can be freely transferable.

Convertible Bonds

Convertible Bonds, also translated into convertible exchangeable bonds, can be converted into the stock shares of the enterprise that issue the bonds. The conversion rate will usually be determined at the time of distribution. Convertible bonds generally have lower nominal interest rates, because the right of being converted into stock shares is a kind of compensation to the bondholders. In addition, when the bonds are converted into ordinary shares, the prices of these shares usually are far higher than the original value of the bonds. In essence, the convertible bonds have an additional option on the basis of the business bonds, and these bondholders are allowed to convert the convertible bonds they have purchased into the stock shares of specific companies during the specific period.

Open Interest

Open Interest refers to the number of open option contracts in the exchange market, also refers to the number of one or series of open option contracts.

Turnover

Turnover refers to the transaction volume of stock shares traded on that certain day.

Delivery

Delivery, its concept comes from futures, can be divided into physical delivery and cash delivery.

Physical delivery refers to the behavior that the vendor and the purchaser finish the open contracts at the end of the term by means of the ownership transfer of the object of futures contracts in accordance with rules and procedures of the stock exchange when the contract expires. The transaction of commodity futures usually adopts the physical delivery.

Cash delivery refers to the way that the two sides finally close their futures contracts by means of cash, with the settlement price used to calculate earnings or loss of the open contracts when the open futures contracts are delivered at the end of term. This kind of delivery is mainly used for futures contracts that their objects can not be dealt with physical delivery such as the financial futures.

第九篇

CHAPTER 9

房地产

REAL ESTATE

表9-1　房地产开发投资
(2014)

单位:亿元

指　标	Indicators	企业个数(个) Enterprises (unit)	本年完成投资 Current Year Investment Completed	建筑工程 Construction Project
总　计	**Total**	**729**	**897.87**	**436.74**
按登记注册类型分	**By Type of Registration**			
内　资	Domestic Investment	620	745.95	382.86
国　有	State-owned	14	10.31	8.13
集　体	Collective-owned	3	2.68	1.44
股份合作	Share-holding			
联　营	Jointly-operated	1		
有限责任公司	Companies with Limited Liabilities	317	492.72	232.87
股份有限公司	Companies Limited by Shares	44	25.69	24.08
私　营	Private	241	214.55	116.34
其　他	Others			
港澳台商投资	Hong Kong/Macao/Taiwan Investment	68	88.51	33.31
#港澳台商独资	Solely Hong Kong/Macao/Taiwan Funded	30	61.25	19.06
外商投资	FIE	41	63.41	20.58
#外商独资	Solely Foreign Funded	20	10.63	3.96
按隶属关系分	**By Subordination**			
中央属	Central Government	12	18.82	8.27
市(局)属	Municipality/Bureau	47	104.61	71.91
区　属	PNA	171	216.91	96.63
其他属	Others	499	557.53	259.93
按企业资质等级分	**By Qualifications of Enterprises**			
一　级	Grade 1	41	9.79	7.49
二　级	Grade 2	153	102.05	81.13
三　级	Grade 3	102	42.41	28.64
无　级	No Grade	433	743.62	319.47

Investment in Real Estate Development

(100 million yuan)

按构成分 By Composition of Completed Investment			按工程用途分 By Project Use of Completed Investment			
安装工程 Installation	设备工器具购置 Equipment Purchasing	其他费用 Other Cost	住　宅 Residential Housing	办公楼 Office Buildings	商业营业用房 Commerce/ Operation	其　他 Others
68.82	**3.03**	**389.27**	**518.60**	**142.27**	**113.77**	**123.22**
64.48	3.03	295.58	412.01	115.34	104.10	114.49
0.07	0.61	1.51	4.74	1.84	0.60	3.13
		1.24	1.52	0.12	1.05	
30.85	2.10	226.89	286.53	82.62	54.02	69.54
0.13	0.02	1.46	4.67	9.81	5.04	6.16
33.43	0.30	64.48	114.55	20.95	43.39	35.65
0.09		55.11	50.27	24.92	6.56	6.76
0.05		42.15	48.42	7.69	4.10	1.04
4.25		38.58	56.32	2.01	3.11	1.97
2.63		4.04	6.57	2.01	1.10	0.96
0.50		10.05	13.82			5.00
16.82	0.02	15.86	48.63	16.79	21.53	17.65
5.61	2.15	112.52	129.32	34.85	17.16	35.58
45.90	0.86	250.84	326.83	90.63	75.07	65.00
1.64	0.09	0.57	3.46	1.08	1.08	4.16
2.86	0.63	17.43	65.31	11.57	8.08	17.09
1.92		11.85	21.12	4.48	7.84	8.97
62.40	2.32	359.42	428.71	125.14	96.76	93.01

表9-2　房地产开发企业投资资金来源
(2014)

单位:亿元

指　标	Indicators	本年资金来源合计 Total Sources of Funds	上年末结余资本 Remnant Capital of Previous Year	本年资金来源小计 Subtotal of Current Year
总　计	**Total**	**1 937.88**	**672.19**	**1 265.69**
按登记注册类型分	**By Type of Registration**			
内　资	Domestic Investment	1 563.83	458.25	1 105.58
国　有	State-owned	30.60	15.32	15.28
集　体	Collective-owned	22.10	7.22	14.88
股份合作	Share-holding			
联　营	Jointly-operated			
有限责任公司	Companies with Limited Liabilities	969.52	344.46	625.06
股份有限公司	Companies Limited by Shares	55.29	3.54	51.75
私　营	Private	486.32	87.71	398.61
其　他	Others			
港澳台商投资	Hong Kong/Macao/Taiwan Investment	223.44	124.93	98.51
#港澳台商独资	Solely Hong Kong/Macao/Taiwan Funded	136.25	52.09	84.15
外商投资	FIE	150.61	89.01	61.61
#外商独资	Solely Foreign Funded	58.65	24.35	34.30
按隶属关系分	**By Subordination**			
中央属	Central Government	41.41	4.19	37.23
市(局)属	Municipality/Bureau	244.35	135.52	108.84
区　属	PNA	335.25	88.78	246.48
其他属	Others	1 316.87	443.71	873.15
按企业资质等级分	**By Qualifications of Enterprises**			
一　级	Grade 1	18.47	2.47	16.00
二　级	Grade 2	267.48	35.72	231.76
三　级	Grade 3	79.70	22.73	56.97
无　级	No Grade	1 572.23	611.26	960.97

Sources of Funds of Investment in Real Estate Development

(100 million yuan)

国内贷款 Domestic Loans	利用外资 Foreign Funds	自筹资金 Self-raised Funds	#自有资金 Self-owned	其他资金来源 Other Funds	本年各项应付款合计 Current Year Total Amount Payable	#工程款 Project Funds
452.37	**18.55**	**363.26**	**171.19**	**431.51**	**158.17**	**85.74**
427.30		301.48	157.50	376.80	140.97	76.97
8.15		2.43	2.43	4.70	0.92	0.79
0.20		13.28		1.40	0.60	0.36
205.59		175.69	103.05	243.78	75.93	45.44
26.39		25.36	16.15		5.85	1.76
186.97		84.72	35.86	126.93	57.67	28.62
8.71	17.50	52.24	13.42	20.05	4.47	2.93
7.92	17.50	44.57	5.75	14.16	3.17	2.53
16.37	1.05	9.54	0.26	34.65	12.74	5.84
8.20	1.05	0.26		24.80	1.09	0.90
14.00		5.08		18.15	2.87	2.87
55.72		20.05	5.30	33.07	2.54	1.39
138.11		82.55	62.49	25.83	25.92	18.21
244.55	18.55	255.59	103.40	354.47	126.85	63.27
8.57		7.41	7.41	0.02	10.85	7.27
123.91		61.52	34.03	46.33	15.81	13.14
18.36		23.91	15.97	14.70	14.25	5.06
301.54	18.55	270.42	113.78	370.46	117.26	60.27

表9-3　房地产开发企业房屋施工面积、竣工面积和销售面积 (2014)

单位:万平方米

指　标	Indicators	施工面积 Floor Area Under Construction	#新开工面积 Floor Area of New Starts	竣工面积 Floor Area Completed
总　计	**Total**	**3 739.22**	**855.75**	**704.86**
按登记注册类型分	**By Type of Registration**			
内　资	Domestic Investment	3 369.56	784.60	678.79
国　有	State-owned	70.25	22.10	30.31
集　体	Collective-owned	25.18	0.27	0.27
股份合作	Share-holding			
联　营	Jointly-operated			
有限责任公司	Companies with Limited Liabilities	2 267.45	547.21	417.88
股份有限公司	Companies Limited by Shares	143.88	7.62	28.63
私　营	Private	862.81	207.39	201.69
其　他	Others			
港澳台商投资	Hong Kong/Macao/Taiwan Invested	212.94	51.18	12.74
#港澳台商独资	Solely Hong Kong/Macao/Taiwan Funded	84.99	36.07	
外商投资	FIE	156.72	19.97	13.34
#外商独资	Solely Foreign Funded	67.93		11.34
按隶属关系分	**By Subordination**			
中央属	Central Government	164.68	19.42	37.60
市(局)属	Municipality/Bureau	472.34	130.46	107.69
区　属	PNA	895.18	242.97	135.05
其他属	Others	2 207.02	462.90	424.52
按企业资质等级分	**By Qualifications of Enterprises**			
一　级	Grade 1	91.25	1.11	13.32
二　级	Grade 2	672.82	125.59	224.43
三　级	Grade 3	259.84	58.02	48.23
无　级	No Grade	2 715.32	671.03	418.88

Floor Space Under Construction, Completed and Sold Floor Space in Real Estate Development

(10 000 sq · m)

			竣工价值(亿元) Completion Value (100 million yuan)	现房销售面积 Sold Floor Space for Completed Housing	期房销售面积 Area of Forward Sale of Future Marketable Housing
#住 宅 Housing	办公楼 Office Building	商业营业用房 Commerce/ Operation			
474.53	**41.39**	**71.08**	**287.70**	**167.80**	**371.34**
467.10	32.69	69.04	271.10	160.42	351.57
25.09		0.30	8.01	12.06	1.27
		0.27	0.06		5.75
292.76	17.83	46.88	156.93	96.09	241.80
8.06	5.11	9.67	20.24	2.86	2.66
141.18	9.75	11.91	85.86	49.40	100.10
6.56		1.88	3.40	3.50	6.17
				0.68	2.52
0.87	8.70	0.16	13.20	3.88	13.60
	8.00		11.53	2.48	3.63
37.60			17.49	2.29	37.05
73.94	3.32	13.86	36.26	14.70	65.05
65.80	19.62	17.24	61.07	41.69	43.98
297.20	18.44	39.98	172.89	109.12	225.25
4.22		0.51	6.37	4.37	
168.04	7.92	12.95	92.71	38.09	39.46
33.10	4.43	2.91	16.32	34.46	30.84
269.17	29.03	54.70	172.31	90.88	301.04

表9-4　历年全社会房屋施工面积、竣工面积
Total Floor Space Under Construction and Completed in Main Years (1992～2014)

年份 Year	施工面积（万平方米） Floor Space Under Construction (10 000 sq·m)	#住宅 Residential Housing	竣工面积（万平方米） Floor Space Completed (10 000 sq·m)	#住宅 Residential Housing	房屋建筑面积竣工率（%） Construction Completion Rate(%)	#住宅 Residential Housing
1992	312.15	123.00	104.70	69.27	33.5	56.3
1993	764.36	285.34	169.44	76.68	22.2	26.9
1994	1 158.24	450.03	458.33	113.92	39.6	25.3
1995	1 577.21	583.96	404.58	199.84	25.7	34.2
1996	2 226.58	904.18	674.49	355.31	30.3	39.3
1997	1 954.70	768.15	581.03	271.64	29.7	35.4
1998	2 014.17	911.68	578.31	301.41	28.7	33.1
1999	1 766.88	856.25	573.20	268.27	32.4	31.3
2000	1 549.57	711.80	544.22	255.21	35.1	35.9
2001	1 526.45	879.01	469.53	249.96	30.8	28.4
2002	2 328.47	1 737.98	611.48	512.11	26.3	29.5
2003	2 242.65	1 607.68	671.70	498.85	29.9	31.0
2004	2 250.62	1 569.76	632.76	453.83	28.1	28.9
2005	2 390.79	1 695.24	684.96	512.42	28.6	30.2
2006	2 204.65	1 589.11	779.65	597.52	35.4	37.6
2007	1 983.86	1 255.32	516.59	419.29	26.0	33.4
2008	1 964.30	1 058.98	477.85	255.77	24.3	24.2
2009	2 977.23	1 792.12	742.28	505.70	24.9	28.2
2010	3 211.12	2 085.07	424.90	296.70	13.2	14.2
2011	3 511.82	2 296.52	487.81	286.14	13.9	12.5
2012	3 527.25	2 280.68	626.96	433.38	17.8	19.0
2013	3 560.04	2 185.40	569.03	350.35	16.0	16.0
2014	3 739.22	2 222.93	704.86	474.53	18.9	21.3

表9-5 主要年份房地产开发企业房屋建筑面积和造价
Floor Space and Cost of Constructions Developed by Real Estate Companies in Main years

指 标	Indicators	1998	2000	2005	2010	2013	2014
房屋施工面积（万平方米）	**Floor Space Under Construction（10 000 sq. m）**	**1 458.94**	**1 119.67**	**2 390.79**	**3 211.12**	**3 560.04**	**3 739.22**
住 宅	Residential Housing	789.35	712.17	1 695.24	2 085.07	2 185.40	2 222.93
#别墅、高档公寓	Villas and Flats	77.46	72.64	490.51	394.58	362.37	412.72
办公楼	Office Buildings	404.07	199.39	196.68	300.14	403.23	475.54
商业营业用房	Commercial Buildings	155.58	106.63	222.13	389.62	356.39	404.39
其 他	Others	109.94	101.48	276.74	436.30	615.02	636.37
房屋竣工面积（万平方米）	**Floor Space Completed（10 000 sq. m）**	**360.36**	**384.03**	**684.96**	**424.90**	**569.03**	**704.86**
住 宅	Residential Housing	231.94	264.91	512.42	296.70	350.35	474.53
#别墅、高档公寓	Villas and Flats	26.10	23.59	168.59	85.58	44.27	38.27
办公楼	Office Buildings	71.15	54.62	54.08	31.61	40.64	41.39
商业营业用房	Commercial Buildings	41.16	28.10	32.85	35.85	66.65	71.08
其 他	Others	16.11	36.40	85.61	60.74	111.39	117.86
房屋竣工价值（亿元）	**Value of Buildings Completed（100 million yuan）**	**141.19**	**110.16**	**204.11**	**173.20**	**302.72**	**287.70**
住 宅	Residential Housing	61.74	55.36	147.55	127.76	165.96	172.47
#别墅、高档公寓	Villas and Flats	16.91	9.86	61.51	71.53	19.84	24.97
办公楼	Office Buildings	53.89	35.25	26.18	13.98	42.92	29.28
商业营业用房	Commercial Buildings	20.61	11.02	10.09	12.98	45.57	42.00
其 他	Others	4.95	8.53	20.29	18.47	48.26	43.94
竣工房屋平均造价（元/平方米）	**Average Construction Cost（yuan/sq. m）**	**3 918**	**2 869**	**2 980**	**4 076**	**5 320**	**4 082**
住 宅	Residential Housing	2 662	2 090	2 879	4 306	4 737	3 635
#别墅、高档公寓	Villas and Flats	6 481	4 179	3 648	8 358	4 481	6 524
办公楼	Office Buildings	7 575	6 454	4 841	4 423	10 562	7 076
商业营业用房	Commercial Buildings	5 007	3 921	3 075	3 622	6 836	5 909
其 他	Others	3 078	2 345	2 371	3 042	4 333	3 728

表9-6 浦东房地产交易中心交易情况
Transactions in Pudong Real Estate Trading Center

指 标 Indicators		单 位 Unit	2010	2013	2014
商品房交易登记	**Registered Transactions of Commodity Housing**				
# 出售套数	Number of Commodity Housing Sold	套 set	73 892	53 172	53 791
出售面积	Floor Space of Commodity Housing Sold	平方米 sq · m	7 197 092	4 921 956	5 015 353
出售金额	Value of Commodity Housing Sold	万元 10 000 yuan	6 799 748	6 073 999	6 419 335
预售套数	Number of Forward Sale of Commodity Housing	套 set	14 905	21 220	18 336
预售面积	Floor Space of Forward Sale of Commodity Housing	平方米 sq · m	1 629 081	2 330 012	1 854 481
预售金额	Value of Forward Sale of Commodity Housing	万元 10 000 yuan	3 283 668	5 085 017	4 390 684
存量房交易登记	**Registered Transactions of Housing at Stock**				
交易过户套数	Trading Number of Housing at Stock	套 set	43 162	68 473	38 445
交易过户面积	Trading Floor Space of Housing at Stock	平方米 sq · m	4 537 343	6 182 764	3 828 179
交易过户金额	Trading Value of Housing at Stock	万元 10 000 yuan	6 277 733	10 543 821	6 997 443

主要统计指标解释

房地产开发投资

指各种登记注册类型的房地产开发公司、商品房建设公司及其他房地产开发法人单位和附属于其他法人单位实际从事房地产开发或经营活动的单位统一开发的包括统代建、拆迁还建的住宅、厂房、仓库、饭店、宾馆、度假村、写字楼、办公楼等房屋建筑物和配套的服务设施，土地开发工程（如道路、给水、排水、供电、供热、通讯、平整场地等基础设施工程）的投资；不包括单纯的土地交易活动。

施工面积

指报告期内施工的全部房屋建筑面积。包括本期新开工的面积和上期开工跨入本期继续施工的房屋面积，以及上期已停建在本期恢复施工的房屋面积。本期竣工和本期施工后又停缓建的房屋，其建筑面积仍计入本期房屋施工面积中。

竣工面积

指在报告期内房屋建筑按照设计要求已经全部完工，达到住人和使用条件，经验收鉴定合格（或达到竣工验收标准），正式移交使用单位的各栋房屋建筑面积的总和。

房屋建筑面积竣工率

指一定时期内房屋竣工面积占同期房屋施工面积的比率。该指标从房屋建筑施工速度的角度反映投资效果的指标。

别墅、高档公寓

指建筑造价和销售价格明显高于一般商品住宅的商品住宅。别墅一般指地处郊区，独立成栋的商品住宅；高档公寓一般指地处市内高尚社区，高层或多层的商品住宅。别墅、高档公寓的确定标准：一是经有房地产投资计划审批权的主管部门审批建设的别墅、高档公寓开发项目；二是销售价格高于当地同等地段商品住宅平均销售价格一倍以上的别墅、公寓开发项目。该指标可以分析房地产投资结构，反映高收入家庭商品住宅的供求平衡情况。

EXPLANATORY NOTES TO MAJOR STATISTICAL INDICATORS

Investment in Real Estate Development

It includes the investment by the real estate development companies, commercial buildings construction companies and other real estate development units of various types of ownership in the construction of house buildings, such as residential buildings, factory buildings, warehouses, hotels, guesthouses, holiday villages, office buildings, and the complementary service facilities and land development projects, such as roads, water supply, water drainage, power supply, heating, telecommunications, land leveling and other projects of infrastructure. It excludes the activities in simple land transactions.

Floor Space under Construction

Floor Space under Construction refers to total floor space of all buildings under construction during the reference period, including floor space of newly started buildings during the reference period, floor space of construction extended from the previous period to the current period, and floor space of construction suspended during the previous period and resumed in the current period. Floor space of construction completed in the current period, and floor space of construction started and then suspended in the current period are also included in the floor space under construction of the current year.

Floor Space of Buildings Completed

Floor Space of Buildings Completed refers to the floor space of all buildings completed in the reference period, which have been appraised and accepted (or come up to the designed standards) and have been transferred to the owners for use.

Completion Rate of Floor Space of Buildings

Completion Rate of Floor Space of Buildings refers to the ratio of the floor space of buildings completed in certain period of time to the floor space of buildings under construction in the same period. This indicator reflects the investment result from the perspective of the speed of construction.

Villas, High-Grade Apartments

Villas, High-Grade Apartments refers to commercial houses whose construction costs and marketing prices are significantly higher than ordinary housing. Villas are independent structures generally located in the suburbs; high-grade apartments are multi-story buildings located in elegant urban neighborhoods. Criteria for villas and high-grade apartments include: 1) projects for the construction of villas or high-grade apartments have to be approved by competent departments in charge of real estate development and investment plans, and 2) prices for projects on villas or high-grade apartments are higher by over 100% compared with the average prices of ordinary commercial housing projects in similar location. This indicator helps to analyze the investment structure of the real estate industry and the demand and supply of housing for high-income households.

第十篇

CHAPTER 10

国内外贸易

DOMESTIC AND FOREIGN TRADES

表10-1　历年商品销售总额
Total Sales of Commercial Goods
(1994～2014)

单位:亿元　　(100 million yuan)

年　份 Year	商品购进总额 Total Value of Goods Purchased	商品销售总额 Total Value of Goods Sold	期末库存 Inventory at Year-end
1994	150.11	171.46	10.40
1995	186.38	200.05	17.03
1996	202.48	242.39	15.90
1997	278.41	274.26	37.23
1998	260.70	306.12	26.75
1999	517.13	593.37	57.62
2000	686.44	752.94	62.63
2001	891.30	1 004.89	64.55
2002	1 152.32	1 787.51	51.08
2003	2 366.49	2 422.87	187.75
2004	2 788.95	2 932.10	258.35
2005	2 499.25	2 807.47	224.16
2006	2 638.45	2 944.96	220.71
2007	3 337.31	3 613.46	245.43
2008	4 174.85	4 646.70	376.29
2009	4 913.26	5 905.20	495.57
2010	8 386.78	8 263.56	1 509.06
2011	12 866.04	10 502.98	2 303.33
2012	12 463.17	14 546.69	1 169.08
2013	24 258.51	24 034.93	1 310.34
2014	27 867.04	27 640.16	1 309.03

注：本篇数据从2013年开始根据第三次全国经济普查数据进行了调整。
Note: The numbers in this chapter are adjusted according to the Third National Economic Census from year 2013.

表10-2 历年社会消费品零售总额
Total Retail Sales of Social Consumer Goods
(1993 ~2014)

单位:亿元 (100 million yuan)

年 份 Year	消费品零售总额 Total Retail Sales of Consumer Goods	#餐 饮 Catering	按商品用途分 By Usage 食 品 Food	衣 着 Clothing	用 品 Articles	燃 料 Fuel	商品销售总额 Total Sales of Retail Goods
1993	41.92		14.04	4.74	22.80	0.34	
1994	82.74	3.18	39.58	6.47	36.08	0.61	171.46
1995	110.00	4.07	49.50	8.36	51.59	0.55	200.05
1996	140.21	4.03	53.13	12.17	74.01	0.90	242.39
1997	162.23	5.41	62.89	12.54	84.72	2.08	274.26
1998	178.97	4.78	65.06	16.61	96.27	1.03	306.12
1999	198.31	19.02	74.17	15.26	104.17	4.71	593.37
2000	215.17	25.80	81.55	13.65	117.94	2.03	752.94
2001	233.02	28.50	81.27	13.99	135.28	2.48	1 004.89
2002	284.24	25.19	75.12	14.08	190.61	4.43	1 787.51
2003	313.24	24.50	72.53	14.49	220.21	6.01	2 422.87
2004	358.21	31.49	83.73	17.84	251.42	5.22	2 932.10
2005	353.69	43.80	111.00	27.53	213.52	1.64	2 807.47
2006	400.02	51.55	125.88	32.24	240.83	1.07	2 944.96
2007	456.04	60.52	128.66	35.63	283.45	8.30	3 613.46
2008	526.89	68.16	167.23	45.39	306.53	7.74	4 646.70
2009	859.63	102.74	256.11	77.78	498.41	27.33	5 905.20
2010	1 036.88	138.03	268.69	92.32	604.08	71.79	8 263.56
2011	1 204.04	152.43	309.09	114.46	650.35	130.14	10 502.98
2012	1 349.73	166.78	341.95	124.25	728.03	155.50	14 546.69
2013	1 598.01	187.48	435.95	166.09	769.63	226.34	24 034.93
2014	1 740.23	199.48	490.44	192.01	829.55	228.23	27 640.16

表 10-3　连锁商业零售额
Retail Sales of Commercial Chains

单位:亿元　　(100 million yuan)

指　标	Indicators	2010	2013	2014
连锁商业零售总额	**Total Retail Sales of Commercial Chains**	**225.96**	**270.79**	**284.08**
超市及大型超市	Supermarkets and Shopping Malls	93.45	101.68	101.23
便利店	Convenience Stores	13.63	22.37	28.64
家居建材商店	Stores of Building Materials for House Decorations	3.60	3.91	4.32
家电连锁店	House Appliance Chain Stores	43.89	34.18	37.38
连锁餐饮	Catering Chains	12.78	14.50	16.63
医药连锁	Pharmcy Chains	1.34	1.77	1.97
成品油连锁	Refined Oil Chains	51.82	86.38	86.81
其他连锁	Other Chains	5.46	6.00	7.10

表 10-4　社会商业商品购、销、存总额
Total Values of Social Products on Purchase, Sales and Inventory

单位:亿元　　(100 million yuan)

指　标	Indicators	2010	2013	2014
商品购进总额	**Total Goods Purchased**	**8 386.78**	**24 258.51**	**27 867.04**
#进　口	Imports	1 632.04	3 565.80	3 396.71
商品销售总额	**Total Goods Sold**	**8 263.56**	**24 034.93**	**27 640.16**
商品零售总额	Total Sales of Retail Goods	1 036.88	1 598.01	1 740.23
商品批发销售总额	Total Sales of Wholesale Goods	7 226.68	22 436.92	25 899.93
#出　口	Exports	663.82	1 103.74	1 074.24
年末库存总额	**Total Inventory at Year-end**	**1 509.06**	**1 310.34**	**1 309.03**

表10-5　社会消费品零售总额
Total Retail Sales of Consumer Goods

单位:亿元　　(100 million yuan)

指　标	Indicators	2010	2013	2014
社会消费品零售总额	**Total Retail Sales of Consumer Goods**	**1 036.88**	**1 598.01**	**1 740.23**
按登记注册类型分	**By Type of Registration**			
内　资	Domestic Funded	694.79	914.91	976.52
国　有	State-owned	69.77	104.82	109.34
集　体	Collective-owned	55.25	31.89	33.26
股份有限公司	Companies with Limited Liability	115.15	164.63	172.86
私　营	Private	215.79	394.41	425.97
其　他	Others	238.83	219.16	235.09
港澳台商投资	Hong Kong/Macao/Taiwan Invested	124.38	346.47	356.61
外商投资	Foreigner Invested	217.70	336.63	407.10
按行业分	**By Sector**			
商业零售额	Commerce	898.85	1 410.53	1 540.75
餐饮业零售额	Catering	138.03	187.48	199.48
按商品用途分	**By Use**			
食品类	Food	268.69	435.95	490.44
衣着类	Clothing	92.32	166.09	192.01
用品类	Articles	604.08	769.63	829.55
燃料类	Fuel	71.78	226.34	228.23
构　成(%)	**Composition (%)**			
总　计	**Total**	**100.0**	**100.0**	**100.0**
按登记注册类型分	**By Type of Registration**			
内　资	Domestic Funded	67.0	57.2	56.1
国　有	State-owned	6.7	6.5	6.3
集　体	Collective-owned	5.3	2.0	1.9
股份有限公司	Company with Limited Liability	11.1	10.3	9.9
私　营	Private	20.8	24.7	24.5
其　他	Others	23.1	13.7	13.5
港澳台商投资	Hong Kong/Macao/Taiwan Invested	12.0	21.7	20.5
外商投资	Foreigner Invested	21.0	21.1	23.4
按行业分	**By Sector**			
商业零售额	Commerce	86.7	88.3	88.5
餐饮业零售额	Catering	13.3	11.7	11.5
按商品用途分	**By Use**			
食品类	Food	25.9	27.3	28.2
衣着类	Clothing	8.9	10.4	11.0
用品类	Articles	58.3	48.1	47.7
燃料类	Fuel	6.9	14.2	13.1

表10-6　限额以上商业企业主要财务指标
Major Financial Indicators of Above-quota Commercial Enterprises

单位:亿元　　(100 million yuan)

指　标	Indicators	2010	2013	2014
企业单位数(个)	**Number of Enterprises (unit)**	**1 524**	**1 754**	**1 783**
年末资产负债	**Assets and Liabilities at Year-end**			
资产总计	Total Assets	3 513.25	7 684.65	8 410.41
#流动资产合计	Total Circulating Assets	2 843.68	5 839.45	6 518.78
#存　货	Goods in Stock	663.75	1 153.40	1 225.93
固定资产合计	Total Fixed Assets	193.64	305.27	325.14
固定资产原价	Original Value of Fixed Assets	271.39	510.17	568.98
累计折旧	Accumulated Depreciation	96.24	211.62	244.49
#本年提取折旧	Depreciation in Current Year	17.76	37.76	38.55
负债总计	Total Liabilities	2 441.40	5 593.90	6 087.29
所有者权益总计	Owner's Equity	1 071.85	2 090.76	2 323.12
#实收资本	Paid-up Capital	411.67	890.00	1 167.94
#国家资本	State-owned Capital Assets	147.05	144.64	198.99
港澳台商资本	Hong Kong/Macao/Taiwan Capital Assets	41.41	113.30	167.51
外商资本	Foreign Capital Assets	81.17	259.38	225.83
法人资本	Legal Person Capital Assets	72.67	253.01	397.21
损益及分配(限批发零售贸易业填)	**Profit, Loss and Distribution (Only for Wholesale and Retails)**			
营业收入	Operating Revenue	83 314.34	19 007.72	24 117.56
#主营业务收入	Main Operation Revenue	82 887.94	18 946.69	23 997.11
主营业务成本	Main Operation Cost	77 084.46	17 340.96	22 336.35
营业费用	Operating Expenses	2 360.98	834.96	903.19
业务税金及附加	Operation Tax & Surtax	111.52	20.47	22.17
主营业务利润	Profit From Main Business	5 691.96	1 585.26	1 638.59
其他业务利润	Other Earnings	331.97	49.47	65.21

表 10-7 商品交易市场基本情况
Commodity Market Transactions
(2014)

指 标	Indicators	市场数（个）Number of Markets(unit)	营业面积（平方米）Business Space(sq·m)	成交额（亿元）Transaction Value (100 million yuan)
合 计	**Total**	**165**	**1 333 957**	**3 672.41**
综合市场	**Integrated Markets**	**58**	**219 317**	**142.23**
生产资料综合市场	Integrated Market for Productive Materials	1	5 000	0.39
农产品综合市场	Integrated Market for Agricultural Products	48	137 112	115.26
其他综合市场	Other Integrated Markets	9	77 205	26.58
专业市场	**Professional Markets**	**107**	**1 114 640**	**3 530.18**
生产资料市场	Market for Productive Materials	8	22 408	3 177.03
农产品市场	Market for Agricultural Products	53	460 957	58.90
食品饮料烟酒市场	Market of Food, Beverage, Tobacco and Liquor	6	16 687	1.95
纺织品服装鞋帽市场	Market of Textiles, Clothes, Shoes and Hats	10	99 519	2.20
日用品及文化用品市场	Market of Commodities and Stationers' Goods	2	5 000	205.00
家俱、五金装饰材料市场	Market of Furniture, Hardware and Decoration Materials	17	438 520	58.81
汽车及零配件市场	Market of Automobiles and Spare and Accessory Parts	2	35 360	24.50
电器、通讯器材市场	Market of Electric Appliances and Communication Equipment	2	11 095	0.45
花、鸟、鱼、虫市场	Market of Flowers, Birds, Fishes and Insects	2	17 740	1.14
其他专业市场	Other Professional Markets	5	7 354	0.20

表 10-8 商品交易市场摊位数量及成交额
Number of Stalls and Transaction Value in Commodity Market (2014)

指 标	Indicators	数 量（个）Stalls (unit)	成交额（亿元）Transaction Value (100 million yuan)
已出租摊位总计	**Total Stalls Leased**	**19 913**	**3 672.41**
食品、饮料、烟酒类	Food, Beverage, Tobacco and Liquor	10 003	143.52
服装、鞋帽、针、纺织品类	Garments, Shoes, Hats and Knitwear	2 604	3.50
化妆品类	Cosmetics	28	0.02
金银珠宝类	Gold, Silver and Jewelry	4	…
日用品类	Articles for Daily Use	589	215.62
五金电料类	Hardware Materials	86	0.23
体育、娱乐用品类	Sports and Recreation Articles	5	0.03
书报杂志类	Books and Newspapers	1	…
电子出版物及音像制品	Electronic Publications and Audio-Video Products	3	…
家用电器和音像器材类	Household Appliances and Audio-Video Equipment	20	0.04
中西药品	Western and Traditional Chinese Medicine	2	…
文化办公用品类	Culture and Office Articles	238	0.88
通讯器材类	Telecommunications Equipment	74	0.09
家具类	Furniture	818	4.32
木材及制品类	Timber and Its Products	20	0.37
石油及制品类	Petroleum and its products	701	1 413.87
金属材料及制品类	Metal Materials and Products	470	1 733.55
建筑及装潢材料类	Building and Decoration Materials	2 374	54.82
汽车类	Automobiles	55	24.50
种子饲料类	Seeds and Feeding Stuff	9	…
其他类	Others	1 809	77.05

表10-9 限额以上主要商品销售量
Sales Amount of Main Above-quota Goods

指 标 Indicators		单 位 Unit	2012	2013	2014
电脑(微型计算机)	Computer (PC)	台 set	2 054 370	2 468 844	2 326 092
煤 炭	Coal	吨 ton	42 694 634	75 372 013	67 034 856
汽 油	Gasoline	吨 ton	2 326 786	2 538 859	7 649 028
柴 油	Diesel Oil	吨 ton	1 769 560	2 932 936	3 351 737
钢 材	Steel Products	吨 ton	7 935 549	23 017 620	24 430 128
铜	Copper	吨 ton	1 222 566	10 830 827	26 400 910
铝	Aluminium	吨 ton	1 790 590	7 227 416	8 412 367
水 泥	Cement	吨 ton	2 912 356	3 076 823	3 992 725
汽 车	Motor Vehicles	辆 unit	1 707 118	1 886 490	2 182 625
#轿 车	Cars	辆 unit	1 455 350	1 543 503	1 822 003

表10-10 电子商务交易情况
Transactions of E-business

单位:亿元 (100 million yuan)

指 标 Indicators		2012	2013	2014
电子商务交易总额	**E-business Trading Total Volume**	**2 792.70**	**3 144.10**	**3 544.15**
B2B	B2B	2 660.50	2 941.20	3 263.15
网络购物(B2C 和 C2C)	Online Shopping(B2C and C2C)	132.20	202.90	281.00
商品类	Commodity	82.60	135.30	205.00
服务类	Service	49.60	67.60	76.00
第三方支付交易额	**Third-party Payment Trading Volume**	**32 120.00**	**55 195.00**	**73 850.70**

注:2013 年起,浦东新区电子商务数据由上海市商务委统一测算,统计口径和计算方法均发生变化。本表 2014 年数据是根据 2013 年数据推算所得。

Note: Since 2013, E-business data is collected and calculated by Shanghai Commission of Commerce, and the statistical calibre and calculation method are both changed. The numbers of year 2014 is back-calculated by those of 2013.

表10－11　历年进出口货物总值

Total Value of Imports and Exports

(1993～2014)

单位:亿美元　　　　(USD 100 million)

年　份 Year	进出口总值 Total Value of Imports and Exports	出口总值 Total Export Value	#一般贸易 Ordinary Trade	加工贸易 Processing Trade	海关特殊监管区域物流货物 Goods for Logistics within Special Supervision of the Customs	进口总值 Total Import Value	#一般贸易 Ordinary Trade	加工贸易 Processing Trade	海关特殊监管区域物流货物 Goods for Logistics within Special Supervision of the Customs
1993	25.92	12.02	6.67			13.90	5.26		
1994	47.35	23.21	13.73			24.14	5.60		
1995	71.96	39.63	24.40			32.34	11.72		
1996	80.78	38.75	21.31			42.03	14.12		
1997	99.01	45.86	23.06			53.15	17.00		
1998	119.82	52.80	25.14			67.02	21.74		
1999	153.65	66.67	28.58			86.98	35.90		
2000	254.86	95.80	44.21			159.06	71.91		
2001	297.83	110.22	49.56			187.61	87.74		
2002	368.98	136.02	62.96			232.96	98.94		
2003	581.33	211.92	102.80			369.41	156.60		
2004	808.07	323.78	145.55			484.29	185.68		
2005	894.75	372.12	175.38			522.63	186.52		
2006	1 073.10	444.71	212.50			628.39	198.72		
2007	1 280.52	528.10	257.50			752.42	248.66		
2008	1 449.59	604.23	300.42			845.36	286.70		
2009	1 389.89	576.50	241.40			813.39	332.19		
2010	1 865.62	738.79	306.50	286.05	127.51	1 126.83	430.70	123.24	506.01
2011	2 260.00	888.98	356.82	339.00	167.03	1 371.02	537.42	152.78	600.65
2012	2 398.93	939.83	361.39	359.28	189.68	1 459.10	542.57	145.04	696.28
2013	2 496.08	958.25	368.20	349.06	212.37	1 537.83	648.54	160.29	630.39
2014	2 678.71	1 006.10	384.88	352.41	241.51	1 672.61	733.49	173.04	644.46

表10－12 重要商品的出口货物总值
Total Value of Important Exported Goods

单位:万美元 (USD 10 000)

指 标	Indicators	2013	2014
总 计	**Total**	**9 582 510**	**10 060 970**
#机电产品	Mechanic and Electric Products	6 571 725	6 880 718
#高新技术产品	Hi-tech Products	4 084 223	4 331 311
电话机	Telephone Sets	781 490	1 199 766
集成电路	Integrated Circuits	859 044	966 071
自动数据处理设备及其部件	Automatic Data Processing Equipment and its Components	1 208 421	791 065
服装及衣着附件	Clothing and its Accessories	748 951	735 784
船 舶	Ships	378 684	387 499
纺织纱线、织物及制品	Textile Yarns, Fabrics and their Products	315 424	317 424
液晶显示板	LCDs	187 908	202 169
医药品	Medicines	181 704	194 128
汽车零配件	Automobile Components	209 836	191 557
成品油	Refined Oils	172 524	176 674
自动数据处理设备的零件	Parts of Automatic Data Processing Equipment	169 486	163 674
通断保护电路装置及零件	Protection Circuit Devices and their Parts	137 421	150 943
二极管及类似半导体器件	Diodes and Similar Semiconductor Devices	118 203	141 113
家具及其零件	Furniture and its Parts	94 512	103 984
箱包及类似容器	Boxes and Similar Containers	94 931	101 216
钢 材	Steel	65 372	86 756
塑料制品	Plastic Products	79 390	84 153
农产品	Agricultural Products	72 221	81 314
珍珠、钻石、宝石及半宝石	Pearls, Diamonds, Precious Stones and Half-precious Stones	76 452	66 273
汽 车	Automobile	107 035	65 487
医疗仪器及器械	Medical Apparatus and Instruments	62 610	65 095
食 品	Food	51 133	59 255

表 10-13 重要商品的进口货物总值
Total Value of Important Imported Goods

单位：万美元 (USD 10 000)

指 标	Indicators	2013	2014
总 计	**Total**	**15 378 282**	**16 726 133**
#机电产品	Mechanic and Electric Products	8 699 578	9 456 610
#高新技术产品	Hi-tech Products	5 774 227	5 849 138
集成电路	Integrated Circuits	2 553 869	2 301 402
汽车(包括整套散件)	Cars (including CKD parts)	959 657	1 418 488
未锻造的铜及铜材	Unwrought Copper and its Bar	897 207	921 328
农产品	Agricultural Products	735 028	759 799
医药品	Medicines	551 766	652 334
初级形状的塑料	Primarily-formed Plastics	554 605	570 630
飞 机	Aeroplanes	369 920	545 575
计量检测分析自控仪器及器具	Automatically-controlled Equipment and Devices for Measuring and Checking Analysis	448 552	472 366
自动数据处理设备及其部件	Automatic Data Processing Equipment and its Components	427 270	451 576
通断保护电路装置及零件	Protection Circuit Device and its Components	293 058	325 843
医疗仪器及器械	Medical Apparatus and Instruments	238 582	276 684
钻 石	Diamonds	214 042	248 152
成品油	Refined Oils	269 025	239 286
汽车零件	Automobile Components	152 279	167 049
粮 食	Grain	84 645	157 203
手 表	Wrist Watches	135 704	139 139
纺织纱线、织物及制品	Textile Yarns, Fabrics and their Products	128 845	132 015
电话机	Telephone Sets	130 684	127 032
自动数据处理设备的零件	Parts of Automatic Data Processing Equipment	138 365	123 368
变压、整流、电感器及零件	Tranformers, Rectifiers, Inductors and their Parts	112 282	122 443
钢 材	Steel	90 203	114 880
服装及衣着附件	Clothing and its Accessories	99 214	113 101

表10－14 主要年份按国别(地区)分的出口货物总值
Total Value of Exports by Country/Region in Main Years

单位:万美元 (USD 10 000)

国别(地区)	Country/Region	2005	2010	2013	2014
总　计	**Total**	**3 721 174**	**7 387 919**	**9 582 510**	**10 060 970**
#亚　洲	**Asia**	**1 697 530**	**3 340 974**	**4 400 962**	**4 866 893**
#中国香港	Hong Kong, China	468 087	717 639	1 008 633	1 181 388
中国澳门	Macao, China	1 789	5 557	1 304	3 337
中国台湾	Taiwan, China	130 197	271 421	243 768	308 564
印　度	India	35 233	133 175	189 216	236 002
孟加拉国	Bangladesh	13 023	24 808	29 379	33 249
印度尼西亚	Indonesia	26 669	71 303	128 736	136 616
日　本	Japan	451 176	774 154	1 022 579	989 941
马来西亚	Malaysia	66 363	244 468	283 662	278 828
巴基斯坦	Pakistan	10 116	15 838	21 993	26 424
菲律宾	Philippines	64 628	71 219	71 410	81 494
沙特阿拉伯	Saudi Arabia	14 897	31 085	52 031	55 529
新加坡	Singapore	109 379	305 192	448 830	512 581
韩　国	Republic of Korea	136 003	260 049	287 550	374 890
斯里兰卡	Sri Lanka	4 348	5 962	18 149	20 488
泰　国	Thailand	33 224	96 554	115 280	128 425
阿拉伯联合酋长国	United Arab Emirates	46 529	100 559	149 753	129 415
欧　洲	**Europe**	**843 460**	**1 893 937**	**1 904 151**	**2 009 069**
#欧　盟	European Union	785 409	1 701 505	1 664 642	1 795 745
#比利时	Belgium	61 105	101 144	69 140	72 086
英　国	United Kingdom	114 380	178 263	236 544	246 532
德　国	Germany	187 924	380 488	335 716	344 793
法　国	France	63 802	166 625	140 113	148 752
爱尔兰	Ireland	15 151	16 467	24 491	20 425
意大利	Italy	51 163	184 868	109 437	100 067
荷　兰	Netherlands	108 070	225 709	345 358	417 981
西班牙	Spain	42 824	78 986	68 584	80 555
波　兰	Poland	12 284	44 788	39 654	45 793
瑞　典	Sweden	22 954	39 060	25 928	28 369
瑞　士	Switzerland	11 441	26 010	30 517	22 046
俄罗斯	Russia	25 442	126 041	154 507	153 127
拉丁美洲	**Latin America**	**144 120**	**384 886**	**451 406**	**471 410**
#阿根廷	Argentina	5 739	24 892	33 624	19 241
巴　西	Brazil	34 310	120 169	136 629	113 679
智　利	Chile	11 408	23 641	37 493	34 621
墨西哥	Mexico	28 773	99 863	115 018	134 464
巴拿马	Panama	19 659	17 688	16 040	28 560
北美洲	**North America**	**863 433**	**1 279 355**	**2 245 327**	**2 171 301**
#加拿大	Canada	92 621	97 013	145 874	124 304
美　国	United States of America	770 807	1 182 329	2 099 437	2 046 981

表 10－15 主要年份按国别(地区)分的进口货物总值
Total Value of Imports by Country/Region in Main Years

单位:万美元 (USD 10 000)

国别(地区)	Country/Region	2005	2010	2013	2014
总 计	**Total**	**5 226 325**	**11 268 269**	**15 378 282**	**16 726 133**
#亚 洲	**Asia**	**3 046 147**	**6 234 946**	**7 397 608**	**7 341 207**
#中国香港	Hong Kong, China	46 910	38 575	57 181	59 785
中国台湾	Taiwan, China	379 850	762 696	899 298	878 400
印 度	India	58 457	184 487	221 289	237 949
印度尼西亚	Indonesia	76 588	84 572	129 899	118 387
日 本	Japan	919 062	1 738 090	1 646 232	1 700 201
马来西亚	Malaysia	220 785	736 065	1 106 392	835 649
新加坡	Singapore	199 594	251 998	352 702	355 844
韩 国	Repubic of Korea	511 641	949 805	1 137 050	1 259 741
泰 国	Thailand	148 120	330 108	256 796	241 220
非 洲	**Africa**	**39 824**	**214 711**	**258 790**	**308 214**
欧 洲	**Europe**	**1 122 993**	**2 515 255**	**4 627 261**	**5 286 138**
#欧 盟	European Union	998 473	2 092 754	3 656 641	4 287 824
#比利时	Belgium	52 002	200 446	185 424	205 189
英 国	United Kingdom	72 078	113 428	598 178	829 827
德 国	Germany	385 695	797 961	1 324 893	1 593 954
法 国	France	159 106	293 253	527 014	535 807
意大利	Italy	102 266	192 625	270 744	318 324
荷 兰	Netherlands	44 876	77 545	135 298	126 482
西班牙	Spain	19 596	50 883	81 167	84 860
波 兰	Poland	4 920	18 727	44 065	46 396
瑞 典	Sweden	34 688	114 719	101 067	103 835
瑞 士	Switzerland	68 211	214 630	750 801	713 686
俄罗斯	Russia	31 450	144 899	108 928	165 335
拉丁美洲	**Latin America**	**127 155**	**645 571**	**847 320**	**962 790**
#巴 西	Brazil	26 441	107 078	97 900	129 454
智 利	Chile	35 236	299 182	303 938	362 612
墨西哥	Mexico	26 439	103 963	176 400	226 750
北美洲	**North America**	**820 607**	**1 420 899**	**1 780 686**	**2 129 525**
#加拿大	Canada	61 936	129 762	167 904	157 912
美 国	United States of America	758 389	1 291 123	1 612 783	1 971 613
大洋洲	**Oceania**	**69 599**	**235 546**	**465 265**	**695 211**
#澳大利亚	Australia	56 073	173 509	400 122	626 410
新西兰	New Zealand	9 197	52 040	64 169	67 041

主要统计指标解释

社会消费品零售总额

指批发和零售业、餐饮业、新闻出版业、邮政业和其他服务业等，售予城乡居民用于生活消费的商品和社会集团用于公共消费的商品之总量。社会消费品零售总额包括：

（1）批发和零售业企业（单位）：

①售予城乡居民的各种生活消费品；

②售予入境旅游的外国人、华侨、港澳台同胞的各类商品；

③售予行政事业单位、社会团体、军队和武警等机构的商品，以及以零售方式售予各类企业的商品。具体包括：用于非生产和社会交往的办公用品，如通讯设备、计算器具和设备、电讯网络设备、文印设备、音像视听器材和设备、纸张、本册、文具及装订文印材料、家具、日用电器、针纺织品、清洁卫生用品、文体用品、奖品、纪念品、礼品等；供内部人员乘坐的交通工具和燃料；用于办公设施修缮的各类配件、材料、工具等；用于取暖和防暑降温的设备、燃料、材料及食品等；专用于教学的用品和设备；非营利医疗机构的中、西药品、中药材和医疗设备器材；非专用的劳动保护用品；不对外营业的内部食堂用的餐具、炊具、设备、清洁卫生工具和食品、燃料等；军队、武警用于其人员生活的衣着品和个人用品；其他各类非生产性设备和用品。

（2）餐饮业出售的主食、菜肴、烟酒饮料和其他商品。

（3）新闻出版业、邮政业售予城乡居民、企事业单位、军队和武警等机构的书报杂志、音像制品、邮品等。

（4）其他服务业出售的食品、烟酒饮料、服装鞋帽、日常生活用品、医药保健用品、艺术品、工艺美术品、玩具、殡葬用品以及其他消费品。

批发零售贸易业商品购、销、存总额

指各种登记注册类型的批发、零售贸易企业（单位）以本企业（单位）为总体的，从上海、上海以外市场购进的商品总量、销售和出口的商品总量、库存商品总量等情况。该指标对促进工农业生产发展、活跃市场、平抑物价、保障供给、满足需求具有举足轻重的作用。该指标可以反映商品流转过程中商品的购进、销售、库存之间的比例关系和存在的问题。

商品购进总额

指从本企业（单位）以外的单位和个人购进（包括从境外直接进口）作为转卖或加工后转卖的商品总额。它反映批发零售贸易业从国内、国外市场上购进商品的总量。商品购进总额包括：①从工农业生产者购进的商品；②从出版社、报社的出版发行部门购进的图书、杂志和报纸；③从各种登记注册类型的批发零售贸易企业（单位）购进的商品；④从其他单位购进的商品，如从机关、团体、企业等单位购进的剩余物资，从餐饮业、服务业购进的商品，从海关、市场管理部门购进的缉私和没收的商品，从居民手中收购的废旧商品等；⑤从国（境）外直接进口的商品。不包括企业（单位）为自身经营用和未通过买卖行为而收入的商品以及销售退回、商品升溢等。

商品销售总额

商品销售总额指对本企业以外的单位和个人出售（包括对国（境）外直接出口）的商品。这个指标反映批发零售贸易业在上海市场以及上海以外市场上销售商品的总量。商品销售总额包括：①售给城乡居民和社会集团消费用的商品；②售给工业、农业、建筑业、运输邮电业、批发零售贸易业、餐饮业、服务业等作为生产、经营使用的商品；③售给批发零售贸易业作为转卖或加工后转卖的商品；④对国（境）外直接出口的商品。不包括：出售本企业自用的废旧包装用品，未通过买卖行为付出的商品，经本单位介绍，由买卖双方直接结算，本单位只收取手续费的业务，购货退出的商品以及商品损耗和损失等。

批发零售贸易业年末库存

是指年末各种经济类型的批发零售贸易企业（单位）已取得所有权的商品，它反映各地区、各批发零售贸易企业的商品库存情况和对市场商品供应的保证程度。期末库存包括：①存放在批发零售贸易业经营单位（如门市部、批发站、经营处）仓库、货场、货柜和货架中的商品；②挑选、整理、包装中的商品；③已记入购进而尚未运到本单位的商品，即发货单或银行承兑凭证已到而货未到部份；④寄放他处的商品，如因购货方拒绝承付而暂存放在购货方的商品和已办完加工成品收回手续而未提回的商品；⑤委托其他单位代销（未作销售或调出）尚未售出的商品；⑥代其他单位购进尚未交付的商品。不包括所有权不属于本单位的商品、拨付除批发零售贸易业以外的其他行业所属独立核算加工厂等加工生产尚未收回成品的商品，代国家物资储备部门保管的商品等。期末库存总额计算方法是：农副产品采购单位按购进价计算；批发单位按进货价计算；零售单位按什么价格核算就按什么价格计算。

主营业务收入

指企业在销售商品、提供劳务等日常活动中所产生的收入总额。

主营业务成本

指企业已销商品应负担的进货原价和商品进价成本。

营业费用

指批发零售贸易企业在购、销、存过程中发生的各项经

营费用。包括运输费、装卸费、包装费、保险费、展览费、差旅费、广告费、商品损耗、进出口商品累计佣金、经营人员的工资及福利费等。

外贸进出口总额

外贸进出口总额是指海关统计中按经营单位即进出口企业在海关注册地的行政区域口径统计的数据，它反映的是上海浦东新区行政辖区内各类具有进出口经营权企业(外贸企业)的进出口。它不包含外省市外贸企业途经上海浦东新区口岸由上海海关结关放行及统计的进出口商品，但包含上海浦东新区外贸企业经由非上海口岸进出口结关放行及统计的商品。

电子商务交易总额

指借助网络订单且实际交割的的商品和服务的总金额，包括商品交易以及住宿旅游、订餐、通信等服务交易，但不包含第三方支付交易。借助网络订单指通过网络发送订单。付款可以是网上，也可以是网下进行。

B2B：指企业对企业的电子商务交易。

B2C：指企业对个人的电子商务交易。

C2C：指个人对个人的电子商务交易。

第三方支付：是指非金融机构作为第三方在收付款人之间作为中介机构通过网络提供货币资金转移服务。

EXPLANATORY NOTES TO MAJOR STATISTICAL INDICATORS

Total Retail Sales of Consumer Goods

Total Retail Sales of Consumer Goods refers to the sum of retail sales of commodities sold by wholesale, retail, catering, publishing, post and telecommunications and other service industries to urban and rural households for private consumption and to social institutions for public consumption. Retail sales of consumer goods include:

(1) Sales by wholesale and retail units:

①of consumer goods sold to urban and rural households;

②of commodities sold to foreigners, overseas Chinese and Chinese compatriots from Hong Kong, Macau and Taiwan visiting in China;

③of commodities sold to government agencies, institutions, social organizations, military and armed police units, and commodities sold to enterprises in the form of retail sales. More specifically, they include: office facilities and articles for non-production purposes such as communications equipment, computing equipment and instruments, TV and network equipment, printing and copying equipment, audio-visual equipment and instruments, paper, notebooks, stationeries, furniture, electric appliances, knitwear, sanitation and cleaning articles, cultural and sport articles, articles for prizes, souvenirs, etc.; transport vehicles and fuels for employees; materials, spare parts and tools for the maintenance of office facilities; equipment, fuels, materials and food for winter heating or summer cooling purposes; articles and equipment for teaching purpose; Chinese and western medicines and medical equipment and facilities purchased by non profit-making medical institutes; non-specialized work safety articles; cooking utensils, tableware, equipment, cleaning articles, food and fuels purchased by internal cafeterias; clothes and personal articles purchased by military or armed police units for their officials and soldiers; and other equipment and articles for non-production purposes.

(2) Sales of stable food, cooked dishes, beverages, tobaccos and other articles by catering units.

(3) Sales of books, newspapers, magazines, audio-visual products and post products by publishing, post and telecommunications departments to urban and rural households and to enterprises, institutions, military and armed police units.

(4) Sales of food, beverages, tobaccos, clothing, hats, footwear, articles for daily use, medicines, medical and health articles, work of art, handicrafts, toys, funeral articles and other articles by other service industries.

Purchase, Sales and Stock of Commodities by Wholesale and Retail Trades

Purchase, Sales and Stock of Commodities by Wholesale and Retail Trades refer to the total volume of commodities purchased, total volume of sales and exports, and the stock of commodities by wholesale and retail enterprises (establishments) of different status of registration from Shanghai and out-of-Shanghai markets. This indicator plays an important role in promoting industrial and agricultural production, thriving market, stabilizing prices, ensuring market supply and meeting the needs of consumers. It also reflects the relationship among purchase, sales and stock of commodities in the circulation of goods and reveals the existing problems.

Total Purchase of Commodities

Total Purchase of Commodities refers to purchase of commodities from other establishments or individuals (including direct import abroad) for the purpose of reselling, either with or without further processing of the commodities purchased. This indicator shows the total value of purchases of commodities by wholesale and retail establishments from domestic and overseas markets, they include: ①agricultural and industrial products purchased from producers; ②books, magazines and newspapers purchased from distribution departments of the publishers; ③commodities purchased from wholesale and retail establishments; ④commodities purchased from other units, such as surplus materials purchased from government agencies, enterprises or institutions, commodities purchased from catering and service establishments, confiscated goods purchased from customs authorities or market management agencies, second hand goods and reusable stuff purchased from residents; ⑤commodities directly imported abroad. Excluded are commodities purchased by establishments for their own business operation, commodities obtained without buying or selling procedures, rejected commodities, etc.

Total Sales of Commodities

Total Sales of Commodities refer to the selling of commodities to other establishments and individuals (including direct export). Reflecting the total value of sales of commodities at Shanghai markets and out-of-Shanghai markets, this indicator includes: ① commodities sold to urban and rural households and institutions for their consumption; ② commodities sold to establishments in industry, agriculture, construction, transportation, post and telecommunications, wholesale and retail trade, catering and service trade and public utility for their production and operation; ③ commodities sold to wholesale and retail establishments for re-selling, with or without further processing; and ④ commodities for direct export to other countries. Excluded are selling of waste packaging materials used by enterprises themselves commodities transferred without buying or selling procedures, commission income from brokerage in transactions whose settlement is directly handled by buyers and sellers, rejected commodities in the purchase, loss in commodities, etc.

Commodities Stock of Wholesale and Retail Enterprises at Year-end

refers to total commodities possessed by wholesale and retail enterprises (units of various ownership, which reflects the commodity stock level of various wholesale and retail enterprises and the potential for market supply. This indicator includes; ①commodities located in storage, rooms, garages, counters, and shelves of operating units(such as sales stores, wholesale stations, and operating offices) of wholesale and retail enterprises; ② commodities in the process of selecting, sorting, and packing; ③commodities not arrived but recorded as purchase in the account, i. e. commodities have not arrived but payment receipts for the commodities from the sellers or the banks have arrived; ④commodities deposited in other places rather than places mentioned above, for instance; commodities in the hold of purchasers temporarily due to the refusal of payment and commodities not taken back after going through processing procedures; ⑤ commodities entrusted to other units to sell but not sold out yet; ⑥ commodities purchased for other units but not delivered yet. Commodities not included as stock are those not owned by enterprises, those allocated to financially independent factories rather than wholesale and retail enterprises for processing but not taken back yet, and finally those put in stock by wholesale and retail enterprises on behalf of the state material reserves units. The value of commodities stock at the end of period, the value is calculated at purchasing price of agricultural goods purchasing units and wholesale units and retail units at accounting prices.

Prime Operating Revenue

Prime Operating Revenue refers to the earnings a corporation receives in daily activity such as selling goods and offering labor service.

Operating Cost

Operating Cost refers to the cost a corporation paid to buy and deliver the commodities.

Operating Expenses

Operating Expenses refer to the spending that a wholesaler or retailer pays in buying, selling or stocking goods. It includes fees incurred in transport, loading and unloading, packaging, insurance, exhibition, business trip, advertisement, commodity wastage, commissions in import and export, salaries and bonus paid to workers involved.

The Volume of Foreign Trade

The Volume of Foreign Trade is offered by Customs authorities, covering the operation units, or the enterprises involved in import and export, that have registered in the administrative regions where the Customs operate. It reflects the import and export of all the enterprises with import and export rights (foreign trade enterprises) under the administration of Shanghai Pudong New Area Municipality. It excludes those commodities of foreign trade enterprises from out of town that underwent customs clearance at Shanghai Pudong New Area ports but includes commodities of foreign trade enterprises of Shanghai Pudong New Area that underwent customs clearance in non-Shanghai ports.

E-business Trading Total Volume

E-business Trading Total Volume refers to the total volume of commodities and services that have been ordered and actually transacted through the network, including commodity transaction and service transactions, such as hotel booking, meal order, tourism service and so on, not including the third-party transaction. The term of "through the network" means sending orders via internet, but the payment can be made both online and offline.

B2B

B2B refers to E-business transactions from business to business.

B2C

B2C refers to E-business transactions from business to consumer.

C2C

C2C refers to E-business transactions from consumer to consumer.

The Third-party Transaction

The Third-party Transaction refers to the online monetary capital transferance in which the non-financial corporations act as the third party between the payee and the payer.

第十一篇

CHAPTER 11

服务、旅游和住宿业

SERVICES, TOURISM AND HOTELS

表 11-1 主要年份社会服务业经济总量(营业收入)
Total Economics of Social Services in Main Years (Operating Revenue)

单位:亿元 (100 million yuan)

指 标	Indicators	2013	2014
总 计	**Total**	**3 961.92**	**4 427.51**
信息传输、软件和信息技术服务业	Information Transmission, Software and Information Technology Service	1 358.49	1 424.43
#软件开发	Software Development	468.38	523.76
租赁和商务服务业	Leasing and Business Services	1 593.57	1 830.31
#商务服务业	Commercial Services	1 465.80	1 686.51
#企业管理服务	Business Management Services	855.35	966.85
咨询与调查	Consulting and Surveys	296.94	354.41
广告业	Advertising	104.40	107.56
科学研究和技术服务业	Scientific Researches and Technology Service	488.44	552.76
水利、环境和公共设施管理业	Water Conservancy, Environment and Public Facilities Management	85.69	110.12
居民服务、修理和其他服务业	Resident Services, Repair and Other Services	56.52	66.36
教 育	Education	160.09	194.06
卫生和社会工作	Health and Social Work	174.39	205.47
文化、体育和娱乐业	Culture, Sports and Entertainment	44.73	44.00

注:本篇社会服务业相关表式自 2012 年起,采用国民经济行业分类(GB/T 4754-2011)。
Note: The relevant forms in this chapter of social services have been classified by the national economical trades (GB/T 4754-2011) since 2012.

表 11-2 社会服务业经济总量
Total Economics of Social Services
(2014)

单位:亿元 (100 million yuan)

指标	Indicators	营业收入 Operating Revenue	增幅(%) Increased by	比重(%) Percentage
总计	**Total**	**4 427.51**	**9.3**	**100.0**
信息传输、软件和信息技术服务业	Information Transmission, Software and Information Technology Service	1 424.43	4.2	32.2
#软件开发	Software Development	523.76	10.8	11.8
租赁和商务服务业	Leasing and Business Services	1 830.31	11.8	41.3
#商务服务业	Commercial Services	1 686.51	11.8	38.1
#企业管理服务	Business Management Services	966.85	9.3	21.8
咨询与调查	Consulting and Surveys	354.41	18.5	8.0
广告业	Advertising	107.56	2.3	2.4
科学研究和技术服务业	Scientific Researches and Technology Service	552.76	12.9	12.5
水利、环境和公共设施管理业	Water Conservancy, Environment and Public Facilities Management	110.12	10.0	2.5
居民服务、修理和其他服务业	Resident Services, Repair and Other Services	66.36	10.1	1.5
教育	Education	194.06	15.0	4.4
卫生和社会工作	Health and Social Work	205.47	13.2	4.6
文化、体育和娱乐业	Culture, Sports and Entertainment	44.00	-1.6	1.0

表11-3　主要年份社会服务业从业人员数
Number of Employees of Social Services in Main Years

单位:万人　　(10 000 persons)

指　标	Indicators	2013	2014
总　计	**Total**	**65.80**	**68.79**
信息传输、软件和信息技术服务业	Information Transmission, Software and Information Technology Service	15.96	16.15
#软件开发	Software Development	8.76	8.87
租赁和商务服务业	Leasing and Business Services	23.73	25.93
#商务服务业	Commercial Services	22.88	24.00
#企业管理服务	Business Management Services	8.60	9.10
咨询与调查	Consulting and Surveys	4.51	4.81
广告业	Advertising	0.53	0.54
科学研究和技术服务业	Scientific Researches and Technology Service	8.21	8.46
水利、环境和公共设施管理业	Water Conservancy, Environment and Public Facilities Management	2.22	2.24
居民服务、修理和其他服务业	Resident Services, Repair and Other Services	3.54	3.56
教　育	Education	6.39	6.52
卫生和社会工作	Health and Social Work	4.21	4.37
文化、体育和娱乐业	Culture, Sports and Entertainment	1.54	1.56

表11-4 社会服务业从业人员数
Number of Employees of Social Services
(2014)

单位:万人 (10 000 persons)

指 标	Indicators	从业人员数 Number of Employees	增 幅(%) Increased by	比 重(%) Percentage
总 计	**Total**	**68.79**	**4.5**	**100.0**
信息传输、软件和信息技术服务业	Information Transmission, Software and Information Technology Service	16.15	1.2	23.5
#软件开发	Software Development	8.87	1.3	12.9
租赁和商务服务业	Leasing and Business Services	25.93	9.3	37.7
#商务服务业	Commercial Services	24.00	4.9	34.9
#企业管理服务	Business Management Services	9.10	5.8	7.0
咨询与调查	Consulting and Surveys	4.81	6.7	7.0
广告业	Advertising	0.54	1.9	0.8
科学研究和技术服务业	Scientific Researches and Technology Service	8.46	3.0	12.3
水利、环境和公共设施管理业	Water Conservancy, Environment and Public Facilities Management	2.24	0.9	3.3
居民服务、修理和其他服务业	Resident Services, Repair and Other Services	3.56	0.6	5.2
教 育	Education	6.52	2.0	9.5
卫生和社会工作	Health and Social Work	4.37	3.8	6.4
文化、体育和娱乐业	Culture, Sports and Entertainment	1.56	1.3	2.3

表 11-5 主要年份接待国内外游客情况
Foreign and Domestic Tourists Received in Main Years

单位:万人次 (10 000 persons-times)

指 标	Indicators	2005	2010	2013	2014
接待游客总数	**Total Tourists Received**	**1 660**	**3 215**	**3 002**	**3 639**
国内游客数	Domestic	1 566	3 085	2 868	3 450
国外游客数	Foreign	94	130	134	189
按接待单位分	By Receiving Agency				
#宾馆接待游客	Hotels	164	278	285	325
旅行社接待游客	Tourist Agencies	111	185	182	157
景点接待游客	Tourist Attractions	1 385	2 752	2 535	3 157
平均每天接待旅游人数(人次/天)	Average Number of Tourists Received Everyday (person-time/day)	45 474	88 094	82 247	99 699

表 11-6 旅游景点经营情况
Operation of Tourist Attractions

指 标	Indicators	单 位 Unit	2005	2010	2013	2014
主要景点营业情况	**Business in Major Tourist Attractions**					
主要景点个数	Main Tourist Attractions	个 in number	23	25	33	34
接待参观人次	Visitors Received	万人次 10 000 person-times	1 908	2 752	2 535	3 157
营业收入	Operation Earnings	万元 10 000 yuan	87 500	144 781	138 976	167 941

表 11－7 主要景点经营情况
The General Development of Main Tourism Spot

指 标 Indicators		营业收入(万元) Operative Income (10 thousand yuan)		接待人数(万人次) Number of Tourists (10 thousand person-time)	
		2014 年	2013 年	2014 年	2013 年
东方明珠	The Oriental Pearl TV Towel	38 432.07	36 523.54	425.87	348.50
上海海洋水族馆	Shanghai Ocean Aquarium	29 122.04	23 450.74	199.27	159.56
上海野生动物园	Shanghai Wild Life Zoo	25 394.20	13 971.48	230.29	119.40
磁悬浮列车	Magnetically Levitated Train	13 285.31	12 298.91	323.99	301.61
上海环球金融中心观光厅	Shanghai World Financial Center Sightseeing Hall	11 401.00	10 877.00	189.36	186.63
上海科技馆	Shanghai Techonology Museum	9 684.05	7 935.70	297.52	357.77
观光隧道	Sightseeing Tunnel	7 847.88	6 258.68	159.33	123.13
上海金茂大厦	Shanghai Jin Mao Tower	6 992.00	6 571.00	123.36	114.05
上海世纪公园	Shanghai Century Park	5 574.33	3 937.94	309.31	183.33
巧克力开心乐园	Chocolate Happy Paradise	5 076.53	1 140.00	38.33	13.03
月亮船(原沙特馆)	Moon Boat	2 016.16	2 068.91	46.77	49.61
鲜花港	Flower Port	1 727.84	1 925.77	50.72	40.88
南汇桃花村	Nanhui Peach Blossom Villiage	1 684.00	1 223.00	11.02	7.23
东方葵园生态农庄	Oriental Sunflower Ecological Farm	1 409.00	1 781.00	11.22	13.91
喜来春国际农庄	Spring Ecological Farm	1 401.51	1 422.75	29.49	11.07
渔乐湾生态园	Fishing Ecological Farm	1 229.25	1 344.04	29.60	30.70
书院人家	Shuyuan Farm	916.51	1 384.30	12.84	17.61
中国航海博物馆	China Maritime Museum	791.15	613.48	28.31	22.03
凌空农艺大观园	Lingkong Agro Museum	780.15	799.66	7.43	8.57

表11-8 旅馆、旅行社经营情况
Operation of Hotels and Travel Agencies

指 标	Indicators	单 位 Unit	2005	2010	2013	2014
旅馆业	Hotel Industry					
接待能力状况	Receiving Capacity					
客房数	Rooms	间 room	12 692	15 780	17 744	18 100
客房床位数	Beds	张 bed	20 245	22 652	25 767	26 272
实际住宿人次数	Actual Staying Guests	万人次 10 000 person-times	163.84	278.33	284.91	324.96
#境外来沪住宿人次数	Overseas Guests	万人次 10 000 person-times	73.03	99.21	102.88	111.57
实际住宿人天数	Actual Staying Days	万人天 10 000 person · days	371.18	491.33	471.67	509.39
#境外来沪住宿人天数	Staying Days of Overseas Guests	万人天 10 000 person · days	195.58	187.84	178.71	182.05
财务经营状况	Financial Operation					
固定资产原值	Original Value of Fixed Assets	亿元 100 million yuan	82.35	119.19	112.60	110.17
营业收入	Operation Earning	亿元 100 million yuan	37.09	55.85	54.91	60.39
#客房收入	Hotel Room Earning	亿元 100 million yuan	21.77	31.87	27.84	31.00
餐饮收入	Catering Earning	亿元 100 million yuan	15.32	19.22	22.30	29.39
旅行社	Travel Agency					
旅行社接待人次数	Persons Received by PNA Travel Agencies	万人次 10 000 person-times	110.69	185.25	181.98	157.68
国内旅行社	Domestic Travel Agencies	万人次 10 000 person-times	89.86	154.52	151.12	117.19
国际旅行社	International Travel Agencies	万人次 10 000 person-times	20.83	30.73	30.86	40.49
旅行社营业收入	Operation Earnings of PNA Travel Agencies	亿元 100 million yuan	14.68	30.00	53.73	53.21
国内旅行社	Domestic Travel Agencies	亿元 100 million yuan	8.44	16.08	25.05	19.34
国际旅行社	International Travel Agencies	亿元 100 million yuan	6.24	13.92	28.68	33.87

表11-9　会议、展览情况
Conferences and Fairs

指　标 Indicators		单　位 Unit	2005	2010	2013	2014
举办展览(博览)	**Number of Exhibitions Hosted**	**次 time**	**114**	**120**	**211**	**220**
#国际性	International	次 time	91	100	173	185
#三万平方米及以上	≥30 000 sq. m	次 time	29	38	79	85
#五万平方米及以上	≥50 000 sq. m	次 time	15	28	44	45
展览面积	Display Area	万平方米 10 000 sq・m	238	400	754	812
参展客商	Exhibition-Attending Investors	个 unit	48 412	69 713	141 502	122 915
接待(参观)人数	Visitors Received	万人次 10 000 person-times	266.90	309.70	632.10	649.99
召开会议	Conferences Hosted	次 time	1 583	1 504	12 932	14 677
#跨省市	Trans-provincial	次 time	61	112		
国际性	International	次 time	199	26	2 164	2 068
参加会议人员	Number of Participants	万人次 10 000 person-times	16.69	17.03	145.83	185.77
#海外与会人员	Overseas Participants	万人次 10 000 person-times	3.00	1.34	19.51	18.35

注：2011 年始会议统计的范围为浦东四星级以上宾馆。
Note： The statistical scope for the conferences since the year of 2011 refers to the hotels with four stars or more in Pudong.

表11－10　四星级以上酒店宾馆基本情况
Basic Information about Hotels above Four-star Level

指　标　Indicators		标　准 Standard	客房数(间) Number of Rooms
浦东新区香格里拉酒店有限公司	Shangri-la Hotel Pudong New Area	五星级 Five-star	952
金茂君悦大酒店	Grand Hyatt Residence	五星级 Five-star	555
上海国际会议中心有限公司大酒店	Shanghai International Conference Center Hotel	五星级 Five-star	273
上海锦江汤臣大酒店有限公司	Shanghai Jinjiang Tangcheng Intercontinental Hotel	五星级 Five-star	398
上海东锦江大酒店有限公司	Shanghai East Jinjiang Hotel (Doubletree by Hilton Shanghai Pudong)	五星级 Five-star	850
喜来登由由酒店	Sheraton Youyou Hotel	五星级 Five-star	666
上海淳大万丽大酒店	Renaissance Shanghai Pudong Hotel	五星级 Five-star	370
上海东郊宾馆有限公司	Shanghai Dongjiao Hotel	五星级 Five-star	262
上海紫金山大酒店	Shanghai Purple Mountain Hotel	五星级 Five-star	368
上海外高桥皇冠假日酒店	Shanghai Waigaoqiao Crowne Plaza	五星级 Five-star	388
上海红塔豪华精选酒店	Shanghai Hongta Luxury Collection	五星级 Five-star	328
裕景大饭店	Yujing Grand Hotel	四星级 Four-star	460
上海浦东华油实业有限责任公司中油大酒店	Zhongyou Hotel of Huayou Real Estate Shanghai Pudong	四星级 Four-star	318
上海通茂大酒店	Shanghai Tongmao Hotel	四星级 Four-star	298
浦东华美达大酒店	Pudong Ramada Hotel	四星级 Four-star	269
证大丽笙大酒店	Radisson Hotel Pudong Century Park	四星级 Four-star	354
福朋喜来登由由酒店	Fupeng Sheraton Youyou Hotel	四星级 Four-star	316
机场华美达大酒店	Ramada Airport Hotel	四星级 Four-star	188
齐鲁万怡大酒店	Courtyard by Marriott Shanghai Pudong	四星级 Four-star	318
上海海神诺富特大酒店	Novotel Atlantis Shanghai	四星级 Four-star	293
浦东假日酒店	Pudong Holiday Inn	四星级 Four-star	352
明城大酒店	Mingcheng Hotel	四星级 Four-star	222
东怡大酒店	Dongyi Hotel	四星级 Four-star	209
上海宝安大酒店有限公司	Shanghai Baoan Hotel	四星级 Four-star	226
上海嘉瑞酒店有限公司	Shanghai Green Garden Hotel	四星级 Four-star	151

主要统计指标解释

接待国外游客人数

指来上海浦东新区参观、访问、旅行、探亲、访友、休养、考察、参加会议和从事经济、科技、文化、教育、体育、宗教等活动的外国人、华侨、港澳和台湾同胞的人数。不包括来上海浦东新区常住1年以上的外国专家、留学生等。上海浦东新区入境的境外旅游人数包括从上海浦东新区口岸入境的境外旅游人数和从我国其他口岸入境的境外旅游人数。

EXPLANATORY NOTES TO MAJOR STATISTICAL INDICATORS

Number of Overseas Tourists

Number of Overseas Tourists refers to the number of foreigners, overseas Chinese, and compatriots from Hong Kong, Macao and Taiwan coming to Shanghai Pudong New Area for sightseeing, visits, tours, family reunions, meeting friends, vacations, study tours, attending meetings and other activities of an economic, scientific and technological, cultural, physical culture and religious nature. This does not include foreign experts and students residing in Shanghai Pudong New Area for over 1 year. The number of overseas tourists to Shanghai Pudong New Area includes those overseas tourists entering China through Shanghai Pudong New Area customs and through customs other than Shanghai.

第十二篇

CHAPTER 12

科学技术

SCIENCE AND TECHNOLOGY

表 12－1　历年科技成果

Achievements in Scientific & Technological Research

(1995～2014)

单位:项　　　　(item)

年　份 Year	获上海市高新技术成果转化百佳项目 Top 100 Projects Which Have Successfully Commercialized Achievements in Scientific & Technological Research	获上海市以上科技进步奖 Shanghai and Above Level Achievement Awards in Scienceand Technology	按奖项分 Award Grade								
			特等奖 Special Award	#国家级 National Grade	一等奖 First Prize	#国家级 National Grade	二等奖 Second Prize	#国家级 National Grade	三等奖 Third Prize	青年科技杰出贡献奖 Youth Science and Technology Outstanding Contribution Award	国际科技合作奖 International Technology Cooperate Award
1995		2					1		1		
1996											
1997		2					1		1		
1998		14					3		11		
1999		12			2		3		7		
2000		11					5		6		
2001		16					5		11		
2002		37			8		13		16		
2003	11	34			8		10		16		
2004	11	45			10		16		19		
2005	25	35			5	1	10	3	20		
2006	17	48			11	1	23	5	14		
2007		73			11	2	31	11	31		
2008		66			10		27	6	29		
2009		50			5		23	5	22		
2010		63			8		29	10	26		
2011	19	92			15		43	12	34		
2012	27	69			19	1	25	3	24	1	
2013	20	70			9		37	12	24		
2014	18	61	1	1	10		21	6	27	1	1

注：上海市高新技术成果转化百佳项目从 2001 年起评比。
Note：We started to appraise the above－mentioned Top 100 Projects since 2001.

表12-2 历年各类技术合同项目
All Kinds of Technical Contracts
(1994～2014)

单位:项 (item)

年 份 Year	各类合同项目 Item of Contracts	技术开发 Technical Development	技术转让 Technology Tranfer	技术咨询 Technical Consultation	技术服务 Technical Service
1994	595	25	43	98	429
1995	924	42	33	147	702
1996	1 525	12	16	215	1 282
1997	1 742	23	56	291	1 372
1998	1 659	57	49	282	1 271
1999	1 998	85	21	406	1 486
2000	1 940	79	24	458	1 379
2001	2 253	260	86	405	1 502
2002	2 281	372	116	465	1 328
2003	2 406	500	284	422	1 200
2004	2 362	580	148	406	1 228
2005	3 034	1 155	225	353	1 301
2006	2 636	1 448	100	204	884
2007	2 545	1 326	118	86	1 015
2008	2 294	1 448	94	262	490
2009	2 518	1 757	112	194	455
2010	2 550	1 774	139	100	537
2011	2 932	2 269	137	181	345
2012	2 722	2 133	124	116	349
2013	2 484	1 876	112	90	406
2014	2 753	1 938	132	8	675

表 12-3 历年各类技术合同成交金额
Business Volume of All Kinds of Technical Contracts
(1994～2014)

单位:万元 (10 000 yuan)

年 份 Year	成交金额 Business Volume	技术开发 Technical Development	技术转让 Technology Tranfer	技术咨询 Technical Consultation	技术服务 Technical Service
1994	6 225	284	404	492	5 045
1995	12 514	3 863	2 105	936	5 610
1996	21 255	599	573	1 772	18 311
1997	15 644	749	1 286	2 386	11 223
1998	21 286	3 924	2 106	2 098	13 158
1999	24 788	7 194	1 509	2 929	13 156
2000	39 707	7 969	15 893	2 524	13 321
2001	62 892	30 778	8 709	3 317	20 088
2002	86 786	51 233	12 303	4 585	18 665
2003	112 355	79 274	12 978	5 217	14 886
2004	221 295	185 897	13 881	4 030	17 487
2005	386 406	335 848	33 096	3 087	14 375
2006	641 015	525 942	96 628	2 952	15 493
2007	839 052	694 197	125 175	2 586	17 094
2008	957 346	870 937	69 244	3 512	13 653
2009	1 299 693	1 145 384	137 907	2 111	14 291
2010	1 210 256	1 023 716	96 063	16 254	74 224
2011	1 269 191	1 125 001	66 825	2 508	74 857
2012	1 578 060	1 247 899	136 211	2 749	191 201
2013	1 747 328	870 741	164 063	22 137	690 387
2014	1 795 142	944 087	89 506	762	760 788

表 12-4 历年专利申请情况
Statistics of Patent Claiming
(1999 ~2014)

单位:项 (item)

年份 Year	专利申请总量 Total Patent Claimings	发明 Inventions	实用新型 Utility Models	外观设计 Design in Appearance
1999	386	67	216	103
2000	718	209	241	268
2001	1 103	222	453	428
2002	2 397	467	591	1 339
2003	2 580	1 064	852	664
2004	2 871	1 676	719	476
2005	3 141	1 794	863	484
2006	6 767	2 557	1 224	2 986
2007	8 435	3 054	1 386	3 995
2008	8 980	3 065	1 893	4 022
2009	14 645	5 372	3 936	5 337
2010	17 587	6 576	4 902	6 109
2011	18 819	9 218	6 973	2 628
2012	21 972	12 902	7 158	1 912
2013	18 331	9 687	6 936	1 708
2014	19 002	10 279	7 127	1 596

表 12-5 历年专利授权情况
Statistics of Patents Authorized
(2001 ~2014)

单位:项 (item)

年份 Year	专利授权总量 Total Patents Authorized	发明 Inventions	实用新型 Utility Models	外观设计 Design in Appearance
2001	519			
2002	668			
2003	1 542			
2004	1 066	95	528	443
2005	1 204	329	576	299
2006	1 432	375	655	402
2007	4 086	409	1 152	2 525
2008	3 677	841	1 442	1 394
2009	8 046	1 557	2 266	4 223
2010	12 764	1 503	3 950	7 311
2011	12 685	2 149	5 423	5 113
2012	11 226	2 789	6 653	1 784
2013	11 073	3 074	6 564	1 435
2014	10 896	3 139	6 454	1 303

表12-6　区属企业、事业单位各类专业技术人员(2014年末)
Professional Personnel Working in Enterprises and Institutions in PNA (Total by the End of 2014)

单位:人　　(person)

指　标	Indicators	合　计 Total	#女　性 Female	按学历分 By Education Level 研究生 Post Graduate	大　学 本　科 University	高　等 专　科 Junior University	中等专科 Specialized Secondary School	高中及以下 Senior High School and Below
总　计	**Total**	**48 255**	**34 578**	**2 782**	**33 567**	**9 455**	**1 805**	**646**
工程技术人员	Engineering	2 645	642	277	1 406	525	164	273
农业技术人员	Agricultural	482	141	41	236	138	59	8
科学研究人员	Research	249	111	44	124	65	11	5
卫生技术人员	Healthcare	12 540	9 180	1 223	6 658	3 448	1 104	107
教学人员	Teaching	28 514	22 376	866	23 327	4 133	181	7
经济人员	Economic	1 351	526	195	583	377	68	128
会计人员	Financial/Accounting	1 330	960	54	652	457	127	40
统计人员	Statistical	175	117	3	91	57	18	6
翻译人员	Interpreter/Translator	14	8	4	7	3		
图书档案文博人员	Librarian/Archivist/Museum Staff	433	320	37	229	131	18	18
新闻、出版人员	News-Reporting/Publishing	76	31	7	60	9		
律师、公证人员	Lawyer/Notary	54	27	9	45			
播音人员	Radio Crew Member							
工艺美术人员	Artisan	23	4		4	6	8	5
体育人员	Sports	63	22		46	16		1
艺术人员	Actor/Actress	83	46	5	28	31	8	11
政工人员	Political	223	67	17	71	59	39	37

表 12-7 区属企业、事业单位各年龄组专业技术职务及专业技术人员(2014 年末)

Technical Professions and Technicians Grouped by Ages in PNA Enterprises and Institutions (Total by the End of 2014)

单位:人 (person)

指 标 Indicators		合 计 Total	按年龄分 By Age					
			35 岁及以下 35 Year-old and Below	36 至 40 岁 36~40 Year-old	41 至 45 岁 41~45 Year-old	46 至 50 岁 46~50 Year-old	51 至 54 岁 51~54 Year-old	55 岁以上 55 Year-old and Above
总 计	**Total**	**44 533**	**16 287**	**8 363**	**8 580**	**6 375**	**3 396**	**1 532**
按专业技术职务分	**By Professional Position**							
高级职务	Senior	4 039	10	338	1 060	1 408	848	375
中级职务	Intermediate	18 851	2 130	4 612	5 581	3 927	1 866	735
初级职务	Junior	19 812	12 362	3 377	1 931	1 038	682	422
未聘职务	Laid-off	1 831	1 785	36	8	2		
按专业技术类别分	**By Profession**							
工程技术人员	Engineering	979	379	186	172	103	78	61
农业技术人员	Agricultural	435	118	36	62	85	61	73
科学研究人员	Scientific	236	56	52	35	49	19	25
卫生技术人员	Healthcare	12 536	5 166	2 604	2 102	1 268	911	485
教学人员	Teaching	28 486	10 108	5 036	5 880	4 595	2 120	747
经济人员	Economic	272	82	51	52	18	36	33
会计人员	Financial/Accounting	767	139	234	149	128	78	39
统计人员	Statistical	127	42	31	25	16	10	3
图书档案文博人员	Librarian/Archivist/Museum Staff	409	110	94	60	73	42	30
政工人员	Political	28	8	1	5	3	4	7
其他专业技术人员	Others	258	79	38	38	37	37	29

表 12-8　工业企业科技活动人员情况
Scientific and Technical Personnel of Industrial Enterprises (2014)

指　标	Indicators	有科技活动企业数(个) Number of Enterprises with Scientific Technical Activities (unit)	从事科技活动人员(人) Total Number of Personnel Undertaking Scientific Technical Activities (person)	#高中级技术职称人员(人) People with Senior and Intermediate Technical Titles (person)
总　计	**Total**	**460**	**70 072**	**18 232**
按注册登记大类分组	**Grouped by Type of Registration**			
国　有	State-owned	7	2 697	1 925
集　体	Collective-owned	1	135	1
股份制及其他有限公司	Share-holding	102	14 914	4 022
私　营	Private	132	7 392	1 754
外商及港澳台投资	Overseas Invested Enterprises	208	41 040	9 064
其　他	Others	10	3 894	1 466
按隶属关系分组	**Grouped by Subordination**			
中央工业	Central	28	14 106	5 871
地方工业	Local	432	55 966	12 361
按企业规模分组	**Grouped by Enterprise Scale**			
#大型企业	Large	64	44 244	12 119
中型企业	Medium	131	16 077	3 829
按工业行业大类分组	**Grouped by Sector**			
农副食品加工业	Farm and Sideline Products Processing	7	401	66
食品制造业	Food Manufacturing	2	108	15
酒、饮料和精制茶制造业	Wine, Beverage and Refined Tea Manufacturing	1	25	11
烟草制品业	Tobacco Manufacturing	1	17	11
纺织业	Textile Industry	3	153	11
家具制造业	Furniture Manufacturing	2	1 366	87
造纸和纸制品业	Papermaking and Paper Products	5	344	154
印刷和记录媒介复制业	Printing and Record Medium Reproduction Industry	10	788	183
文教、工美、体育和娱乐用品制造业	Culture, Art, Sports and Recreation Supplies Manufacturing	3	80	38
石油加工、炼焦和核燃料加工业	Oil Processing, Coking and Nuclear Fuel Processing	3	137	101
化学原料和化学制品制造业	Raw Chemical Materials and Chemical Products	32	2 815	431
医药制造业	Medicine Manufacture	40	4 585	632
化学纤维制造业	Chemical Fiber Manufacturing	2	72	14
橡胶和塑料制品业	Rubber and Plastic Products Industry	16	788	267
非金属矿物制品业	Nonmetal Mineral Products	14	642	152
黑色金属冶炼和压延加工业	Smelting and Rolling of Nonferrous Metals	1	9	1
有色金属冶炼和压延加工业	Smelting and Rolling of Ferrous Metals	4	259	57
金属制品业	Metal Products	18	1 320	227
通用设备制造业	General Equipment Manufacture	61	4 883	1 886
专用设备制造业	Special Purpose Equipment Manufacturing	50	4 102	1 442
汽车制造业	Automobile Manufacturing	46	15 717	3 676
铁路、船舶、航空航天和其他运输设备制造业	Railroad, Ship, Aviation and Other Transportation Equipment Manufacturing	12	2 736	1 063
电气机械和器材制造业	Electric Equipment and Machinery Manufacturing	54	5 744	1 086
计算机、通信和其他电子设备制造业	Computer, Communications and Other Electronic Equipment Manufacturing	43	19 101	4 315
仪器仪表制造业	Instrument Manufacturing	18	1 243	312
废弃资源综合利用业	Comprehensive Utilization of Waste Resources	1	20	3
金属制品、机械和设备修理业	Metal Products, Machinery and Equipment Repair Industry	1	20	14
电力、热力生产和供应业	Production and Supply of Electricity and Thermal Power	7	2 546	1 944
燃气生产和供应业	Production and Supply of Fuel Gas	1	15	10
水的生产和供应业	Production and Supply of Water	2	36	23

注：本篇工业数据为年主营业务收入 2000 万及以上企业。
Note: In this chapter, industry data refer to enterprises with annual main business income of 20 million yuan and above.

表12-9 工业企业技术开发项目和人员情况
Technical Development Projects and Personnel of Industrial Enterprises
(2014)

指 标	Indicators	项目数(项) Number of Projects (item)	从事技术开发人数(人) Number of Technical Development Personnel (person)	科技项目经费内部支出(万元) Internal Expenditure for Projects of Science and Technology (10 000 yuan)
总 计	**Total**	**6 325**	**59 577**	**2 335 079**
按注册登记大类分组	**Grouped by Type of Registration**			
国 有	State-owned	335	2 553	35 380
集 体	Collective-owned	9	130	54
股份制及其他有限公司	Share-holding	1 000	13 017	500 579
私 营	Private	893	6 472	120 142
外商及港澳台投资	Overseas Invested Enterprises	3 893	33 826	1 521 759
其 他	Others	195	3 579	157 165
按隶属关系分组	**Grouped by Subordination**	**6 325**	**59 577**	**2 335 079**
中央工业	Central	1 045	12 116	462 687
地方工业	Local	5 280	47 461	1 872 392
按企业规模分组	**Grouped by Enterprise Scale**			
#大型企业	Large	2 692	37 460	1 712 615
中型企业	Medium	1 781	13 625	394 174
按工业行业大类分组	**Grouped by Sector**			
农副食品加工业	Farm and Sideline Products Processing	34	373	13 448
食品制造业	Food Manufacturing	16	63	3 696
酒、饮料和精制茶制造业	Wine,Beverage and Refined Tea Manufacturing	2	11	42
烟草制品业	Tobacco Manufacturing	2	13	342
纺织业	Textile Industry	13	107	2 754
家具制造业	Furniture Manufacturing	185	1 059	36 847
造纸和纸制品业	Papermaking and Paper Products	31	308	6 775
印刷和记录媒介复制业	Printing and Record Medium Reproduction Industry	76	756	12 184
文教、工美、体育和娱乐用品制造业	Culture, Art, Sports and Recreation Supplies Manufacturing	12	73	647
石油加工、炼焦和核燃料加工业	Oil Processing, Coking and Nuclear Fuel Processing	51	126	2 072
化学原料和化学制品制造业	Raw Chemical Materials and Chemical Products	325	2 338	89 352
医药制造业	Medicine Manufacture	682	3 971	119 152
化学纤维制造业	Chemical Fiber Manufacturing	7	57	981
橡胶和塑料制品业	Rubber and Plastic Products Industry	73	710	15 113
非金属矿物制品业	Nonmetal Mineral Products	76	591	18 677
黑色金属冶炼和压延加工业	Smelting and Rolling of Ferrous Metals	2	9	1
有色金属冶炼和压延加工业	Smelting and Rolling of Nonferrous Metals	39	149	12 859
金属制品业	Metal Products	139	1 210	24 081
通用设备制造业	General Equipment Manufacture	908	3 996	184 259
专用设备制造业	Special Purpose Equipment Manufacturing	361	3 498	102 059
汽车制造业	Automobile Manufacturing	1 327	13 455	715 527
铁路、船舶、航空航天和其他运输设备制造业	Railroad, Ship, Aviation and Other Transportation Equipment Manufacturing	317	2 155	106 530
电气机械和器材制造业	Electric Equipment and Machinery Manufacturing	380	5 154	113 529
计算机、通信和其他电子设备制造业	Computer, Communications and Other Electronic Equipment Manufacturing	883	15 728	690 748
仪器仪表制造业	Instrument Manufacturing	93	1 125	25 673
废弃资源综合利用业	Comprehensive Utilization of Waste Resources	1	18	307
金属制品、机械和设备修理业	Metal Products,Machinery and Equipment Repair Industry	6	18	173
电力、热力生产和供应业	Production and Supply of Electricity and Thermal Power	277	2 459	35 687
燃气生产和供应业	Production and Supply of Fuel Gas	2	14	18
水的生产和供应业	Production and Supply of Water	5	33	1 549

表 12-10　工业科技活动经费支出情况
(2014)

单位:万元

指　标	Indicators	企业内部科技活动支出合计 Total Expenditures of Scientific and Technological Activities Within Enterprises
总　计	**Total**	**2 594 785**
按注册登记大类分组	**Grouped by Type of Registration**	
国　有	State-owned	35 734
集　体	Collective-owned	755
股份制及其他有限公司	Share-holding	593 775
私　营	Private	131 773
外商及港澳台投资	Overseas Invested Enterprises	1 662 709
其　他	Others	170 039
按隶属关系分组	**Grouped by Subordination**	
中央工业	Central	491 675
地方工业	Local	2 103 110
按企业规模分组	**Grouped by Enterprise Scale**	
#大型企业	Large	1 874 262
中型企业	Medium	472 198
按工业行业大类分组	**Grouped by Sector**	
农副食品加工业	Farm and Sideline Products Processing	13 792
食品制造业	Food Manufacturing	3 717
酒、饮料和精制茶制造业	Wine, Beverage and Refined Tea Manufacturing	472
烟草制品业	Tobacco Manufacturing	471
纺织业	Textile Industry	3 341
家具制造业	Furniture Manufacturing	48 981
造纸和纸制品业	Papermaking and Paper Products	7 098
印刷和记录媒介复制业	Printing and Record Medium Reproduction Industry	12 484
文教、工美、体育和娱乐用品制造业	Culture, Art, Sports and Recreation Supplies Manufacturing	652
石油加工、炼焦和核燃料加工业	Oil Processing, Coking and Nuclear Fuel Processing	2 406
化学原料和化学制品制造业	Raw Chemical Materials and Chemical Products	92 561
医药制造业	Medicine Manufacture	129 525
化学纤维制造业	Chemical Fiber Manufacturing	1 002
橡胶和塑料制品业	Rubber and Plastic Products Industry	15 429
非金属矿物制品业	Nonmetal Mineral Products	19 631
黑色金属冶炼和压延加工业	Smelting and Rolling of Ferrous Metals	1
有色金属冶炼和压延加工业	Smelting and Rolling of Nonferrous Metals	13 266
金属制品业	Metal Products	25 675
通用设备制造业	General Equipment Manufacture	197 645
专用设备制造业	Special Purpose Equipment Manufacturing	119 664
汽车制造业	Automobile Manufacturing	811 299
铁路、船舶、航空航天和其他运输设备制造业	Railroad, Ship, Aviation and Other Transportation Equipment Manufacturing	115 097
电气机械和器材制造业	Electric Equipment and Machinery Manufacturing	160 938
计算机、通信和其他电子设备制造业	Computer, Communications and Other Electronic Equipment Manufacturing	734 654
仪器仪表制造业	Instrument Manufacturing	26 927
废弃资源综合利用业	Comprehensive Utilization of Waste Resources	378
金属制品、机械和设备修理业	Metal Products, Machinery and Equipment Repair Industry	192
电力、热力生产和供应业	Production and Supply of Electricity and Thermal Power	35 877
燃气生产和供应业	Production and Supply of Fuel Gas	18
水的生产和供应业	Production and Supply of Water	1 594

Expenditures of Industrial Science and Technology Activities

(10 000 yuan)

委托外单位科技活动支出合计 Total Expenditures of Scientific and Technological Activities Organized by Other Enterprises	其他技术活动费用支出 Expenses of Other Technological Activities			
	技术改造经费支出 Expenditures on Technical Transformation	技术引进经费支出 Expenditures on Technical Introdnction	消化吸收经费支出 Expenditures on Technical Digestion and Absorption	购买国内技术经费支出 Expenditure in Buying Domestic Technology
256 464	**454 778**	**292 158**	**151 517**	**21 127**
9 162	10 666			
114 723	109 247	71 283	5 055	20 621
654	1 091			71
124 124	291 045	215 200	146 461	20
7 800	42 729	5 675		415
54 462	138 252	19 511	4 350	415
202 002	316 526	272 647	147 167	20 713
238 841	392 513	268 464	150 616	1 888
11 644	45 173	21 434	901	19 189
1 371	187			
15				
52	500			
3 878				
	1 123			
	69 541			
581	22 210	1 192	461	39
6 356				50
10	330	124		
64	762			
5	6 769			
12	1 176			
3 360	3 885	12 888	532	
1 435	398	1 461	3 819	21
152 430	265 292	241 266	102 201	427
7 028	33 650	5 485		415
19 130	8 461	18 139	13 369	
51 041	9 474	11 603	31 135	20 176
5				
22				
9 626	21 163			
23	8 196			
20	1 662			

表12-11　工业企业技术开发机构情况

Technical Development Institutions of Industrial Enterprises (2014)

指　标　Indicators		企业办技术开发机构数（个）Technical Development Institutions in Enterprises (unit)	技术开发机构科技活动人数（人）Technical Development Personnel (person)	技术开发机构科技经费内部支出(万元) Expenditure of Technical Development (10 000 yuan)
总　计	**Total**	**301**	**36 493**	**1 661 158**
按注册登记类型分	**Grouped by Type of Registration**			
国　有	State-owned	4	600	15 652
股份制及其他有限公司	Share-holding	70	7 784	342 244
私　营	Private	89	3 499	62 291
外商及港澳台投资	Overseas Invested Enterprises	132	22 273	1 162 180
其　他	Others	6	2 337	78 791
按隶属关系分	**Grouped by Subordination**			
中央工业	Central	21	9 089	385 267
地方工业	Local	280	27 404	1 275 891
按企业规模分	**Grouped by Enterprise Scale**			
#大型企业	Large	72	25 460	1 351 401
中型企业	Medium	86	7 127	219 082
按行业大类分	**Grouped by Sector**			
农副食品加工业	Farm and Sideline Products Processing	1	131	1 821
食品制造业	Food Manufacturing	4	83	3 305
酒、饮料和精制茶制造业	Wine, Beverage and Refined Tea Manufacturing			
烟草制品业	Tobacco Manufacturing			
纺织业	Textile Industry	1	56	1 723
家具制造业	Furniture Manufacturing	1	583	40 557
造纸和纸制品业	Papermaking and Paper Products	4	285	6 301
印刷和记录媒介复制业	Printing and Record Medium Reproduction Industry	5	198	7 979
文教、工美、体育和娱乐用品制造业	Culture, Art, Sports and Recreation Supplies Manufacturing	2	40	50
石油加工、炼焦和核燃料加工业	Oil Processing, Coking and Nuclear Fuel Processing			
化学原料和化学制品制造业	Raw Chemical Materials and Chemical Products	19	735	22 698
医药制造业	Medicine Manufacture	28	1 737	63 525
化学纤维制造业	Chemical Fiber Manufacturing	1	32	955
橡胶和塑料制品业	Rubber and Plastic Products Industry	9	402	9 029
非金属矿物制品业	Nonmetal Mineral Products	5	243	7 884
黑色金属冶炼和压延加工业	Smelting and Rolling of Ferrous Metals			
有色金属冶炼和压延加工业	Smelting and Rolling of Nonferrous Metals	4	241	964
金属制品业	Metal Products	11	465	9 066
通用设备制造业	General Equipment Manufacture	46	3 299	140 655
专用设备制造业	Special Purpose Equipment Manufacturing	29	1 914	71 922
汽车制造业	Automobile Manufacturing	27	10 803	640 751
铁路、船舶、航空航天和其他运输设备制造业	Railroad, Ship, Aviation and Other Transportation Equipment Manufacturing	8	2 280	68 303
电气机械和器材制造业	Electric Equipment and Machinery Manufacturing	40	1 834	64 360
计算机、通信和其他电子设备制造业	Computer, Communications and Other Electronic Equipment Manufacturing	48	10 429	482 074
仪器仪表制造业	Instrument Manufacturing	5	182	3 511
废弃资源综合利用业	Comprehensive Utilization of Waste Resources			
金属制品、机械和设备修理业	Metal Products, Machinery and Equipment Repair Industry			
电力、热力生产和供应业	Production and Supply of Electricity and Thermal Power	2	511	13 596
燃气生产和供应业	Production and Supply of Fuel Gas			
水的生产和供应业	Production and Supply of Water	1	10	128

表12-12 工业企业专利情况
Patents Utilized by Industrial Enterprises
(2014)

单位:件 (item)

指 标	Indicators	专利申请数 Patent Applications	#发明专利数 Patents of Creations and Inventions	有效发明专利数 Number of Effective Patents	#境外授权 Authorized Overseas
总 计	**Total**	**8 878**	**5 460**	**7 662**	**802**
按注册登记大类分组	**Grouped by Type of Registration**				
国 有	State-owned	757	433	492	
集 体	Collective-owned	10	1		
股份制及其他有限公司	Share-holding	2 483	1 657	1 625	85
私 营	Private	875	283	649	7
外商及港澳台投资	Overseas Invested Enterprises	4 515	3 019	4 732	705
其 他	Others	238	67	164	5
按隶属关系分组	**Grouped by Subordination**				
中央工业	Central	1 584	1 042	1 543	34
地方工业	Local	7 294	4 418	6 119	768
按企业规模分组	**Grouped by Enterprise Scale**				
#大型企业	Large	5 809	3 993	4 602	473
中型企业	Medium	1 438	803	1 532	178
按工业行业大类分组	**Grouped by Sector**				
农副食品加工业	Farm and Sideline Products Processing	24	20	18	
食品制造业	Food Manufacturing	1	1	16	9
酒、饮料和精制茶制造业	Wine, Beverage and Refined Tea Manufacturing				
烟草制品业	Tobacco Manufacturing	1	1		
纺织业	Textile Industry	41	7	4	
家具制造业	Furniture Manufacturing	44	23	29	
造纸和纸制品业	Papermaking and Paper Products	11	4	9	
印刷和记录媒介复制业	Printing and Record Medium Reproduction Industry	53	30	37	
文教、工美、体育和娱乐用品制造业	Culture, Art, Sports and Recreation Supplies Manufacturing	167	6	5	1
石油加工、炼焦和核燃料加工业	Oil Processing, Coking and Nuclear Fuel Processing	10	10	10	
化学原料和化学制品制造业	Raw Chemical Materials and Chemical Products	168	109	284	27
医药制造业	Medicine Manufacture	237	154	321	13
化学纤维制造业	Chemical Fiber Manufacturing	38	19	7	
橡胶和塑料制品业	Rubber and Plastic Products Industry	123	29	79	
非金属矿物制品业	Nonmetal Mineral Products	30	23	77	9
黑色金属冶炼和压延加工业	Smelting and Rolling of Ferrous Metals	2	1		
有色金属冶炼和压延加工业	Smelting and Rolling of Nonferrous Metals	24	3	18	
金属制品业	Metal Products	87	20	65	3
通用设备制造业	General Equipment Manufacture	481	182	353	20
专用设备制造业	Special Purpose Equipment Manufacturing	524	293	550	28
汽车制造业	Automobile Manufacturing	1292	357	455	19
铁路、船舶、航空航天和其他运输设备制造业	Railroad, Ship, Aviation and Other Transportation Equipment Manufacturing	165	73	157	
电气机械和器材制造业	Electric Equipment and Machinery Manufacturing	456	112	266	5
计算机、通信和其他电子设备制造业	Computer, Communications and Other Electronic Equipment Manufacturing	4 044	3 503	4 331	665
仪器仪表制造业	Instrument Manufacturing	115	41	99	3
废弃资源综合利用业	Comprehensive Utilization of Waste Resources				
金属制品、机械和设备修理业	Metal Products, Machinery and Equipment Repair Industry	1			
电力、热力生产和供应业	Production and Supply of Electricity and Thermal Power	732	435	457	
燃气生产和供应业	Production and Supply of Fuel Gas	2	1	3	
水的生产和供应业	Production and Supply of Water	1	1	12	

表12-13 工业企业新产品产出情况
Output of New Products of Industrial Enterprises
(2014)

单位:万元 (10 000 yuan)

指 标	Indicators	新产品产 值 Output of New Products	新产品销售收入 Sales Revenue	#出 口 Export
总 计	**Total**	**22 849 192**	**32 746 904**	**4 500 684**
按注册登记大类分组	**Grouped by Type of Registration**			
国 有	State-owned	44 997	40 701	
集 体	Collective-owned	34 748	34 748	
股份制及其他有限公司	Share-holding	1 847 831	1 934 731	231 178
私 营	Private	715 710	834 021	90 251
外商及港澳台投资	Overseas Invested Enterprises	17 230 541	26 513 708	2 589 968
其 他	Others	2 975 366	3 388 996	1 589 286
按隶属关系分组	**Grouped by Subordination**			
中央工业	Central	4 292 408	4 375 428	2 446 558
地方工业	Local	18 556 784	28 371 476	2 054 126
按企业规模分组	**Grouped by Enterprise Scale**			
#大型企业	Large	19 095 707	28 897 870	4 058 755
中型企业	Medium	2 670 053	2 703 835	303 192
按工业行业大类分组	**Grouped by Sector**			
农副食品加工业	Farm and Sideline Products Processing	49 791	49 968	
食品制造业	Food Manufacturing	5 256	5 256	3 329
酒、饮料和精制茶制造业	Wine, Beverage and Refined Tea Manufacturing	4 958	4 692	
烟草制品业	Tobacco Manufacturing			
纺织业	Textile Industry	51 451	47 285	1 459
家具制造业	Furniture Manufacturing	273 718	273 718	
造纸和纸制品业	Papermaking and Paper Products	178 498	175 711	
印刷和记录媒介复制业	Printing and Record Medium Reproduction Industry	110 419	181 620	2 606
文教、工美、体育和娱乐用品制造业	Culture, Art, Sports and Recreation Supplies Manufacturing	6 838	6 838	6 811
石油加工、炼焦和核燃料加工业	Oil Processing, Coking and Nuclear Fuel Processing	8 017	18 535	
化学原料和化学制品制造业	Raw Chemical Materials and Chemical Products	801 861	393 702	36 410
医药制造业	Medicine Manufacture	1 029 947	959 519	11 447
化学纤维制造业	Chemical Fiber Manufacturing			
橡胶和塑料制品业	Rubber and Plastic Products Industry	167 158	173 905	63 204
非金属矿物制品业	Nonmetal Mineral Products	68 518	53 689	3 105
黑色金属冶炼和压延加工业	Smelting and Rolling of Ferrous Metals			
有色金属冶炼和压延加工业	Smelting and Rolling of Nonferrous Metals	17 877	17 845	1 505
金属制品业	Metal Products	92 336	93 704	15 251
通用设备制造业	General Equipment Manufacture	2 148 236	2 245 752	873 737
专用设备制造业	Special Purpose Equipment Manufacturing	489 097	482 114	21 333
汽车制造业	Automobile Manufacturing	10 681 741	20 739 121	248 049
铁路、船舶、航空航天和其他运输设备制造业	Railroad, Ship, Aviation and Other Transportation Equipment Manufacturing	2 274 384	2 307 906	1 589 286
电气机械和器材制造业	Electric Equipment and Machinery Manufacturing	1 590 764	1 609 194	607 972
计算机、通信和其他电子设备制造业	Computer, Communications and Other Electronic Equipment Manufacturing	2 661 632	2 769 793	1 001 594
仪器仪表制造业	Instrument Manufacturing	136 697	137 039	13 587
废弃资源综合利用业	Comprehensive Utilization of Waste Resources			
金属制品、机械和设备修理业	Metal Products, Machinery and Equipment Repair Industry			
电力、热力生产和供应业	Production and Supply of Electricity and Thermal Power			
燃气生产和供应业	Production and Supply of Fuel Gas			
水的生产和供应业	Production and Supply of Water			

表 12-14 主要年份科技企业主要经济指标
Major Economic Indicators of Technology Enterprises in Main Years

指 标	Indicators	单 位 Unit	2000	2005	2010	2011	2013	2014
企业单位数	Number of Enterprises	个 unit	828	700	2 525	4 083	1 773	2 035
企业专利总数	Number of Enterprise Patents	项 item			4 918	2 572	6 630	5 574
职工人数	Number of Employees	万人 10 000 persons	3.04	5.76	9.47	26.63	27.09	27.66
从事科技活动人员	Persons Employed in Science and Technology	万人 10 000 persons			1.59	6.39	11.60	12.81
资产总额	Total Assets	亿元 100 million yuan	122.40	575.47	766.56	3 854.86	5 655.14	6 208.57
技工贸销售总额	Total Sales	亿元 100 million yuan	82.01	521.45	858.06	2 071.63	8 346.95	4 318.22
产品销售收入	Income for Selling Products	亿元 100 million yuan			770.89	1 976.35	8 237.57	4 150.83
利润总额	Total Profits	亿元 100 million yuan	4.64	35.58	64.99	169.50	321.71	378.53
上交税收	Tax Payable	亿元 100 million yuan	2.70	18.22	44.66	117.58	182.43	509.96
创汇总额	Total Foreign Exchange	亿美元 USD 100 million	0.95	12.65	25.67	88.38	115.59	114.44
投入科研开发费	Investment in Research and Development	亿元 100 million yuan	4.18	34.72	26.56	155.77	300.44	393.41

注：2011 年起表中数据均为年营业收入 2000 万及以上科技企业。
Note：Since 2011，data in this sheet include technology enterprises that have the output value of more than 20 million yuan.

主要统计指标解释

专　利

是专利权的简称，是对发明人的发明创造经审查合格后，由专利局依据专利法授予发明人和设计人对该项发明创造享有的专有权。包括发明、实用新型和外观设计。反映拥有自主知识产权的科技和设计成果情况。

发　明

指对产品、方法或者其改进所提出的新的技术方案。是国际通行的反映拥有自主知识产权技术的核心指标。

实用新型

指对产品的形状、构造或者其结合所提出的适于实用的新的技术方案。反映具有一定技术含量的技术成果情况。

外观设计

指对产品的形状、图案、色彩或者其结合所作出的富有美感并适于工业上应用的新设计。反映拥有自主知识产权的外观设计成果情况。

专业技术人员

专业技术人员指事业、企业单位中已被聘任专业技术职务的从事专业技术工作和专业技术管理的人员，以及虽未被聘任专业技术职务，但现在专业技术岗位上工作的人员。

国有企业

指企业全部资产归国家所有，并按《中华人民共和国企业法人登记管理条例》规定登记注册的非公司制的经济组织。不包括有限责任公司中的国有独资公司。

集体企业

集体企业指企业资产归集体所有，并按《中华人民共和国企业法人登记管理条例》规定登记注册的经济组织。

科技活动

指在自然科学、农业科学、医药科学、工程与技术科学、人文与社会科学领域（简称科学技术领域）中，与科技知识的产生、发展、传播和应用密切相关的有组织的活动。可分为研究与试验发展（R&D）、研究与试验发展成果应用及相关的科技服务三类活动。该定义是联合国教科文组织考虑成员国特别是发展中国家开展科技统计工作的需要，而对科技活动所作的统计界定。

科技活动人员

指直接从事科技活动、以及专门从事科技活动管理和为科技活动提供直接服务，累计从事科技活动的时间占全年制度工作时间10%及以上的人员。（1）直接从事科技活动的人员，包括：在独立核算的科学研究与技术开发机构、高等学校、各类企业及其他事业单位内设的研究室、实验室、技术开发中心及中试车间（基地）等机构中从事科技活动的研究人员、工程技术人员、技术工人及其它人员；虽不在上述机构工作，但编入科技活动项目（课题）组的人员；科技信息与文献机构中的专业技术人员；从事论文设计的研究生等。（2）专门从事科技活动管理和为科技活动提供直接服务的人员包括：独立核算的科学研究与技术开发机构、科技信息与文献机构、高等学校、各类企业及其他事业单位主管科技工作的负责人，专门从事科技活动的计划、行政、人事、财务、物资供应、设备维护、图书资料管理等工作的各类人员，但不包括保卫、医疗保健人员、司机、食堂人员、茶炉工、水暖工、清洁工等为科技活动提供间接服务的人员。该指标用来反映投入科技活动人力的规模。

科学家和工程师

科学家与工程师指科技活动人员中具有高、中级技术职称（职务）的人员和不具有高、中级技术职称（职务）的大学本科及以上学历人员。

科技活动经费筹集

指从各种渠道筹集到的计划用于科技活动的经费，包括政府资金、事业资金、企业资金、银行贷款和其他收入等。反映各社会经济主体对促进科技进步所作的努力。

政府资金

指从各级政府部门获得的计划用于科技活动的经费，包括科学事业费、科技三项费、科研基建费、科学基金、教育等部门事业费中计划用于科技活动的经费以及政府部门预算外资金中计划用于科技活动的经费等。

新产品

指采用新技术原理、新设计构思研制、生产的全新产品，或在结构、材质、工艺等某一方面比原有产品有明显改进，从而显著提高了产品性能或扩大了使用功能的产品。既包括政府有关部门认定并在有效期内的新产品，也包括企业自行研制开发、在统计规定的新产品跟踪期限内的产品。跟踪期限规定如下：装备类跟踪五年，消费品类跟踪二年，其他类跟踪三年。用来反映科技产出及对经济增长的直接贡献。

R&D

是“科学研究与试验发展”(Research and Development)的英文缩写。其含义是指在科学技术领域,为增加知识总量,以及运用这些知识去创造新的应用进行的系统的创造性的活动。R&D 包括基础研究、应用研究、试验发展三类活动。

EXPLANATORY NOTES TO MAJOR STATISTICAL INDICATORS

Patent

Patent is an abbreviation for the patent right and refers to the exclusive right of ownership by the inventors or designers for the creation or inventions, given from the patent offices after due process of assessment and approval in accordance with the Patent Law. Patents are granted for inventions, utility models and designs. This indicator reflects the achievements of S&T and design with independent intellectual property.

Invention

Inventions refer to the new technical proposals to the products or methods or their modifications. This is universal core indicator reflecting the technologies with independent intellectual property.

Utility Models

Utility Models refer to the practical and new technical proposals on the shape and structure of the product or the combination of both. This indicator reflects the condition of technological results with certain technical content.

Exterior Design

Designs refer to the aesthetics and industrially applicable new designs for the shape, pattern and color of the product, or their combinations. This indicator reflects the appearance design achievements with independent intellectual property.

Professional and Technical Personnel

Professional and Technical Personnel refer to professional, technical and managerial staff members in institutions or enterprises who not only have professional and technical titles but also hold professional and technical posts. They also include those who work on professional and technical posts but do not have professional and technical titles.

State-owned Enterprises

State-owned Enterprises refer to non-corporation economic units where the entire assets are owned by the state and which have registered in accordance with the Regulation of the People's Republic of China on the Management of Registration of Corporate Enterprises. Excluded from this category are sole state-funded corporations in the limited liability corporations.

Collective-owned Enterprises

Collective-owned Enterprises refer to economic units where the assets are owned collectively and which have registered in accordance with the Regulation of the People's Republic of China on the Management of Registration of Corporate Enterprises.

Scientific and Technological Activities (S&T Activities)

Scientific and Technological Activities (S&T Activities) refer to organized activities which are closely related with the creation, development, dissemination and application of the scientific and technical knowledge in the fields of natural sciences, agricultural sciences, medical sciences, engineering and technological sciences, humanities and social sciences (referred to as scientific and technological fields). S&T activities can be classified into 3 categories: research and development (R&D) activities, application of R&D results, and related S&T services. This statistical definition is made by UNICHIEF for scientific and technological activities to meet the need of carrying out statistical work in this field for its member countries in particular those developing countries.

Personnel Engaged in S&T Activities

Personnel Engaged in S&T Activities refer to personnel directly engaged in S&T activities, in the management of S&T activities, and in providing direct service to S&T activities, who spend over 10% of the total working hours in a year in S&T activities. (1) Personnel directly engaged in S&T activities include researchers, engineers, technicians and other related personnel engaged in S&T activities in independent-accounting R&D institutions, institutions of higher learning, and in research institutes, laboratories, technology development centers and central experiment workshops under enterprises and institutions. Also included are people working in S&T information archiving institutes, and graduate students working on the design of their thesis. (2) Personnel engaged in the management of S&T activities and in providing direct service to S&T activities include senior management people responsible for S&T activities in independent-accounting R&D institutions, S&T information archiving institutes, institutions of higher learning, and in enterprises and institutions where S&T activities are undertaken. Also included are people responsible for the planning, administration, personnel management, financial management, logistics supply, equipment maintenance, information and library management that are related with S&T activities. People providing indirect services are excluded, such as security, medical service, drivers, plumbers, cleaners and those providing catering and related service. This indicator reflects the size of personnel engaged in S&T activities.

Scientists and Engineers

Scientists and Engineers refer to persons engaged in S&T activities who have obtained titles of senior and middle level professional positions, and those without such position but have completed university or higher education.

Funding for S&T Activities

Funding for S&T Activities refers to funds obtained from various sources for S&T activities, including government funds, self-raised funds by institutions, self-raised funds by enterprises, loans from banks and other funds. This indicator reflects the efforts made by various social economic entities in promoting the development of S&T.

Government Funds

Government Funds refer to funds obtained from government agencies at all levels to be used for S&T activities, including fund for scientific undertakings, 3 kinds of fund for S&T activities, fund for capital construction for scientific researches, science fund, funds from education expenditures by education departments for S&T activities, and extra-budget fund from government agencies for S&T activities.

New Products

New Products refer to new products produced with new technology and new design, or products that represent noticeable improvement in terms of structure, material, or production process so as to improve significantly the character or function of the older versions. They include new products certified by relevant government agencies within the period of certification, as well as new products designed and produced by enterprises within the new product track time limit prescribed by the statistical regulations. The new product track time limit is prescribed as following: equipment products 5 years, consumption products 2 years, other products 3 years. This indictor reflects the direct contribution of S&T output to economic growth.

R&D

R&D is an abbreviation which stands for 'Science Research and Experimental Development', which means systematic and creative endeavors aimed at expanding the overall volume of knowledge and applying the knowledge in systematic creation. R&D includes basic studies, application research and experimental development.

第十三篇

CHAPTER 13

2015上海浦东新区统计年鉴
SHANGHAI PUDONG NEW AREA STATISTICAL YEARBOOK

人民生活

PEOPLE' SLIVELIHOOD

表13-1 从业人员工资总额
Wages of Employees
(2014)

单位:亿元 (100 million yuan)

指 标 Indicators		合 计 Total	国有单位 State-owned Enterprises	集体单位 Collective-owned Enterprises	港澳台及外商投资单位 Overseas Invested Enterprises	其他单位 Others
总 计	**Total**	**2 415.90**	**244.75**	**9.68**	**1 495.24**	**666.23**
按产业分	**By Industry**					
第一产业	Primary Industry	1.36	0.52			0.84
第二产业	Secondary Industry	835.80	14.69	3.15	534.94	283.02
第三产业	Tertiary Industry	1 578.74	229.54	6.53	960.30	382.37
按行业分	**By Sector**					
农、林、牧、渔业	Farming, Forestry, Animal Husbandry and Fishery	1.36	0.52			0.84
采矿业	Mining	0.61				0.61
制造业	Manufacturing	672.20	12.21	2.19	498.40	159.40
电力、热力、燃气及水生产和供应业	Production and Supply of Electricity, Heat, Gas and Water	17.70	0.82		3.98	12.90
建筑业	Construction	145.29	1.66	0.96	32.56	110.11
批发和零售业	Wholesale and Retail	459.70	1.86	0.90	419.07	37.87
交通运输、仓储和邮政业	Transportation, Warehousing and Post Service	169.41	17.56	0.03	42.15	109.67
住宿和餐饮业	Hotel and Catering	18.77	1.29	0.48	9.00	8.00
信息传输、软件和信息技术服务业业	Information Transmission, Software and Information Technology Services	132.59	0.47	0.02	97.73	34.37
金融业	Banking	441.38	55.62	0.19	256.34	129.23
房地产业	Real Estate	56.26	4.38	0.09	31.82	19.97
租赁和商务服务业	Leasing and Business Service	86.53	2.23	0.35	64.12	19.83
科学研究和技术服务业	Scientific Research and Technology Services	63.01	16.70		36.11	10.20
水利、环境和公共设施管理业	Water Conservancy, Environment and Public Facilities Administration	9.30	4.96	0.01	0.09	4.24
居民服务、修理和其他服务业	Residents Service, Repair and other Services	2.28	0.46		1.01	0.81
教 育	Education	59.46	52.79	0.59		6.08
卫生和社会工作	Healthcare and Social Work	39.80	36.32	2.77		0.71
文化、体育和娱乐业	Culture, Sports and Entertainment	7.75	3.64	1.10	2.86	0.15
公共管理、社会保障和社会组织	Public Management, Social Guarantee and Social Organizations	32.50	31.26			1.24

表13-2 从业人员平均工资
Average Wages of Employees
(2014)

单位:元 (yuan)

指 标	Indicators	合 计 Total	国有单位 State-owned Enterprises	集体单位 Collective-owned Enterprises	港澳台及外商投资单位 Overseas Invested Enterprises	其 他 单 位 Others
总 计	**Total**	**116 726**	**112 545**	**43 328**	**134 119**	**98 340**
按产业分	**By Industry**					
第一产业	Primary Industry	34 726	50 090	32 113	49 575	33 546
第二产业	Secondary Industry	83 726	90 461	41 496	85 077	81 978
第三产业	Tertiary Industry	135 038	114 317	44 126	172 928	106 311
按行业分	**By Sector**					
农、林、牧、渔业	Farming, Forestry, Animal Husbandry and Fishery	37 335	53 505	31 776	49 575	36 464
采矿业	Mining	118 140				118 140
制造业	Manufacturing	83 660	89 902	41 415	83 505	85 567
电力、热力、燃气及水生产和供应业	Production and Supply of Electricity, Heat, Gas and Water	136 582	82 861	58 435	121 184	147 108
建筑业	Construction	80 208	29 849	41 132	165 822	74 258
批发和零售业	Wholesale and Retail	144 670	61 452	34 502	162 987	82 770
交通运输、仓储和邮政业	Transportation, Warehousing and Post Service	104 500	72 693	24 265	90 878	110 795
住宿和餐饮业	Hotel and Catering	50 332	42 770	30 195	52 482	49 302
信息传输、软件和信息技术服务业	Information Transmission, Software and Information Technology Services	197 427	67 172	10 000	219 102	168 887
金融业	Banking	182 390	183 598		246 260	156 071
房地产业	Real Estate	77 665	96 827	41 911	89 096	70 687
租赁和商务服务业	Leasing and Business Service	136 573	41 268	29 314	223 434	68 856
科学研究和技术服务业	Scientific Research and Technology Services	166 678	129 496	67 299	203 333	110 824
水利、环境和公共设施管理业	Water Conservancy, Environment and Public Facilities Administration	63 051	64 396	33 083	107 927	64 848
居民服务、修理和其他服务业	Residents Service, Repair and other Services	40 482	68 952	33 501	49 404	23 053
教 育	Education	85 858	93 220	67 211	127 164	61 693
卫生和社会工作	Healthcare and Social Work	95 096	119 604	70 311	111 254	48 694
文化、体育和娱乐业	Culture, Sports and Entertainment	88 341	101 988	37 403	92 183	73 340
公共管理、社会保障和社会组织	Public Management, Social Guarantee and Social Organizations	92 801	97 227	68 896		84 540

表 13-3　城镇居民家庭基本情况
Background of Urban Families

指　标	Indicators	单　位　Unit	2010	2013	2014
调查户数	Households Surveyed	户 household	600	600	800
调查户总人口	Total Population of Households Surveyed	人 person	1 704	1 520	2 004
调查户就业人口	Employed Persons in Households Surveyed	人 person	918	786	1 020
#国有单位就业人口	Employed by State-owned Enterprises	人 person	402	235	232
平均每户常住人口	Average Number of Permanent Residents Per Household	人 person	2.84	2.53	2.50
平均每户就业人口	Average Number of Employed Persons Per Household	人 person	1.53	1.31	1.28
平均每户就业面	Average Employment Rate Per Household	% %	53.9	51.7	50.9
平均每一就业者赡养人口	Number of Persons Supported by Each Employed Person	人 person	1.86	1.93	1.96
恩格尔系数	Engel's Coefficient	% %	34.8	36.5	35.3
平均消费倾向	Average Propensity to Consumption	% %	67.7	58.3	57.8
平均每人年实际收入	Annual Actual Income Per Capita	元 yuan	36 399	50 294	56 448
平均每人年可支配收入	Annual Disposable Income Per Capita	元 yuan	32 330	45 199	49 629
平均每人年消费性支出	Annual Consumption Spending Per Capita	元 yuan	21 897	26 352	28 652

注：1. 本表至表 13－12 为住户调查资料。
　　2. 根据国家住户调查城乡划分口径调整，原郊区部分 200 户 2014 年划分为城镇部分。

Note：1. The contents in from this table to Table 13－12 are the survey data of households in Pudong.
　　2. The statistical caliber is adjusted according to the urban and rural division in the National Household Survey. The original 200 suburban households are divided to rural ones from year 2014.

表13-4　主要年份城乡居民收支情况
Income and Expenditure of Urban and Suburban Residents in Main Years

单位:元　　(yuan)

指　标	Indicators	2010	2012	2013	2014
城镇居民人均可支配收入	**Disposable Income of Urban Residents**	**32 330**	**40 901**	**45 199**	**49 629**
工资性收入	Wage Income	21 706	27 159	29 872	31 584
经营净收入	Net Operational Income	869	1 170	1 205	1 277
财产净收入	Net Property Income	715	1 073	1 387	1 755
转移净收入	Net Transferable Income	9 040	11 499	12 735	15 013
城镇居民人均消费支出	**Total Expenses Per Capita of Urban Residents**	**21 897**	**24 723**	**26 352**	**28 652**
食品烟酒	Foodstuff,tobacoo,and alcohol	7 631	9 278	9 609	10 126
衣　着	Clothing	1 831	2 010	1 879	2 055
生活用品及服务	Household Appliances and Services	1 695	1 716	1 745	1 832
医疗保健	Medical Care	1 143	1 123	1 333	1 481
交通通信	Traffic and Communications	3 456	3 552	4 052	4 392
教育文化娱乐	Education,Culture,and Amusement	3 324	3 936	4 211	4 762
居　住	Habitation	1 649	1 907	2 207	2 646
其他用品和服务	Miscellaneous Stuff and Services	1 167	1 201	1 316	1 358
社会保障支出	Social Security Expenses	2 941	3 665	4 819	2 629
农村居民人均可支配收入	**Disposable Income of Suburban Residents**	**13 898**	**17 641**	**19 529**	**21 814**
工资性收入	Wage Income	10 223	12 543	13 610	14 688
经营净收入	Net Operational Income	743	555	569	720
财产净收入	Net Property Income	1 314	1 540	1 756	1 972
转移净收入	Net Transferable Income	1 618	3 003	3 594	4 434

表13-5 城镇居民家庭人均收入与支出状况(按收入水平分)

Average Income and Expenses of Urban Families(by Income Level) (2014)

单位:元 (yuan)

指 标	Indicators	总平均 Overall Average	低收入户 Low-income Household	较低收入户 Lower-income Household	中等收入户 Medium-income Household	较高收入户 Medium Higher-income Household	高收入户 High-income Household
人均可支配收入	**Disposable Income Per Capita**	**49 629**	**19 895**	**38 572**	**54 456**	**77 859**	**138 975**
工资性收入	Wage Income	31 584	17 155	25 925	38 337	38 830	57 053
经营净收入	Net Operational Income	1 277	93	1 071	128	3 258	3 322
财产净收入	Net Property Income	1 755	450	1 140	807	1 269	4 242
转移净收入	Net Transferable Income	15 013	472	4 403	7 461	25 428	59 746
人均消费支出	**Consumption Expenses**	**28 652**	**16 227**	**22 856**	**32 377**	**37 063**	**49 874**
食品烟酒	Foodstuff, tobacoo, and alcohol	10 126	6 504	9 265	10 574	12 446	15 833
衣 着	Clothing	2 055	1 273	1 772	2 167	2 668	4 007
生活用品及服务	Household Appliances and Services	1 832	686	1 236	2 003	2 953	4 019
医疗保健	Medical Care	1 481	744	1 112	1 831	2 224	1 612
交通通信	Traffic and Communications	4 392	2 586	3 242	5 144	4 473	7 927
教育文化娱乐	Education, Culture, and Amusement	4 762	1 831	3 290	5 760	6 496	9 815
居 住	Habitation	2 646	2 078	2 063	3 428	3 631	4 058
其他用品和服务	Miscellaneous Stuff and Services	1 358	523	877	1 470	2 171	2 603
财产性支出	Property Expenses	782	215	1 027	1 423	1 437	1 305
转移性支出	Transferable Expenses	4 389	2 353	3 425	5 478	5 367	8 510
社会保障支出	Social Security Expenses	2 629	1 495	2 295	3 492	3 109	4 295
购、建房支出	Expenses for Purchasing/ Building Houses	403			70	1 768	370

注：收入水平根据居民家庭人均可支配收入由低到高排序,分别按家庭数量的20%分为5组。

Note: Income levels are sorted from the low to the high according to the disposable income per capita of urban families. They are divided into five groups from 20% of the total number of families respectively.

表13-6 每百户城镇居民家庭年末耐用消费品拥有量
Possession of Durable Consumer Goods Per 100 Urban Households at Year-end

指 标	Indicators	单 位 Unit	2010	2013	2014
摩托车	Mototrcycle	辆 in number	9	5	6
助力车	Scooter	辆 in number	22	27	43
家用汽车	Household Car	辆 in number	18	24	23
洗衣机	Washing Machine	台 set	100	96	85
电冰箱	Household Refrigerator	台 set	102	100	90
彩色电视机	Color TV Set	台 set	198	181	166
家用电脑	Personal Computer	台 set	116	126	106
组合音响	Stereo System	套 set	47	16	13
摄像机	Video Camera	架 set	15	14	11
照相机	Camera	架 set	72	54	46
中高档乐器	Medium and High-grade Musical Instrument	架 set	5	9	7
微波炉	Microwave Oven	台 set	95	93	78
空调器	Air Conditioner	台 set	206	201	175
淋浴热水器	Water Heater	台 set	104	97	82
健身器材	Fitness Goods	套 set	9	5	3
普通电话	Fixed Telephone	部 set	96	73	73
移动电话	Mobile Phone	部 set	216	208	204

表13-7 城镇居民家庭生活质量
Living Conditions of Urban Families

指标	Indicators	单位 Unit	2010	2013	2014
生活用水	**Tap Water for Residential Use**				
独用自来水	Private Tap Water	%	100.0	100.0	98.2
公用自来水	Shared Tap Water	%			1.8
居室卫生设备	**Sanitary Equipment**				
无卫生设备	Without any Sanitary Equipment	%		0.7	0.4
有厕所浴室	With Lavatory	%	98.2	91.9	87.0
有厕所无浴室	With Lavatory but no Bathroom	%	1.4	2.6	6.6
公　用	Shared Sanitary Equipment	%	0.4	4.8	6.0
居室取暖设备	**Heating Equipment**				
无取暖设备	Without any Heating	%	2.3	4.1	13.1
冷暖空调	Air Conditioner	%	97.1	95.9	86.9
其　他	Others	%	0.6		
炊用燃气	**Gas for Cooking**				
天然气	Natural Gas	%	92.1	87.7	66.8
液化石油气	Liquefied Petroleum Gas	%	6.9	7.0	25.6
煤	Coal	%	0.6	0.7	
其　他	Others	%	0.4	4.6	7.6
通信设备	**Telecommunications Equipment**				
固定电话	Fixed Telephone	部/百户 set / hundred households	95.7	75.8	73.1
移动电话	Mobile Telephone	部/百户 set / hundred households	216.2	215.0	204.0

表13-8 城镇居民家庭人均可支配收入
Annual Disposable Income Per Capita for Urban Families

按人均年可支配收入分组 Grouped by Annual Disposable Income Per Capita		比 重 Proportion	2010	2013	2014
总 计	**Total**	%	**100.0**	**100.0**	**100.0**
6 000元以下	Below 6 000 yuan	%		0.3	1.7
6 000~12 000元	6 000~12 000 yuan	%	4.7	1.2	4.4
12 000~18 000元	12 000~18 000 yuan	%	12.8	6.8	9.9
18 000~24 000元	18 000~24 000 yuan	%	20.5	12.0	8.6
24 000~30 000元	24 000~30 000 yuan	%	19.0	15.6	9.5
30 000~36 000元	30 000~36 000 yuan	%	11.2	15.8	10.1
36 000~42 000元	36 000~42 000 yuan	%	10.5	10.0	7.7
42 000~48 000元	42 000~48 000 yuan	%	5.8	9.0	5.1
48 000元以上	Above 48 000 yuan	%	15.5	29.3	43.0

表13-9 城镇居民家庭人均消费性支出
Annual Consumer Spending Per Capita for Urban Families

按人均年消费性支出分组 Grouped by Annual Nonproductive Expenditure Per Capita		比 重 Proportion	2010	2013	2014
总 计	**Total**	%	**100.0**	**100.0**	**100.0**
6 000元以下	Below 6 000 yuan	%	1.7	2.0	4.0
6 000~12 000元	6 000~12 000 yuan	%	19.3	14.6	15.6
12 000~18 000元	12 000~18 000 yuan	%	28.6	19.1	18.9
18 000~24 000元	18 000~24 000 yuan	%	21.7	18.5	15.1
24 000~30 000元	24 000~30 000 yuan	%	11.7	14.1	10.9
30 000~36 000元	30 000~36 000 yuan	%	4.3	9.2	7.9
36 000~42 000元	36 000~42 000 yuan	%	3.0	5.5	5.9
42 000~48 000元	42 000~48 000 yuan	%	3.0	4.0	4.6
48 000元以上	Above 48 000 yuan	%	6.7	13.0	17.1

表 13-10　城镇居民家庭人均年消费支出状况
Annual Consumption Expenditure Per Capita for Urban Families

单位:元　　　　　　　　　　　　　　　　　　　　　　　　　　　　　　　　　　　　　　　(yuan)

指　标	Indicators	2010	2013	2014
总　计	**Total**	**21 896**	**26 352**	**28 652**
食品烟酒	**Food, tobacoo, and alcohol**	**7 631**	**9 609**	**1 026**
#粮油类	Cereals & Oils	772	841	785
肉禽蛋水产品	Meat Poultry Eggs and Aquatic Products	2 018	2 539	2 214
蔬菜类	Vegetables	640	857	749
糖烟酒饮料类	Sugar Tobacco Alcoholic Drinks and Other Beverages	923	909	948
干鲜瓜果类	Dry and Fresh Fruits	654	843	687
糕点、奶及奶制品	Cakes Milk and Dairy Products	599	874	914
衣　着	**Clothing**	**1 831**	**1 879**	**2 055**
#服　装	Clothes	1 350	1 409	1 625
鞋　类	Shoes	389	381	430
生活用品及服务	**Household Appliances and Service**	**1 695**	**1 745**	**1 832**
#耐用消费品	Durable Consumer Goods	685	619	259
室内装饰品	Household Ornaments	55	19	32
家具材料	Furniture and Materials	4	3	11
家庭服务	Household Services	176	322	244
医疗保健	**Health Care**	**1 143**	**1 333**	**1 481**
#药品费	Medicines	424	153	163
滋补保健品	Nutritious Health Products	313	258	306
医疗费	Medical Treatment	330	883	976
交通通信	**Transportation and Telecommunications**	**3 456**	**4 052**	**4 392**
交　通	Transportation	2 310	2 917	3 050
通　信	Telecommunications	1 146	1 135	1 342
教育文化娱乐	**Education, Culture, and Entertainment**	**3 324**	**4 211**	**4 762**
文化娱乐用品	Cultural and Entertainment Products	968	727	708
文化娱乐服务	Cultural and Entertainment Services	1 429	2 061	2 376
教　育	Education	927	1 423	1 678
居　住	**Housing**	**1 649**	**2 207**	**2 646**
住　房	Accommodation	742	1 303	1 062
水电燃料及其他	Water Electricity Fuel and Others	727	714	907
居住服务费	Accommodation Services	180	190	677
其他用品和服务	**Miscellancous Stuff and Services**	**1 167**	**1 316**	**1 358**

表 13-11 农村居民家庭基本情况
Basic Information of Rural Families

指 标 Indicators		单 位 Unit	2010	2013	2014
调查户数	Households Surveyed	户 household	500	400	200
调查户总人口	Total Population of Households Surveyed	人 person	1 453	1 036	473
调查户总劳动力	Total Number of Laborers in the Household Surveyed	人 person	1 002	772	382
调查户就业人口	Employed Persons in Households Surveyed	人 person	897	696	297
#纯务农	Totally Engaged in Agriculture	人 person	48	41	28
平均每户人口	Average Number of Residents Per Household	人 person	2.91	2.58	2.37
平均每户劳动力	Average Number of Laborers Per Household	人 person	2.00	1.93	1.91
平均每户就业人口	Average Employed Persons Per Household	人 person	1.79	1.74	1.485
平均每户就业面	Average Employed Persons Per Household	%	61.7	67.5	52.8
平均每一就业者赡养人口	Number of Persons Supported by Each Employed Person	人 person	1.63	1.49	1.59

注：由于国家城乡划分口径调整,原郊区部分 200 户 2014 年划分为城镇部分。
Note: The statistical caliber is adjusted according to the urban and rural division in the National Household Survey. The original 200 suburban households are divided to rural ones from year 2014.

表13-12 农村居民收支情况
Incomes and Expenses of Suburban Citizens

单位:元 (yuan)

指 标	Indicators	2010	2013	2014
人均可支配收入	Disposable Income	13 898	19 529	21 814
工资性收入	Wage Income	10 223	13 610	14 688
经营净收入	Net Operation Income	743	569	720
财产净收入	Net Property Income	1 314	1 756	1 972
#股 息	Stock Dividend			
租 金	Rent	1 014	1 818	1 804
红 利	Dividend	34		12
转移净收入	Net Transfer Income	1 618	3 594	4 434
#农村以外亲友赠送	Gifts from Relatives and Friends in Urban Area	23	23	
救济金、保险年金	Relief and Life Annuity	13	61	82
退休金、抚恤金	Pension and Compensation	1 902	3 083	4 811
人均消费性支出	Consumption Expenses	10 225	13 393	15 067
#食 品	Foodstuff	3 807	5 112	5 667
衣 着	Clothing	554	1 059	874
家庭设备用品及服务	Family Appliances and Services	528	708	633
医疗保健	Medical Care	585	1 221	1 390
交通和通信	Traffic and Communications	1 459	1 705	2 289
教育文化娱乐服务	Education Culture and Amusement Services	1 012	1 504	1 571
居 住	Habitation	2 070	1 664	2 098
其他商品及服务	Miscellaneous Commodities and Services	210	420	545
财产性支出	Property Expenditure	4	156	6
转移性支出	Transfer Expenditure	1 060	918	1 117

主要统计指标解释

从业人员工资总额

从业人员工资总额指各单位在一定时期内直接支付给本单位全部从业人员的劳动报酬总额。包括在岗职工工资总额和本单位其他从业人员劳动报酬两部分。

从业人员平均工资

平均工资指企业、事业、机关单位的职工在一定时期内平均每人所得的货币工资额。它表明一定时期从业人员工资收入的高低程度,是反映工资水平的主要指标。计算公式为:

平均工资 = 报告期实际支付的全部从业人员工资总额/报告期全部从业人员平均人数

城镇居民可支配收入

城镇居民可支配收入指居民可用于最终消费支出和其他非义务性支出以及储蓄的总和,即居民家庭可以用来自由支配的收入。它是家庭总收入扣除交纳的所得税、个人交纳的社会保障费以及调查户的记账补贴后的收入。不包括出售财物和借贷收入。

城镇居民家庭消费支出

指城镇居民家庭用于日常生活的全部支出,包括食品、衣着、家庭设备用品及服务、医疗保健、交通和通信、教育文化娱乐服务、居住、杂项商品和服务等八大类。

城镇居民家庭人均服务性消费支出

指调查户用于本家庭支付社会提供的各种文化和生活方面的非商品性服务费用。服务性消费的特点在于其劳动过程和消费过程在时间与空间上的统一。在居民家庭八大类消费中,服务消费支出包括:(1)食品类中加工服务费和部分在外饮食费用;(2)衣着类中衣着加工服务费;(3)家庭设备用品及服务类中家庭服务(如家政服务费用);(4)医疗保健类中医疗费(如诊疗费、上门出诊费、护工费用);(5)交通和通信类中交通工具服务费(如汽车使用、维修费用)、交通费中使用飞机、轮船、火车等交通工具费用、通信服务费(如电信费、邮费);(6)教育文化娱乐服务类中文化娱乐服务费(如参观、游览费用、健身活动费、团体旅游、其他文娱活动费)、文娱用品修理服务费、教育费(如义务、非义务教育支出)、成人教育支出、家教费、培训班费用、择校费;(7)居住类中租赁费用、部分房屋装潢费用(人工费用)、居住服务费(如物业管理、维修费用);(8)杂项商品和服务(如美容、洗澡、理发费用,旅馆住宿等费用)。

农村居民可支配收入

指一定时期内农村居民总收入中,扣除家庭经营费用支出、生产性固定资产折旧、交纳税金和上交承包金、公益性及转移支付后的(包括养老、失业、合作医疗、保险基金及罚款等支付),可用于生活消费、生产投资和储蓄的收入。它与纯收入的主要区别是扣除了转移性支付,加上实际得到的公益性及转移性收入后的余额。农村居民可支配收入包括:工资性收入、家庭经营净收入、财产性收入、转移性净收入。

农村居民家庭生活消费支出

指农村住户用于物质生活和精神生活方面的支出。包括食品、衣着、居住、家庭设备用品及服务、医疗保健、交通和通信、文化教育娱乐用品及服务、其他商品和服务等消费支出。

财产性收入

指金融资产或有形非生产性资产的所有者向其他机构单位提供资金或将有形非生产性资产供其支配,作为回报而从中获得的收入。

转移性收入

指农村住户和住户成员无须付出任何对应物而获得的货物、服务、资金或资产所有权等,不包括无偿提供的用于固定资本形成的资金。一般情况下,是指农村住户在二次分配中的所有收入。

基本养老保险

(1)参加保险人数:指报告期末按照国家法律、法规和有关政策规定参加基本养老保险的职工人数。包括不能正常缴费、已中断缴费但未终止保险关系的职工人数。

(2)社会统筹基金收入:指根据国家规定,由纳入基本养老保险范围的单位,按照国家规定的缴费基数和缴费比例缴纳的社会统筹基金,以及通过其他方式取得的形成基金来源的收入,包括:单位缴纳的社会统筹基金收入、财政补贴收入、利息收入、其他收入。

(3)社会统筹基金支出:指按照国家政策规定的开支范围和开支标准从社会统筹基金中支付给参加基本养老保险的离休、退休、退职人员个人的养老金、丧葬抚恤补助,以及由于保险关系转移、上下级之间调剂资金等原因而发生的支出。包括:基础性养老金、过渡性养老金、离休金、退休金、退职金、补贴、丧葬抚恤补助、其他支出。

(4)社会统筹基金结余:指截止报告期末基本养老保险

的社会统筹基金结余金额。包括银行存款、财政专户、债券投资和其他。

城镇登记失业人员

城镇登记失业人员指有非农业户口,在一定的劳动年龄内(16 岁以上及男 50 岁以下、女 45 岁以下),有劳动能力,无业而要求就业,并在当地就业服务机构进行求职登记的人员。

EXPLANATORY NOTES TO MAJOR STATISTICAL INDICATORS

Total Wages of Employees

Total Wages of Employees refers to total payment by various units to their employees during a certain period of time, including wages to permanent staff and workers and payment to other employees.

Average Wage

Average Wage refers to the average wage in money terms per person during a certain period of time for staff and workers in enterprises, institutions, and government agencies, which reflects the general level of wage income during a certain period of time and is calculated as follows: Average Wage = Total Wages of Staff and Workers at Reference Time / Average Number of Staff and Workers at Reference Time.

Disposable Income of Urban Households

Disposable Income of Urban Households refers to the actual income at the disposal of members of the households which can be used for final consumption, other non-compulsory expenditure and savings, which is part of the urban households´income that can be disposed by the urban households themselves. It is the income after deducting personal income tax, social insurance paid by individuals and investigation allowance from the total income of the households. The income from selling properties and borrowing are not included.

Consumption Expenditures of Urban Households

Consumption Expenditures of Urban Households refer to all the expenditures paid by urban households for consumption in daily life, including 8 categories as follows: food; clothing; household facilities, articles and services; medical care; traffic and telecommunication; education, culture and recreation services; housing; miscellaneous commodities and services.

Urbanities'per-capita Spending on Services

Urbanities'per-capita spending on services refers to urbanites pay for services rather than commodities. Services are offered and consumed at the same time and place. The service spending for an urban family falls into the following eight types: (1)Money paid for food processing and money spent while eating out; (2)Money paid for clothing processing; (3)Domestic services and services for home amenities; (4) Medical cost (including medical diagnosis and treatment, in-home medical services and nursing cost); (5)Transport tool service fees (such as for the use of a car and maintenance fee thereby arising), transport tools (plane, ship, train) fees, post and telecommunications fees; (6)Fees for culture and entertainment services (such as tour and fitness building), fees for repair of sports and entertainment items, education cost (spending on obligatory and non-obligatory education), adult education cost, tutor fees, training courses fees and extra money paid as sponsorship fee to a school a student outside his or her education community; (7)Housing rents, some interior decoration cost (for labor), residence service fees (such as for property management and repairs); (8)Fees for other services (such as at a beauty salon, bathhouse, hairdresser´s and hotels).

Disposable Income of Rural Households

Disposable Income of Rural Households refers to the part of the rural households´income in a certain period after deducting family business expenditure, depreciation of productive fixed assets, taxes, contract expenditure, welfare funds and transferred expenditure, (including pensions, unemployment relief, cooperative medical funds, premiums and fines), which can be used for personal consumption, production investment and deposit. It differs from the net income in that it is the balance of the actual welfare and transferred income after deducting transferred expenditure. The disposable income includes: wages and salaries, net income from household business, property income, net transferred income.

Living Expenditures for Consumption of Rural Households

Living Expenditures for Consumption of Rural Households refer to expenditures of material and culture life of rural household, including expenses on food, clothing, housing, household appliances and service, medical and health care, traffic and communication items, cultural, education and recreation items and service and other commodities and service.

Income from Properties

Income from Properties refers to the income received as returns by owners of financial assets or tangible non-productive assets by providing capitals or tangible non-productive assets to other institutional units.

Income from Transfers

Income from Transfers refers to the receipt by rural households and their members of goods, services, capitals or rights of assets without giving or repaying accordingly, excluding capitals provided to them for the formation of fixed assets. In general, it refers to all income received by rural households through redistribution.

Basic Endowment Insurance

(1) Number of people participating in the insurance program: by the end of reference period, number of staff and workers partici-

pating in the insurance program in line with national laws, regulations and related policies, including those who can not make regular payment or interrupt payment but not terminate the insurance program.

(2) Revenue of social comprehensive funds: according to national provision, payments made by units covered in basic endowment insurance program, and income from other resources, including: income of social comprehensive funds paid by unites, financial subsidies, interest income and others.

(3) Expenditure of social comprehensive funds: refer to payment made to those retired and resigned people covered in endowment insurance program in terms of pension or compensation within the expenditure scope and standards according to related national policies, and the expenditure occurred due to shift of the insurance relationship or adjustment funds among agencies, including: basic pension, transitional pension, pension for resigned people, pension for retired people, pension for people quitting jobs, subsidies, funeral subsidies and other expenditure.

(4) Balance of social comprehensive funds: refer to the balance of basic endowment insurance of social comprehensive funds at the end of the reference period, including: bank savings, special fiscal account, investment in bonds and others.

Registered Urban Unemployment

Registered Urban Unemployment refers to those non-agricultural population within working age (16 – 50 years for male and 16 – 45 years for females) who arc able and willing to work but unemployed and have registered for job in local employment service agencies.

第十四篇

CHAPTER 14

就业与社会保障

EMPLOYMENT AND SOCIAL SECURITY

表 14－1　历年全社会从业人员数
Number of Whole Society Employees
(1993～2014)

单位:人　　　　　　　　　　　　　　　　　　　　　　　　　　　　　　(person)

年　份 Year	从业人员 Employed Persons	国有、集体、其他经济单位从业人员 Employed Persons in State-owned, Collective-owned and Other Economic Institutions	其　他 Others
1993	1 043 985	788 821	255 164
1994	1 049 985	767 146	282 839
1995	1 079 744	798 884	280 860
1996	1 039 692	759 936	279 756
1997	981 826	703 890	277 936
1998	963 211	638 707	324 504
1999	983 401	645 583	337 818
2000	1 040 411	636 923	403 488
2001	1 114 514	650 633	463 881
2002	1 199 864	686 637	513 227
2003	1 268 717	674 381	594 336
2004	1 302 723	643 628	659 095
2005	1 440 763	746 714	694 049
2006	1 467 145	720 105	747 040
2007	1 490 809	708 308	782 501
2008	1 507 631	749 400	758 231
2009	2 009 539	920 081	1 089 458
2010	2 351 115	1 004 078	1 347 037
2011	2 806 796	1 488 778	1 318 018
2012	2 970 091	1 584 025	1 386 066
2013	2 905 942	1 547 059	1 358 883
2014	3 023 905	2 069 720	954 185

注：2014 年从业人员数据根据第三次经济普查数据进行调整。
Note: The data of employed persons in 2014 has adapted according to the third economic census.

表14-2 全社会各行业从业人员数
Number of Whole Society Employees by Sectors

单位:人 (person)

指 标	Indicators	2012	2013	2014
总 计	**Total**	**2 970 091**	**2 905 942**	**3 023 905**
按产业分	**By Industry**			
第一产业	Primary Industry	137 109	133 905	136 340
第二产业	Secondary Industry	1 669 882	1 555 064	1 503 262
第三产业	Tertiary Industry	1 163 100	1 216 973	1 384 303
按行业分	**By Sector**			
农、林、牧、渔业	Farming, Forestry, Animal Husbandry and Fishery	137 109	134 226	136 340
采矿业	Mining	163	170	191
制造业	Manufacturing	1 255 085	1 269 976	1 258 765
电力、热力、燃气及水生产和供应业	Production and Supply of Electricity, Heat, Gas and Water	26 932	37 971	35 159
建筑业	Construction	387 702	271 891	209 147
批发和零售业	Wholesale and Retail	306 296	317 844	352 262
交通运输、仓储和邮政业	Transportation, Warehousing and Post Service	162 046	197 078	206 172
住宿和餐饮业	Hotel and Catering	58 268	39 722	40 105
信息传输、软件和信息技术服务业业	Information Transmission, Software and Information Technology Services	56 737	53 950	60 958
金融业	Banking	190 550	194 200	205 850
房地产业	Real Estate	50 983	57 388	58 109
租赁和商务服务业	Leasing and Business Service	45 896	45 450	48 860
科学研究和技术服务业	Scientific Research and Technology Services	39 295	34 341	35 046
水利、环境和公共设施管理业	Water Conservancy, Environment and Public Facilities Administration	11 983	12 825	134 163
居民服务、修理和其他服务业	Residents Service, Repair and other Services	130 062	129 047	130 197
教 育	Education	46 133	47 169	47 459
卫生和社会工作	Healthcare and Social Work	28 576	29 134	29 782
文化、体育和娱乐业	Culture, Sports and Entertainment	10 531	7 294	8 983
公共管理、社会保障和社会组织	Public Management, Social Guarantee and Social Organizations	25 744	26 266	26 357

表 14-3　历年职工人数
Staff and Workers
(1993~2014)

单位：人　　(person)

年　份 Year	职工人数 Staff and Workers	按登记注册类型分 Classified by Registration Categories			
		国有经济单位 State-owned Enterprises	集体经济单位 Collective-owned Enterprises	港澳台及外商投资单位 Overseas Investment Enterprises	其他单位 Others
1993	788 821	597 417	84 811		106 592
1994	767 146	582 477	76 023		108 646
1995	798 884	571 398	85 955		141 531
1996	719 634	469 966	85 030		164 638
1997	663 163	405 349	77 072	52 405	128 337
1998	661 406	354 408	60 633	111 015	135 350
1999	677 348	355 607	56 824	126 897	138 020
2000	677 544	340 605	44 654	137 332	154 953
2001	687 694	299 186	37 756	134 732	216 020
2002	701 949	276 876	33 390	160 884	230 799
2003	671 434	249 461	25 549	136 212	260 212
2004	614 014	238 073	23 217	119 658	233 066
2005	701 553	233 350	20 431	129 890	317 882
2006	665 680	173 204	16 196	145 534	330 746
2007	631 720	188 892	16 278	186 480	240 070
2008	667 882	175 428	11 823	225 566	255 065
2009	797 302	193 246	20 408	297 093	286 555
2010	850 176	201 002	17 155	336 022	295 997
2011	1 385 342	275 135	13 728	627 996	468 483
2012	1 451 359	282 539	24 766	695 262	448 792
2013	1 528 417	211 685	21 634	749 439	545 659
2014	1 978 127	177 932	29 731	999 677	770 787

表14-4 各行业职工人数
Staff and Workers by Sectors
(2014)

单位:人 (person)

指标	Indicators	职工人数 Staff and Workers	按登记注册类型分 Classified by Registration Categories			
			国有经济单位 State-owned Enterprises	集体经济单位 Collective-owned Enterprises	港澳台及外商投资单位 Overseas Investment Enterprises	其他单位 Others
总计	**Total**	**1 978 127**	**177 932**	**29 731**	**999 677**	**770 787**
按三次产业分	**By Industry**					
第一产业	Primary Industry	9 955	188	286	616	8 865
第二产业	Secondary Industry	679 955	13 573	7 793	438 320	220 269
第三产业	Tertiary Industry	1 288 217	164 171	21 652	560 741	541 653
按行业分	**By Sector**					
农、林、牧、渔业	Farming, Forestry, Animal Husbandry and Fishery	10 609	196	307	616	9 490
采矿业	Mining	429				429
制造业	Manufacturing	576 610	14 612	7 322	430 754	123 922
电力、热力、燃气及水生产和供应业	Production and Supply of Electricity, Heat, Gas and Water	8 721	407	146	2 145	6 023
建筑业	Construction	100 067	546	548	7 363	91 610
批发和零售业	Wholesale and Retail	288 568	2 005	2 414	226 203	57 946
交通运输、仓储和邮政业	Transportation, Warehousing and Post Service	170 005	4 432	421	41 343	123 809
住宿和餐饮业	Hotel and Catering	21 385	972	517	10 895	9 001
信息传输、软件和信息技术服务业业	Information Transmission, Software and Information Technology Services	129 826	436	4	75 432	53 954
#软件和信息技术服务业	Software and Information Technology Services	15 477	156		2 278	13 043
金融业	Banking	178 305	35 544		38 575	104 186
房地产业	Real Estate	64 652	3 504	3 856	25 228	32 064
租赁和商务服务业	Leasing and Business Service	188 875	5 094	4 811	85 463	93 507
科学研究和技术服务业	Scientific Research and Technology Services	60 250	9 192	210	35 722	15 126
水利、环境和公共设施管理业	Water Conservancy, Environment and Public Facilities Administration	15 631	4 510	1 939	688	8 494
#公共设施管理业	Public Facilities Administration	13 378	3 871	1 939	213	7 355
居民服务、修理和其他服务业	Residents Service, Repair and other Services	22 793	723	952	12 926	8 192
教育	Education	54 443	38 982	1 233	1 890	12 338
卫生和社会工作	Healthcare and Social Work	35 259	23 363	3 353	232	8 311
文化、体育和娱乐业	Culture, Sports and Entertainment	9 411	2 323	398	4 202	2 488
公共管理、社会保障和社会组织	Public Management, Social Guarantee and Social Organizations	42 288	31 091	1 300		9 897

表 14-5　应届毕业生构成及就业基本情况
Composition of Fresh Graduates and Employment

指　标	Indicators	单　位　Unit	2005	2010	2013	2014
毕业生按性别分	**By Sex of Graduates**					
男性比重	Proportion of Male Graduates	%	48.9	46.8	49.1	49.3
女性比重	Proportion of Female Graduates	%	51.1	53.2	50.9	50.7
毕业生按学历分	**By Educational Qualifications of Graduates**					
三校毕业生比重	Proportion of Graduates from Three Kinds of Colleges	%	37.0	17.0	16.1	12.1
大专毕业生比重	Proportion of Junior College Graduates	%	38.4	40.7	32.6	33.5
本科及以上毕业生比重	Proportion of University Graduates or Those with Higher Degrees	%	24.7	42.3	51.3	54.4
毕业生总体就业率	**Overall Employment Rate of Graduates**	**%**	**65.8**	**64.1**	**74.8**	**75.1**
就业率按性别分	**Employment Rate, By Sex of Graduates**					
男性就业率	Employment Rate of Male Graduates	%	62.6	61.8	71.7	73.7
女性就业率	Employment Rate of Female Graduates	%	68.7	66.2	77.8	76.5
就业率按学历分	**Employment Rate, by Educational Qualifications**					
三校生	Graduates from Three Kinds of Colleges	%	53.3	49.2	61.4	62.1
大专生	Graduates of Junior Colleges	%	69.1	60.6	72.4	72.5
本科生及以上	Graduates of Universities or those with Higher Degrees	%	74.8	72.4	79.2	79.6
首份工作薪酬收入均值	**Average Monthly Salaries of First Jobs**	**元**	**1 617**	**2 370**	**3 429**	**3 682**
三校生	Graduates from Three Kinds of Colleges	元	1 101	1 773	2 844	3 193
大专生	Graduates of Junior Colleges	元	1 404	2 093	2 984	3 311
本科生及以上	Graduates of Universities or those with Higher Degrees	元	2 327	2 718	3 786	4 018

注：数据取自对新区各类应届毕业生进行的抽样调查。调查对象为常住人口口径，居住在抽中居（村）委会、应届毕业的大专院校毕业生和三校毕业生。自 2010 年起，调查抽样范围覆盖新浦东的城乡全部村居委，且调查时点改为当年 7 月 1 日零时。2012 年起调查对象改为具有浦东户籍、应届毕业的大专院校毕业生和三校毕业生。

Note: These data come from sample surveys to fresh graduates of different colleges and universities in PNA. The surveyed graduates are graduated from junior colleges and three kinds of colleges who are de jure population and live in the selected urban/rural residential committees. The area of survey sampling covered all of the village and neighborhood committees in new PNA since 2010 and the survey time changed to 0:00 of June 1 of that current year. Since 2012, the surveyed have been changed to those who graduated from junior colleges and three kinds of colleges registered in Pudong in current year.

表14-6 享受居民最低生活保障人数
Number of Residents Benefiting from Guarantee of Minimum Standard of Living (2014)

单位:人 (person)

指 标	Indicators	保障对象 Residents to be Guaranteed	城镇低保 Guarantee of Minimum Standard of Living in Urban Area	农村贫困户 Poverty Households in Rural Area
总 计	**Total**	**38 694**	**33 843**	**4 851**
潍坊新村街道	Weifangxincun Subdistrict	785	785	
陆家嘴街道	Lujiazui Subdistrict	1 703	1 703	
周家渡街道	Zhoujiadu Subdistrict	2 220	2 220	
塘桥街道	Tangqiao Subdistrict	863	863	
上钢新村街道	Shanggangxincun Subdistrict	1 558	1 558	
南码头路街道	Nanmatoulu Subdistrict	825	825	
沪东新村街道	Hudongxincun Subdistrict	1 147	1 147	
金杨新村街道	Jinyangxincun Subdistrict	1 266	1 266	
洋泾街道	Yangjing Subdistrict	1 014	1 014	
浦兴路街道	Puxinglu Subdistrict	1 748	1 748	
东明路街道	Dongminglu Subdistrict	888	888	
花木街道	Huamu Subdistrict	1 768	1 768	
川沙新镇	Chuansha New Town	2 877	2 273	604
高桥镇	Gaoqiao Town	694	663	31
北蔡镇	Beicai Town	1 825	1 808	17
合庆镇	Heqing Town	507	367	140
唐 镇	Tangzhen Town	236	198	38
曹路镇	Caolu Town	1 495	1 314	181

单位:人　　　　表 14－6　续表　Continued　　　　(person)

指　标 Indicators		保障对象 Residents to be Guaranteed	城镇低保 Guarantee of Minimum Standard of Living in Urban Area	农村贫困户 Poverty Households in Rural Area
金 桥 镇	Jinqiao Town	204	202	2
高 行 镇	Gaohang Town	629	629	
高 东 镇	Gaodong Town	389	333	56
张 江 镇	Zhangjiang Town	965	965	
三 林 镇	Sanlin Town	1 781	1 728	53
惠 南 镇	Huinan Town	1 536	1 161	375
周 浦 镇	Zhoupu Town	595	549	46
新 场 镇	Xinchang Town	840	576	264
大 团 镇	Datuan Town	1 155	526	629
康 桥 镇	Kangqiao Town	449	446	3
航 头 镇	Hangtou Town	546	392	154
祝 桥 镇	Zhuqiao Town	3 133	2 201	932
泥 城 镇	Nicheng Town	770	532	238
宣 桥 镇	Xuanqiao Town	617	453	164
书 院 镇	Shuyuan Town	616	185	431
万 祥 镇	Wanxiang Town	357	196	161
老 港 镇	Laogang Town	508	176	332
南汇新城镇	Nanhui New Town	185	185	

表 14－7　劳动就业及社会保障
Employment and Social Security

指　标	Indicators	单　位 Unit	2010	2013	2014
劳动就业	**Employment**				
期末城镇登记失业人数	Actual Number of Those Registered as Unemployed at Year-end	人 person	43 453	43 963	41 759
招工录用总数	Total Recruitment	人 person	287 873	272 826	264 446
征地劳动力安置	Recruitment of Those Who Have Lost Jobs Because of Requisition of Land	人 person	29 310	4 328	3 401
新增就业岗位	Number of Newly Increased Employment	人 person	140 440	150 984	150 714
扶持创业人数	Number of Entrepreneurship Support	人 person		1 875	1 959
国家职业资格培训人数	Number of National Occupation Qualification Training	人 person		89 331	83 811
社 会 保 险	**Social Security**				
失业保险金发放人次	Unemployment Insurance Payment Distribution	人次 person-time	294 180	244 535	230 566
失业保险金发放金额	Unemployment Insurance Payment	万元 10 000yuan	17 156	20 297	26 572
农村社会养老保险期末参保人数	Number of Persons Who Joined Endowment Insurance Program in Rural Area at Year end	人 person	91 747	134 321	130 355
农村社会养老保险期末享受人数	Number of Persons Who Benefited from Endowment Insurance Program in Rural Area at Year end	人 person	58 432	71 652	73 713
社会救助	**Social Relief**				
城镇居民低保人数	Urban Residents Who Benefit from Subsistence Allowances from the State	人 person	72 424	37 006	33 843
城镇居民低保金额	Subsistence Allowances to Urban Residents	万元 10 000yuan	24 902	22 171	23 457
农村居民低保人数	Number of Rural Population Benefiting from Subsistence Allowance	人 person	11 119	4 974	4 851
农村居民低保金额	Amount of Subsistence Allowance for Rural Population	万元 10 000yuan	2 285	2 310	2 913

表 14－8　收养性单位基本情况
Background of Welfare Facilities
(2014)

指　标	Indicators	单　位 Unit	合　计 Total	社会福利院 Welfare Homes	敬老院 Homes for Senior Citizens
单位数	**Total Number**	**个 unit**	**125**	**2**	**123**
年末职工人数	**Number of Staff and Workers (Year End)**	**人 person**	**5 646**	**206**	**5 440**
#医护人员	Medical Personnel and Nurses	人 person	348	25	323
年末床位数	**Number of Beds**	**张 bed**	**23 459**	**858**	**22 601**
年末在院人数	**Persons Housed (Year End)**	**人 person**	**16 071**	**362**	**15 709**
#女　性	Female	人 person	10 563	213	10 350
#自费人员	Those at Their Own Expenses	人 person	15 744	362	15 382
在院人员按年龄分	Persons Housed by Age				
老　人	Old People	人 person	15 587	362	15 225
青壮年	Young and Middle-aged People	人 person	484		484
儿　童	Children	人 person			

表 14－9　残疾人事业及居家养老情况
Statistics of Disabled Persons & Home-based Care for the Aged

指　标	Indicators	单　位 Unit	2010	2013	2014
残疾人事业	**Disabled Persons**				
白内障复明手术	Operations for Recovery from Cataract	例 in number	2 281	830	628
低视力配用助视器人数	Number of Bad Eyesighted Persons Equipped with Typoscope	人 person	153	68	619
低听力配用助听器人数	Number of Bad Auditioned Persons Equipped with Haudiphone	人 person	336	395	939
精神病人数	Number of Mental Patients	人 person	15 735	23 787	23 856
监护精神病人数	Number of Mental Patients Supervised	人 person	15 230	23 434	23 450
城镇残疾人就业人数	Employed Disabled Persons in Towns and Subdistricts	人 person	125	447	452
居家养老	**Life of Disabled Persons Including the Aged**				
期末养老机构床位数	Number of Beds in Old-Aged Institutions at End of Term	张 bed	22 096	23 025	23 459
居家养老护理人员数	Number of Care Workers for the Old-Aged Living at Home	人 person	3 953	4 355	4 187
居家养老服务总数	Number of Services for the Old-Aged Living at Home	人 person	47 610	55 981	58 345
#补贴数	Number of the Old Disabled Persons	人 person	41 596	44 629	46 773
新增安康通安装数	Number of New Installations for Ankangtong SIM Cards	人次 persons-time	1 776		

表 14－10 红十字会基本情况
Statistics of Red Cross

指 标 Indicators		单 位 Unit	2010	2013	2014
救 灾	**Providing Disaster Relief**				
捐赠款物	Donation of Money and Clothes	万元 10 000Yuan	2 790	408	102
救 助	**Salvage**				
救助款物	Salvation of Money and Clothes	万元 10 000Yuan	1 186	5 744	4 259
受益人次	Number of Persons Benefited	人次 person-time	14 031	48 862	47 395
救 护	**Rescue**				
师资培训	Teachers Trained	人 person	29	8	132
救护员培训	Rescue Workers Trained	人 person	4 501	5 722	5 208
救护防病知识普及	Popularization of Rescue and Disease Protection	人次 person-time	59 265	112 560	127 756
预防艾滋病	Protection of AIDS	人次 person-time	31 520	518 116	524 492
遗体捐献登记	Registration of Body Donations	例 in number	202	213	273
基层组织	Grassroot Organizations	个 in number	281	286	296
社区公益服务站点	Community Public Service Stations	个 in number	523	1 013	1 197
志愿者	Volunteers	人 in number	6 491	10 823	19 547

表 14－11 保障性住房
Indemnificatory Housing

指 标 Indicators		单 位 Unit	2005	2010	2013	2014
廉租住房	**Low Rent Housing**					
人均居住面积认定标准	Approved Standard for Living Space Per Capita	平方米 sq·m	≦7	≦7	≦7	≦7
人均月收入认定标准	Approved Standard for Monthly Income Per Capita	元 yuan	300	≦1100	≦2100	≦2500
累计受益户数	Number of Households Registered	户 household	1 670	6 450	8 744	9 850
配租金额	Total Rent of Assisted Households	万元 10 000yuan	780	12 059	22 785	27 283
动迁房	**Resettlement Housing**					
动迁房套数	Number of Resettlement Housing	套 household			15 000	15 673
动迁房面积	Area of Resettlement Housing	万平方米 10 000 sq·m			120.00	137.74
共有产权房	**Limited-property-rights Housing**					
共有产权房套数	Number of Limited-property-rights Housing	套 household			3 595	262
共有产权房面积	Area of Limited-property-rights Housing	万平方米 10 000 sq·m			27.64	2.01
临港限价房	**Capped-Price Housing**					
临港限价房套数	Number of Capped-Price Housing	套 household			1 432	
临港限价房面积	Area of Capped-Price Housing	万平方米 10 000 sq·m			11.00	

表 14－12　社会捐赠与帮困
Social Donations and Financial Aids

指　标	Indicators	单位　Unit	2010	2013	2014
社会捐赠	**Social Donations**				
捐赠款金额	Amount of Donations	万元 10 000yuan	12 416	14 607	9 910
捐赠衣被	Clothes and Quilts for Donation	万件 10 000unit	88	24	4
医疗救助	**Medical Assistance**				
医疗救助人次	Number of Medical Assistance	人次 person-time	13 096	52 102	68 494
医疗救助金额	Amount of Medical Assistance	万元 10 000yuan	5 122	4 666	6 725
帮困助学	**Financial Aids for Students**				
帮困助学人次	Number of Financial Aids for Students	人次 person-time	18 136	11 933	21 070
帮困助学金额	Amount of Financial Aids for Students	万元 10 000yuan	907	1 030	1 608

表 14－13　社会保障标准
Standard for Social Security

单位：元　　(yuan)

指　标	Indicators	2010	2013	2014
职工月最低工资标准	Standard of Minimum Monthly Salary for Employees	1 120	1 620	1 820
城镇居民月最低生活保障标准	Standard of Minimum Monthly Living Expenses for Urban Residents	450	640	710
农村居民月最低生活保障标准	Standard of Minimum Monthly Living Expenses for Rural Residents	300	500	620
农村社会养老保险金月最低标准	Minimum Monthly Pension Insurance for Rural Residents in PNA		625	725

主要统计指标解释

从业人员

从业人员指从事一定社会劳动并取得劳动报酬或经营收入的人员,包括在岗职工、再就业的离退休人员、私营业主、个体户主、私营和个体从业人员、乡镇企业从业人员、农村从业人员、其他从业人员(包括民办教师、宗教职业者、现役军人等)。这一指标反映了一定时期内全部劳动力资源的实际利用情况,是研究我国基本国情国力的重要指标。

各单位的从业人员指在各级国家机关、政党机关、社会团体及企业、事业单位中工作,取得工资或其他形式的劳动报酬的全部人员。包括在岗职工、再就业的离退休人员、民办教师以及在各单位中工作的外方人员和港澳台方人员、兼职人员、借用的外单位人员和第二职业者。不包括离开本单位仍保留劳动关系的职工。各单位的就业人员反映了各单位实际参加生产或工作的全部劳动力。

职　工

职工指在国有、城镇集体、联营、股份制、外商和港、澳、台投资、其他单位及其附属机构工作,并由其支付工资的各类人员。不包括下列人员:(1)乡镇企业就业人员;(2)私营企业就业人员;(3)城镇个体劳动者;(4)离休、退休、退职人员;(5)再就业的离、退休人员;(6)民办教师;(7)在城镇单位中工作的外方及港、澳、台人员;(8)其他按有关规定不列入职工统计范围的人员。(1998 年及以后的数据均为在岗职工数据,其他相关指标如职工工资总额,职工平均工资等指标也从 1998 年按此口径进行了相应调整)。

登记注册类型

登记注册类型是以工商行政管理机关登记注册的具有法人资格的各类企业为划分对象。产业活动单位和行政机关、事业单位、社会团体及其他经济组织参照执行。

国有企业指企业全部资产归国家所有,并按《中华人民共和国企业法人登记管理条例》规定登记注册的非公司制的经济组织。不包括有限责任公司中的国有独资公司。

集体企业指企业资产归集体所有,并按《中华人民共和国企业法人登记管理条例》规定登记注册的经济组织。

股份合作企业指以合作制为基础,由企业职工共同出资入股,吸收一定比例的社会资产投资组建,实行自主经营,自负盈亏,共同劳动,民主管理,按劳动分配与按股份分红相结合的一种集体经济组织。

联营企业指两个及两个以上相同或不同所有制性质的企业法人或事业单位法人,按自愿、平等、互利的原则,共同投资组成的经济组织。联营企业包括国有联营企业、集体联营企业、国有与集体联营企业和其他联营企业。

有限责任公司指根据《中华人民共和国公司登记管理条例》规定登记注册,由 2 个以上,50 个以下的股东共同出资,每个股东以其所认缴的出资额对公司承担有限责任,公司以其全部资产对其债务承担责任的经济组织。有限责任公司包括国有独资公司以及其他有限责任公司。

股份有限公司指根据《中华人民共和国公司登记管理条例》规定登记注册,其全部注册资本由等额股份构成并通过发行股票筹集资本,股东以其认购的股份对公司承担有限责任,公司以其全部资产对其债务承担责任的经济组织。

私营企业指由自然人投资设立或由自然人控股,以雇佣劳动为基础的营利性经济组织。包括按照《公司法》、《合伙企业法》、《私营企业暂行条例》规定登记注册的私营有限责任公司、私营股份有限公司、私营合伙企业和私营独资企业。

与港澳台商投资合资经营企业指港澳台地区投资者与内地企业依照《中华人民共和国中外合资经营企业法》及有关法律的规定,按合同的比例投资设立、分享利润和分担风险的企业。

港澳台商投资合作经营企业指港澳台地区投资者与内地企业依照《中华人民共和国中外合资经营企业法》及有关法律的规定,依照合同的约定进行投资或提供条件设立、分享利润和分担风险的企业。

港澳台商独资经营企业指依照《中华人民共和国外资企业法》及有关法律的规定,在内地由港澳台商地区投资者全额投资设立的企业。

港澳台商投资股份有限公司指根据国家有关规定,经外经贸部依法批准设立,其中港、澳、台商的股本占公司注册资本的比例达 25% 以上的股份有限公司。凡其中港、澳、台商的股本占公司注册资本的比例小于 25% 的,属于内资企业中股份有限公司。

中外合资经营企业指外国企业或外国人与中国内地企业依照《中华人民共和国中外合资经营企业法》及有关法律的规定,按合同规定的比例投资设立、分享利润和分担风险的企业。

中外合作经营企业指外国企业或外国人与中国内地企业依照《中华人民共和国中外合作经营企业法》及有关法律的规定,依照合作合同的约定进行投资或提供条件设立、分享利润和分担风险的企业。

外资企业指依照《中华人民共和国外资企业法》及有关法律的规定,在中国内地由外国投资者全额投资设立的企业。

外商投资股份有限公司指根据国家有关规定,经外经贸部依法批准设立,其中外资的股本占公司注册资本的比例达 25% 以上的股份有限公司。凡其中外资股本占公司注册资本的比例小于 25% 的,属于内资企业中的股份有限公司。

国民经济行业分类

《国民经济行业分类》国家标准于1984年首次发布，1994年对其进行了第一次修订，2011年新修订。

本年鉴的行业分类使用2011年修订的行业分类标准。

2011年新行业分类标准按照国际通行的经济活动同质性原则划分行业，进一步打破了部门管理界限，对原标准中不符合这一原则的分类进行了调整；根据我国社会经济活动的发展状况，重点加强了第三产业的分类，新增了大量服务业方面的活动类别；对新标准的每一个行业小类，全部与国际标准产业分类的最细一层分类建立了对应关系。新修订的《国民经济行业分类》主要目的之一是与联合国的《全部经济活动的国际标准产业分类》接轨，准确反映一定时期内国民经济行业的构成状况。

失业保险

①参加保险人数：指报告期末按照国家法律、法规和有关政策规定参加了失业保险的城镇企业事业单位的职工及地方政府规定参加失业保险的其他人员的人数。

②失业保险金：指为保障失业人员的基本生活而按规定支付的失业保险金金额。

社会福利事业单位

社会福利事业单位指集中收养社会孤老、残、幼的机构。包括由民政部门管理的社会福利院、儿童福利院、精神病人福利院和城镇集体办的福利院，以及农村集体办的敬老院。

优抚对象

优抚指政府对革命烈士家庭、病故残疾工作人员以及参战负伤致残的民兵、民工的抚恤和人民群众对其的优待。优抚对象包括革命烈士家属、因公牺牲和病故军人家属、革命伤残人员、现役军属、退伍红军老战士、红军失散人员、复员军人、退伍军人、在职退役军人、在乡退役军人、带病回乡退伍军人、复退军人精神病员、孤老优抚对象等。

EXPLANATORY NOTES TO MAJOR STATISTICAL INDICATORS

Employees

Employees refer to the persons who are engaged in social working and receive remuneration payment or earn business income, including total staff and workers, re-employed retirees, employers of private enterprises, self-employ ed workers, employees in private enterprises and individual economy, employees in township enterprises, employed persons in the rural areas , and other employed persons (including teachers in the schools run by the local people, people engaged in religious profession and the servicemen, etc.). This indicator reflects the actual utilization of total labor force during a certain period of time and is often used for the research on China' s economic situation and national power.

Employees in Various Units refer to all the persons working in government agencies of various levels, political and party organizations, social organizations, enterprises and institutions, and receiving wages or other forms of payment. They include fully-employed staff and workers, re-employed retirees, teachers in schools run by the local people, foreigners and Chinese compatriots from Hong Kong, Macao, and Taiwan working in various units, part-time employees, employees of other units working temporarily at current post s, and employees holding the second job, but exclude staff and workers who have left their working units while keeping their labor contract (employment relation) unchanged. This indicator reflects the total number of laborers actually engaged in production or other operations in various units.

Staff and Workers

Staff and Workers refer to persons working in, and receive payment from units of state ownership, collective ownership, joint ownership, share holding ownership, foreign ownership, and ownership by entrepreneurs from Hong Kong, Macao, and Taiwan, and other types of ownership and their affiliated units. They do not include 1) persons employed in township enterprises, 2) persons employed in private enterprises, 3) urban self-employed persons, 4) retirees, 5) re-employed retirees, 6) teachers in the schools run by the local people, 7) foreigners and persons from Hong Kong, Macao and Taiwan who work in urban units, and 8) other persons not to be included by relevant regulations. (Data of 1998 and afterward refer to fully employed staff and workers. Other related statistics such as total wages and average wage are adjusted since 1998 accordingly).

Registration Categories

Registration Categories are used to classify all kinds of enterprises that have the legal person status and have registered with the industrial and commercial administrations. The classification of business units, administrative and public institutions, social organizations and other economical bodies may refer to it.

The state-owned enterprises are economic organizations whose assets are solely owned by the state and whose registrations are made according to "Regulations of the People's Republic of China for Controlling the Registration of Enterprises as Legal Persons" excluding the state-owned liability limited companies.

The collective-owned enterprises are economic organizations whose assets are owned by collecting and whose registration are made according to "Regulations of the People's Republic of China for Controlling the Registration of Enterprises as Legal Persons."

Share-holding cooperative enterprises are a kind of collective economic organizations based on a cooperative system. In addition to the shares bought by their workers and staff, the enterprises also absorb a certain percentage of social capital. They enjoy the autonomy in operation and are responsible for their own losses and profits. The share-holders work together, conduct democratic management, and combine labor-based distribution with share-based dividends.

Joint-owned enterprises refer to economic organizations set up with joint investment from legal persons of two or more enterprises of different ownerships or institutions according to principle of voluntary participation, equality and mutual benefit. They include state-owned joint operation enterprises, collective joint operation enterprises, state-collective joint operation enterprises and other types of joint operation enterprises.

A company with limited liability is a company registered in accordance with the "Regulations of the People's Republic of China on Administration of Company Registration." Its investment comes from more than 2 and less than 50 shareholders. Each shareholder assumes limited liability for the company according to his subscription to capital stock. The company assumes liabilities for its debts according to all its assets. Such economic organizations include solely state – invested companies and other types of companies with limited liability.

A share-holding company with limited liability refers to economic organizations registered in accordance with the "Regulations of the People's Republic of China on Administration of Company Registration". All its registered capital is composed of shares of equal value and its capital is collected through share issuing. The shareholders bear limited liability for the company according to the amount of shares they have bought from the company and the company assumes liabilities for its debts according all its assets.

A private enterprise refers to profit-making economic organizations set up with investment from natural persons or with controlling interest in the hands of natural persons who employ laborers for operation. Such enterprises include private companies with limited liability private joint stock companies limited private partnership enterprises and solely individual-invested enterprises, which are registered according to the "Company Law," "Partnership Enterprises Law" and "Interim Regulations of Private Enterprises."

The joint ventures with investment from Hong Kong, Macao and Taiwan refer to those established according to the "Law of the People's Republic of China on Chinese-foreign Joint Ventures" and regulations stipulated in relevant laws, by investors from those regions and the Chinese mainland enterprises with contracted share of investment and sharing profits and ventures between the parties.

Cooperative businesses with investment from Hong Kong, Macao and Taiwan refer to enterprises jointly set up by investors from Hong Kong, Macao and Taiwan and mainland enterprises according to the "Law of the People's Republic of China on Chinese-foreign Contractural Joint Ventures" and other relevant regulations. They invest or provide conditions for establishment, decide profit distribution, and share risks according to provisions prescribed in the cooperative venture contracts.

Solely Hong Kong, Macao and Taiwan Funded enterprises refer to enterprises set up on the mainland according to the "Law of the People's Republic of China on Foreign Capital Enterprises and solely invested by investors from Hong Kong, Macao and Taiwan."

A share-holding company with limited liability with investment from Hong Kong, Macao and Taiwan refers to any joint stock company limited that is set up according relevant state regulations and is approved by the Ministry of Foreign Economic Relations and Trade. The investment from Hong Kong, Macao and Taiwan investors must account more than 25 per-cent of the company's total capital. If such investment is less than 25 percent, it shall be classified as a joint stock company limited invested by domestic investors.

A Sino-foreign joint venture refers to any enterprise that is jointly set up by foreign enterprises or foreigners with Chinese enterprises in accordance with the "Law of the People's Republic of China on Joint Ventures with Chinese and Foreign Investment." The investors shall put in investment, share profits and risks according to the contract on the joint venture.

Sino-foreign cooperative Businesses refer to the enterprises set up by foreign enterprises or foreigners with Chinese enterprises as their partners, in line with "The Sino-foreign Cooperative Ventures Law of the People's Republic of China" and other relevant laws and regulations. The partners of the cooperative ventures will invest, take profits and share risks according to the requirements of stipulated in the contract.

A Solely Foreign-Funded enterprises refers to any enterprise that is set up on the Chinese mainland according to the "Law of the People's Republic of China on Foreign-Capital Enterprises" and with all its investment coming from foreign investors.

The foreign-invested joint stock company limited refers to any joint stock company limited that is set up according to relevant state regulations and is approved by the Ministry of Foreign Economic Relations and Trade. The foreign investment must account more than 25 per-cent of the company's total capital. If such investment is less than 25 percent, it shall be classified as a joint stock company limited invested by Chinese investors.

Classification of the Sectors of the National Economy

Classification of the Sectors of the National Economy was first published in 1984 and revisions were made into it in 2011.

This Yearbook follows standards in the 2011 version of the Classification of the Sectors of the National Economy.

In the 2011 version, economic sectors are classified in accordance with the international categories of the economic activities, abolishing in definition between different administrative departments. Given the development of China's social and economic activities, more detailed classification is made of the service sector. The further breakdown of each economic sector in the latest version is geared to the most specific categorization in international practice. The latest version aims at, among others, an objective and precise presentation of the composition of the national economy in a certain period.

Unemployment Insurance

1. Number of people participated in unemployment insurance program: the number of staff and workers in urban enterprises or institutions and other people according to local government regulations participated in unemployment insurance program in line with national law, regulations and related policies by the end of the reference period.

2. Sum of Unemployment Insurance: refers to total amount of insurance paid to un-employees to guarantee their basic lives according to related regulations.

Social Welfare Institutions

Social Welfare Institutions refer to institutions taking care of old people without children, handicapped people and orphans. They include social welfare institutions run by civil affairs departments, children's welfare institutions, welfare institutions for mental patients, and collectively-run old people's homes in rural areas.

Special Care

Special Care is offered by the government to the family member of the martyrs, disabled or demobilized servicemen or laborers who were injured on duty. Entitled to the special care are family members of the revolutionary martyrs, family members of servicemen who dies on duty or died of an illness, disabled servicemen, family members of servicemen on active service, retired veteran Red Army soldiers, scattered Red Army soldiers, demobilized servicemen, ex-servicemen, servicemen who were demobilized while on duty, ex-servicemen back to their rural homes, ex-servicemen who were demobilized because of an illness and have gone back to their rural homes, ex-servicemen who suffer from mental illness and elderly persons with no family.

第十五篇

CHAPTER 15

教育

EDUCATION

表15－1　各级各类学校基本情况
Schools by Education Level and Type
(2014)

单位:人　　(person)

指　标	Indicators	学校(所) Schools (unit)	毕业生数 Graduates	招生数 Student Enrollment	在校学生数 Students Enrolled	教职员工数 Faculty and Staff	#专任教师 Full-time Faculty
总　计	**Total**	**367**	**111 573**	**125 155**	**537 255**	**43 357**	**33 970**
高等学校	Institutions of Higher Education	29	34 915	33 844	168 501	13 752	8 428
中等技术学校	Secondary Technical Schools	9	5 632	3 874	12 043	1 267	612
普通中学	High Schools	154	33 894	40 919	139 424	14 194	11 955
职业中学	Vocational Schools	7	5 449	4 717	15 273	1 103	936
小　学	Primary Schools	165	31 593	41 726	201 261	12 842	11 853
特殊教育学校	Special Education Schools	3	90	75	753	199	186

注：高等学校的毕业生数和招生数仅包括本、专科学生数，研究生的毕业生数和招生数未统计在内。
Note: The number of enrolment and that of graduates of higher education only include the number of undergraduate students in universities and colleges, not including those who study master's and doctor's degree.

表15－2　各级各类学校占地面积和校舍建筑面积
Ground Space of Schools and Floor Space of School Buildings by Education Level and Type
(2014)

单位:万平方米　　(10 000 sq·m)

指　标	Indicators	学校(所) Schools (unit)	占地面积 Ground Space	校舍建筑面积 Floor Space of School Buildings
总　计	**Total**	**367**	**1 536.97**	**843.71**
高等学校	Institutions of Higher Education	29	694.61	345.19
中等技术学校	Secondary Technical Schools	9	24.87	25.19
普通中学	High Schools	154	533.11	307.31
职业中学	Vocational Schools	7	34.81	25.82
小　学	Primary Schools	165	245.53	137.20
特殊教育学校	Special Education Schools	3	4.04	3.00

表 15-3 各级各类学校女学生和女教师
Female Students and Teachers by Education Level and Type
(2014)

单位:人 (person)

指 标 Indicators		女学生 Female Students		女教师 Female Faculty	
		人 数 Students	占学生总数(%) of Students(%)	人 数 Teachers	占教师总数(%) of Teachers(%)
总 计	**Total**	**256 626**	**47.8**	**22 989**	**67.7**
高等学校	Institutions of Higher Education	84 164	49.9	4 205	49.9
中等专业学校	Secondary Specialized Schools	5 073	42.1	350	57.2
普通中学	High Schools	67 416	48.4	8 178	68.4
职业中学	Vocational Schools	6 939	45.4	637	68.1
小 学	Primary Schools	92 776	46.1	9 465	79.9
特殊教育学校	Special Education Schools	258	34.3	154	82.8

表 15-4 幼儿园基本情况
Statistics of Kindergartens
(2014)

指 标 Indicators		幼儿园(所) Kindergartens (unit)	班级数(个) Classes (unit)	幼儿数(人) Children Enrolled (person)	教职员(人) Faculty and Staff (person)	#专任教师 Full-time Faculty
总 计	**Total**	**280**	**3 776**	**109 807**	**9 987**	**7 398**
教育部门办	Run by Government Education Department	181	2 915	86 736	6 394	5 608
民 办	Run by Entrepreneurs	98	857	22 971	3 573	1 779
其他部门办	Run by Other Organizations	1	4	100	20	11

表15-5　市、区实验性示范性中学基本情况一览
(2014)

指　标	Indicators	班级数(个) Classes (in Number)	初　中 Junior Schools	高　中 High Schools
总　计	**Total**	**899**	**148**	**751**
市实验性示范性中学	**Experimental and Demonstrative High Schools in Shanghai**	**380**	**77**	**303**
华东师范大学第二附属中学	Second High School Affiliated to Huadong Normal University	28		28
上海市浦东复旦附中分校	Shanghai Pudong High School Affiliated to Fudan University	8		8
上海市建平中学	Shanghai Jianping High School	38		38
上海市进才中学	Shanghai Jincai High School	38		38
上海师范大学附属中学	High School Affiliated to Shanghai Normal University	24		24
上海市洋泾中学	Shanghai Yangjing High School	38		38
上海南汇中学	Shanghai Nanhui High School	58	4	54
上海市川沙中学	Shanghai Chuansha High School	38	2	36
上海市实验学校	Shanghai Experimetnal High School	33	15	18
上海外国语大学附属浦东外国语学校	Pudong Foreign Languages High School Affiliated to Shanghai Foreign Languages University	45	32	13
上海中学东校	Shanghai High School East Campus	32	24	8
区实验性示范性中学	**Experimental and Demonstrative High Schools in Pudong**	**519**	**71**	**448**
华东师范大学附属东昌中学	Dongchang High School Affiliated to Huadong Normal University	37		37
上海市上南中学	Shanghai Shangnan High School	36		36
上海市高桥中学	Shanghai Gaoqiao High School	36		36
上海市三林中学	Shanghai Sanlin High School	30		30
上海市杨思高级中学	Shanghai Yangsi High School	24		24
上海海事大学附属北蔡高级中学	Beicai High School Affiliated to Shanghai Maritime University	18		18
上海市浦东中学	Shanghai Pudong High School	18		18
上海市陆行中学	Shanghai Luhang High School	24		24
上海市高行中学	Shanghai Gaohang High School	36	24	12
上海市香山中学	Shanghai Xiangshan High School	27	15	12
上海市建平世纪中学	Shanghai Jianping Century High School	18		18
上海市新川中学	Shanghai Xinchuan High School	24		24
上海交通大学附属中学浦东实验高中	Pudong Experimental High School Affiliated to Shanghai Jiaotong University	27		27
上海市文建中学	Shanghai Wenjian High School	18		18
上海海洋大学附属大团高级中学	Datuan High School Affiliated to Shanghai Maritime University	30		30
上海市新场中学	Shanghai Xinchang High School	30		30
华东师范大学附属周浦中学	Zhoupu High School Affiliated to Huadong Normal University	36		36
上海市南汇第一中学	Shanghai Nanhui First HIgh School	50	32	18

Statistics of Municipal and PNA Experimental and Demonstrative High Schools

在校学生(人) Students Enrolled (Persons)	初中 Junior Schools	高中 High Schools	教职员工(人) Faculty (Persons)	专任教师(人) Full-time Teachers	高中 High Schools	初中 Junior Schools	占地面积(平方米) Ground Space (sq. m)	校舍建筑面积(平方米) Floor Space of School Buildings (sq. m)	运动场地面积(平方米) Floor Space of Sports Grounds (Stadiums) (sq. m)
33 699	**5 676**	**28 023**	**3 816**	**3 165**	**2 749**	**416**	**1 686 650**	**969 103**	**413 279**
14 320	**2 890**	**11 430**	**1 710**	**1 398**	**1 183**	**215**	**1 004 306**	**596 787**	**206 750**
1 157		1 157	177	130	130		100 000	59 133	23 900
230		230	20	20	20		50 640	39 990	11 152
1 481		1 481	152	137	137		41 385	33 459	7 075
1 425		1 425	188	158	158		114 146	73 411	35 504
797		797	150	120	120		99 999	49 815	4 012
1 398		1 398	160	135	135		51 811	43 482	8 300
2 205	164	2 041	247	200	200		259 064	102 992	36 092
1 514	80	1 434	170	122	122		32 503	27 137	11 400
1 215	540	675	177	121	72	49	73 724	29 081	17 600
1 775	1 263	512	165	152	53	99	81 004	72 178	21 000
1 123	843	280	104	103	36	67	100 030	66 109	30 715
19 379	**2 786**	**16 593**	**2 106**	**1 767**	**1 566**	**201**	**682 344**	**372 316**	**206 529**
1 335		1 335	137	111	111		30 690	17 845	10 384
1 336		1 336	146	126	126		46 347	27 187	15 400
1 334		1 334	141	116	116		41 675	24 206	11 582
1 143		1 143	132	118	118		34 185	20 593	13 737
884		884	104	89	89		37 715	18 757	10 259
678		678	61	54	54		25 338	15 561	11 013
691		691	71	64	64		29 093	19 295	9 847
894		894	95	66	66		40 766	21 033	11 410
1 336	886	450	126	114	48	66	37 077	17 694	12 659
912	458	454	103	93	51	42	21 242	16 987	7 800
671		671	70	65	65		27 328	15 653	9 699
920		920	84	82	82		21 940	12 836	10 200
860		860	129	97	97		21 871	21 104	9 573
609		609	70	64	64		17 267	18 031	5 700
1 142		1 142	171	101	101		64 414	24 954	19 980
1 136		1 136	120	112	112		46 220	19 930	14 572
1 365		1 365	164	143	143		79 695	39 220	8 000
2 133	1 442	691	182	152	59	93	59 481	21 430	14 714

表 15-6 普通中学和小学专任教师学历情况
Education Level of Full-time Teachers at Junior and High Schools and Primary Schools (2014)

单位:人 (person)

指 标	Indicators	教师数 Faculty Contracts	大学本科毕业及以上 Graduated from University or Above	大学专科毕业 Graduated from Junior University	高中阶段毕业 Graduated from Senior High School	高中毕业以下 Below Senior High School or below
教师学历分布	**Education Level of Teachers**	**23 808**	**20 400**	**3 225**	**182**	**1**
高 中	High Schools	3 596	3 573	20	3	
初 中	Junior Schools	8 359	8 197	161	1	
小 学	Primary Schools	11 853	8 630	3 044	178	1
教师学历构成(%)	**Education Level Composition of Teachers (%)**	**100.0**	**85.7**	**13.5**	**0.8**	…
高 中	High Schools	100.0	99.4	0.5	0.1	
初 中	Junior Schools	100.0	98.1	1.9	…	
小 学	Primary Schools	100.0	72.8	25.7	1.5	…

表 15-7 民工子弟学校基本情况
Statistics of Schools for Children of Migrant Workers

指 标	Indicators	单 位 Unit	2005	2010	2013	2014
学校数	Total of Schools	所 in number	23	41	41	40
班级数	Total of Classes	个 in number	394	553	606	552
教职员工人数	Number of Teaching Staff	人 persons	851	1 526	1 618	1 504
在校学生人数	Total of Students	人 persons	20 520	25 768	27 735	24 019

主要统计指标解释

学　校

指按国家规定的设置标准和审批程序批准设立的，招收适龄人口实施各级各类教育活动的教育机构。

普通高等学校

指按照国家规定的设置标准和审批程序批准举办的，通过全国普通高等学校统一招生考试，招收高中毕业生为主要培养对象，实施高等教育的全日制大学、独立设置的学院和高等专科学校、高等职业学校和其他机构。

大学、独立设置的学院主要实施本科层次以上教育，高等专科学校、高等职业学校实施专科层次教育，其他机构是承担国家普通招生计划任务不计校数的机构。包括普通高等学校分校和批准筹建的普通高等学校等。

成人高等学校

指按国家规定的设置标准和审批程序举办的，通过全国成人高等教育统一招生考试，招收高中毕业或同等学历的人员为主要培养对象，利用函授、业余、脱产的多种形式对其实施高等学历教育的学校。包括：职工高等学校、农民高等学校、管理干部学院、教育学院、独立函授学院、广播电视大学、其他机构等。

民办的其他高等教育机构

指经省、自治区、直辖市教育行政部门审批并颁发办学许可证，但不具有颁发学历文凭资格的实施高等教育的单位。学历文凭考试机构是指民办的经教育行政部门专门批准，进行全日制高等教育的其他高等教育机构。

中等专业学校

指经县或县以上教育行政部门批准设立，招收初中毕业生实施中等专业课程教育的教学机构。

职业中学（职业高中、职业初中）

指经县或县以上教育行政部门批准设立，招收小学或初中毕业生实施中等职业技术教育的教学机构。按学校性质类别可分为：独立设置的职业中学（包括：职业初中、职业高中、职业初高中合设学校）；附设有普通中学班的职业中学。

普通中学（普通高中、普通初中）

普通中学分为普通高级中学和普通初级中学两个阶段。普通初级中学是指独立设置的招收小学毕业的适龄人口进行初级中等基础教育的机构；普通高级中学是指独立设置的招收初中毕业的适龄人口进行高级中等基础教育的机构；完全中学是指普通初、高中合设的教育机构；一贯制学校是指在一所学校连续实施中小学教育的机构。其中包括实施九年义务教育的九年一贯制学校和实施高中教育的十二年一贯制学校。（说明：一贯制学校的办学条件如能划分为小学、初中、高中，则分开填报；如不能划分清楚，可按就高不就低的方法填入初中、高中报表中，不能重复填写。）

普通小学

指由区或区以上教育行政部门批准，招收学龄儿童实施初等教育的教学机构。

幼儿园

指招收三周岁以上（含三周岁）学龄前幼儿，对其进行保育和教育的单位。

特殊教育学校

指本市独立设置的招收盲聋哑和智残儿童，以及其他特殊需要的儿童、青少年进行普通或职业初、中等教育的教学机构。

EXPLANATORY NOTES TO MAJOR STATISTICAL INDICATORS

School Institutions

School Institutions refer to education establishment set up according to the government evaluation and approval procedures, enrolling population of the right age, providing various phase education activity.

Regular Institutions of Higher Education

Regular Institutions of Higher Learning refer to educational establishments set up according to the government evaluation and approval procedures, enrolling graduates from senior secondary schools and providing higher education courses and training for senior professionals. They include full-time universities, colleges, high professional schools, high professional vocational schools and others.

Universities and colleges are mainly providing undergraduate courses; those high professional schools and high professional vocational schools are mainly providing professional trainings; and others refer to educational establishments, which are responsible for enrolling students but not covered in the total number of schools, including: branch schools of universities and colleges, and universities and colleges that have been proved and prepared to construct.

Institutions of Higher Education for Adults

Institution of Higher Learning for Adults refer to educational establishments, set up in line with relevant rules approved by the government, enrolling personnel with senior secondary schools or equivalent education, and providing higher education courses in many forms of correspondence, spare time, or full time for adults. Institutions of higher schools for adults include schools of higher educations for staff and workers, schools of higher education for peasants, colleges for management cadres, pedagogical colleges, independent correspondence colleges, Radio and TV universities and other educational establishment, etc.

Civil Other Institution of Higher Education

Civil Other Institution of Higher Education refer to educational establishment set up according to rules approved and permitted by educational administration department of municipal government and not be provided with qualification to awarding diploma.

Specialized Secondary schools

Specialized Secondary Schools refer to educational establishment set up according to approval and permission by educational administration department of district and above government, enrolling graduates from junior secondary schools and providing secondary professional education courses.

Vocational Secondary Schools (Senior Secondary Schools and Junior Secondary Schools)

Vocational Secondary Schools refer to educational establishment set up according to approval and permission by educational administration department of district and above government, enrolling graduates from primary schools and junior secondary schools and providing secondary vocational education courses.

Regular Secondary Schools (Senior Secondary Schools and Junior Secondary Schools)

Regular Secondary Schools are classified as senior secondary schools and junior secondary schools. Junior Secondary Schools refer to educational establishment enrolling graduates from primary schools and providing junior secondary educational courses. Senior Secondary Schools refer to educational establishment enrolling graduates from junior secondary schools and providing higher secondary educational courses.

Regular Primary Schools

Regular Primary Schools refer to educational establishment set up according to approval and permission by educational administration department of district and above government, enrolling graduates from children of school age and providing primary educational courses.

Kindergartens

Kindergartens refer to nursery and education establishment, enrolling children in 3 years old and above.

Special Education Schools

Special Education Schools refer to educational establishments set up independently, enrolling blind, deaf, dumb, amentia or other special children, and educational establishment, providing regular or vocational junior and senior secondary education for hobbledehoy.

第十六篇

CHAPTER 16

文化和体育

CULTURE AND SPORTS

表 16-1 文化事业
Cultural Establishments

指 标	Indicators	单 位 Unit	2010	2013	2014
街道、镇社区文化活动中心	Culture and Activity Center for Sub-district and Town	个 unit	38	37	37
行政村(居委)综合文化活动室	Comprehensive Culture and Activity Room for Administrative Village (Neighborhood Committee)	个 unit	1 117	1 135	1 135
街镇图书馆藏书量	Number of Books Collected in Sub-district and Town Libraries	万册 10 000 Books	104.57	124.00	130.00
文化资源	**Cultural Resources**				
区属文化基层单位	PNA Grassroot Cultural Institutions	个 unit	16	15	15
公共文化设施数	Number of Public Cultural Facilities	个 unit	1 280	1 302	1 302
公益电影放映次数	Number of Welfare Films Screened	场次 in number	21 553	16 930	15 509
业余文艺团队个数	Number of Amateur Literary and Artistic Teams	个 unit	3 261	4 470	4 057
文化交流	**Cultural Exchanges**				
赴境外演出、展览次数	Number of Performances and Exhibitions in Foreign Countries and Regions	次 time	1	2	
境外艺术团来访个数	Number of Overseas Artist Teams Visited	个 unit	18	69	7
境外艺术团演出场次	Number of Overseas Artist Teams Performed	场次 in number	54	102	4
文艺创作演出情况	**Literary and Artistic Creations and Performances**				
群众文艺创作数	Number of Literary and Artistic Creations	个 unit	1 169	899	1 297
获奖个数	Number of Prizes	个 unit	198	225	293
获奖人次	Number of Person-times Who Get the Prizes	人次 person-time	2 500	2 631	2 521
获奖单位	Number of Units Who Get the Prizes	个 unit	198	54	90

表16-2 公共图书馆基本情况
Statistics of Public Libraries

指 标	Indicators	单 位 Unit	2005	2010	2013	2014
机构数	Number of Institutions	个 unit	1	3	3	3
职工人数	Staff and Workers	人 person	110	188	202	217
公用房屋建筑面积	Floor Space of Buildings for Public Use	平方米 sq · m	18 343	74 221	74 160	74 160
#书 库	Stack Rooms	平方米 sq · m	6 040	16 515	5 695	5 695
阅览室面积	Floor Space of Reading Rooms	平方米 sq · m	7 550	38 882	27 877	27 877
阅览室座席	Seats in Reading Rooms	个 unit	1 366	3 764	4 329	4 329
总藏书量	Total Book Volume	万册 10 000 volumes	126	290	318	371
#本年新购藏书	New Books Purchased in Current Year	万册 10 000 volumes	12	24	29	42
累计有效借书证数	Library Cards Distributed	张 in number			212 503	266 142
#当年发证数	Library Card distributed in Current Year	张 in number	10 524	56 598	65 197	72 064
图书流通人次	Books Circulation Persons-Time	万人次 10 000 person-times	150	242	441	484
图书外借册次	Borrowed Books-time	万册次 10 000 volume-times	99	177	405	469

表 16－3　广播电视事业基本情况
Statistics of Broadcasting and Television

指　标	Indicators	单 位 Unit	2005	2010	2013	2014
区广播电视台	PNA Radio and TV Station	座 unit	1	1	1	1
区有线网络中心	PNA Cabled Networking Center	座 unit	1	1	1	1
市属有线电视管理站	Municipal CATV Management Station	个 unit	10	10	10	10
区属有线电视管理站	PNA CATV Management Station	个 unit	3	7	2	2
广电工作从业人员	Persons Employed in Sectors of Broadcasting and Television	人 person	342	544	632	620
区台无线广播发射塔	Radio Broadcasting and TV Tower of PNA	座 unit	1	1	1	1
区台使用频率	Frequency Occupied by PNA	兆赫 MHz	106.5	106.5/100.1	106.5/100.1	106.5/100.1
区台无线广播覆盖率	Radio Broadcasting Coverage of PNA	%	100.0	100.0	100.0	100.0
有线广播电视专线	Cabled Broadcasting and Television Line	杆公里 pole. km	1 858	6 097	7 034	7 186
有线电视管道干线	CATV Trunk Line	公里 km	223	1 211	1 810	1 835
广播电视台播出节目时间	Broadcasting Duration of Radio and Television Stations	小时/日 hour/day		18	18	18
有线电视用户	CATV Subscribers	万户 10 000 households	73	131	142	150
村通播率	Rate of Villages Access to Broadcasting	%	100.0	100.0	100.0	100.0
区台平均日播音时间	Average Broadcasting Hours of PNA Radio Stations	小时 hour	1/14.5	1/21.0	2/36.0	2/36.0

表16-4 文化馆基本情况
Statistics of Cultural Centers
(2014)

指 标 Indicators		单 位 Unit	合 计 Total	浦东文化馆 Pudong Cultural Center	浦南文化馆 Punan Cultural Center	川沙文化馆 Chuansha Cultural Center	文化艺术指导中心 Art Consulting Center
机构数	Number of Centers	个 unit	4	1	1	1	1
职工人数	Staff and Workers	人 person	173	23	28	23	99
公用房屋建筑面积	Floor Space of Buildings for Public Use	平方米 sq. m	36 447	7 392	2 510	5 000	21 545
组织文艺活动次数	Performances Organized	次 time	897	202	260	150	285
举办业余文艺训练班班次	Training Courses for Amateurs	班次 class-time	370	7	35	5	323
结业人数	Persons Graduated	人次 person-time	101 621	240	21 600	120	79 661

表16-5 参加市级以上体育竞赛成绩情况
Sport Prize in State-level and International-level Competitions
(2014)

单位:次 (time)

指 标 Indicators		第1名 First Place Winners	第2名 Second Place Winners	第3名 Third Place Winners	第4名 Fourth Place Winners	第5名 Fifth Place Winners	第6名 Sixth Place Winners	第7名 Seventh Place Winners
合 计	**Total**	**295**	**280**	**279**	**106**	**104**	**96**	**60**
市 级	Municipal Level	254	240	255	103	100	96	54
全 国	State Level	41	40	24	3	4		6
团 体	**Team**	**24**	**16**	**14**	**6**	**5**	**1**	**2**
市 级	Municipal Level	20	15	14	4	4	1	
全 国	State Level	4	1		2	1		2
个 人	**Individual**	**271**	**264**	**265**	**100**	**99**	**95**	**58**
市 级	Municipal Level	234	225	241	99	96	95	51
全 国	State Level	37	39	24	1	3		7

表16-6　举(承)办各级体育比赛情况
Sports Games of All Levels Held or Undertaken
(2014)

比赛级别	Levels	次数(次) Times (in number)	参加人次数(人次) Athletes (person-time)
总　计	**Total**	**193**	**63 940**
区级比赛	PNA Games	124	31 941
市级比赛	Shanghai Games	51	31 199
全国比赛及以上	National or Above Games	18	800

表16-7　等级运动员和裁判员情况
Graded Athletes and Referees
(2014)

单位:人　　(person)

项　目	Item	二级运动员 Grade-Ⅱ Athletes	裁判员 Referees 二级 Grade-Ⅱ	裁判员 Referees 三级 Grade-Ⅲ
合　计	**Total**	**141**	**135**	**90**
田　径	Track and Field	29		
排　球	Volleyball	8		
武　术	Martial Art	11		
篮　球	Basketball	20		
射　击	Shooting	1		
足　球	Soccer	15		
游　泳	Swimming	3		
棒　球	Baseball	3		
散　打	Free Boxing			
击　剑	Fence-play			
围　棋	Go	1	9	39
象　棋	Chinese Chess			
国际象棋	Chess	1		
乒乓球	Table Tennis	21	1	
举　重	Weight Lifting	1		
垒　球	Softball			
羽毛球	Badminton	1	41	34
台　球	Billiards		15	
门　球	Croquet			
健美操	Aerobics			
皮划艇	Canoeing/Kayaking	2		
赛　艇	Racing Boat	12		
摔　跤	Wrestling	2		
中国式摔跤	Chinese-style Wrestling			
花样游泳	Synchronized Swimming			
网　球	Tennis			
风　筝	Kite Flying			
航空模型	Model Plane			
车辆模型	Model Vehicle			
体育舞蹈	Ballroom Dancing			
拳　击	Boxing	6		
柔　道	Judo	2		
射　箭	Archery			
航海模型	Model Ship			
信　鸽	Carrier Pigeon		56	5
桥　牌	Bridge			
健身秧歌	Fitness Yangko Dance			
马　术	Equestrianism	1		
跆拳道	Taekwondo	1		
毽　球	Shuttlecock		13	12

表16-8 全民健身活动设施情况
Facilities for Fitness Activities

指 标	Indicators	单 位 Unit	2010	2013	2014
农民健身家园	**Fitness Garden for Farmers**				
篮球场	Basketball Court	片 in number	206	251	254
羽毛球场	Badminton Court	片 in number	5	5	5
网球场	Tennis Court	片 in number	2	3	3
门球场	Croquet Court	片 in number	68	82	89
社区公共运动场	**Community Public Sports Ground**				
篮球场	Basketball Court	片 in number	69	87	91
门球场	Croquet Court	片 in number	26	37	37
网球场	Tennis Court	片 in number	16	21	21
足球场	Soccer Field	片 in number	1	1	1
羽毛球场	Badminton Court	片 in number	3	3	5
健身苑(点)数量	**Number of Fitness Court (Center)**	**个 in number**	**1 689**	**1 689**	**3 079**
健身苑	Fitness Court	个 in number	67	67	67
街道、镇	Subdistrict or Town	个 in number	63	63	63
体育系统	Sports System	个 in number	2	2	2
学 校	School	个 in number	2	2	2
健身点	Fitness Center	个 in number	1 622	1 622	3 012
街道、镇	Subdistrict or Town	个 in number	1 622	1 622	3 012
健身苑(点)面积	**Floor Space for Fitness Court (Center)**	**万平方米 10 000 sq. m**	**91.95**	**91.95**	**122.91**
健身苑	Fitness Court	万平方米 10 000 sq. m	15.15	15.15	15.15
街道、镇	Subdistrict or Town	万平方米 10 000 sq. m	14.00	14.00	14.00
体育系统	Sports System	万平方米 10 000 sq. m	0.60	0.60	0.60
学 校	School	万平方米 10 000 sq. m	0.55	0.55	0.55
健身点	Fitness Center	万平方米 10 000 sq. m	76.80	76.80	107.76
街道、镇	Subdistrict or Town	万平方米 10 000 sq. m	76.80	76.80	107.76
健身器材配置数	**Number of Body Fitness Apparatus**	**件 set**	**20 803**	**20 803**	**31 296**
街 道	Subdistrict	件 set	6 125	6 125	8 786
镇	Town	件 set	14 582	14 582	22 414
专业体育场馆	Professional Stadium and Gymnasium	件 set	60	60	60
学 校	School	件 set	36	36	36

主要统计指标解释

文化机构

是指专门从事文化工作具有法人资格，独立核算的事业，企业单位，以及单独核算，附属于事业单位的经营性专业文化活动单位。包括从事艺术、图书馆、档案馆、群众文化、文物保护、艺术教育、艺术研究、文化娱乐、新闻出版等机构，以及其他文化机构。

等级运动员人数

指经考核正式批准授予等级运动员称号的人数。运动员等级分为国际级运动健将、运动健将、一级运动员、二级运动员、三级运动员、少年级运动员。该指标主要反映运动员队伍的技术质量水平。

等级裁判员人数

指经考核正式批准授予等级裁判员称号的人数。裁判员等级分为国际裁判、国家级裁判、一级裁判、二级裁判、三级裁判。该指标主要反映裁判员队伍的技术质量水平。

EXPLANATORY NOTES TO MAJOR STATISTICAL INDICATORS

Cultural Institutions

Cultural Institution refers to undertaking and business institutions which specialize in cultural work and have legal personality and independent accounting system, and those professional cultural institutions attached to undertaking institutions and have independent accounting system. It includes institutions specialize in art, library, archives, mass culture, historical relic protection, art education, art research, entertainment, news and publication and other cultural institutions.

Number of Athletes in Grades

Number of Athletes in Grades refers to the number of athletes who have been given titles through examination. The titles of athletes include international masters of sports, masters of sports, first-grade, second-grade and third-grade sportsmen and young athletes. This indicator reflects skill of the athletes.

Number of Referees in Grades

Number of Referees in Grades refers to the number of referees who have been given titles after examination. They are classified as international referees, national referees and referees of the first, second and third grades. This indicator reflects the skill of referees.

第十七篇

CHAPTER 17

卫生

PUBLIC HEALTH

表 17-1 各类卫生机构、床位及人员数
Healthcare Institutions, Hospital Beds and Professionals by Institution Type (2014)

指 标	Indicators	机构数(个) Institution (unit)	床位数(张) Beds (bed)	人员数(人) Staff (person)	#卫生技术人员 Healthcare Professional	管理人员 Administrator
总 计	**Total**	**1 044**	**20 043**	**34 675**	**28 341**	**1 776**
卫生部门合计	**Total by Healthcare Departments**	**171**	**15 762**	**27 090**	**22 609**	**1 181**
医院合计	Total of Hostpitals	25	12 542	19 330	16 375	936
综合性医院	Comprehensive Hospital	10	7 238	12 297	10 383	586
中医医院	Hospital of Traditional Chinese Medicine	4	1 389	2 344	1 980	116
中西医结合医院	Integrated Hospital of Traditonal Chinese and Western Medicine	1	690	1 234	1 088	59
专科医院	Special Hospital	8	2 497	2 219	1 863	109
妇幼保健院	Maternity and Pediatric Hospital	2	728	1 236	1 061	66
社区卫生服务中心(站)	Community Healthcare Service Center (Station)	138	3 220	6 562	5 513	181
妇幼保健所	Maternity and Pediatric Clinic	1		94	80	4
眼病牙病防治所	Visual and Dental Clinic	1		55	49	5
疾病预防控制中心	Disease Prevention and Control Center	1		292	256	2
卫监监督所	Health Supervision Institution	1		141	123	6
急救中心	First-Aid Center	1		451	116	19
采供血机构	Blood Sampling and Supply Institution	1		77	49	12
其 他	Others	2		88	48	16
工业及其他部门合计	**Total by Industry and other Departments**	**873**	**4 281**	**7 585**	**5 732**	**595**
医院合计	Total of Hospitals	39	4 281	4 939	3 378	484
工业医院	Industrial Hospital	5	2 249	1 472	1 025	267
综合性医院	Comprehensive Hospital	3	673	899	582	203
专科医院	Special Hospital	1	420	134	87	12
护理院	Nursing Home	1	1 156	439	356	52
民办医院	Private Hospital	34	2 032	3 467	2 353	217
诊所(含内设医疗机构)	Clinic (medical establishments inside)	528		2 646	2 354	111
村卫生室	Village Clinic	306				

表17-2 各类卫生技术人员数
Number of Healthcare Professionals
(2014)

单位:人 (person)

指 标 Indicators		合 计 Total	执 业 医 师 Medical Practitioners	执业助理医师 Assistant Medical Practitioners	注 册 护 士 Registered Nurses	药 师 (士) Pharmacist	检 验 技 师 (士) Inspect technician	摄 像 技 师 (士) Video technician	其他卫生技术人员 Other Healthcare Professionals
总 计	**Total**	**28 341**	**10 309**	**343**	**12 283**	**1 605**	**1 180**	**418**	**2 203**
卫生部门合计	**Total by Healthcare Departments**	**22 609**	**7 863**	**232**	**10 133**	**1 362**	**987**	**338**	**1 694**
医院合计	Hostpitals	16 375	5 263	21	8 191	827	626	291	1 156
综合性医院	Comprehensive Hospital	10 383	3 361	5	5 164	438	367	199	849
中医医院	Hospital of Traditional Chinese Medicine	1 980	690	7	937	189	82	42	33
中西医结合医院	Integrated Hospital of Traditonal Chinese and Western Medicine	1 088	383	2	562	49	40	16	36
专科医院	Special Hospital	1 863	496	7	1 016	117	78	29	120
妇幼保健院	Maternity and Pediatric Hospital	1 061	333		512	34	59	5	118
社区卫生服务中心(站)	Community Healthcare Service Center (Station)	5 513	2 303	208	1 870	530	239	46	317
妇幼保健所	Maternity and Pediatric Clinic	80	47		17	4	4	1	7
眼病牙病防治所	Visual and Dental Clinic	49	29		12	1	1		6
疾病预防控制中心	Disease Prevention and Control Center	256	166		5		60		25
卫监监督所	Health Supervision Institution	123							123
急救中心	First-Aid Center	116	48	3	9				56
采供血机构	Blood Sampling and Supply Institution	49	5		29		14		1
其 他	Others	48	2				43		3
工业及其他部门合计	**Total by Industry and other Departments**	**5 732**	**2 446**	**111**	**2 150**	**243**	**193**	**80**	**509**
医院合计	Hospitals	3 378	1 186	34	1 386	181	135	41	415
工业医院	Industrial Hospital	1 025	219	6	418	50	43	16	273
综合性医院	Comprehensive Hospital	582	170	5	260	34	36	6	71
专科医院	Special Hospital	87	14	1	60	5	2	1	4
护理院	Nursing Home	356	35		98	11	5	9	198
民办医院	Private Hospital	2 353	967	28	968	131	92	25	142
诊所(含内设医疗机构)	Clinic (medical establishments inside)	2 354	1 260	77	764	62	58	39	94

注：以上含浦东区域内市属三级医院及分院数据。
Note: The above-mentioned data include those of municipal Grade III hospitals and their affiliated hospitals located in Pudong.

表17-3 区级医院基本情况
Statistics of PNA-level Hospitals
(2014)

指 标 Indicators		人员数（人） Staff (person)	#卫生技术人员 Healthcare Professionals	建筑面积（平方米） Floor Space (sq·m)	#业务用房 Floor Space for Treatment	床位数（张） Beds (bed)	全年诊疗人次（万人次） Annual Patients Treated (10 000 person-times)
总 计	**Total**	**12 417**	**10 524**	**758 429**	**661 998**	**8 655**	**1 397.37**
综合医院	**Comprehensive Hospitals**	**10 270**	**8 693**	**632 087**	**559 199**	**5 982**	**1 149.56**
东方医院	Oriental Hospital	2 797	2 344	157 584	148 911	1 479	271.88
第七人民医院	No. 7 People's Hospital	1 234	1 088	79 603	78 104	690	140.53
华山医院南汇分院	Nanhui Branch of Huashan Hospital	1 391	1 213	91 015	91 015	1 000	165.39
浦东新区人民医院	PNA People's Hospital	1 380	1 205	95 106	61 828	844	184.38
浦东新区公利医院	PNA Gongli Hospital	1 373	1 154	72 472	68 076	680	170.62
第九人民医院周浦分院	Zhoupu Branch of Shanghai No.9 People's Hospital	1 096	883	102 891	77 849	678	132.12
浦南医院	Punan Hospital	999	806	33 416	33 416	611	84.63
专科医院	**Specialized Hospitals**	**2 147**	**1 831**	**126 342**	**102 799**	**2 673**	**247.81**
传染病院	Infectious Disease Control Hospital	88	69	7 380	4 500	100	5.51
浦东新区中医医院	Hospital of Traditional Chinese Medicine, PNA	492	413	24 331	22 531	275	91.80
妇幼保健院	Maternity and Pediatric Hospital	385	336	20 031	15 770	200	35.25
光明中医医院	Guangming Chinese Medicine Hospital	508	447	16 000	13 800	325	90.84
南汇精神卫生中心	Nanhui Mental Health Center	118	95	12 500	10 725	340	4.63
浦东新区精神卫生中心	Mental Health Centre, PNA	210	183	21 771	18 219	800	8.49
南华医院	Nanhua Hospital	139	119	7 398	6 101	153	7.75
老年医院	Laonian Hospital	121	100	10 678	6 960	300	1.74
肺科医院	Pulmonary Disease Hospital	86	69	6 253	4 193	180	1.81

表 17－4 综合医院工作质量情况
Workload in Comprehensive Hospitals

指 标	Indicators	手术人数(人次) Operations (person-time) 2013	2014	入院病人数(人次) Inpatients(person-time) 2013	2014	出院病人数(人次) Inpatients Leaving for Home(person-time) 2013	2014
总 计	**Total**	**94 855**	**117 718**	**181 216**	**216 210**	**180 476**	**216 464**
东方医院	Oriental Hospital	23 570	34 018	38 653	58 217	38 467	58 238
第七人民医院	No. 7 People's Hospital	9 864	12 603	20 247	26 358	20 134	26 456
上海市浦东医院	Shanghai Pudong Hospital	15 845	16 813	35 282	36 813	35 188	36 833
浦东新区人民医院	PNA People's Hospital	13 868	15 140	29 195	31 553	29 088	31 553
浦东新区公利医院	PNA Gongli Hospital	12 921	14 698	23 929	25 231	23 853	25 291
浦东新区周浦医院	Zhoupu Hospital in Pudong New District	10 373	16 210	17 582	21 462	17 449	21 491
浦南医院	Punan Hospital	8 414	8 236	16 328	16 576	16 297	16 602

表 17－4 续表 Continued

指 标	Indicators	出院者平均住院日数(日) Average Days of Inpatients at Hospital(day) 2013	2014	平均病床工作日(日) Average Beds Exploitation(day) 2013	2014	病床使用率(%) Rate of Beds Exploitation(%) 2013	2014
总 计	**Total**	**9.55**	**9.17**	**350.02**	**343.76**	**95.90**	**94.18**
东方医院	Oriental Hospital	7.71	8.18	377.33	339.59	103.38	93.04
第七人民医院	No. 7 People's Hospital	11.75	9.30	347.82	354.39	95.29	97.09
上海市浦东医院	Shanghai Pudong Hospital	9.65	9.62	352.00	353.28	96.44	96.79
浦东新区人民医院	PNA People's Hospital	9.74	9.51	352.16	358.80	96.48	98.30
浦东新区公利医院	PNA Gongli Hospital	9.13	8.71	356.36	319.05	97.63	87.41
浦东新区周浦医院	Zhoupu Hospital in Pudong New District	8.54	8.77	319.81	360.25	87.62	98.70
浦南医院	Punan Hospital	12.33	12.05	328.08	318.76	89.88	87.33

注：1. 原华山医院南汇分院更名为上海市浦东医院。
2. 原第九人民医院周浦分院更名为浦东新区周浦医院。

Note：1. Nanhui Branch of Huashan Hospital has changed its name into Shanghai Pudong Hospital.
2. Zhoupu Branch of Shanghai No. 9 People's Hospital Has changed its name into Zhoupu Hospital of Pudong New Area.

表17－5　医院诊疗人次和入院人数
Outpatients and Inpatients Treated
(2014)

指　标 Indicators		诊疗人次（万人次） Total Patients Treated (10 000 person-times)	#门、急诊 Outpatients or Emergency Treatment	入院人数（人次） Inpatients (person-times)	每百诊次的入院人数(人) Inpatients Per 100 Total Patient/time (person)	出院人数（人次） Inpatients Leaving for Home (person-times)
总　计	**Total**	**4 655.82**	**4 563.34**	**365 928**	**0.79**	**524 487**
卫生部门合计	**Total by Healthcare Departments**	**3 998.67**	**3 931.11**	**318 425**	**0.80**	**476 995**
医院合计	Hostpitals	2 143.32	2 114.50	278 687	1.30	450 634
综合性医院	Comprehensive Hospital	1 338.46	1 309.94	201 420	1.50	286 265
中医医院	Hospital of Traditional Chinese Medicine	388.58	388.58	16 973	0.44	58 139
中西医结合医院	Integrated Hospital of Traditonal Chinese and Western Medicine	140.53	140.23	26 358	1.88	26 456
专科医院	Special Hospital	180.16	180.16	33 936	1.88	38 488
妇幼保健院	Maternity and Pediatric Hospital	95.59	95.59	13 608	1.42	41 286
社区卫生服务中心(站)	Community Healthcare Service Center (Station)	1 846.13	1 807.39	26 130	0.14	26 361
专业公共卫生机构	Special Public Health Institution	9.21	9.21			
工业及其他部门合计	**Total by Industry and other Departments**	**657.15**	**632.24**	**47 503**	**0.72**	**47 492**
医院合计	Hospitals	411.52	386.61	47 503	1.15	47 492
工业医院	Industrial Hospital	45.38	45.38	13 450	2.96	13 473
综合性医院	Comprehensive Hospital	43.76	43.76	8 058	1.84	8 060
专科医院	Special Hospital			25		21
护理院	Nursing Home	1.62	1.62	5 367	33.23	5 392
民办医院	Private Hospitals	366.14	341.23	34 053	0.93	34 019
诊　所（含门诊部）	Clinics (including health rooms)	245.63	245.63			

注：1. 业务指标不包括村卫生室。
2. 以上数据除入院人数指标外均包含浦东地域市属三级医院分院数据。

Note: 1. Business indicators exclude those of village health rooms.
2. Except the number of inpatients, the above mentioned data include those of municipal Grade III hospitals and their affiliated hospitals located in Pudong.

表17-6 医疗业务效益指标
Indicators of Medical Results

指 标 Indicators		单 位 Unit	2005	2010	2013	2014
医院(卫生部门)	**Hospitals (Healthcare Departments)**					
手术人次数	Operation Person-times	人次 person-time	32404	69354	119740	144884
病床周转率	Turnover of Beds	次/床 time/bed	26.77	24.95	28.50	30.73
病床平均工作日	Average Bed in Service	日/床 day/bed	374.72	344.26	352.26	355.23
病床使用率	Rate of Bed Exploitation	%	102.66	94.32	96.51	97.32
出院者平均住院日	Average Days of Inpatient at Hospital	日 day	13.37	13.06	11.26	10.83
综合医院出院病人平均医疗费	**Average Medical Fee of Inpatients at Comprehensive Hospitals**	**元/人 yuan/person**	**7 499.06**	**10 362.34**	**12 513.12**	**13 857.31**

注：1. 2009 年始，平均每张处方费用不作统计。
2. 本表不含浦东区域内市属三级医院分院数据

Note：1. The average expense of every medical prescription has not been put into statistics since 2009.
2. Data in this table exclude those of municipal Grade III hospitals and their affiliated hospitals located in Pudong.

表17-7 公民义务献血、用血情况
Voluntary Blood Donation and Blood Transfusion

指 标 Indicators		单 位 Unit	2010	2013	2014
献血人次	Number of Person-times Who Voluntarily Donate Their Blood	人份 in number	49 902	49 238	53 073
无偿献血占献血人次比重	Ratio of Person-times Who Voluntarily Donate Their Blood in Total Number of Blood Donations	%	93.0	97.0	97.0
用血量	Amount of Blood Transfusion				
#全 血	Whole Blood	人次 person-time	96	51	60
红细胞	Red Blood Cell	人次 person-time	41 729	44 592	47 254
血 浆	Blood Plasma	人次 person-time	37 740	46 802	51 093

表 17-8 主要年份前十位疾病死亡原因及构成
Death Causes of 10 Major Diseases and Their Composition in Main Years

单位:% (%)

疾病死亡原因 Cause of Death		构成比 Composition Rate					
		1997	2000	2005	2010	2013	2014
循环系统病	Circulatory System Disease	35.85	32.40	34.55	34.24	35.83	36.98
肿 瘤	Tumor	26.87	30.40	31.04	32.52	32.48	32.15
呼吸系病	Respiratory Disease	16.11	13.80	11.00	9.66	9.10	9.68
损伤和中毒	Trauma & Toxicosis	5.86	6.30	5.48	5.73	4.77	4.61
消化系病	Digestive Disease	2.57	2.90	2.70	2.78	3.03	2.49
内分泌代谢免疫病	Internal Secretion, Metabolic and Immunity Diseases	2.64	2.70	4.10	4.03	4.45	4.66
传染病寄生虫病	Infectious Disease and Pardsitic Disease	1.94	2.10	1.52	1.19	1.08	0.98
精神病	Mental Disease	1.66	1.90	0.97	0.65	0.56	0.45
泌尿生殖系病	Genitourinary Disease	1.10	1.11	0.93	0.85	0.69	0.67
神经系病	Neuro Disease	0.66	0.62	0.78	1.05	1.22	1.22

表 17-9 主要年份婴儿疾病死亡原因及构成
Disease Cause of Infant Death in Main Years

单位:% (%)

主要疾病死亡原因 Main Cause of Death		构成比 Composition Rate					
		2005	2010	2011	2012	2013	2014
新生儿病	Disease of the New-borns	34.2	40.98	54.55	45.61	49.26	49.43
先天异常	Congenital Anomaly	43.9	40.98	32.73	36.84	47.76	37.93
呼吸系病	Respiratory Disease	4.9	4.92	1.82	5.26	1.49	
传染病寄生虫病	Infectious Disease and Pardsitic Disease		3.28	1.82	5.26		
神经系统疾病	Nervous System Disease					1.49	3.45
损伤中毒	Trauma & Toxicosis	7.3	3.28	3.64	3.51		3.45
肿 瘤	Tumor	2.40	1.64				1.15
血液系病	Blood System Disease		1.82				

表 17-10 家庭病床情况
Statistics of Family Ward Beds

指 标	Indicators	单 位 Unit	2005	2010	2013	2014
中西医师(士)赴家庭病床诊疗总人次	Total Number of Doctors of Traditional Chinese Medicine and ofWestern Medicine Treating Patients in Family Ward Beds	人次 person-times	109 579	162 608	112 821	112 616
期初原有家庭病床数	Number of Family Ward Beds at Beginning of Term	张 bed	2 097	2 555	2 285	2 857
期内新建家庭病床数	Number of New Established Family Ward Beds During the Term	张 bed	4 340	5 005	5 323	6 461
期内撤床病人数	Number of Patients Leaving Family Ward Beds During the Term	人 person	4 260	4 928	5 169	6 194
治 愈	Patients Cured	人 person	1	2	8	16
好 转	Patients Getting Better	人 person	149	264	348	574
稳 定	Patients Turning Stablized	人 person	3 452	3 711	3 835	4 362
转 院	Patients Turning to Another Hospital	人 person	419	618	722	690
要求撤床	Patients Asking to Cancel the Ward Beds	人 person	204	279	162	468
死 亡	Dead Patients	人 person	35	54	94	84
期末实有家庭病床数	Acutual Number of Family Ward Beds at End of Term	张 bed	2 177	2 632	2 439	3 124
期内家庭病床病人住床总床日数	Total Bed-days of Patients Staying in Familiy Ward Beds During the Term	天 day	777 590	1 042 073	983 057	979 701
期内撤床病人住床总床日数	Total Bed-days of Patients Who Have Stayed in Ward Beds Asking to Cancel Ward Beds During the Term	天 day	610 522	589 302	582 334	599 794
期内撤床病人诊疗总人次数	Total person-times of Patients Who Have Taken Medical Care Asking to Cancel Ward Beds During the Term	人次 person-times	90 942	100 068	69 750	70 157

主要统计指标解释

卫生机构

卫生机构是指从卫生行政部门取得《医疗机构执业许可证》，或从民政、工商行政、机构编制管理部门取得法人单位登记证书，为社会提供医疗保健、疾病控制、卫生监督服务或从事医学研究、医学教育等卫生单位和卫生社会团体。

医疗机构

医疗机构是指根据《医疗机构管理条例》的规定，经登记取得《医疗机构执业许可证》的机构。包括医院、社区卫生服务中心（站）、卫生院、门诊部、诊疗所、医务室、村卫生室、妇幼保健院（所、站）、专科疾病防治院（所、站）、急救中心、临床检验中心。

医　院

医院指设有固定床位，能收容病人住院并能为病人提供医疗、护理服务的医疗机构，包括县及县以上医院、农村乡卫生院和其他医院三部分。县及县以上医院按业务性质不同分为综合医院和专科医院。

卫生技术人员

卫生技术人员指从事卫生技术工作并在卫生事业机构领取劳动报酬的专业人员。包括中医师、西医师、中西医结合高级医师、护师、中药师、西药师、检验师、其他技师、中医士、西医士、护士、助产士、中药剂士、西药剂士、检验士、其他技士、其他中医、护理员、中药剂员、西药剂员、检验员、其他初级卫生技术人员。

医　生

医生指在医疗、预防保健机构工作且取得《执业医师证书》的执业医师和执业助理医师。

EXPLANATORY NOTES TO MAJOR STATISTICAL INDICATORS

Health Care Institutions

Health Care Institution refers to medical institutions and corporations providing health care, disease control and medical supervision service or engaged in medical research and medical education, which obtain Medical Institution Practice License from Medical Administration or Corporative Registration Certificate from Civil Administration, Commercial Administration or Organizational Management Administration.

Medical Organizations

Medical Institution refers to institutions which register Medical Institution Practice License according to Medical Institution Management Regulation, including hospitals, community medical service centers, medical house, clinics, dispensaries, medicine rooms, village medicine rooms, hospitals for maternity and kids care, special disease cure hospitals, first-aid center, clinical inspection centers.

Hospitals

Hospitals refer to medical institutions with permanent hospital beds, which are able to take in patients and provide them with medical and nursing services. Hospitals are classified into three categories: hospitals at or above the county level, hospitals of rural townships, and other hospitals. Hospitals at or above county level are divided into comprehensive and specialized hospitals.

Medical Professionals

Medical Professionals refers to those professionals engaged in medical work and receive salaries from medical institutions, including doctors of Chinese and Western medicine, senior doctors of integrated Chinese-Western medicine, head nurses, pharmacists of Chinese and Western medicine, laboratory specialists , other specialists, junior doctors of Chinese and Western medicine, nurses, midwives, druggists of Chinese and Western medicine, laboratory technicians, other technicians, other practitioners of Chinese medicine, nursing attendants, pharmacological workers of Chinese and Western medicine, laboratory workers and other primary medical personnel.

Doctors

Doctors refer to certified physicians and certified assistant physicians with certifications working in medical and health care and prevention agencies.

第十八篇

CHAPTER 18

法律、社会治安及其他

LAWS, PUBLIC ORDER AND OTHERS

表18-1　主要年份律师、公证及调解工作基本情况
Lawyers, Notaries and Mediations in Main Years

指　标	Indicators	单 位 Unit	2010	2013	2014
律师事务所	**Law and Lawyers'Offices**	**个 unit**	**214**	**216**	**229**
合伙所	Partner Offices	个 unit	172	169	181
个人所	Individual Offices	个 unit	42	47	48
律师工作人员	**Lawyer Staff**	**人 person**	**2 958**	**3 845**	**4 136**
#专职律师	Full-time Lawyers	人 person	2 842	3 693	3 989
兼职律师	Part-time Lawyers	人 person	116	152	147
律师办理各类法律事务	**All Kinds of Legal Affairs Handled by Lawyers**				
担任法律顾问	Legal Advisers	家 unit	9 170	9 080	9 258
刑事诉讼辩护及代理	Litigation Defense and Legal Representation in Criminal Cases	件 unit	2 392	4 199	5 940
民事案件诉讼代理	Legal Representation in Civil Cases	件 unit	6 152	7 884	23 977
行政案件诉讼代理	Legal Representation in Administrative Cases	件 unit	98	90	389
非诉讼法律事务	Non-Litigation Legal Affairs	件 unit	5 741	7 290	15 621
法律援助工作	**Legal Aid Work**				
办理法律援助案件数	Number of Legal Aid Work Transaction	件 unit		3 472	4 314
刑事案件法律援助	Number of Criminal Case Legal Aid Work	件 unit		1 721	1 686
民事案件法律援助	Number of Civil Case Legal Aid Work	件 unit		1 751	2 628
公证工作	**Notarization**				
公证处	Notary Offices	个 unit	1	1	1
公证人员	Notarization Staffs	人 person	40	46	52
#公证员	Notaries	人 person	26	37	37
办理各类公证文件	All Kinds of Notarial Documents Conducted	件 unit	27 535	40 931	45 240
国内公证	Notarization for Domestic Affairs	件 unit	13 205	19 896	19 835
涉外公证	Notarization Concerning Foreign Affairs	件 unit	13 447	20 127	24 389
涉港澳台公证	Notarization Concerning Affairs in Macao, Hong Kong and TaiWan	件 unit	883	908	1 016
人民调解工作	**Mediation Work**				
专职司法助理员	Full-time Judicial Assistants	人 person	124	152	152
人民调解委员会	People's Mediation Commission	个 person	1 142	1 201	1 201
调解员	Mediators	人 person	5 386	5 417	5 417
调解民间纠纷	Mediation for Disputes among the People	件 unit	41 622	50 528	59 574

表 18－2 道路交通事故
Road Traffic Accidents

指 标 Indicators		单 位 Unit	2013	2014
次 数	Number of Traffic Accidents	起 in number	17 952	15 406
死亡人数	Death Toll	人 person	252	286
伤残人数	Number of Wounded and Disabled	人 person	18 559	15 647

注：统计口径改变，上述数据为浦东新区所有产生伤亡的交通事故数。
Note：Statistical caliber has changed. Numbers in this chart include all the wounded and death traffic in Pudong New Area.

表 18－3 火灾事故
Fire Accidents

指 标 Indicators		单 位 Unit	2010	2013	2014
次 数	Number	起 in number	1 274	1 684	1 051
#纵 火	Arson	起 in number	19	31	19
电 气	Electric	起 in number	500	724	406
违章操作	False Operations	起 in number	59	53	34
吸 烟	Cigarette Smoking	起 in number	38	65	43
生活用火不慎	Careless Use of Fire in Daily Life	起 in number	218	277	164
玩 火	Playing with Fire	起 in number	33	17	19
自 燃	Spontaneous Ignition	起 in number	8	11	18
死亡人数	Death Toll	人 person	8	19	7
伤残人数	Number of Wounded and Disabled	人 person	6	27	15
损失折款	Amount Converted from the Losses	万元 10 000yuan	1 083	3 588	2 058

表 18－4 社会治安
Public Order

指 标 Indicators		单 位 Unit	2010	2013	2014
刑事案件立案数	Number of Registered Criminal Cases	件 piece	23 517	29 050	23 968
行政(治安)案件查处	Investigation and Prosecution of Administrative (Public Order) Cases	件 piece	622 580	1 498 530	1 810 596
治安案件查处数	Number of Investigation and Prosecution of Public Order Cases	件 piece	95 669	121 653	140 994

表18-5　档案管理
Archives Management

指　标　Indicators		单 位 Unit	2010	2013	2014
机构数	**Number of Institutions**	**个 Unit**	**1**	**1**	**1**
档案局(馆)	Archives Bureaus (Chanceries)	个 unit	1	1	1
从业人员	**Employees**	**人 person**	**93**	**89**	**83**
专　职	Full-time Employees	人 person	93	89	83
馆藏档案	**Collected Files**				
全　宗	Whole File	个 unit	359	362	362
案　卷	Rolls	万卷 10 000rolls	235	269	272
录音、录像、影片档案	Archives of Records, Videos and Films	万盘 10 000discs	0.16	0.16	0.17
照片档案	Photo Archives	万张 10 000pieces	12.91	16.57	19.00
底　图	Base Maps	万张 10 000pieces	0.21	0.21	0.21
电子档案	**Electric Archives**				
磁　盘	Discs	万盘 10 000discs	0.03	0.03	0.03
光　盘	Compact Discs	万盘 10 000discs	0.43	0.43	0.76
微缩胶片	**Microfiches**				
平　片	Plain Films	万张 10 000Pieces	0.20	0.20	0.20
卷　片	Coiled Films	万米 10 000meters	12.93	12.97	13.08
档案利用情况	**Utilization of Archives**				
利用卷次	Number of Roll-times Utilized	万卷次 10 000roll-times	6.89	4.78	4.71
利用人次	Number of Person-times Utilized	万人次 10 000Person-times	5.71	6.73	6.71
综合档案开放利用情况	**Open and Utilization of Comprehensive Archives**				
建国前案卷	Rolls Archived Before Liberation	卷 roll	425	2 951	2 951
建国后案卷	Rolls Archived After Liberation	万卷 10 000rolls	5.88	5.88	6.19
建筑面积	**Floor Space**	**平方米 sq · m**	**17 524**	**17 524**	**17 524**
#库　房	Storeroom	平方米 sq · m	8 200	8 200	8 200

表 18-6 信访情况
Complaint Letters and Visits

指 标	Indicators	单 位 Unit	2010	2013	2014
信访办受理人民来信、来访	**People's Letters and Visits Handled by Offices of Complaint Letters and Visits**	**件(批) piece (batch)**	**27 741**	**26 360**	**25 180**
来信数	Number of People's Letters	件(批) piece (batch)	12 453	9 971	8 810
电子邮件	E-mails	件(批) piece (batch)	9 452	7 541	9 139
来访数	Number of Visits	件(批) piece (batch)	1 893	3 514	6 306
来电数	Number of Calls	件(批) piece (batch)	3 943	1 644	925
进京非正常上访人次数	Number of Person-times Visiting Beijing in Secret	人次 person-times		130	604
到市政府集体上访批次	Number of Patch-times Visiting Municipal Government	批次 batch-times	145	69	174
到市政府集体上访人次数	Number of Person-times with Three and More Persons Visiting Municipal Government	人次 person-times	2 947	1 700	4 752

表18-7　法院收、结案情况
Cases Accepted and Ended by Courts

指　标	Indicators	单位 Unit	2010	2013	2014
法院收案数	Number of Cases Accepted by Courts	件 piece	76 028	92 473	103 436
#刑　事	Criminal	件 piece	3 406	5 239	6 059
民　事	Civil	件 piece	52 356	62 314	69 185
#经　济	Economic	件 piece	11 091	14 588	21 342
婚姻家庭类	Marriage and Family	件 piece	6 746	5 740	5 753
行　政	Administrative	件 piece	381	362	521
法院结案数	Number of Cases Ended by Courts	件 piece	75 899	92 423	102 917
法院未结案数	Number of Cases Not Ended by Courts	件 piece	8 556	8 336	8 801
同期结案率	Corresponding Claim Settlement Rate	%		99.9	92.1
均衡结案度	Balanced Claim Settlement Rate	%		1.2	4.9
法院上诉率	Rate of Appeals by Courts	%	23.4	20.1	16.9
法院实际执行率	Rate of Actual Executions by Courts	%	82.5	93.9	73.7
法院审限内结案率	Rate of Cases Ended by Courts Within Time Limit	%	98.3	99.5	99.5

表18-8 外事活动情况
Activities in Foreign Affairs

指 标 Indicators		2013 批 数 (批) Delegations (in number)	2013 人 数 (人) Visitors (person)	2014 批 数 (批) Delegations (in number)	2014 人 数 (人) Visitors (person)
接待外国人来访总计	**Foreigners Received**	**213**	**1 479**	**218**	**1 421**
#副总理以上国宾团	Deputy Prime Ministers and Above	3	58	3	20
部长级(含副部长)团	Ministers (Including Deputy Ministers)	12	88	7	88
其他政界人士团	Persons of Other Political/Government Circles	30	307	46	435
经贸界团	Businessmen	89	389	101	486
新闻界团	Newsreporters	3	17	6	33
其他团	Others	76	620	55	359
邀请外国人来访总计	**Foreigners Invited**	**10 809**	**12 193**	**10 765**	**12 205**
按签证性质分	By Type of Visa				
#多次签证	Multi-Entry	2 127	2 187	2 156	2 192
一次性签证	One-Entry	5 443	6 413	2 977	3 295
按国别(地区)分	By Country/Region				
#美 国	United States of America	1 122	1 338	1 166	1 417
德 国	Germany	1 076	1 170	947	1 073
日 本	Japan	1 525	1 626	1 428	1 529
审批因公出国访问总计	**Approved Overseas Visits on State Missions**	**1 013**	**3 118**	**943**	**2 442**
按出国性质分	By Purpose				
经 贸	Business	954	2 839	832	2 048
非经贸	Non-Business	59	279	111	394
按出访国家(地区)分	By Country/Region				
#美 国	United States of America	204	535	234	509
日 本	Japan	24	80	30	74
中国香港	Hong Kong, China	69	183	80	189

表18-9 主要年份人大情况
Statistics of Deputies to the People's Congress in Main Years

指 标 Indicators		单 位 Unit	2005	2010	2013	2014
全国人大代表人数	Number of Deputies to the National People's Congress	人 person	1			
全国人大代表提出议案	Proposals Suggested by Deputies to NPC	件 piece	5			
市人大代表人数	Number of Deputies to the Municipal People's Congress	人 person	80	118	120	117
#女 性	Female	人 person	19	37	47	47
市人大常委人数	Number of Standing Committee Members in MPC	人 person	4	6	5	5
市人大代表提出议案	Proposals Suggested by Deputies to MPC	件 piece	4	8	11	5
新区人大代表人数	Number of Deputies to PNA People's Congress	人 person	436	443	430	440
#女 性	Female	人 person	158	136	141	139
新区人大常委人数	Number of Standing Committee Members in PPC	人 person	28	34	33	30
#女 性	Female	人 person	4	11	8	8
新区人大代表提出议案	Proposals Suggested by Deputies to PPC	件 piece	9	4	4	2

表18-10 主要年份政协情况
Statistics of Political Consultative Conference Affairs in Main Years

指 标 Indicators		单 位 Unit	2005	2010	2013	2014
全国政协委员人数	National Political Consultative Conference Commissioners	人 person	7	10	17	17
市政协委员人数	Municipal Political Consultative Conference Commissioners	人 person	58	66	105	105
#女 性	Female	人 person	6	8	25	25
新区政协委员人数	PNA Political Consultative Conference Commissioners	人 person	379	645	538	536
#女 性	Female	人 person	84	161	145	148
新区政协常委人数	Standing Commissioners of PNA Political Consultative Conference	人 person	55	93	86	83
#女 性	Female	人 person	8	13	18	16
新区政协委员提案	Proposals Submitted by PNA Political Consultative Conference Commissioners	件 piece	205	528	262	265
#被采纳提案	Proposals Accepted	件 piece	165	467	166	152

注："全国政协委员人数"和"市政协委员人数"均指在浦东工作的政协委员人数。
Note: Both the item of "National Political Consultative Conference Commissioners" and that of "Municipal Political Consultative Conference Commissioners" refer to those who work in Pudong New Area.

表 18－11 主要年份精神文明建设情况
Construction of Role Models in Main Years

单位：个 (unit)

指 标	Indicators	2005	2010	2013	2014
市级文明社区	Model Communities at Municipal Level	6	12	12	12
市级文明镇	Model Towns at Municipal Level	6	16	16	16
文明小区	Model Quarters	393	908	729	874
#市 级	Municipal-level	208	414	291	340
文明村	Model Villages	101	254	209	206
#市 级	Municipal-level	53	112	78	93
文明开发园区	Model Development Parks	6	11	10	14
文明大厦	Model Mansions	22	45	47	48
文明单位	PNA Model Institutions	484	1 081	1 039	1 025
#市 级	Municipal-level	113	245	277	305
军民共建先进集体(对)	Model Collectives of Army-civilian (pair)	76	97	103	
#市 级	Municipal-level	24	22		
五好文明家庭(户)	Model Families (household)	203	241	500	580
"三八"红旗手(人)	Female Models (person)	306	192	39	40
#国 家	State Level		1		
市 级	Municipal-level	32	41	39	40
"三八"红旗集体	Female Model Groups	99	88	10	11
#国 家	State Level		3		
市 级	Municipal-level	11	10	10	11
文明班组	Model Crews	338	479	508	483
#市 级	Municipal-level	12			
区文明岗位	PNA-level Model Posts	202	227	254	229
市级文明岗	Municipal Model Posts				

注：表列各项均为每两年评选一次。
Note: All the items in the listed table are choosen through public appraisal every two years.

主要统计指标解释

律　师

指依法取得律师执业证书,担任法律顾问,民事(刑事、行政)案件代理人、刑事案件辩护人、办理非诉讼业务,解答法律询问,代写法律事务文书等,为社会提供法律服务的人员。

公证人员

指在国家机关依法办理公证事务的司法人员。包括公证员、助理公证员和在公证处工作的其他人员。

公证文书

指公证处根据当事人申请,依照事实和法律,按照法定程序制作的,具有法律效力的司法证明文书。根据公证书用途和使用地,公证书分为国内公证书、国内经济公证书、涉外民事公证书、涉外经济公证书四类。

调解民间纠纷

指调解委员会按照法律规定,根据自愿原则,用说服教育的方法调解民间发生的有关民事权利和义务争执的件数,包括调解成功数和调解未成功数。该指标主要反映人民调解委员会的工作量。

立　案

指人民检察院对受理的报案、控告、举报或自首及自行发现的犯罪线索、犯罪嫌疑人进行初步调查后,认为存在职务犯罪事实和应追究刑事责任,并决定作为刑事案件进行侦查的诉讼活动,是追究犯罪的开始。该指标主要反映人民检察院依法将职务犯罪线索作为刑事案件进行侦查的诉讼活动。

EXPLANATORY NOTES TO MAJOR STATISTICAL INDICATORS

Lawyers

Lawyers are certified legal workers according to law, and who are employed by legal counseling firms to act as legal advisers, agents in criminal or civil lawsuits, or defenders in criminal lawsuits, or to handle non-litigious legal affairs, to advise on matters of law or to write legal papers for others, and provide service to the public.

Notary Personnel

Notary Personnel are judicial workers of the state notary organs handling notarization work according to law. They include notaries, assistant notaries, and other people working in notary firms.

Notary Documents

Notary Documents refer to the judicatory notary documents drawn up by the request of the party and are in accordance with facts and laws and following certain legal proceedings. According to usage and locality, the notary documents are divided into following 4 types: domestic notary documents, domestic economic notary documents, foreign-related civil notary documents and foreign-related economic notary documents.

Mediation of Civil Disputes

Mediation of Civil Disputes refers to number of cases made by mediation committees in mediating in civil disputes concerning civil rights and duties through persuasion and education in accordance with the provisions of law on a voluntary basis, so as to solve disputes by helping the parties involved come to an agreement and understanding, including those unsuccessful ones. This indicator reflects the workload of the mediation committees.

Acceptance of Case

Acceptance of Case refers to the decision made by the people′s procuratorate office on reported cases, prosecution, impeachment, surrender, self-found criminal clues or suspects after initial investigation to confirm the act of crime and to start legal proceedings of the case as criminal case.

第十九篇

CHAPTER 19

城市建设和环境保护

URBAN CONSTRUCTION AND ENVIRONMENTAL PROTECTION

表 19-1　八层以上房屋分布(至 2014 年累计)
Distribution of 8-storey and Above Buildings (Total by the End of 2014)

单位:万平方米　　(10 000 sq · m)

指　标 Indicators		总　计 Total	8～10 层 8～10 Storeys	11～15 层 11～15 Storeys	16～19 层 16～19 Storeys	20～29 层 20～29 Storeys	30 层及以上 30 Storeys and Above
幢	In number	8 784	1 054	4 694	1 905	850	281
面　积	Area	8 566	820	3 220	1 886	1 541	1 099

表 19-2　市政工程设施
Public Utilities

指　标	Indicators	单　位 Unit	2005	2010	2013	2014
城市道路长度	Length of Urban Roads	公里 km	960	1 224	1 356	1 274
城市道路面积	Area of Urban Roads	万平方米 10 000 sq · m	1 704	2 463	2 784	2 773
城市桥梁	Urban Bridges	座 unit	169	370	555	649
雨水、污水泵站	Pump Stations for Rain/Sewage	座 unit	148	176	163	171
雨水、污水管长度	Length of Rain/Sewage Pipe	公里 km	1 858	2 805	3 067	3 150
公路里程	Length of Rural Highways	公里 km	905	1 937	2 095	2 278
公路面积	Area of Rural Highways	万平方米 10 000 sq · m	1 360	3 173	3 023	3 316
公路桥梁	Highway Bridges	座 unit	635	1 533	1 718	1 979

注：1. 2007 年起道路长度和道路面积统计口径改变。
　　2. 2013 年起雨水、污水泵站数的统计口径为排水所的设施量。
Note：1. The statistical approach has changed for the length and coverage of roads since 2007.
　　2. The data of pump stations for rain water and sewage is calculated by the number of facilities in sewage institutions since 2013.

表 19-3 环境保护
Environmental Protection

指 标	Indicators	单 位 Unit	2005	2010	2013	2014
工业固体废物产生量	Amount of Industrial Solid Waste	万吨/年 10 000 tons/year	250	268	232	239
工业固体废物综合利用量	Comprehensive Utilization of Industrial Solid Waste	万吨 /年 10 000 tons/year	242	243	221	227
工业废水排放量	Discharge of Industrial Waste Water	万吨/年 10 000 tons/year	7 103	6 679	5 848	5 939
工业废气排放总量	Total Emission of Industrial Waste Gases	亿标立方米/年 100 million cu · m/year	1 112	1 696	2 049	1 987
二氧化硫日平均值	Daily Average Amount of Sulphur Dioxide	毫克/立方米 milligram / cu · m	0.056	0.035	0.028	0.019
二氧化氮日平均值	Daily Average Amount of Nitrogen Dioxide	毫克/立方米 milligram / cu · m	0.046	0.041	0.039	0.037
可吸入颗粒物日平均值	Daily Average Amount of Inhalable Particles	毫克/立方米 milligram / cu · m	0.081	0.071	0.069	0.064
PM2.5 日平均值	Daily Average Amount of PM2.5	毫克/立方米 milligram / cu · m			0.057	0.048
区域环境噪声平均值	Average Value of Regional Ambient Noise	分贝 decibel	57.4	54.8	56.5	56.3
空气质量优良率	Rate of Fine Air Quality	%	89.3	92.6	68.2	76.7
污水纳管率	Rate of Sewage Piping	%	70.4	81.9	87.9	89.0

注：2013 年空气质量优良率评价的主要污染物因子由原来的 PM10 改为 PM2.5。
Note: The main measurement of the rate of fine air quality has changed from PM10 to PM2.5.

表 19-4 城市环境卫生
Urban Environmental Sanitation

指 标	Indicators	单 位 Unit	2005	2010	2013	2014
清运垃圾	**Garbage Disposal**	**万吨 10 000 tons**	**104.22**	**169.86**	**210.66**	**215.56**
生活垃圾	Domestic Waste	万吨 10 000 tons	103.10	168.98	151.21	145.56
建筑垃圾	Construction Refuse	万吨 10 000 tons	1.12	0.88	59.45	70.00
清运粪便	**Night Soil Disposal**	**万吨 10 000 tons**	**31.45**	**35.31**	**27.70**	**24.06**
环境卫生设施	**Facilities of Environmental Sanitation**					
公共厕所	Public Restrooms	所 unit	219	900	1 016	1 016
垃圾箱	Garbage Bins/Cans	只 unit	9 216	4 013	3 881	3 837
废物箱	Litterbins	只 unit	8 317	19 384	28 837	28 837
倒粪站	Manure-Dumping Stations	个 unit	89	102	101	98
化粪池	Septic Tanks	个 unit	4 711	5 855	5 837	5 834
垃圾处理	**Trash Disposal**					
垃圾焚烧	Trash Burning	万吨 10 000 tons	44.49	44.40	46.54	88.65
焚烧垃圾发电量	Power Output by Trash Burning	万千瓦·时 10 000 kw·h	10 841	12 619	13 800	27 662
环卫机械总数	**Machineries Used in Environmental Sanitation**	**辆 set**	**598**	**1 191**	**1 248**	**1 203**

注：1. 2009 年起，垃圾箱统计口径作调整。
2. 2013 年起，清运垃圾的分类方法有调整，含装修垃圾、集贸垃圾、地沟油等。

Note：1. The statistical approach for garbage bins has been readjusted since 2009.
2. Since 2013, the diversification of garbage disposal has changed, including decoration garbage, trading garbage, and illegal cooking oil.

表 19-5 园林绿化
Parks,Gardens and Green Space

指　标	Indicators	单　位 Unit	2005	2010	2013	2014
园林绿地面积	Total Area of Parks, Gardens and Green Space	万平方米 10 000 sq · m	8 439.52	12 019.49	13 166.00	13 456.00
#公共绿地	Public Green Space	万平方米 10 000 sq · m	4 154.71	5 565.51	6 152.25	6 242.00
单位附属绿地	Green Space of Organizations	万平方米 10 000 sq · m	1 508.15	2 479.00	2 728.00	2 828.00
居住区绿地	Residential Green Space	万平方米 10 000 sq · m	1 139.81	2 834.12	3 131.00	3 231.00
建成区绿化覆盖面积	Green Coverage of Built Area	万平方米 10 000 sq · m	6 426.88	12 283.46	13 625.00	14 118.00
建成区绿化覆盖率	Coverage Rate of Urban Green Areas (%) in PNA	%	37.8	36.1	36.0	36.2
新辟、扩大各类绿地	New and Extended Green Space	万平方米 10 000 sq · m	199.50	516.76	328.22	290.00
#公共绿地	Public Green Space	万平方米 10 000 sq · m	78.97	294.71	128.22	90.00
公园个数	Parks	个 unit	17	20	25	26
#免费公园	Ticket-free Parks	个 unit	15	17	21	22
公园面积	Area of Parks	万平方米 10 000 sq · m	214.25	486.27	551.17	563.91
#免费公园	Ticket-free Parks	万平方米 10 000 sq · m	68.88	78.31	143.21	155.95
人均公共绿地	Public Green Space Per Capita	平方米/人 sq · m/person	24.42	22.71	24.02	24.00
行道树年末累计数	Accumulated Trees on Streets at Year-end	万株 10 000 pcs	36.79	23.20	34.32	36.25

表19-6 水、电、煤气供应
Supply of Tap Water, Electricity and Gas

指 标 Indicators		单 位 Unit	2005	2010	2013	2014
自来水	**Tap Water**					
水厂生产能力	Capacity of Tap Water Plants	万立方米/日 10 000 cu · m/day	171.20	241.00	228.00	228.00
供水管道总长度	Length of Water Supply Pipes	公里 km	3 100	8 471	11 975	13 250
全年售水总量	Total Annual Volume of Water Sold	万立方米 10,000 cu · m	41 926	60 088	60 539	60 860
#工业用水	Industrial Water	万立方米 10 000 cu · m	10 526	14 541	12 009	11 473
生活用水	Domestic Water	万立方米 10 000 cu · m	21 749	21 876	22 506	22 587
每日平均售水量	Average Daily Tap Water Consumption	万立方米 10 000 cu · m	115	165	165	167
电 力	**Electricity**					
用电最高日负荷	Maximum Daily Load of Electricity	万千瓦 10 000 kw	285.70	553.00	664.76	657.70
全年售电量	Annual Electricity Sold	亿千瓦 · 时 100 million kwh	128.19	229.71	263.67	261.01
各类用电户数	Various Electricity Users	万户 10 000 households	117.91	190.03	210.08	215.73
天然气	**Natural Gas**					
管线长度	Length of Gas Pipes	公里 km	3 574	6 463	6 404	6 701
全年销售量	Annual Volume of Gas Sold	万立方米 10 000 cu · m	44 300	64 200	71 673	74 872
#生活用气	Domestic Use	万立方米 10 000 cu · m	18 700	23 926	29 745	32 058
家庭用天然气户数	Natural Gas-using Households	万户 10 000 households	75.50	121.25	139.63	148.78
液化石油气	**Liquified Petroleum Gas (LPG)**					
全年销售量	Annual Volume of Gas Sold	吨 ton	52 000	66 700	98 136	118 300
#生活用气	Domestic Use	吨 ton	50 000	54 000	80 614	57 300
家庭用液化气户数	LPG-using Households	万户 10 000 households	45.90	69.11	105.10	80.89

表19－7 交通运输
Transportation

指 标	Indicators	单 位 Unit	2005	2010	2013	2014
公共交通	**Public Transport**					
年末实有公交线路条数	Routes of Public Transport at year-end	条 route	108	232	311	331
年末运营线路长度	Length of Public Transport Routes at year－end	公里 km	2 125	4 770	5 054	5 242
年末运营公共车辆	Buses in Operation at year-end	辆 vehicle	2 041	3 450	3 891	3 877
全年运客量	Annual Passengers Carried	万人次 10 000 person-times	34 894	60 317	61 257	59 736
郊区行政村通达率	Rate of Village Access in Rural Area	%			98	100
公交线网密度	Density of Bus Net	公里/平方公里			1.4	1.5
专线客运	**Public Feeder Bus System**					
专线客运线路条数	Routes of Public Feeder Buses	条 route	68	43	20	19
年末营运线路长度	Length of Routes in Operation at year end	公里 km	2 069	1 623	1 067	1 035
运营专线车辆	Public Feeder Buses in Operation	辆 vehicle	1 575	1 023	490	453
全年运客量	Annual Passengers Carried	万人次 10 000 person-times	28 293	14 879	10 002	9 864
隧道大桥	**Tunnels and Bridges**					
越江隧道条数	Tunnels across the Huangpu River	条 route	6	12	12	12
越江大桥座数	Bridges across the Huangpu River	座 in number	4	4	4	4
越江桥隧道车道数	Number of Lanes on Tunnels and Bridges across the Huangpu River	条 lane	54	84	84	84
轨　道	**City Railways**					
运营条数	Number of Railways in Operation	条 route		7	12	13
运营线路里程	Length of Routes in Operation	公里 km		109	179	186
站点数	Number of City Railway Stations	个 Unit		73	95	97
港　口	**Ports**					
港口货物吞吐量	Volume of Cargo Handled at Ports	万吨 10 000 tons		22 470	28 697	29 918
外高桥港区货物吞吐量	Volume of Cargo Handled at Waigaoqiao Port	万吨 10 000 tons		13 570	15 178	15 762
洋山港货物吞吐量	Volume of Cargo Handled at Yangshan Port	万吨 10 000 tons		8 900	13 519	14 156
集装箱吞吐量	Volume of Containers Handled	万标箱 10 000 TEUs		2 510	3 059	3 237
外高桥港区集装箱吞吐量	Volume of Containers Handled at Waigaoqiao Port	万标箱 10 000 TEUs		1 499	1 622	1 716
洋山港集装箱吞吐量	Volume of Containers Handled at Yangshan Port	万标箱 10 000 TEUs		1 011	1 437	1 520
民用航空	**Civil Aviation**					
浦东机场旅客吞吐量	Passenger Capacity at Pudong International Airport	万人次 10 000 person-times	2 358	4 041	4 719	5 169
浦东机场货邮吞吐量	Volume of Cargo and Post Handled at Pudong International Airport	万吨 10 000 tons	185	322	291	318

表 19-8　邮电通信设施和邮电业务量
Post and Telecommunications Facilities and the Volume of Business

指　标	Indicators	单　位 Unit	2005	2010	2013	2014
邮政设施	**Postal Facilities**					
邮电局、所	Post Offices	个 unit	93	136	104	102
信筒、信箱	Mailboxes	处 unit	624	641	632	632
报刊发行站	Newpaper and Magazine Distributors	个 unit	728	392	1 245	1 309
邮路单程长度	Length of Single-Way Post	公里 km	3 282	822	644	684
农村投递路线总长度	Total Length of Postal Routes	公里 km	3 691	6 688	5 820	5 464
邮运汽车	Postal Vehicle	辆 vehicle	108	144	264	267
邮政业务总量	**Business Value of Postal Service**					
邮政业务收入	Postal Service Income	万元 10 000 yuan	35 300	43 990	56 754	64 230
函　件	Mails	万件 10 000 pieces	5 409	15 112	24 061	26 480
包　件	Parcels	万件 10 000 pieces	94	93	278	476
汇　票	Drafts	万张 10 000 pieces	98	162	132	103
订销报刊累计数	Accumulated Circulation of Newspapers and Magazines	万份 10 000 pieces	11 750	7 326	17 508	17 970
特快专递	Special Express	万份 10 000 pieces	281	618	61	47
集邮业务	Stamp-collecting Business	万枚 10 000 pieces	354	663	783	938
邮政储蓄年末收储余额	Postal Savings Balance at Year-end	万元 10 000 yuan	235 230	1 008 020	1 480 932	1 554 994
电讯设施、用户及业务收入	**Telecommunication Facilities, Subscribers and Operating Income**					
本地电话局用交换机容量	Urban Switchboard Capacity	万门 10 000 units	146	218	228	205
本地电话用户数	Local Telephone Users	万户 10 000 households	118	161	146	136
电信宽带用户数	Subscribers of Telecommunication Broad-Band	门 unit	281 408	806 341	1 013 398	1 071 202
电信业务收入	Telecommunication Income	万元 10 000 yuan	119 250	353 092	395 684	409 745
网络互动电视(IPTV)	Internet Interactive TV Network	线 Line		263 280	313 705	332 516
"我的 e 家"用户	"My e-Home" Subscribers	户 Household		625 799	721 367	329 454
光纤入户(FTTH)	Fiber To The Home(FTTH)	户 Household		53 731	717 652	768 383

注：电信业务收入，不包括移动通信和中国联通以及与其结算的业务量。报刊发行站、邮路单程长度、订销报刊不包括邮政投递的业务量。

Note: The business value of China Mobile and China Unicom as well as the related business is not included in the Telecommunication Income. Fields of newspaper distribution stations, one-way length of postal routes, subscriptions and unsubscriptions of newspapers and magazines exclude the postal delivery volume.

表 19-9 房屋拆迁情况
Housing Demolition and Resettlement

指　标	Indicators	单　位 Unit	2005	2010	2013	2014
房屋完成拆迁总户数	**Total Households Domolished and Resettled**	**户 household**	**23 294**	**3 725**	**4 041**	**2 240**
重大项目拆迁	Demolished Because of Key Investment Projects	户 household	18 288	1 175	299	126
企事业单位	Enterprises and Institutions	户 household	351	77	8	8
公　房	Public Housing	户 household	4 487			
私　房	Private Housing	户 household	13 361	1 085	291	118
个体工商	Individuals Engaged in Industry and Commerce	户 household	89	13		
旧城改造拆迁	Demolished Because of Renovation of Old Towns	户 household	211		197	50
其　他	Others	户 household	4 795	2 550	3 545	2 064
完成拆迁总面积	Tota Area of Demolition Finished	万平方米 10 000 sq · m	474.63	139.78	67.03	36.46
重大项目拆迁	Demolished Because of Key Investment Projects	万平方米 10 000 sq · m	363.14	26.79	5.58	2.61
企事业单位	Enterprises and Institutions	万平方米 10 000 sq · m	59.67	5.06	0.94	0.94
公　房	Public Housing	万平方米 10 000 sq · m	22.34			
私　房	Private Housing	万平方米 10 000 sq · m	277.46	18.83	4.64	1.67
个体工商	Individuals Engaged in Industry and Commerce	万平方米 10 000 sq · m	3.67	2.90		
旧城改造拆迁	Demolition Because of Renovation of Old Towns	万平方米 10 000 sq · m	5.83		2.84	0.45
# 企事业单位	Enterprises and Institutions	万平方米 10 000 sq · m	3.81		0.59	
其　他	Others	万平方米 10 000 sq · m	105.66	112.99	58.61	33.40

主要统计指标解释

城市基础设施

城市基础设施包括电力建设、交通运输、邮电通信、市内公共交通、自来水、煤气、市政建设、园林绿化、环境卫生等。

道路长度

道路长度指除土路外，路面经过铺装宽度在3.5米以上的道路，包括高级、次高级道路和普通道路。

城市园林绿地面积

指报告期末用作园林和绿化的各种绿地面积。包括公共绿地、居住区绿地、单位附属绿地、防护绿地、生产绿地、道路绿地和风景林地面积。

不包括：

(1)屋顶绿化、垂直绿化、阳台绿化和室内绿化。

(2)以物质生产为主的林地、耕地、牧草地、果园和竹园等。

(3) 城市总体规划中不列入绿地的水域。

公共绿地

公共绿地指向公众开放的市级、区级、居住区级各类公园、街旁游园，包括其范围内的水域。其中居住区级公园应不小于1万平方米，街旁游园的宽度不小于8米，面积不小于400平方米。

供水管道长度

指从送水泵至用户水表之间所有管道的长度。不包括新安装尚未使用的管道。

生活用水

生活用水包括公共服务用水和居民家庭用水。公共服务用水指为城市社会公共生活服务的用水。包括行政事业单位、部队营区和公共设施服务、社会服务业、批发零售贸易业、旅馆饮食业以及其他公共服务业等单位的用水。居民家庭用水指城市范围内所有居民家庭的日常生活用水。包括城市居民、农民家庭、公共供水站用水。

工业固体废弃物产生量

指报告期内企业在生产过程中产生的固体状、半固体状和高浓度液体状废弃物的总量，包括危险废物、冶炼废渣、粉煤灰、炉渣、煤矸石、尾矿、放射性废物和其他废物等；不包括矿山开采的剥离废石和掘进废石(煤矸石和呈酸性或碱性的废石除外)。酸性或碱性废石指采掘的废石其流经水、雨淋水的pH值小于4或pH值大于10.5者。

工业固体废物综合利用量

指通过回收、加工、循环、交换等方式，从固体废物中提取或者使其转化为可以利用的资源、能源和其他原材料的固体废物量(包括当年利用往年的工业固体废物累计贮存量)，如用作农业肥料、生产建筑材料、筑路等。综合利用量由原产生固体废物的单位统计。

工业废水排放量

工业废水排放量指经过企业厂区所有排放口排到企业外部的工业废水量。包括生产废水、外排的直接冷却水、超标排放的矿井地下水和与工业废水混排的厂区生活污水，不包括外排的间接冷却水(清污不分流的间接冷却水应计算在内)。

工业废水排放达标量

指报告期内废水中各项污染物指标都达到国家或地方排放标准的外排工业废水量，包括未经处理外排达标的，经废水处理设施处理后达标排放的，以及经污水处理厂处理后达标排放的。

工业废气排放量

工业废气排放量指企业厂区内燃料燃烧和生产工艺过程中产生的各种排入空气的含有污染物的气体总量，按标准状态〔273K，101 325Pa〕计算。测算公式为：

工业废气排放量 = 燃料燃烧过程中废气排放量 + 生产工艺过程中废气排放量

生活垃圾清运量

指报告期内收集和运送到垃圾处理厂(场)的生活垃圾数量。生活垃圾指城市日常生活或为城市日常生活提供服务的活动中产生的固体废物以及法律行政规定的视为城市生活垃圾的固体废物。包括：居民生活垃圾、商业垃圾、集市贸易市场垃圾、街道清扫垃圾、公共场所垃圾和机关、学校、厂矿等单位的生活垃圾。

运营公交车辆数

指年末公交企业(单位)用于运营业务的全部车辆数。以企业(单位)固定资产台帐中已投入运营的车辆数为准。

邮政业务总量

指以货币表现的邮政部门用于邮政服务的总数量。它综合反映了一定时期邮政工作的总成果，是研究邮政业务量构成和发展趋势的重要指标。它用各种邮政分类业务量，如函件件数、电报份数、订销报刊累计份数等，分别乘以相应的平均单位（不变价），加总后再加上其他业务收入求得。

局用交换机容量

指安装在电信企业用于接续本地固定电话的电话交换机容量。

住宅电话用户

指安装在居民住宅或农民家里并按照住宅电话用户登记注册和收费的电话用户。包括私人付费、单位付费和按规定免费安装的住宅电话用户。

EXPLANATORY NOTES TO MAJOR STATISTICAL INDICATORS

Urban Infrastructure Facilities

Urban Infrastructure Facilities include facilities for power generating, transportation, post and telecommunication, urban public transportation, supply of tap water and gas, development of municipal engineering, city landscaping and sanitation.

Length of Roads

Length of Roads refers to the roads with a paved surface, and with a width of more than 3 – 5 meters, including high quality, medium quality and ordinary roads.

Area of Urban Gardens and Green Areas

Area of Urban Gardens and Green Areas refers to the total area occupied for green projects at the end of the reference period, including public green land, green land in residential quarters, green land attached to institutions, protection green land, production green land, roadside green land and forest in scenic spots. It does not include the following:

(1) Greenery and plants on roofs, balconies, indoors and vertical green areas;

(2) Forest, cultivated land grassland, orchards and bamboo grooves that are for production purpose and etc.;

(3) Water areas that are not included in urban master plan as green land.

Public Green Area

Public Green Area refers to green areas open to the public such as municipal, community and neighborhood parks and roadside parks, including waters within parks. Neighborhood parks should occupy an area larger than 10,000 square meters, and the width of roadside parks should occupy an area larger than 400 square meters, with a width of more that 8 meters.

Length of Water Supply Pipelines

Length of Water Supply Pipelines refers to the total length of all the pipelines between the water pumps and the user's water meters, excluding pipelines newly installed but not used yet.

Consumption of Water for Residential Use

Consumption of Water for Residential Use refers to the water consumption of households for daily life and the water consumption of public service facilities. The latter refers to water consumption for urban public services, including the consumption of government agencies and public institutions, military barracks, public facilities, wholesale and retail outlets, restaurants, hotels, and other units providing public services. Household water consumption refers to consumption of water for daily life of all households in the boundary of cities, including households of urban residents and farmers, and public water supply stations.

Industrial Solid Wastes Produced

Industrial Solid Wastes Produced refers to total volume of solid, semi-solid and high concentration liquid residues produced by industrial enterprises from production process in a given period of time, including hazardous wastes, slag, coal ash, gangue, tailings, radioactive residues and other wastes, but excluding stones stripped or dug out in mining (gangue and acid or alkaline stones not included). A stone is acid or alkaline depending on the pH value of the water below 4 or above 10.5 when the stone is in, or soaked by, the water.

Volume of Industrial Solid Wastes Utilized in a Comprehensive Way

Volume of Industrial Solid Wastes Utilized in a Comprehensive Way refers to the volume of solid wastes from which useful materials can be extracted or which can be changed into utilizable resources, energy or other materials, including the volume of industrial solid wastes stored up in previous years and utilized in the current year, such as the solid wastes utilized as fertilizers, building materials, for making roads or for other purposes. Statistical data on utilization of industrial solid wastes are collected by solid wastes producing units.

Volume of Industrial Waste Water Discharged

Volume of Industrial Waste Water Discharged refers to the volume of industrial waste water discharged, through all outlets, to the outside of industrial enterprises, including waste water produced, direct-cooling water, underground water from mines that does not meet the standard of discharge, and the domestic sewage mixed up with industrial waste water when discharged, but excluding discharged indirect-cooling water.

Industrial Waste Water Meeting Discharge Standards

Industrial Waste Water Meeting Discharge Standards refers to volume of industrial waste water discharge which, with or without treatment, reaches national or local standards with regard to all pollutants.

Volume of Waste Industrial Gas Emission

Industrial Waste Air Emission refers to discharge into atmosphere of waste air containing pollutants generated from fuel burning and production process in enterprises within a given period of time. It is calculated at standard status (273K, 101325Pa) as:

Industrial waste air emission = emission through fuel burning + emission through production process

Consumption Wastes Transported

Consumption Wastes Transported refers to volume of consumption wastes collected and transported to disposal factories or sites. Consumption Wastes are solid wastes produced from urban households or from seryice activities for urban households , and solid wastes regarded by laws and regulations as urban consumption wastes, including those from households, commercial activities, markets cleaning of streets, public sites, offices, schools, factories, mining units and other sources.

Number of Vehicles under Operation

Number of Vehicles under Operation refers to the total number of vehicles under operation by public transport enterprises (units) at the end of the year, based on the records of operational vehicles by the enterprises (units).

Volume of Post Business

Volume of Post Business refers to the total amount of post services provided by the post department, which reflects the total achievements by the post departments during a given period of time in a comprehensive way, and is an important indicator to study the composition and development of the post business. It is arrived by first multiplying the business volume of different types, such as number of letters, telegrams and accumulated number of newspaper and journals subscribed and sold, etc. by their respective average unit price (fixed price) and then adding these products together, plus the income from other business revenues.

Capacity of Office Telephone Exchanges

Capacity of Office Telephone Exchanges refers to the capacity of telephone exchanges installed in the office of telecommunication service providers for communication between fixed telephones.

Household Telephone Subscribers

Household Telephone Subscribers refer to telephone sets installed in the dwelling units of urban or rural residents, and registered as residence subscribers for payment, including 3 types of payment for the service: private payment, public payment and free service.

第二十篇

CHAPTER 20

重点开发区和街镇

KEY DEVELOPMENT ZONES AND SUBDISTRICTS AND TOWNS

表20-1 陆家嘴金融贸易区主要经济指标
Major Economic Indicators in Lujiazui Finance and Trade Zone

指 标 Indicators		单 位 Unit	2013	2014
税收总额(税务部门口径)	Total Amount of Tax Revenues (from the Tax Departments)	亿元 100 million yuan	512.12	570.77
一般公共预算收入	Local Fiscal Revenue	亿元 100 million yuan	146.25	165.23
固定资产投资额	Investment in Fixed Assets	亿元 100 million yuan	224.76	231.07
#房地产开发投资额	Investment in Real Estate	亿元 100 million yuan	203.13	200.96
#办公楼及商业营业用房	Office and Commercial Buildings	亿元 100 million yuan	127.20	84.32
房地产新开工面积	Floor Space of New Construction of Buildings	万平方米 10 000 sq·m	92.08	49.26
房地产竣工面积	Floor Space of Completed Buildings	万平方米 10 000 sq·m	101.86	20.16
外商直接投资项目	Projects of Foreign Direct Investment	个 unit	212	175
外商直接投资合同金额	Contracted Amount of Foreign Direct Investment	亿美元 USD 100 million	22.70	21.10
外商直接投资实际到位金额	Actual Paid Amount of Foreign Direct Investment	亿美元 USD 100 million	15.96	12.65
新增内资企业注册户数	Number of New Domestic Enterprises Registered	个 unit	1115	1983
新增内资企业注册资本	Capital of New Domestic Enterprises Registered	亿元 100 million yuan	320.78	543.34
金融业增加值	Added Value of Finance Industry	亿元 100 million yuan	1 045.08	1 288.05
期末金融机构数	Number of Financial Institutions at End of Term	个 unit	698	728
#外资银行法人行	Foreign Banks and Corporate Banks	个 unit	18	18
基金总公司	Head Office of Funds	个 unit	38	46
期末认定跨国公司地区总部个数	Number of Approved Regional Headquarters of Transnational Companies at End of Term	个 unit	85	87
举办展览(博览)次数	Number of Exhibitions (Fairs) Hosted	次 time	124	135
商品销售总额(限额以上)	Gross Sales of Commodities (Above Quota)	亿元 100 million yuan	9 394.38	12 974.02
社会消费品零售总额(限额以上)	Total Volume of Retail Sales for Social Consumer Goods (Above Quota)	亿元 100 million yuan	471.45	521.36
期末星级宾馆个数	Number of Star Hotels at End of Term	个 unit	34	34
主要景点接待人次	Person-times Received by Main Sight Spots	万人次 10 000 persom-times	1 791.86	2 046.80
商办楼宇数	Number of Office Buildings	幢 in number	233	235
商办楼宇建筑面积	Floor Space of Office Buildings	万平方米 10 000 sq·m	1 422.92	1 432.40
商办楼宇平均入驻率	Average Occupancy Rate of Office Buildings	%	95.6	96.8

注：地方财政收入即为原“地方税收”口径,后续相关指标口径相同。
Note: The local fiscal revenue is the former local tax approach. The relevant indicators hereinafter have the same statistical approach.

表20-2 金桥经济技术开发区主要经济指标
Major Economic Indicators in Jinqiao Economy and Technology Zone

指 标 Indicators		单 位 Unit	2013	2014
税收总额(税务部门口径)	Total Amount of Tax Revenues (from the Tax Departments)	亿元 100 million yuan	348.04	335.95
一般公共预算收入	Local Fiscal Revenue	亿元 100 million yuan	39.54	37.27
固定资产投资额	Investment in Fixed Assets	亿元 100 million yuan	77.75	60.51
#房地产开发投资额	Investment in Real Estate	亿元 100 million yuan	17.55	11.99
工业投资额	Investment in Industries	亿元 100 million yuan	49.76	42.10
房地产新开工面积	Floor Space of New Construction of Buildings	万平方米 10 000 sq·m	10.01	9.24
房地产竣工面积	Floor Space of Completed Buildings	万平方米 10 000 sq·m	43.68	13.32
外商直接投资项目	Projects of Foreign Direct Investment	个 unit	44	35
外商直接投资合同金额	Contracted Amount of Foreign Direct Investment	亿美元 USD 100 million	2.14	4.92
外商直接投资实际到位金额	Actual Paid Amount of Foreign Direct Investment	亿美元 USD 100 million	3.12	1.95
新增内资企业注册户数	Number of New Domestic Enterprises Registered	个 unit	193	349
新增内资企业注册资本	Capital of New Domestic Enterprises Registered	亿元 100 million yuan	4.25	25.84
工业总产值	Gross Value of Industrial Output	亿元 100 million yuan	1 976.31	2 047.94
#高技术产业产值	Output Value of High-tech Industries	亿元 100 million yuan	615.71	540.73
工业重点发展行业产值	Output Value of Key Industrial Sectors for Development	亿元 100 million yuan	1 628.24	1 730.70
#电子信息产品制造业	Manufacturing of Electronic and Information Products	亿元 100 million yuan	525.99	463.68
汽车制造业	Automobile Industry	亿元 100 million yuan	820.74	1 138.03
成套设备制造业	Manufacturing of Complete Equipment	亿元 100 million yuan	142.45	100.25
生物医药制造业	Manufacturing of Biological Medicine	亿元 100 million yuan	40.00	97.97
工业出口交货值	Delivery Value of Industrial Exports	亿元 100 million yuan	325.39	353.92
生产性服务业经营收入	Operating Income of Productive Services	亿元 100 million yuan	2 347.64	3 154.43
期末从业人员数	Number of Employed Persons at End of Term	万人 10 000 persoms	14.90	13.94

注：工业总产值为规模以上口径。后续相关指标口径相同。
Note: The gross value of industrial output has the approach for enterprises above certain scales. The relevant indicators hereinafter have the same statistical approach.

表 20-3　南汇工业园区主要经济指标
Major Economic Indicators in Nanhui Industrial Park

指　标　Indicators		单　位　Unit	2013	2014
税收总额(税务部门口径)	Total Amount of Tax Revenues (from the Tax Departments)	亿元 100 million yuan	6.66	7.39
一般公共预算收入	Local Fiscal Revenue	亿元 100 million yuan	1.71	2.04
固定资产投资额	Investment in Fixed Assets	亿元 100 million yuan	15.75	17.85
#工业投资额	Investment in Industries	亿元 100 million yuan	8.90	4.97
外商直接投资项目	Projects of Foreign Direct Investment	个 unit	7	6
外商直接投资合同金额	Contracted Amount of Foreign Direct Investment	亿美元 USD 100 million	0.75	0.69
外商直接投资实际到位金额	Actual Paid Amount of Foreign Direct Investment	亿美元 USD 100 million	0.58	0.22
新增内资企业注册户数	Number of New Domestic Enterprises Registered	个 unit	52	87
新增内资企业注册资本	Capital of New Domestic Enterprises Registered	亿元 100 million yuan	15.09	2.64
工业总产值	Gross Value of Industrial Output	亿元 100 million yuan	137.37	142.24
#高技术产业产值	Output Value of High-tech Industries	亿元 100 million yuan	18.42	13.72
工业重点发展行业产值	Output Value of Key Industrial Sectors for Development	亿元 100 million yuan	82.75	86.19
#电子信息产品制造	Manufacturing of Electronic and Information Products	亿元 100 million yuan	35.08	34.69
汽车制造业	Automobile Industry	亿元 100 million yuan	15.07	16.46
成套设备制造业	Manufacturing of Complete Equipment	亿元 100 million yuan	28.29	30.42
生物医药制造业	Manufacturing of Biological Medicine	亿元 100 million yuan	2.35	2.48
工业出口交货值	Delivery Value of Industrial Exports	亿元 100 million yuan	33.51	33.99
工业利润总额	Total Amount of Industrial Profits	亿元 100 million yuan	3.69	4.54

表20-4 张江高科技园区主要经济指标
Major Economic Indicators in Zhangjiang High-tech Park

指 标 Indicators		单 位 Unit	2013	2014
税收总额(税务部门口径)	Total Amount of Tax Revenues (from the Tax Departments)	亿元 100 million yuan	159.62	169.79
一般公共预算收入	Local Fiscal Revenue	亿元 100 million yuan	42.45	47.09
固定资产投资额	Investment in Fixed Assets	亿元 100 million yuan	125.33	131.37
#房地产开发投资额	Investment in Real Estate	亿元 100 million yuan	11.28	40.93
工业投资额	Investment in Industries	亿元 100 million yuan	83.18	50.32
外商直接投资项目	Projects of Foreign Direct Investment	个 unit	73	85
外商直接投资合同金额	Contracted Amount of Foreign Direct Investment	亿美元 USD 100 million	10.07	10.31
外商直接投资实际到位金额	Actual Paid Amount of Foreign Direct Investment	亿美元 USD 100 million	8.05	6.80
新增内资企业注册户数	Number of New Domestic Enterprises Registered	个 unit	595	991
新增内资企业注册资本	Capital of New Domestic Enterprises Registered	亿元 100 million yuan	69.27	56.26
工业总产值	Gross Value of Industrial Output	亿元 100 million yuan	619.69	758.37
#高技术产业产值	Output Value of High-tech Industries	亿元 100 million yuan	413.95	603.31
工业重点发展行业产值	Output Value of Key Industrial Sectors for Development	亿元 100 million yuan	578.62	714.52
#电子信息产品制造业	Manufacturing of Electronic and Information Products	亿元 100 million yuan	213.36	392.12
汽车制造业	Automobile Industry	亿元 100 million yuan	134.80	72.22
生物医药制造业	Manufacturing of Biological Medicine	亿元 100 million yuan	197.82	207.76
工业出口交货值	Delivery Value of Industrial Exports	亿元 100 million yuan	221.18	266.04
信息传输、计算机服务和软件业营业收入	Operating Income of Information Transmission, Computer Services and Software Industry	亿元 100 million yuan	569.88	762.21
文化产业营业收入	Operating Income of Cultural Industry	亿元 100 million yuan	706.07	988.79
知识产权授权数	Number of Authorizations for Intellectual Property	件 item	2 621	5 247
#专利授权数	Number of Patent Authorizations	件 item	2 195	4 015
技术交易数量	Number of Technology Transfers	件 item	919	1 051
技术合同金额	Contracted Value of Technologies	亿元 100 million yuan	79.21	57.48
经认定高新技术企业数	Number of Approved High-tech Enterprises	个 unit	550	596
期末从业人员数	Number of Employed Persons at End of Term	万人 10 000 persons	22.65	23.99

表20-5　康桥工业开发区主要经济指标
Major Economic Indicators in Kangqiao Industrial Development Zone

指　标　Indicators		单　位　Unit	2013	2014
税收总额（税务部门口径）	Total Amount of Tax Revenues (from the Tax Departments)	亿元 100 million yuan	40.20	34.72
一般公共预算收入	Local Fiscal Revenue	亿元 100 million yuan	8.90	7.59
固定资产投资额	Investment in Fixed Assets	亿元 100 million yuan	78.53	52.68
#工业投资额	nvestment in Industries	亿元 100 million yuan	39.64	40.42
外商直接投资项目	Projects of Foreign Direct Investment	个 unit	12	5
外商直接投资合同金额	Contracted Amount of Foreign Direct Investment	亿美元 USD 100 million	1.14	1.02
外商直接投资实际到位金额	Actual Paid Amount of Foreign Direct Investment	亿美元 USD 100 million	0.72	0.36
新增内资企业注册户数	Number of New Domestic Enterprises Registered	个 unit	162	235
新增内资企业注册资本	Capital of New Domestic Enterprises Registered	亿元 100 million yuan	18.52	16.84
工业总产值	Gross Value of Industrial Output	亿元 100 million yuan	1 565.25	1 496.47
#高技术产业产值	Output Value of High-tech Industries	亿元 100 million yuan	1 069.72	986.64
工业重点发展行业产值	Output Value of Key Industrial Sectors for Development	亿元 100 million yuan	1 340.06	1 281.19
#电子信息产品制造	Manufacturing of Electronic and Information Products	亿元 100 million yuan	1 070.93	986.13
汽车制造业	Automobile Industry	亿元 100 million yuan	123.40	142.25
成套设备制造业	Manufacturing of Complete Equipment	亿元 100 million yuan	120.12	124.15
工业出口交货值	Delivery Value of Industrial Exports	亿元 100 million yuan	1 051.97	1 013.03
工业利润总额	Total Amount of Industrial Profits	亿元 100 million yuan	77.59	80.08

表20-6 国际医学园区主要经济指标
Major Economic Indicators in International Medical Park

指 标 Indicators		单 位 Unit	2013	2014
税收总额(税务部门口径)	Total Amount of Tax Revenues (from the Tax Departments)	亿元 100 million yuan	3.53	4.17
一般公共预算收入	Local Fiscal Revenue	亿元 100 million yuan	1.06	1.17
固定资产投资额	Investment in Fixed Assets	亿元 100 million yuan	30.08	30.21
#工业投资额	Investment in Industries	亿元 100 million yuan	2.06	5.72
#医疗仪器设备及器械投资额	Investment in Medical Equipment, Apparatus and Appliances	亿元 100 million yuan	2.06	5.72
外商直接投资项目	Projects of Foreign Direct Investment	个 unit	14	7
外商直接投资合同金额	Contracted Amount of Foreign Direct Investment	亿美元 USD 100 million	0.47	0.39
外商直接投资实际到位金额	Actual Paid Amount of Foreign Direct Investment	亿美元 USD 100 million	0.21	0.10
新增内资企业注册户数	Number of New Domestic Enterprises Registered	个 unit	52	87
新增内资企业注册资本	Capital of New Domestic Enterprises Registered	亿元 100 million yuan	7.89	2.73
工业总产值	Gross Value of Industrial Output	亿元 100 million yuan	37.73	41.75
#高技术产业产值	Output Value of High-tech Industries	亿元 100 million yuan	35.68	39.54
工业重点发展行业产值	Output Value of Key Industrial Sectors for Development	亿元 100 million yuan	37.20	41.20
#生物医药制造业	Manufacturing of Biological Medicine	亿元 100 million yuan	75.64	37.08
工业出口交货值	Delivery Value of Industrial Exports	亿元 100 million yuan	16.56	18.80
生物医药产业营业收入	Operating Income of Bio-medicine Industry	亿元 100 million yuan	75.64	96.23
期末生物医药企业签约个数	Number of Contracted Bio-medicine Enterprises at End of Term	个 unit	100	133
期末医院签约个数	Number of Contracted Hospitals at End of Term	个 unit	8	11
期末在建医院个数	Number of Hospitals under Construction at End of Term	个 unit	2	

表20-7　外高桥保税区主要经济指标
Major Economic Indicators in Waigaoqiao Free Trade Zone

指　标	Indicators	单　位　Unit	2013	2014
税收总额(税务部门口径)	Total Amount of Tax Revenues (from the Tax Departments)	亿元 100 million yuan	449.53	519.10
一般公共预算收入	Local Fiscal Revenue	亿元 100 million yuan	94.54	117.54
海关部门税收	Tax Revenues by Customs Departments	亿元 100 million yuan	552.70	588.39
固定资产投资额	Investment in Fixed Assets	亿元 100 million yuan	28.21	25.58
外商直接投资项目	Projects of Foreign Direct Investment	个 unit	310	1 893
外商直接投资合同金额	Contracted Amount of Foreign Direct Investment	亿美元 USD 100 million	14.21	81.82
外商直接投资实际到位金额	Actual Paid Amount of Foreign Direct Investment	亿美元 USD 100 million	6.61	6.56
新增内资企业注册户数	Number of New Domestic Enterprises Registered	个 unit	3 462	8 622
新增内资企业注册资本	Capital of New Domestic Enterprises Registered	亿元 100 million yuan	669.28	3 067.07
港口货物吞吐量	Cargo Handling Capacity	万吨 10 000 tons	15 178	15 762
集装箱吞吐量	Container Handling Capacity	万标箱 10 000 TEUs	1 622	1 716
商品销售总额(限额以上)	Gross Sales of Commodities (Above Quota)	亿元 100 million yuan	2 477.14	2 499.57
商品销售总额(注册地口径)	Gross Sales of Commodities (Approach of Registered Place)	亿元 100 million yuan	11 623.26	12 786.96
保税市场交易额	Volume of Transactions in Free Trade Markets	亿美元 USD 100 million	1 294.80	1 454.15
交通运输业营业收入(注册地口径)	Operating Income of Transportation Industry (Approach of Registered Place)	亿元 100 million yuan	102.00	108.00
仓储业营业收入(注册地口径)	Operating Income of Storage Industry (Approach of Registered Place)	亿元 100 million yuan	66.00	72.00
工业总产值	Gross Value of Industrial Output	亿元 100 million yuan	646.16	572.70
#高技术产业产值	Output Value of High-tech Industries	亿元 100 million yuan	436.95	351.80
工业重点发展行业产值	Output Value of Key Industrial Sectors for Development	亿元 100 million yuan	564.83	485.86
#电子信息产品制造业	Manufacturing of Electronic and Information Products	亿元 100 million yuan	440.06	352.95
汽车制造业	Automobile Industry	亿元 100 million yuan	51.31	59.42
石化及精细化工制造业	Manufacturing of Petrochemical Industry and Refined Industry	亿元 100 million yuan	41.68	43.25
工业出口交货值	Delivery Value of Industrial Exports	亿元 100 million yuan	170.56	210.79
进出口总额	Total Volume of Foreign Trade	亿美元 USD 100 million	989.42	1 042.71
出口额	Amount of Exports	亿美元 USD 100 million	238.58	262.57
进口额	Amount of Imports	亿美元 USD 100 million	750.84	780.14
期末从业人员数(注册地口径)	Number of Employed Persons at End of Term (Approach of Registered Place)	万人 10 000 persoms	26.15	26.44
期末历年累计竣工房屋面积	Floor Space of Accumulated Completed Buildings in Main Years at End of Term	万平方米 10 000 sq·m	871.52	904.61

表 20-8　洋山保税港区主要经济指标
Major Economic Indicators in Yangshan Bonded Area Port

指　标	Indicators	单　位　Unit	2013	2014
税收总额（税务部门口径）	Total Amount of Tax Revenues (from the Tax Departments)	亿元 100 million yuan		53.68
一般公共预算收入	Local Fiscal Revenue	亿元 100 million yuan		
海关部门税收	Tax Revenues by Customs Departments	亿元 100 million yuan	376.90	382.91
固定资产投资额	Investment in Fixed Assets	亿元 100 million yuan	5.07	2.74
外商直接投资项目	Projects of Foreign Direct Investment	个 unit	37	88
外商直接投资合同金额	Contracted Amount of Foreign Direct Investment	亿美元 USD 100 million	3.83	16.30
外商直接投资实际到位金额	Actual Paid Amount of Foreign Direct Investment	亿美元 USD 100 million	0.42	0.03
新增内资企业注册户数	Number of Actual Registered Domestic Enterprises at End of Term	个 unit	446	542
新增内资企业注册资本	Registered Capital of Actual Domestic Enterprises at End of Term	亿元 100 million yuan	159.04	231.72
港口货物吞吐量	Cargo Handling Capacity at Port	万吨 10 000 tons	13 519	14 156
集装箱吞吐量	Container Handling Capacity	万标箱 10 000 TEUs	1 436.50	1 520.20
#洋山港国际中转量	International Transferring Amount at Yangshan Port	万标箱 10 000 TEUs	158.90	167.00
#洋山港水水中转	Ship-to-ship Transferring Amount at Yangshan Port	万标箱 10 000 TEUs	715.00	755.50
进出口总额	Total Volume of Foreign Trade	亿美元 USD 100 million	106.08	121.82
出口额	Amount of Exports	亿美元 USD 100 million	42.61	44.17
进口额	Amount of Imports	亿美元 USD 100 million	63.47	77.65

表20-9 临港产业区主要经济指标
Major Economic Indicators in Lingang Industrial Park

指 标 Indicators		单 位 Unit	2013	2014
税收总额(税务部门口径)	Total Amount of Tax Revenues (from the Tax Departments)	亿元 100 million yuan		57.86
一般公共预算收入	Local Fiscal Revenue	亿元 100 million yuan		
固定资产投资额	Investment in Fixed Assets	亿元 100 million yuan	123.48	183.11
#工业投资额	Investment in Industries	亿元 100 million yuan	31.50	66.71
外商直接投资项目	Projects of Foreign Direct Investment	个 unit	50	86
外商直接投资合同金额	Contracted Amount of Foreign Direct Investment	亿美元 USD 100 million	1.18	1.55
外商直接投资实际到位金额	Actual Paid Amount of Foreign Direct Investment	亿美元 USD 100 million	0.61	0.06
新增内资企业注册户数	Number of New Domestic Enterprises Registered	个 unit	1211	3626
新增内资企业注册资本	Capital of New Domestic Enterprises Registered	亿元 100 million yuan	31.00	339.01
工业总产值	Gross Value of Industrial Output	亿元 100 million yuan	231.41	249.17
#高技术产业产值	Output Value of High-tech Industries	亿元 100 million yuan	2.94	3.94
工业重点发展行业产值	Output Value of Key Industrial Sectors for Development	亿元 100 million yuan	103.14	146.24
#汽车制造业	Automobile Industry	亿元 100 million yuan	12.50	12.18
成套设备制造业	Manufacturing of Complete Equipment	亿元 100 million yuan	83.12	105.08
工业出口交货值	Delivery Value of Industrial Exports	亿元 100 million yuan	39.30	36.28
工业利润总额	Total Amount of Industrial Profits	亿元 100 million yuan	10.30	11.42

表20－10 各镇财政收入及工业总产值
Fiscal Revenue and Gross Output Value of Industry in Towns

单位:亿元　　100 million yuan

镇 Town		财政收入 Financial Revenue			工业总产值 Gross Output Value of Industry		
		2012	2013	2014	2012	2013	2014
总　计	**Total**	**384.69**	**412.20**	**474.81**	**2 134.52**	**2 313.69**	**2 261.42**
川沙新镇	Chuansha New Town	19.41	21.92	19.06	142.14	132.36	134.05
高桥镇	Gaoqiao Town	18.21	20.86	22.71	122.83	129.41	133.26
北蔡镇	Beicai Town	25.62	23.11	27.01	61.23	65.75	73.14
合庆镇	Heqing Town	12.39	12.64	14.74	178.97	180.40	184.37
唐　镇	Tangzhen Town	23.08	24.60	27.01	50.42	47.80	49.62
曹路镇	Caolu Town	22.82	20.81	22.94	176.93	203.14	194.54
金桥镇	Jinqiao Town	24.80	24.04	23.13	18.01	22.66	24.85
高行镇	Gaohang Town	23.04	23.97	29.32	171.63	148.16	139.46
高东镇	Gaodong Town	28.13	29.69	32.26	343.79	315.60	197.36
张江镇	Zhangjiang Town	16.29	15.70	18.84	40.67	38.38	36.35
三林镇	Sanlin Town	27.70	40.52	55.57	39.36	42.05	39.09
惠南镇	Huinan Town	9.76	9.29	13.23	13.86	13.48	13.09
周浦镇	Zhoupu Town	15.53	17.68	20.69	85.34	94.45	99.58
新场镇	Xinchang Town	7.54	8.38	9.33	85.55	88.00	89.03
大团镇	Datuan Town	3.27	3.05	3.65	14.08	14.26	14.77
南汇新城	Nanhui New Town	6.32	18.18	31.65	13.57	174.57	202.40
康桥镇	Kangqiao Town	26.56	21.14	21.90	198.49	200.35	210.17
航头镇	Hangtou Town	13.56	12.63	12.84	85.25	96.75	107.28
祝桥镇	Zhuqiao Town	33.00	33.90	33.64	145.80	150.95	145.17
泥城镇	Nicheng Town	9.88	11.28	12.54	11.28	11.41	12.21
宣桥镇	Xuanqiao Town	4.23	3.82	4.44	54.97	56.08	52.74
书院镇	Shuyuan Town	5.77	6.19	7.16	21.04	22.49	22.98
万祥镇	Wanxiang Town	4.79	5.24	6.37	20.52	22.95	21.06
老港镇	Laogang Town	2.99	3.57	4.78	38.82	42.14	64.85

主要统计指标解释

货物流量包括货物运输总量和货物进出仓量

货物运输总量

指在报告期内，以重量单位吨位计算的各种运输工具实际完成运输过程的货物数量，公路和水路的货运量按报告期到达货物数量统计，即报告期内已送达目的地并投卸完的货物数量为该报告期的货物运输总量。

货物进仓量

指在报告期内进入本企业仓库和堆放场地的各种货物的重量。按来源分为来自国外、来自国内一般地区和来自国内特殊监管区域（即保税区、出口加工区、保税物流园区等海关特殊监管区域）。

货物出仓量

指在报告期内运出本企业仓库和堆放场地的各种货物的重量。按流向分为流向国外、流向国内一般地区和流向国内特殊监管区域（即保税区，出口加工区、保税物流园区等海关特殊监管区域）。

上海市高新技术企业认定条件

（一）在本市注册的企业，近三年内通过自主研发、受让、受赠、并购等方式，或通过在全球范围内5年以上的独占许可方式，对其主要产品（服务）的核心技术拥有在中国内地得到中国法律保护的自主知识产权；

（二）产品（服务）属于高新技术企业认定管理办法的附件《国家重点支持的高新技术领域》规定的范围；

（三）具有大学专科以上学历的科技人员占企业当年职工总数的30%以上，其中研发人员占企业当年职工总数的10%以上；

（四）企业为获得科学技术（不包括人文、社会科学）新知识，创造性运用科学技术新知识，或实质性改进技术、产品（服务）而持续进行了研究开发活动，且近三个会计年度的研究开发费用总额占销售收入总额的比例符合如下要求：

1、最近一年销售收入小于5000万元的企业，比例不低于8%；

2、最近一年销售收入在5000万元至20000万元的企业，比例不低于4%；

3、最近一年销售收人在20000万元以上的企业，比例不低于3%。

其中，企业在中国内地发生的研究开发费用总额占全部研究开发费用总额的比例不低于60%。企业注册成立时间满一年但不足三年的，按实际经营年限计算；

（五）高新技术产品（服务）收入占企业当年总收入的60%以上；

（六）企业研究开发组织管理水平、科技成果转化能力、自主知识产权数量、销售与总资产成长性等指标符合《高新技术企业认定管理工作指引》的要求。

EXPLANATORY NOTES TO MAJOR STATISTICAL INDICATORS

The Flow of Goods Includes the Total of Goods and the Amount of Goods Entered and Left the Warehouse

Total of Cargo Transport

Refers to the number of cargoes that have been completely finished by all kinds of transportation means that are calculated by weight with the unit of ton during the reference period. The transport volume by road and that by water are calculated by the number of cargoes that have actually arrived during the reference period, namely the volume of goods that has been transported to its destination and discharged during the reference period is the total of cargo transport during the reference period.

Amount of Goods Entered the Warehouse

Refers to the weight of all kinds of goods that have entered the warehouse and storage space of this enterprise during the reference period. Grouped by its sources, they are from the overseas, ordinary domestic regions and specially-supervised domestic regions (namely special regions supervised by the Customs House such as bonded zones, export processing zones, bonded logistics parks).

Amount of Goods Left the Warehouse

Refers to the weight of all kinds of goods that have left the warehouse and storage space of this enterprise during the reference period. Grouped by its flows, they are to the overseas, ordinary domestic regions and specially-supervised domestic regions (namely special regions supervised by the Customs House such as bonded zones, export processing zones, bonded logistics parks).

Conditions for Identification of High-tech Enterprises in Shanghai

(I) Enterprises, which have registered in Shanghai, possess independent intellectual property rights protected by Chinese laws in China for the core technology of their main products or services, by means of independent research and development, transferring, donation and purchasing, or in possession of exclusive licenses for over five years all over the world.

(II) Their products or services belong to the scope specified in the Appendix: High-tech Fields Key Supported by the State of Identification and Management Methods of High-tech Enterprises.

(III) High-tech employees with education levels of college degrees or above occupy over 30% of the total number of employees in that year, in which R&D persons are over 10%.

(IV) In order to obtain the new knowledge of science and technology (excluding human studies), take advantage of the new knowledge of science and technology in a creative way, or improve their products or services in a substantial way, enterprises have continued to conduct R&D activities and the ratios of the sum of expenses for research and development in the total sales revenue during the current three fiscal years should accord with the following requirements:

1. This ratio is not less than 8% for enterprises with its sales revenue of the previous year less than RMB 50 million.

2. This ratio is not less than 4% for enterprises with its sales revenue of the previous year between RMB 50 million and RMB 200 million.

3. This ratio is not less than 3% for enterprises with its sales revenue of the previous year over RMB 200 million.

Which the sum expenses for research and development in domestic regions of China of the enterprise should account for more than 60% of the total R&D expenses. If the enterprise has registered for more than one year and less than three years, we will calculate its actual operation period.

(V) The revenue of high-tech products or services accounts for over 60% of the total income of the enterprise at the year.

(VI) Indicators such as the level of R&D organization and management, the transferring capability of scientific and technical achievements, the number of independent intellectual property rights, and sales and total assets growth accord with the requirements of the Working Guidance of Identification and Management for High-tech Enterprises.

第二十一篇

CHAPTER 21

上海市统计资料

STATISTICS OF SHANGHAI MUNICIPALITY

表21－1　主要年份人口、从业人员、工资和婚姻情况
Population,Employment,Wages and Marriage in Main Years

指　标	Indicators	1990	2000	2010	2013	2014
年末户籍总人口（万人）	**Year-end Household Registered Population (10 000 persons)**	**1 283.35**	**1 321.63**	**1 412.32**	**1 432.34**	**1 438.69**
按性别分	Grouped by Sex					
男	Male	647.13	665.51	703.57	711.93	714.71
女	Female	636.22	656.12	708.75	720.41	723.99
按农业、非农业分	Grouped by Agriculture and Non-agriculture					
农业人口	Agriculture	418.89	335.47	157.37	142.76	139.19
非农业人口	Non-agriculture	864.46	986.16	1 254.95	1 289.58	1 299.50
常住人口(万人)	Year-end Resident Population (10 000 persons)	1 334.00	1 608.60	2 302.66	2 415.15	2 425.68
人口密度(人/平方公里)	Density of Population (persons/sq. km)	2 104	2 537	3 632	3 809	3 826
总户数(万户)	Total Households (10 000 household)	415.28	475.73	519.27	527.52	532.55
每户平均人口(人)	Average Persons Per Household (persons)	3.1	2.8	2.7	2.7	2.7
人口自然变动	**Natural Change**					
出生人口(万人)	Number of Birth (10 000 persons)	13.12	6.95	10.02	10.89	12.41
出生率(‰)	Birth Rate (‰)	10.20	5.30	7.13	7.62	8.64
死亡人口(万人)	Number of Death (10 000 persons)	8.63	9.45	10.87	11.67	11.95
死亡率(‰)	Death Rate (‰)	6.70	7.20	7.73	8.16	8.32
自然增长率(‰)	Natural Growth Rate (‰)	3.51	-2.50	-0.60	-0.54	0.32
人口迁徙变动	**Migration Change**					
迁入人口(万人)	Inflows (10 000 persons)	12.18	15.16	17.22	12.12	11.55
迁入率(‰)	Rate of Inflows (‰)	9.52	11.51	12.24	8.48	8.05
迁出人口(万人)	Outflows (10 000 persons)	10.72	5.32	4.97	6.06	5.78
迁出率(‰)	Rate of Outflows (‰)	8.38	4.04	3.53	4.24	4.02
从业人员(万人)	**Employment (10 000 persons)**	**787.72**	**828.35**	**1 090.76**	**1 368.91**	**1 365.63**
职工工资总额(亿元)	Wages of Staff and Workers (100 million yuan)	146.78	614.53	3 018.55	6 183.93	7 643.73
职工年平均工资(元)	Average Annual Wages of Staff and Workers (yuan)	2 917	15 420	46 757	60 435	65 417
婚姻登记	**Registered Marriage**					
准予登记结婚(万对)	Marriage Registration Permitted (10 000 couples)	10.77	9.31	13.03	14.95	14.19
初　婚(万人)	First Marriage (10 000 persons)	19.49	15.08	20.10	22.17	20.14
再　婚(万人)	Remarriage (10 000 persons)	2.04	2.89	5.96	7.74	8.25
离婚件数(万件)	Divorce (10 000 persons)	1.64	3.18	4.67	6.96	6.15

表21-2　主要年份上海市生产总值和指数
Value Added and Index in Main Years

指　标	Indicators	1990	2000	2010	2013	2014
上海市生产总值(亿元)	**Gross Domestic Product (100 million yuan)**	**781.66**	**4 771.17**	**17 165.98**	**21 818.15**	**23 567.70**
第一产业	Primary Industry	34.24	76.68	114.15	124.89	124.26
第二产业	Secondary Industry	505.60	2 207.63	7 218.32	7 907.81	8 167.71
#工　业	Industry	469.83	1 998.96	6 536.21	7 139.18	7 362.84
建筑业	Construction	35.77	208.67	682.11	791.08	831.86
第三产业	Tertiary Industry	241.82	2 486.86	9 833.51	13 785.45	15 275.73
构　成(%)	**Composition (%)**					
第一产业	Primary Industry	4.3	1.8	0.7	0.6	0.5
第二产业	Secondary Industry	63.8	47.6	42.0	36.2	34.7
#工　业	Industry	59.1	43.0	38.0	32.7	31.2
建筑业	Construction	4.7	4.6	4.0	3.6	3.5
第三产业	Tertiary Industry	31.9	50.6	57.3	63.2	64.8
人均生产总值(元)	**Average GDP Per Capita (yuan)**	**5 911**	**30 047**	**76 074**	**90 993**	**97 370**
上海市生产总值指数(以1990年为100)	**Indices of GDP (1990=100)**	**100.0**	**319.1**	**953.0**	**1 195.2**	**1 278.9**
第一产业	Primary Industry	100.0	126.8	112.8	109.0	109.0
第二产业	Secondary Industry	100.0	305.0	915.8	1063.2	1107.8
第三产业	Tertiary Industry	100.0	375.9	1143.6	1511.2	1644.2
上海市生产总值指数(以上年为100)	**Indices of GDP (preceding year=100)**	**103.5**	**111.0**	**110.3**	**107.7**	**107.0**
第一产业	Primary Industry	104.3	103.4	93.4	96.7	100.1
第二产业	Secondary Industry	102.8	109.8	116.8	105.9	104.2
第三产业	Tertiary Industry	105.3	113.5	105.7	109.0	108.8

表21-3 主要年份全社会固定资产投资主要指标
Major Indicators of Total Investment in Fixed Assets in Main Years

指 标	Indicators	1990	2000	2010	2013	2014
投资总额(亿元)	**Total Investment (100 million yuan)**	**227.08**	**1 869.67**	**5 317.67**	**5 647.79**	**6 016.43**
#房地产	Real Estate	8.16	566.17	1 980.68	2 819.59	3 206.48
按构成分	Grouped by Use of Funds					
#建筑安装工程	Construction and Installation	127.63	882.91	2 820.17	3 440.47	3 713.25
设备、工具、器具购置	Purchase of Equipment, Tools and Instrument	79.51	482.47	991.10	787.55	624.83
按建设性质分	Grouped by Type of Construction					
#新 建	New Construction	78.01	730.76	2 052.69	1 739.51	1 913.30
改建和技改	Reconstruction and Technical Renovation	70.48	216.40	513.80	428.57	335.59
扩 建	Expansion	47.50	216.71	368.07	310.61	303.63
按三次产业分	Grouped by Type of Industry					
第一产业	Primary Industry	3.20	7.87	16.40	18.45	11.86
第二产业	Secondary Industry	133.00	615.94	1 435.37	1 242.02	1 157.27
第三产业	Tertiary Industry	90.88	1 245.86	3 865.90	4 387.32	4 847.30
按经济类型分	Grouped by Economic Types					
#国有经济	State-owned	192.24	829.98	2 234.12	1 926.89	1 796.22
集体经济	Collective-owned	18.29	156.34	183.07	102.81	55.07
联营经济	Joint Owned		41.20	11.52	13.99	6.11
股份制经济	Share-holding		421.53	1 200.26	1 601.33	1 812.77
外商投资经济	Foreign Funded		222.86	439.28	602.5	637.9
港澳台投资经济	Hong Kong, Macao and Taiwan Funded		96.19	247.67	291.96	465.14
房屋建筑面积(万平方米)	**Floor Space of Buildings (10 000 sq. m)**					
施工面积	Floor Space Under Construction	3 801.46	8 636.31	15 020.76	17 180.27	18 010.06
#住 宅	Residential Housing	2 269.06	4 804.12	7 344.07	8 188.56	8 573.04
竣工面积	Floor Space Completed	2 138.44	3 266.52	2 776.21	2 698.35	2 682.42
#住 宅	Residential Housing	1 339.02	1 724.02	1 415.44	1 439.20	1 549.64
房屋建筑面积竣工率(%)	Rate of Floor Space of Buildings Completed (%)	56.3	37.8	18.5	15.7	14.9
资金来源合计(亿元)	**Total Capital Source (100 million yuan)**	**261.46**	**2 061.66**	**7 997.62**	**9 997.36**	**10 524.10**
上年末结余资金	A Balance at End of Previous Year	28.85	241.05	1 440.57	2 169.14	2 562.48
当年资金来源小计	Sub-total Capital Source of the Year	232.61	1 820.61	6 557.05	7 828.22	7 961.62
国家预算内资金	Capital Within the State Budget	14.39	48.30	116.71	368.25	417.89
国内贷款	Domestic Loans	62.52	379.21	1 568.79	1 782.39	2 068.08
债 券	State Treasury Bond		4.85	10.06		
利用外资	Foreign Capital Absorbed	35.46	161.83	239.18	172.52	205.05
自筹资金	Self-raised Capital	94.13	905.46	3 273.11	3 284.39	3 243.55
其他资金	Other Capital	26.11	320.96	1 349.21	2 220.67	2 027.05

表21-4 主要年份城市基础设施投资额和公用事业
Investment in Urban Infrastructure and Public Utilities in Main Years

指 标	Indicators	1990	2000	2010	2013	2014
城市基础设施投资额（亿元）	**Investment in Urban Infrastructure (100 million yuan)**	**47.22**	**449.90**	**1 497.46**	**1 043.31**	**1 057.25**
电力建设	Electric Construction	17.53	64.61	148.50	110.35	134.22
交通邮电	Traffic and Post	10.06	117.52	866.20	550.42	422.48
公用设施	Public Facilities	19.63	267.77	482.76	382.54	412.61
公用事业	Public Utilities	10.83	104.43	86.58	47.57	32.80
自来水	Tap Water	1.06	5.35	61.63	24.83	20.00
燃 气	Gas	1.81	6.88	24.95	22.74	12.80
市政建设	Municipal Construction	8.80	163.34	396.18	334.97	379.81
#园林建设	Parks, Gardens and Green Areas	0.11	38.76	35.87	27.16	56.46
环境卫生	Environment Sanitation	0.37	19.34	10.80	12.52	9.41
市政工程	Urban Municipal Engineering	8.31	102.36	349.27	292.48	313.94
自来水	**Tap Water**					
自来水管道长度（公里）	Length of Tap Water Pipelines (km)	3 483	15 943	31 182	36 217	35 068
自来水供应能力（万立方米/日）	Tap Water Supply (10 000 cu · m/day)	462	1 048	1 131	1 124	1 137
售水量（亿立方米）	Sales of Tap Water (100 milion cu · m)	12.25	19.75	24.44	24.92	24.82
#生产用水	Industrial Use	5.90	5.49	5.80	5.23	5.16
生活用水	Residential Use	6.11	11.88	18.64	19.69	19.66
燃气、液化气	**Gas and Liquefied Gas**					
管道燃气	Pipeline Gas					
管线长度（公里）	Length of Gas Pipelines (km)	2 700	6 606	5 517	2 962	2 109
燃气销售量（亿立方米）	Sales of Coal Gas (100 million cu · m)	12.15	20.56	55.51	71.19	69.40
#家庭用	Family Use	7.63	16.22	14.07	26.11	26.57
家庭用液化气户数（万户）	Household of Family Use Petroleum Gas (10 000 households)	113.19	255.89	316.37	330.46	334.68
道 路	**Road**					
铺装道路长度（公里）	Length of Road Paved (km)	1 631	6 641	16 687	17 498	17 797
铺装道路面积（万平方米）	Area of Road Paved (10 000 sq. m)	1 787	8 147	25 607	27 290	27 918
交 通	**Traffic**					
年末实有公交线路条数（条）	Lines of Public Traffic (year-end) (route)	390	978	1 165	1 338	1 377
年末实有公交线路长度（公里）	Lines of Public Traffic Routes (year-end) (km)	18 593	23 260	23 131	23 824	23 897
年末运营公交车辆（辆）	Public Transportation Vehicles (year-end) (vehicle)	6 264	17 939	17 455	16 717	16 155
客运总量（亿人次）	Passengers Carried (100 million person-times)	54.37	26.49	28.08	27.10	26.65
出租汽车运营车辆数（辆）	Taxi in Operation (vehicle)	11 298	42 943	50 007	50 612	50 738
隧 道	**Tunnels**					
越江隧道条数（条）	Routes of Tunnels Across the Huangpu River (route)	2	2	12	13	13
越江大桥座数（座）	Number of Bridges Across the Huangpu River (unit)	1	5	10	10	10
城市绿化	**Urban Greenbelt**					
城市绿地面积（公顷）	Area of Parks, Gardens and Green Areas (hectare)	3 570	12 601	120 148	124 295	125 741
人均公共绿地面积（平方米/人）	Public Green Area Per Capita (sq. m/person)	1.02	4.60	13.00	13.38	13.79
绿化覆盖率（%）	Green Area Coverage (%)	12.4	22.2	38.2	38.4	38.4
公园数（个）	Number of Parks (unit)	83	122	148	158	161

注：2009年原园林绿地面积改为城市绿地面积，统计分类作了调整。
Note: As the field of green-land area was changed into that of urban green space in 2009, the classification has been readjusted thereafter.

表21-5　主要年份农业主要指标
Major Indicators of Agriculture in Main Years

指　标	Indicators	1990	2000	2010	2013	2014
农业总产值(亿元)	**Gross Output Value of Agriculture (100 million yuan)**	**68.16**	**216.50**	**287.03**	**323.48**	**322.22**
#种植业	Planting	29.09	89.82	155.27	172.28	169.51
林　业	Forestry	0.37	1.41	7.53	9.65	8.78
牧　业	Animal Husbandry	30.25	87.35	62.90	69.97	69.93
渔　业	Fishery	8.04	37.92	52.62	59.89	62.50
主要农副产品产量	**Output of Major Farm and Sideline Products**					
粮　食(万吨)	Grain (10 000 tons)	244.36	174.00	118.40	114.15	112.89
油菜籽(万吨)	Rapeseed (10 000 tons)	18.17	15.71	2.04	1.28	1.05
蔬　菜(万吨)	Vegetables (10 000 tons)	186.79	377.00	380.35	385.34	377.95
食用菌(万吨)	Edible Fungus(10 000 tons)			8.73	13.08	15.23
水　果(万吨)	Fruit (10 000 tons)	9.42	22.54	44.16	37.01	45.85
年末圈存量(万头)	Hogs at year-end(10 000 in number)	237.53	241.60	171.87	184.75	171.68
猪肉产量(万吨)	Pork (10 000 tons)	23.32	25.96	17.87	18.33	18.83
牛奶产量(万吨)	Cow Milk (10 000 tons)	22.68	25.95	24.71	26.53	27.05
鲜蛋上市量(万吨)	Poulty Eggs (10 000 tons)	15.07	16.64	6.28	5.66	5.23
水产品(万吨)	Aquatic Products (10 000 tons)	27.36	28.87	28.97	27.13	30.90
淡水产品	Freshwater Aquatic Products	10.32	16.64	16.82	13.48	13.03
海水产品	Seawater Aquatic Products	17.04	12.23	12.15	13.65	17.87
农业机械总动力(万千瓦)	**Total Power of Agricultural Machinery (10 000 kw)**	**276.50**	**142.50**	**28.97**	**115.84**	**117.76**

表21-6　规模以上工业企业主要指标
Major Indicators of the Above-certain-scale Industrial Enterprises (2014)

指　标	Indicators	单位数（个）Number of Enterprises (unit)	从业人员（万人）Employees (10 000 persons)	工业总产值（亿元）Gross Output Value of Industry (100 million yuan)	年末资产总计（亿元）Total Assets (year-end) (100 million yuan)	利润总额（亿元）Total After-tax Profits (100 million yuan)	税金总额（亿元）Total Tax and Duties (100 million yuan)
总　计	**Total**	**9 469**	**242.45**	**32 665.19**	**35 512.24**	**2 650.00**	**1 877.90**
按隶属关系分	**Grouped by Subordination**						
中央工业	Central Government	150	16.90	6 323.65	9 035.41	393.07	1 011.29
地方工业	Local Government	9 319	225.55	26 341.54	26 476.82	2 256.93	866.60
按登记注册类型分	**Grouped by Registration Categories**						
内　资	Domestic	5 423	101.05	12 627.61	18 782.03	1 076.83	1 136.05
国　有	State-owned	77	3.54	976.35	2 057.30	49.23	40.19
集　体	Collective-owned	92	1.11	76.54	71.15	2.44	2.70
股份合作	Share-holding Coorperation	48	0.57	29.60	27.35	1.08	0.91
联　营	Joint Owned	13	0.16	17.50	11.06	-0.06	0.45
有限责任公司	Companies with Limited Liabilities	1 013	31.62	5 492.75	7 501.01	413.89	844.24
股份有限公司	Share-holding Companies with Limited Liabilities	162	9.89	2 125.89	5 180.76	381.92	139.48
私　营	Private	4 008	54.07	3 901.69	3 927.03	228.03	107.90
其　他	Others	10	0.11	7.30	6.37	0.28	0.17
港澳台商投资	Hong Kong, Macao and Taiwan Funded	1 167	39.94	5 103.67	4 113.62	221.72	178.67
外商投资	Foreign Funded	2 879	101.46	14 933.90	12 616.59	1 351.46	563.17
按企业规模分	**Grouped by Size of Enterprises**						
大型企业	Large	293	87.08	17 338.81	18 785.83	1 642.26	1 451.17
中型企业	Medium	1 336	70.39	6 969.54	7 572.79	548.90	194.78
小型企业	Small	7 840	84.97	8 356.83	9 153.62	458.84	231.95

注：本表为国有企业及销售收入在2000万元以上的非国有企业。
Note: Data in this table is collected from state-owned enterprises and non-state-owned enterprises with revenue of sales more than 20 million yuan.

表21-7 主要年份国内外贸易主要指标
Major Indicators of Domestic and Foreign Trade in Main Years

指标	Indicators	1990	2000	2010	2013	2014
社会消费品零售总额(亿元)	**Total Retail Sales Value of Consumer Goods (100 million yuan)**	**333.86**	**1 865.28**	**6 070.50**	**8 052.00**	**9 303.49**
按用途分	Grouped by Type of Goods					
吃的商品	Food	142.15	743.31	1 830.64	2 241.19	2 065.56
穿的商品	Clothing	52.33	248.94	686.15	933.26	1 313.05
用的商品	Articles	137.23	858.33	3 197.85	4 410.85	5 210.09
烧的商品	Fuels	2.15	14.70	355.86	466.70	714.79
按行业分	Grouped by Sector					
#批发零售贸易业	Wholesale and Retail Trade	265.67	1 493.13	5 391.59	8 258.27	8 414.81
住宿餐饮业	Hotels and Catering Trade	17.08	134.12	678.91	793.73	888.68
外贸出口商品总额(亿美元)	Total Value of Exports (USD 100 million)	53.21	253.54	1 807.84	2 042.44	2 102.77
外贸进口商品总额(亿美元)	Total Value of Imports (USD 100 million)	21.10	293.56	1 880.85	2 371.54	2 563.45
外商直接投资签约项目数(个)	Projects of Foreign Direct Investment (unit)	203	1 814	3 906	3 842	4 697
#中外合资	Joint Venture	161	441	445	656	887
中外合作	Cooperative Operation	12	226	14	5	7
外商独资	Foreign Enterprise	30	1 146	3 443	3 075	3 796
外商直接投资合同金额(亿美元)	Contracted Foreign Capital of Foreign Direct Investment (USD 100 million)	3.75	63.90	153.07	246.30	316.09
#中外合资	Joint Venture	1.98	13.86	21.54	36.09	70.13
中外合作	Cooperative Operation	0.40	5.86	1.11	5.31	1.91
外商独资	Foreign Enterprise	1.36	44.14	128.17	203.95	230.19

表21-8 主要年份口岸进出口商品总额
Total Export and Import at Port in Main Years

单位:亿美元 (USD 100 million)

指 标	Indicators	1990	2000	2010	2013	2014
口岸进出口总额	**Total Value of Import and Export**	**172.89**	**1 093.11**	**6 846.45**	**8 121.37**	**8 634.55**
出口总额	**Total Value of Export**	**86.62**	**615.72**	**4 233.40**	**4 991.29**	**5 232.12**
#一般贸易	Original Trade	51.39	341.02	2 183.98	2 857.73	3 112.37
来料加工装配贸易	Processing and Assembly Trade	3.20	64.21	178.52	130.46	126.18
进料加工贸易	Processing Trade of Imported Material	30.67	205.13	1 639.70	1 642.18	1 601.78
对外承包工程货物	Contracted Projects in Foreign Countries	0.41	1.25	60.55	80.16	85.04
进口总额	**Total Value of Import**	**86.27**	**477.39**	**2 613.05**	**3 130.08**	**3 402.43**
#一般贸易	Original Trade	51.79	212.65	1 209.42	1 628.68	1 777.08
来料加工装配贸易	Processing and Assembly Trade of Import	2.40	44.87	169.36	135.19	164.31
进料加工贸易	Processing Trade of Imported Material	19.70	125.13	552.83	524.14	568.61
租赁贸易	International Leasing		2.47	18.56	23.68	40.52
外商投资进口设备	Imported Equipment of Foreign Funded Enterprise	6.11	40.26	43.81	23.58	26.63

表21－9　主要年份财政收支和保险
Major Indicators of Fiscal Revenue and Expenditure and Insurance in Main Years

单位:亿元　　(100 million yuan)

指　标	Indicators	1990	2000	2010	2013	2014
全市财政收入	**Fiscal Revenue**	**284.36**	**1 752.70**			
#中央财政收入	Central Fiscal Revenue	114.33	1 246.47			
一般公共预算收入	Local Fiscal Revenue	170.03	497.96	2 873.58	4 109.51	4585.55
#增值税	Value-added Tax		93.55	388.62	848.47	969.14
营业税	Sales Tax		153.81	933.91	962.72	1 001.92
企业所得税	Enterprise Income Tax		103.03	606.05	837.44	942.46
个人所得税	Individual Income Tax		60.24	261.20	355.22	408.61
市级财政收入	Fiscal Revenue at Prefectural Level		215.81	1 393.23	1 977.03	2 209.25
区县级财政收入	Fiscal Revenue at District (County) Level		282.15	1 480.35	2 132.48	2 376.30
一般公共预算支出	**Local Fiscal Expenditure**	**75.56**	**622.84**	**3 302.89**	**4 528.61**	**4 923.44**
保险费收入	**Premium Income**	**8.99**	**127.23**	**883.86**	**821.43**	**986.75**
赔款及给付	Indemnity Expenditure and Payment	2.23	36.20	194.54	301.95	378.66
赔款率(%)	Indemnity and Premium Ratio(%)	24.7	28.5	22.0	36.8	38.4

表21-10 主要年份交通运输
Transportaion in Main Years

指标	Indicators	1990	2000	2010	2013	2014
铁路运输	**By Railway**					
运营里程(公里)	Operations in Length (km)	259	257	414	456	456
正线延展里程(公里)	Extension of Main Tracks in Length (km)	356	397	697	825	825
旅客发送量(万人次)	Volume of Passengers Carried (10 000 person-times)	2 476	2 980	6 095	7 972	9 194
旅客周转量(亿人·公里)	Volume of Passengers Circulated (100 million persons·km)	26.85	35.40	60.16	75.26	84.46
货物运输量(万吨)	Volume of Goods Transported (10 000 tons)	1 257	1 055	959	694	549
货物周转量(亿吨·公里)	Volume of Goods Circulated (100 million tons·km)	111	122	26	14	12
公路运输	**By Road**					
通车里程(公里)	Available for Traffic in Length (km)	3 050	6 078	11 974	12 633	12 945
#高速公路	Expressway	36	98	775	815	825
旅客发送量(万人次)	Volume of Passengers Carried (10 000 person-times)	605	2 482	3 634	3 720	3 754
旅客周转量(亿人·公里)	Volume of Passengers Circulated (100 million persons·km)	8.42	16.44	115.44	108.71	124.34
货物运输量(万吨)	Volume of Goods Transported (10 000 tons)	605	2 482	40 890	43 809	42 848
货物周转量(亿吨·公里)	Volume of Goods Circulated (100 million tons·km)	11	56	266	299	301
水路运输	**By Water**					
旅客周转量(亿人·公里)	Volume of Passengers Circulated (100 million persons·km)	40.84	6.77	3.69	0.82	1.04
货物运输量(万吨)	Volume of Goods Transported (10 000 tons)	12 864	18 442	38 803	46 697	46 583
#远洋运输(万吨)	Ocean Transportation (10 000 tons)	2 246	7 022	15 172	15 255	16 541
货物周转量(亿吨·公里)	Volume of Goods Circulated (100 million tons·km)	3 236	6 430	15 818	17 497	18 320
#远洋运输(亿吨·公里)	Ocean Transportation (100 million tons·km)	1 957	5 285	14 535	13 562	14 487
港　口	**Ports**					
港口旅客发送量(万人次)	Volume of Passengers Carried at Ports (10 000 person-times)	555	539	85	68	90
民用航空	**Civil Aviation**					
旅客发送量(万人次)	Volume of Passengers Carried (10 000 person-times)	199	892	3642	4 173	4 522
旅客周转量(亿人·公里)	Volume of Passengers Circulated (100 million persons·km)	37.84	176.11	1 034.96	1 158.95	1 217.26
货物运输量(万吨)	Volume of Goods Transported (10 000 tons)	13	88	371	335	361
货物周转量(亿吨·公里)	Volume of Goods Circulated (100 million tons·km)	1	12	63	57	57

注：港口旅客发送量从2006年起不包含海港到内河部分。
Note: The volume of Passenger Departures excludes those from seaports to freshwater since 2006.

表21-11 主要年份教育、卫生事业情况
Statistics of Education and Healthcare in Main Years

指 标	Indicators	1990	2000	2010	2013	2014
学校(所)	**School (unit)**					
高等学校	Institutions of Higher Education	50	37	66	68	68
中等专业学校	Special Secondary Schools	110	84	65	55	54
职业中学	Vocational Middle Schools	80	60	26	28	28
普通中学	Regular Secondary Schools	712	861	755	762	768
小 学	Primary Schools	2630	1021	766	759	757
特殊教育学校	Special Schools	29	34	29	29	29
在校学生数(万人)	**Student Enrollment (10 000 persons)**					
高等学校	Institutions of Higher Education	12.13	22.68	51.57	50.48	50.66
中等专业学校	Special Secondary Schools	6.17	11.89	10.91	9.23	7.74
职业中学	Vocational Middle Schools	3.66	8.48	3.77	3.24	2.72
普通中学	Regular Secondary Schools	48.31	79.54	59.44	79.72	58.42
小 学	Primary Schools	110.19	78.86	70.16	79.25	80.30
特殊教育学校	Special Schools	0.33	0.54	0.50	0.47	0.46
教职员工(万人)	**Staff and Workers (10 000 persons)**					
高等学校	Institutions of Higher Education	7.06	6.08	7.42	7.34	7.34
中等专业学校	Special Secondary Schools	1.49	1.27	0.91	0.82	0.80
职业中学	Vocational Middle Schools	0.53	0.66	0.43	0.40	0.39
普通中学	Regular Secondary Schools	6.62	7.66	6.73	6.82	6.95
小 学	Primary Schools	7.48	6.13	5.58	5.81	5.96
特殊教育学校	Special Schools	0.11	0.16	0.16	0.16	0.16
卫生机构数(个)	**Health Care Institutions(unit)**	**7 690**	**4 400**	**3 270**	**4 929**	**4 987**
#医 院	Hospital	462	459	306	328	332
医院床位数(张)	**Hospital Beds (bed)**	**62 100**	**73 070**	**84 825**	**114 314**	**98 261**
卫生技术人员(万人)	**Medical Technical Personnel (10 000 persons)**	**15.85**	**10.71**	**13.54**	**15.64**	**16.40**
#执业医生	Medical Parctitioners	5.82	4.99	5.13	5.81	6.13
护师、护士	Senior and Junior Nurses	3.27	3.68	5.59	6.79	7.19
医院治疗人次(万人次)	**Total Patients Treated (10 000 person-times)**	**8 395.00**	**8 631.67**	**21 002.46**	**24 093.28**	**25 834.62**
#门、急诊	Out-patients and Emergency Patients		8 432.29	20 676.24	22 423.53	24 043.26
医院入院人数(万人次)	**In Patients (10 000 person-times)**	**95.28**	**122.79**	**285.68**	**314.66**	**345.08**
医院每百诊次的入院人数(人)	**In Patients Per 100 Patient-times (person)**	**1.10**	**1.40**	**1.40**	**1.31**	**1.34**

表21-12 居民消费价格指数(以上年价格为100)
Consumer Price Index of Residents(Preceding Year = 100)

指标	Indicators	2014
居民消费价格指数	**Overall Residents Consumer Price Index**	**102.7**
食品	**Food**	**103.2**
粮食	Grain	102.4
淀粉及制品	Starch and Related Products	102.5
干豆类及豆制品	Dry Beans and Bean Products	100.4
油脂	Oil and Fat	95.5
肉禽及其制品	Meat Poultry and Their Products	101.4
蛋	Eggs	106.0
水产品	Aquatic Products	102.7
菜	Vegetables	101.5
#鲜菜	Fresh Vegetables	100.5
调味品	Flavoring	103.1
糖	Sugar	102.0
茶及饮料	Tea and Beverages	103.2
干鲜瓜果	Dried and Fresh Fruits	111.6
#鲜瓜果	Fresh Fruits	116.6
糕点饼干面包	Cakes, Biscuits and Bread	102.6
液体乳及乳制品	Milk and Its Products	110.1
在外用膳食品	Out-of-home Food	101.9
其他食品	Other Food	103.4
烟酒	**Tobacco, Alcohol and Related Products**	**101.0**
烟草	Tobacco	101.2
酒	Liquor	100.7
衣着	**Clothing**	**103.7**
服装	Garments	102.4
男式服装	Men's Wear	102.7
女式服装	Women's Wear	102.7
儿童服装	Children's Wear	99.1
衣着材料	Clothing Materials	103.1
鞋袜帽	Shoes, Socks and Hats	108.5
#鞋	Shoes	109.5
衣着加工服务	Garment Processing Service	110.0
家庭设备用品及维修服务	**Home Appliances and Required Service**	**101.8**
耐用消费品	Durable Consumer Goods	100.9
室内装饰品	Interior Decorations	93.6
床上用品	Bed Articles	98.4
家庭日用杂志	Daily Use Household Articles	100.5
家庭服务及加工维修服务	Other Daily Use Articles	110.7
医疗保健和个人用品	**Medicine, Medical Services and Personal Articles**	**100.4**
医疗保健	Medicine and Medical Services	101.7
#中药材及中成药	Chinese Medicinal Crop and Patent Medicine	103.0
西药	Western Medicine	99.9
保健器具及用品	Healthcare and Equipment	104.4
医疗保健服务	Medical and Healthcare Services	101.9
个人用品及服务	Personal Articles and Service	99.2
交通和通信	**Means of Transportation and Communication**	**100.1**
交通	Transport	100.6
#交通工具	Transport Tools	98.3
通信	Communications	98.7
通信工具	Communications Tools	93.7
通信服务	Communications Service	99.2
娱乐教育文化用品及服务	**Recreation, Education and Culture Articles**	**101.8**
文娱用耐用消费品及服务	Durable Consumer Goods for Recreational Use	93.7
教育	Education	102.4
文化娱乐用品	Recreation and Culture Articles	101.0
旅游	Tourism	107.9
居住	**Residence**	**104.6**
建房及装修材料	Housing Construction And Finishing Materials	99.8
住房租金	Rents	105.2
自有住房	Self-owned House	105.3
水电燃料	Tap Water, Electricity and Fuels	105.9
#水	Tap Water	119.0
电	Electricity	102.6
液化石油气	LPG	103.2
管道燃气	Pipelined Gas	104.3

表21－13　主要年份商品零售价格指数（以上年价格为100）
Classified Retail Price Index in Main Years (Preceding Year = 100)

指　标	Indicators	2001	2004	2005	2010	2013	2014
商品零售价格指数	**Overall Retail Price Index**	**98.6**	**100.9**	**99.4**	**101.7**	**100.2**	**100.9**
食品类	Food	98.4	108.6	104.7	107.6	104.5	103.2
粮　食	Grain	100.1	128.8	102.1	112.0	103.6	102.0
淀粉及制品	Starch and Related Products	100.4	107.2	105.2	95.5	101.6	102.5
干豆类及豆制品	Dry Beans and Bean Products	111.3	124.8	103.6	108.7	103.1	100.4
油　脂	Oil or Fat	81.4	114.4	91.2	105.6	97.5	95.0
肉禽及其制品	Meat Poultry and Their Products	100.4	117.6	105.5	104.2	103.7	101.4
蛋	Eggs	110.7	118.6	105.8	106.1	102.2	106.0
水产品	Aquatic Products	90.1	107.7	114.4	116.1	105.0	102.7
菜	Vegetables	107.1	95.5	103.4	111.0	108.0	101.5
调味品	Flavoring	99.5	103.0	102.1	106.5	102.4	103.1
糖	Sugar	104.4	103.1	103.8	103.8	102.0	102.0
干鲜瓜果	Dried and Fresh Fruits	107.3	118.3	99.4	112.1	107.3	111.6
糕点饼干面包	Cakes, Biscuits and Bread	99.8	100.9	98.4	100.5	101.7	102.6
液体乳及乳制品	Milk and Its Products	99.8	99.6	100.8	102.3	108.1	110.1
在外用膳食品	Out-of-home Food	100.7	103.1	104.4	105.6	103.3	101.9
其它食品	Other Food	99.5	96.9	101.1	105.0	102.6	103.4
饮料、烟酒	Beverages, Tobacco and Liquor	98.4	98.8	99.6	101.9	100.1	101.4
服装、鞋帽	Garments, Shoes and Hats	107.7	93.9	92.6	98.4	99.9	103.6
纺织品	Textiles	98.8	102.2	99.4	103.9	100.6	99.1
家用电器及音像器材	Household Appliances and Audio-video Appliances	95.0	93.4	93.1	92.4	94.9	96.5
文化办公用品	Cultural and Office Articies	98.7	91.9	91.6	97.7	94.9	98.2
日用品	Daily Use Articles	99.0	98.4	100.5	100.3	100.2	99.9
体育娱乐用品	Sports and Recreation Goods	99.1	96.8	94.7	95.9	98.6	98.6
交通、通信用品	Transportation and Communication Goods	97.4	90.2	88.5	94.0	96.8	98.8
家　具	Furniture	90.4	98.2	100.1	101.1	99.7	102.6
化妆品	Cosmetics	100.7	99.0	96.1	101.0	100.8	102.3
金银珠宝	Jewelry	87.2	107.9	107.3	111.7	93.7	93.7
中西药品及医疗保健用品	Traditional Chinese and Western Medicines	98.7	95.6	97.7	99.8	101.0	101.7
书报杂志及电子出版物	Books, Newspapers, Magazines and Electronic Publications	99.5	99.6	98.0	103.2	100.9	100.6
燃　料	Fuels	111.4	107.0	109.1	112.8	99.3	99.8
建筑材料及五金电料	Building Materials and Hardwares	101.8	104.7	104.0	103.3	100.6	99.3

主要统计指标解释

居民消费价格指数

居民消费价格指数是度量一组代表性消费商品及服务项目价格水平随着时间而变动的相对数,反映居民家庭购买的消费品及服务价格水平的变动情况。它是宏观经济分析和决策、价格总水平监测和调控以及国民经济核算的重要指标。其按年度计算的变动率通常被用来作为反映通货膨胀或紧缩程度的指标。

现行的居民消费价格指数按用途分为八个大类,包括食品、烟酒及用品、衣着、家庭设备用品及维修服务、医疗保健和个人用品、交通和通信、娱乐教育文化用品及服务、居住。

商品零售价格指数

商品零售价格指数是反映一定时期内城乡商品零售价格变动趋势和程度的相对数。商品零售价格的变动直接影响城乡居民的生活支出和国家的财政收入,影响居民购买力和市场供需的平衡,影响消费与积累的比例关系。因此,该指数可以从一个侧面对上述经济活动进行观察和分析。

EXPLANATORY NOTES TO MAJOR STATISTICAL INDICATORS

Consumer Price Index

The Consumer Price Index is an index that reflects the time-based change of prices of a group of representative consumption commodities and services. It is an important reference factor for macro-economic analysis and strategy, monitoring and adjustment of overall price level and the national economic budgeting. The year-on-year change of the index is often a norm reflecting the inflation or deflation.

The current CPI covers eight categories of goods and services: food; tobacco, liquor and related articles; garments; household facilities, articles and repair services; medical and health care and personal items; traffic and telecommunications; education, culture and recreation articles and services and residence.

Retail Price Index

Retail Price Index reflects the trend and degree of change in retail prices of commodities during a given period. The change in retail prices of commodities directly affect the living expenditure of urban and rural residents, government revenue, purchasing power of residents and the equilibrium of market supply and demand, and the ratio of consumption to accumulation. Therefore, the retail price indices are useful to analyze the changes of the above economic activities.

中国统计出版社最新图书简目

（仅供参考，以实际出版为准）

统计资料

中国统计年鉴　中国统计摘要　中国发展报告
中国经济普查年鉴2013　国际统计年鉴　金砖国家联合统计手册
中国-东盟国家统计手册　中国区域经济统计年鉴　中国县域统计年鉴
中国城市统计年鉴　中国农村统计年鉴　中国地区经济监测报告
中国贸易外经统计年鉴　中国对外直接投资统计公报　中国商品交易市场统计年鉴
大中型批发零售和住宿餐饮企业统计年鉴　中国零售和餐饮连锁企业统计年鉴　中国住户调查年鉴
中国价格统计年鉴　中国农产品价格调查年鉴　全国农产品成本收益资料汇编
中国环境统计年鉴　中国能源统计年鉴　国外资源、能源和环境统计资料汇编
中国工业统计年鉴　中国建筑业统计年鉴　中国房地产统计年鉴
中国城市建设统计年鉴　中国城乡建设统计年鉴　中国第三产业统计年鉴
中国证券期货统计年鉴　中国科技统计年鉴　中国高技术产业统计年鉴
工业企业科技活动资料　中国劳动统计年鉴　中国人口和就业统计年鉴
中国人才资源统计报告　中国社会统计年鉴　中国文化及相关产业统计年鉴
文化及相关产业统计概览　中国教育经费统计年鉴　中国民政统计年鉴
中国民族统计年鉴　中国工会统计年鉴　中国残疾人事业统计年鉴
中国妇女儿童状况统计资料（英）　中国乡镇街道行政区域简册

省级综合统计年鉴系列

北京 天津 河北 山西 内蒙古 辽宁 吉林 黑龙江 上海 江苏 浙江 安徽 福建 江西 山东 河南 湖北 湖南 广东 广西 海南 重庆 四川 贵州 云南 西藏 陕西 甘肃 青海 宁夏 新疆 新疆生产建设兵团

市(县)级综合统计年鉴系列

天津滨海新区 石家庄 唐山 邯郸 保定 沧州 邢台 廊坊 承德 衡水 秦皇岛 张家口 太原 大同 阳泉 长治 晋城 朔州 晋中 运城 忻州 临汾 呼和浩特 呼和浩特新城区 鄂尔多斯 包头 沈阳 大连 长春 四平 哈尔滨 齐齐哈尔 黑龙江垦区 上海浦东新区 南京 无锡 徐州 常州 苏州 南通 连云港 淮安 盐城 扬州 镇江 泰州 宿迁 江阴 丹阳 杭州 宁波 温州 嘉兴 绍兴 金华 衢州 舟山 台州 丽水 合肥 安庆 马鞍山 福州 厦门 宁德 南昌 九江 上饶 新余 抚州 济南 青岛 枣庄 滕州 郑州 洛阳 平顶山 三门峡 南阳 商丘 济源 武汉 十堰 荆州 宜昌 荆门 咸宁 长沙 广州 深圳 惠州 东莞 南宁 柳州 桂林 来宾 海口 三亚 成都 贵阳 昆明 西安 兰州 庆阳 银川 乌鲁木齐 兵团一师 兵团十师

调查年鉴系列

天津 山西 内蒙古 辽宁 吉林 上海 福建 河南 湖北 湖南 广西 重庆 四川 云南 甘肃 宁夏 新疆

“十二五”规划教材

统计学（经济管理类专业本科适用，单薇 等）　抽样调查理论与方法（冯士雍 等）
贝叶斯统计（茆诗松 等）　统计学（黄良文 等）　试验设计（茆诗松 等）
统计学：从数据到结论（吴喜之）　医学统计学（于浩）　统计学（经济、管理类专业基础教材，张小斐）
概率论与数理统计三十三讲（魏振军）　概率论与数理统计三十三：学习指导与习题解答（魏振军）
非参数统计（吴喜之 等）　统计学：经济与管理中的数据分析（李慧云 等）
卫生管理统计学（新编医学院校基础课教材，尚磊）　医院统计学（新编医学院校基础课教材，徐天和 等）
社会统计学（蒋萍 等）　现代金融投资统计分析（李腊生 等）
国民经济核算初级教程（经济类、统计类、管理类专业适用，蒋萍 等）

重点图书

图解中国经济2015　新编英汉汉英统计大词典　中华医学统计百科全书
挑大学选专业2016—考研择校指南　挑大学选专业2015—高考志愿填报指南

图书在版编目(CIP)数据

上海浦东新区统计年鉴．2015 / 上海市浦东新区统计局，国家统计局浦东调查队编．
-- 北京 ：中国统计出版社，2015.8
ISBN 978-7-5037-7524-6

Ⅰ．①上…
Ⅱ．①上… ②国…
Ⅲ．①统计资料－浦东新区－2015－年鉴
Ⅳ．①C832.513-54

中国版本图书馆CIP数据核字(2015)第185504号

上海浦东新区统计年鉴—2015

作　　者/上海市浦东新区统计局　国家统计局浦东调查队
责任编辑/陈越月
执行编辑/施湘君　计勤敏
封面设计/蔡旭洲
出版发行/中国统计出版社
通信地址/北京市西城区月坛南街57号
邮　　编/100826
办公地址/北京市丰台区西三环南路甲6号
邮政编码/100073
电　　话/邮购（010）63376909　书店（010）68783171
网　　址/http://csp.stats.gov.cn
印　　刷/上海万卷印刷有限公司
经　　销/新华书店
开　　本/890×1240毫米1/16
字　　数/915.2千字
印　　张/22
印　　数/1～1500册
版　　别/2015年8月第1版
版　　次/2015年8月第1次印刷
书　　号/ISBN 978-7-5037-7524-6
定　　价/320.00元

如有印装错误，本社发行部负责调换。